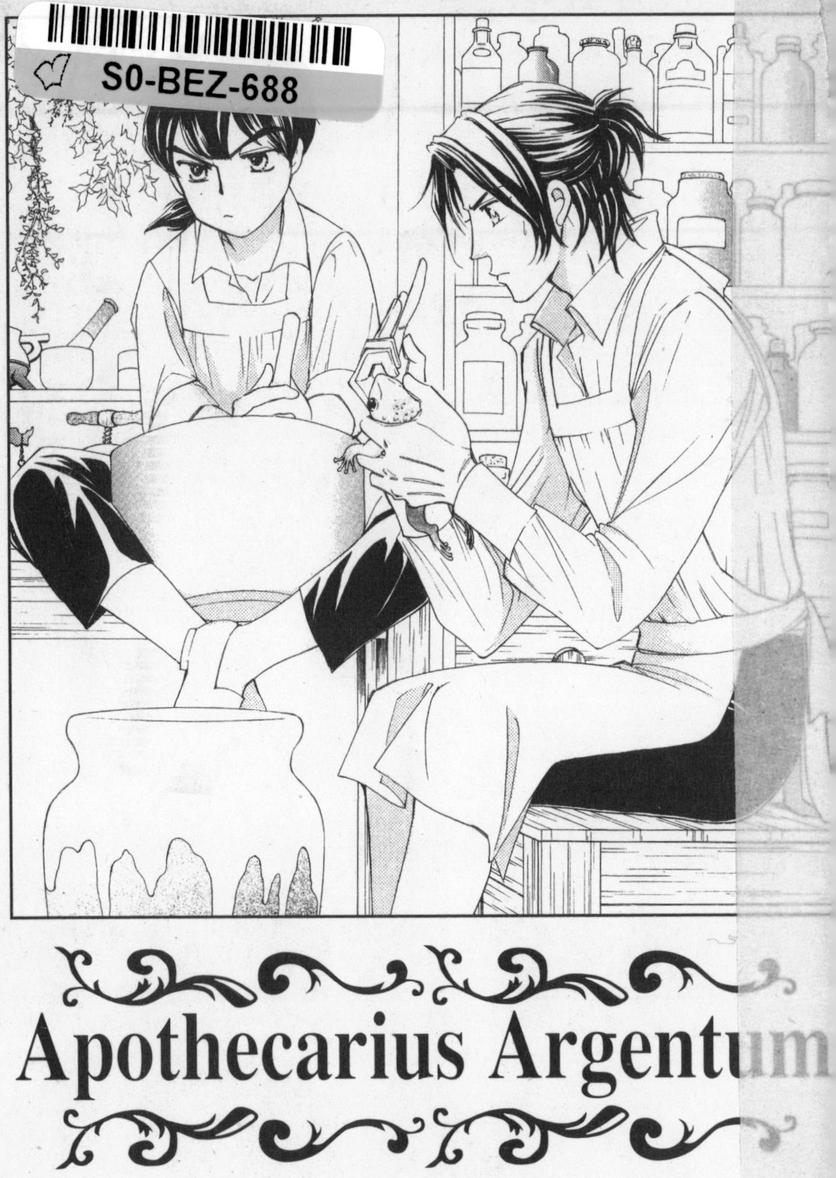

Apothecarius Argentum

Volume 6

By Tomomi Yamashita

Apothecarius Argentum

Character Introductions
and Summary of Previous Volume

Lady Primula
The daughter of the King of Beazol. A strong-minded woman, she's known as the "Princess of Steel."

Argent
The Royal Apothecary and Lady Primula's former food taster.

Carli
Lady Primula's etiquette instructor.

Soda
Argent's assistant and pupil.

Lorca
The Prince of Navara, a neighboring kingdom. He wants to marry Lady Primula.

Adona, the First Prince of Navara,
Daniel, the Second Prince of Navara.

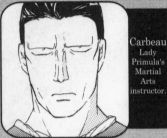

Carbeau
Lady Primula's Martial Arts instructor.

King of Beazol
He's known as a ruthless ruler, but he loves his daughter dearly.

Garna
The royal chef.

Argent was fed poison during his youth to turn him into the ultimate assassin. The King of Beazol bought Argent to be the food taster for his young daughter. However, the Princess freed Argent and instructed him to flee from the palace.

Several years later, Argent reappeared as a skilled healer and saved the Princess from an assassination attempt. As a result, he was promoted to the position of Royal Apothecary. Along with Soda, his apprentice, Argent works tirelessly for the people...

One day, Prince Lorca from Navara crashed a party and proposed to Lady Primula! The King of Navara was assassinated, and Beazol and Navara quickly moved to establish a peace treaty.

Argent discovered that in Castoria, there might be a way to detoxify his body so that he could lead a normal life. He set out to Castoria with Soda, but...

Apothecarius Argentum

Contents

Recipe 21 The Girl from Castoria.....................7
Recipe 22 Mino Valley.................................55
Recipe 23 The Doctor and The Apothecary...99
Recipe 24 Storm...149

Afterword..............................191

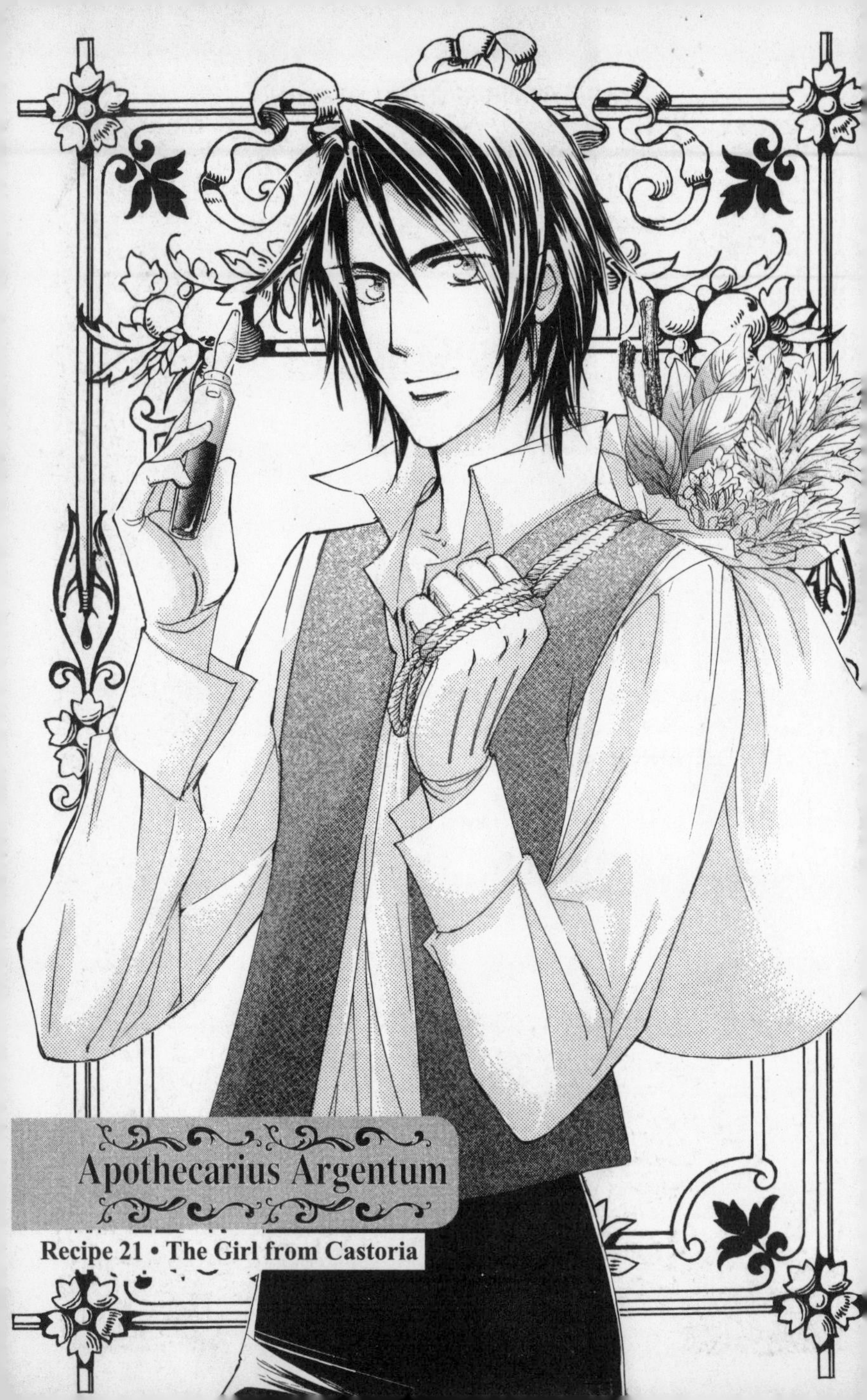
Apothecarius Argentum
Recipe 21 • The Girl from Castoria

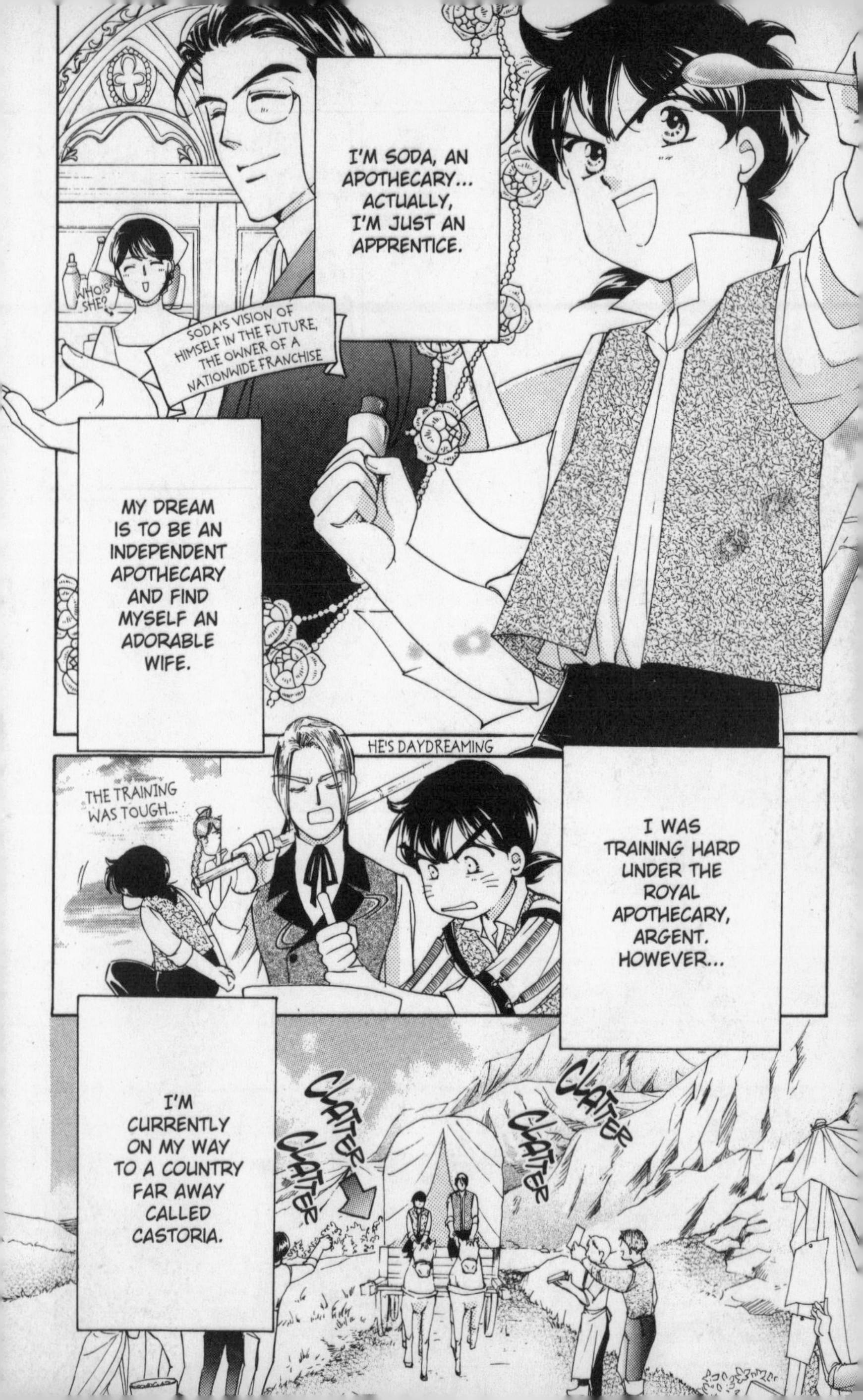
I'M SODA, AN APOTHECARY... ACTUALLY, I'M JUST AN APPRENTICE.
WHO'S SHE?
SODA'S VISION OF HIMSELF IN THE FUTURE, THE OWNER OF A NATIONWIDE FRANCHISE
MY DREAM IS TO BE AN INDEPENDENT APOTHECARY AND FIND MYSELF AN ADORABLE WIFE.
HE'S DAYDREAMING
I WAS TRAINING HARD UNDER THE ROYAL APOTHECARY, ARGENT. HOWEVER...
THE TRAINING WAS TOUGH...
CLATTER CLATTER
CLATTER CLATTER
I'M CURRENTLY ON MY WAY TO A COUNTRY FAR AWAY CALLED CASTORIA.

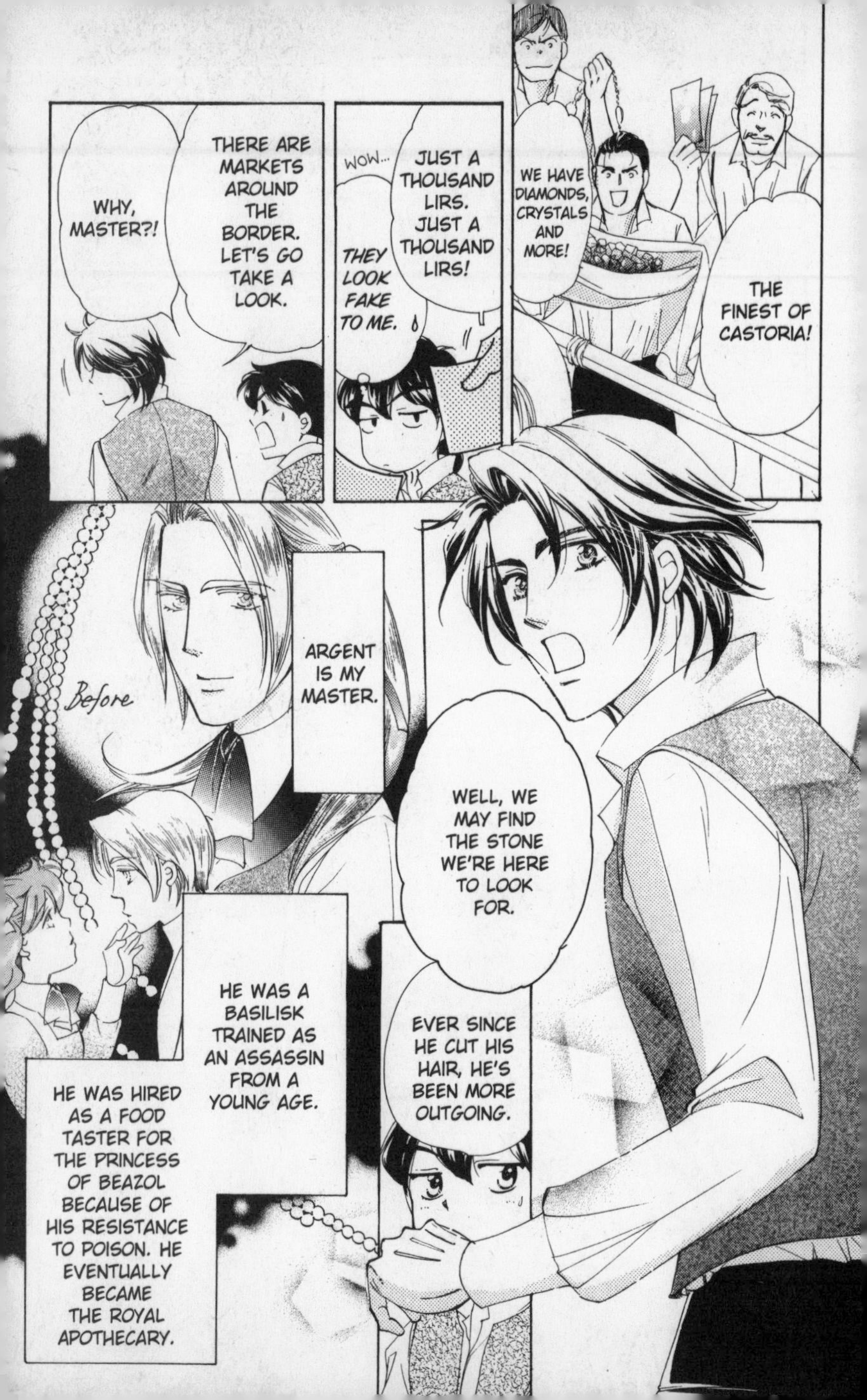
WE HAVE DIAMONDS, CRYSTALS AND MORE!
THE FINEST OF CASTORIA!
JUST A THOUSAND LIRS. JUST A THOUSAND LIRS!
WOW...
THEY LOOK FAKE TO ME.
THERE ARE MARKETS AROUND THE BORDER. LET'S GO TAKE A LOOK.
WHY, MASTER?!
WELL, WE MAY FIND THE STONE WE'RE HERE TO LOOK FOR.
EVER SINCE HE CUT HIS HAIR, HE'S BEEN MORE OUTGOING.
ARGENT IS MY MASTER.
Before
HE WAS A BASILISK TRAINED AS AN ASSASSIN FROM A YOUNG AGE.
HE WAS HIRED AS A FOOD TASTER FOR THE PRINCESS OF BEAZOL BECAUSE OF HIS RESISTANCE TO POISON. HE EVENTUALLY BECAME THE ROYAL APOTHECARY.

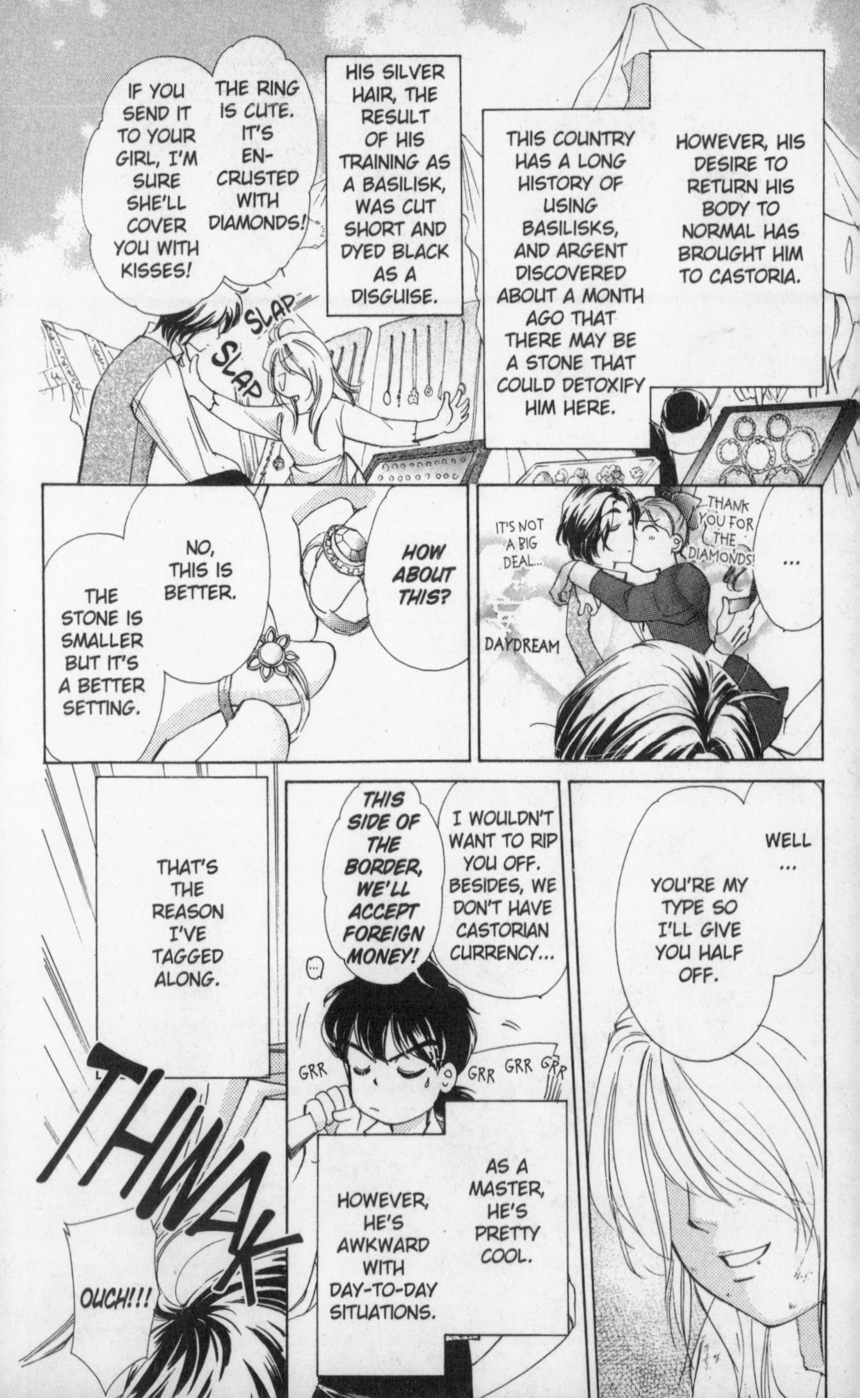
HOWEVER, HIS DESIRE TO RETURN HIS BODY TO NORMAL HAS BROUGHT HIM TO CASTORIA.
THIS COUNTRY HAS A LONG HISTORY OF USING BASILISKS, AND ARGENT DISCOVERED ABOUT A MONTH AGO THAT THERE MAY BE A STONE THAT COULD DETOXIFY HIM HERE.
HIS SILVER HAIR, THE RESULT OF HIS TRAINING AS A BASILISK, WAS CUT SHORT AND DYED BLACK AS A DISGUISE.
THE RING IS CUTE. IT'S EN-CRUSTED WITH DIAMONDS!
IF YOU SEND IT TO YOUR GIRL, I'M SURE SHE'LL COVER YOU WITH KISSES!
SLAP
SLAP
...
THANK YOU FOR THE DIAMONDS!
IT'S NOT A BIG DEAL...
DAYDREAM
HOW ABOUT THIS?
NO, THIS IS BETTER.
THE STONE IS SMALLER BUT IT'S A BETTER SETTING.
WELL ...
YOU'RE MY TYPE SO I'LL GIVE YOU HALF OFF.
I WOULDN'T WANT TO RIP YOU OFF. BESIDES, WE DON'T HAVE CASTORIAN CURRENCY...
THIS SIDE OF THE BORDER, WE'LL ACCEPT FOREIGN MONEY!
...
GRR GRR GRR GRR
AS A MASTER, HE'S PRETTY COOL.
HOWEVER, HE'S AWKWARD WITH DAY-TO-DAY SITUATIONS.
THAT'S THE REASON I'VE TAGGED ALONG.
THWAK
OUCH!!!

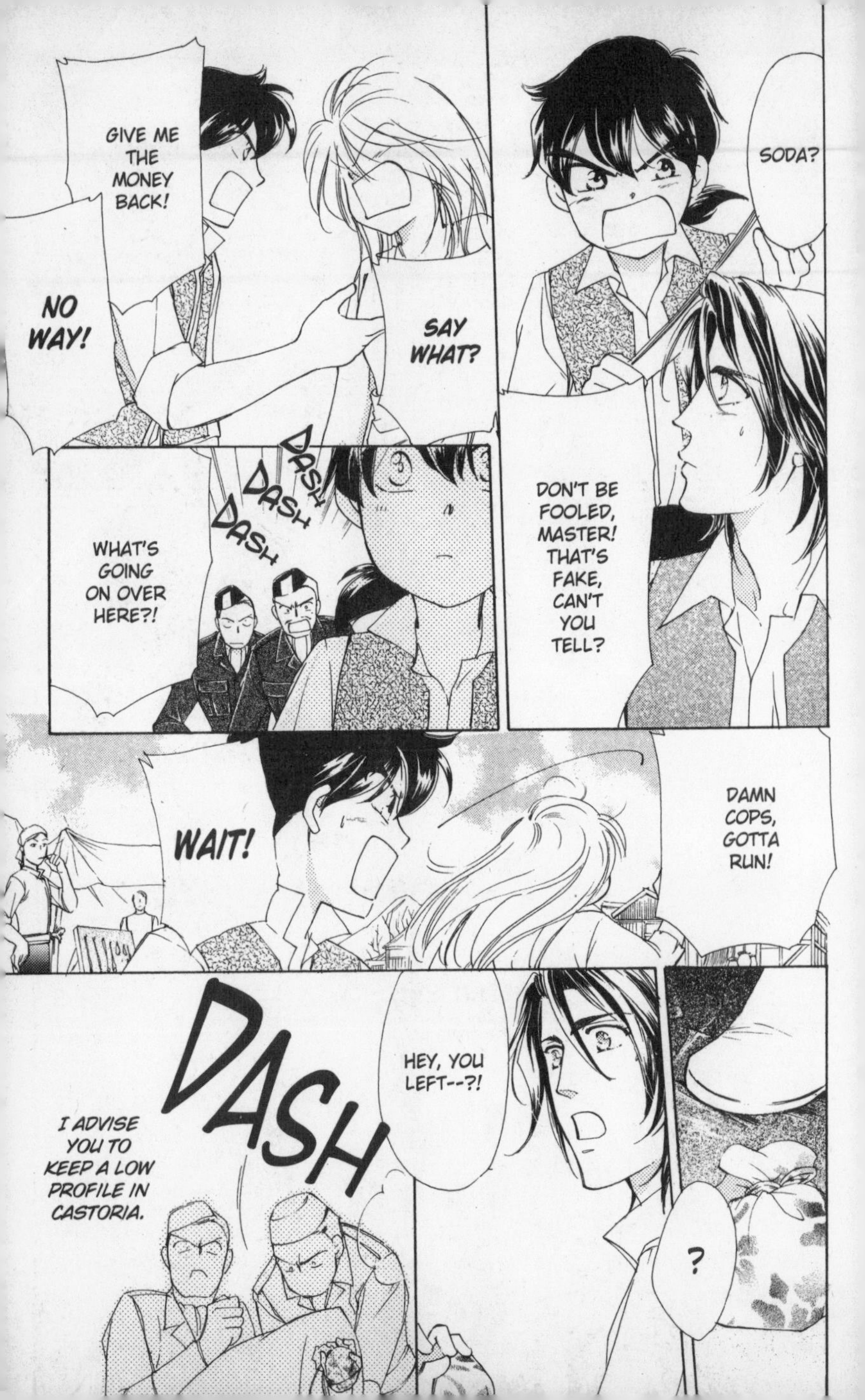
SODA?
DON'T BE FOOLED, MASTER! THAT'S FAKE, CAN'T YOU TELL?
GIVE ME THE MONEY BACK!
SAY WHAT?
NO WAY!
DASH DASH DASH
WHAT'S GOING ON OVER HERE?!
DAMN COPS, GOTTA RUN!
WAIT!
HEY, YOU LEFT--?!
?
DASH
I ADVISE YOU TO KEEP A LOW PROFILE IN CASTORIA.

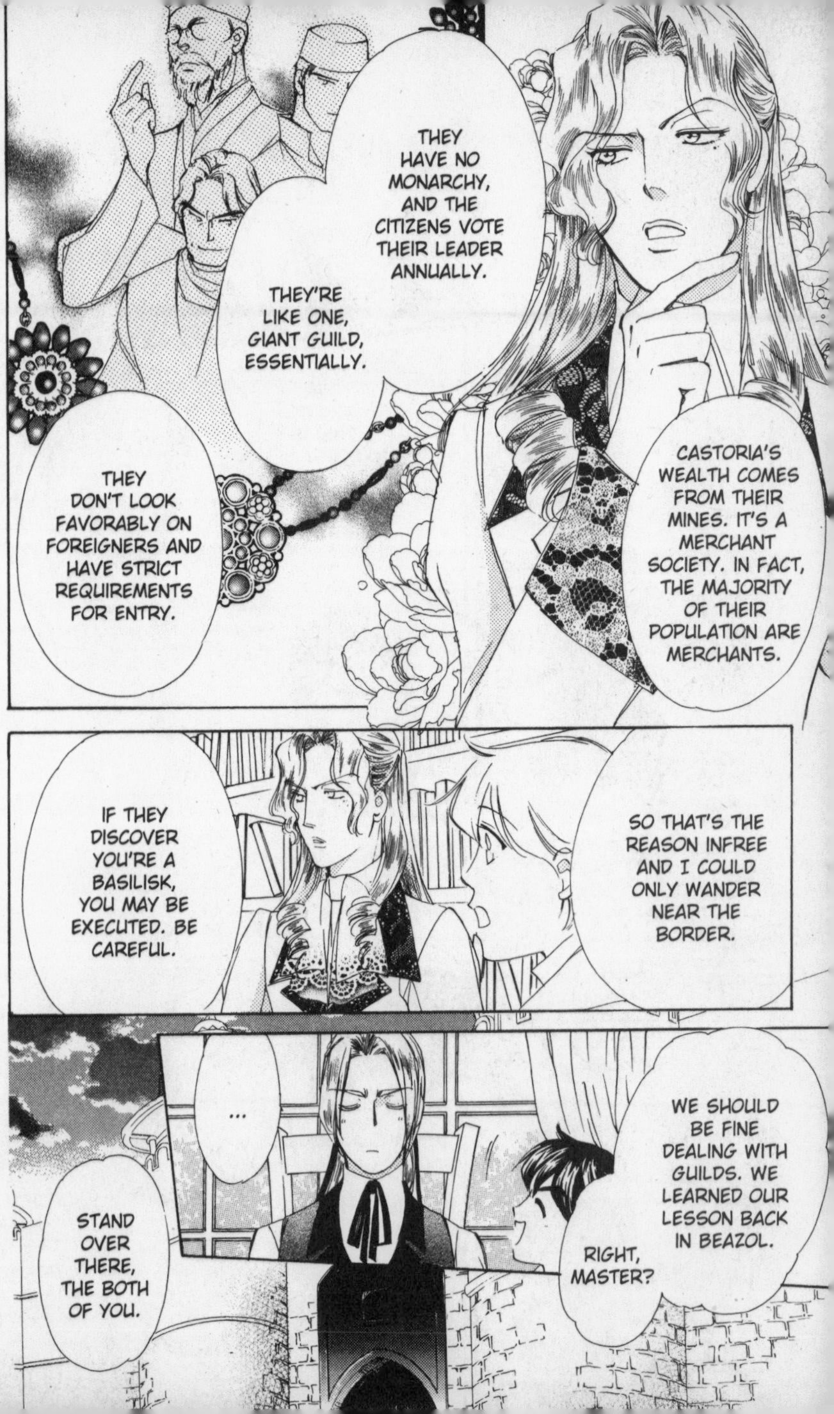
CASTORIA'S WEALTH COMES FROM THEIR MINES. IT'S A MERCHANT SOCIETY. IN FACT, THE MAJORITY OF THEIR POPULATION ARE MERCHANTS.
THEY HAVE NO MONARCHY, AND THE CITIZENS VOTE THEIR LEADER ANNUALLY.
THEY'RE LIKE ONE, GIANT GUILD, ESSENTIALLY.
THEY DON'T LOOK FAVORABLY ON FOREIGNERS AND HAVE STRICT REQUIREMENTS FOR ENTRY.
SO THAT'S THE REASON INFREE AND I COULD ONLY WANDER NEAR THE BORDER.
IF THEY DISCOVER YOU'RE A BASILISK, YOU MAY BE EXECUTED. BE CAREFUL.
WE SHOULD BE FINE DEALING WITH GUILDS. WE LEARNED OUR LESSON BACK IN BEAZOL.
RIGHT, MASTER?
...
STAND OVER THERE, THE BOTH OF YOU.

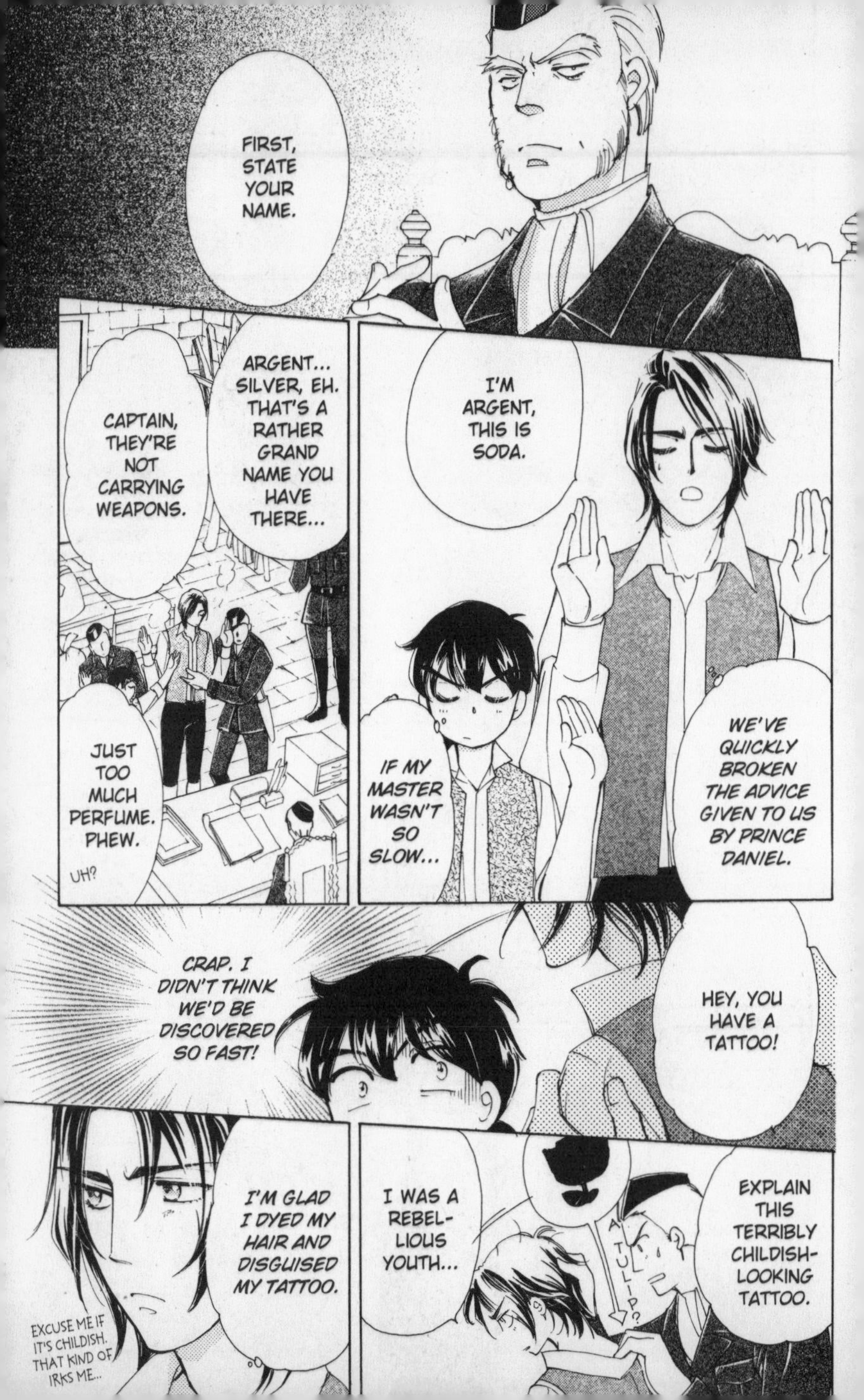

FIRST, STATE YOUR NAME.
I'M ARGENT, THIS IS SODA.
WE'VE QUICKLY BROKEN THE ADVICE GIVEN TO US BY PRINCE DANIEL.
IF MY MASTER WASN'T SO SLOW...
ARGENT... SILVER, EH. THAT'S A RATHER GRAND NAME YOU HAVE THERE...
CAPTAIN, THEY'RE NOT CARRYING WEAPONS.
JUST TOO MUCH PERFUME. PHEW.
UH?
HEY, YOU HAVE A TATTOO!
CRAP. I DIDN'T THINK WE'D BE DISCOVERED SO FAST!
EXPLAIN THIS TERRIBLY CHILDISH-LOOKING TATTOO.
A TULIP?
I WAS A REBEL-LIOUS YOUTH...
I'M GLAD I DYED MY HAIR AND DISGUISED MY TATTOO.
EXCUSE ME IF IT'S CHILDISH. THAT KIND OF IRKS ME...

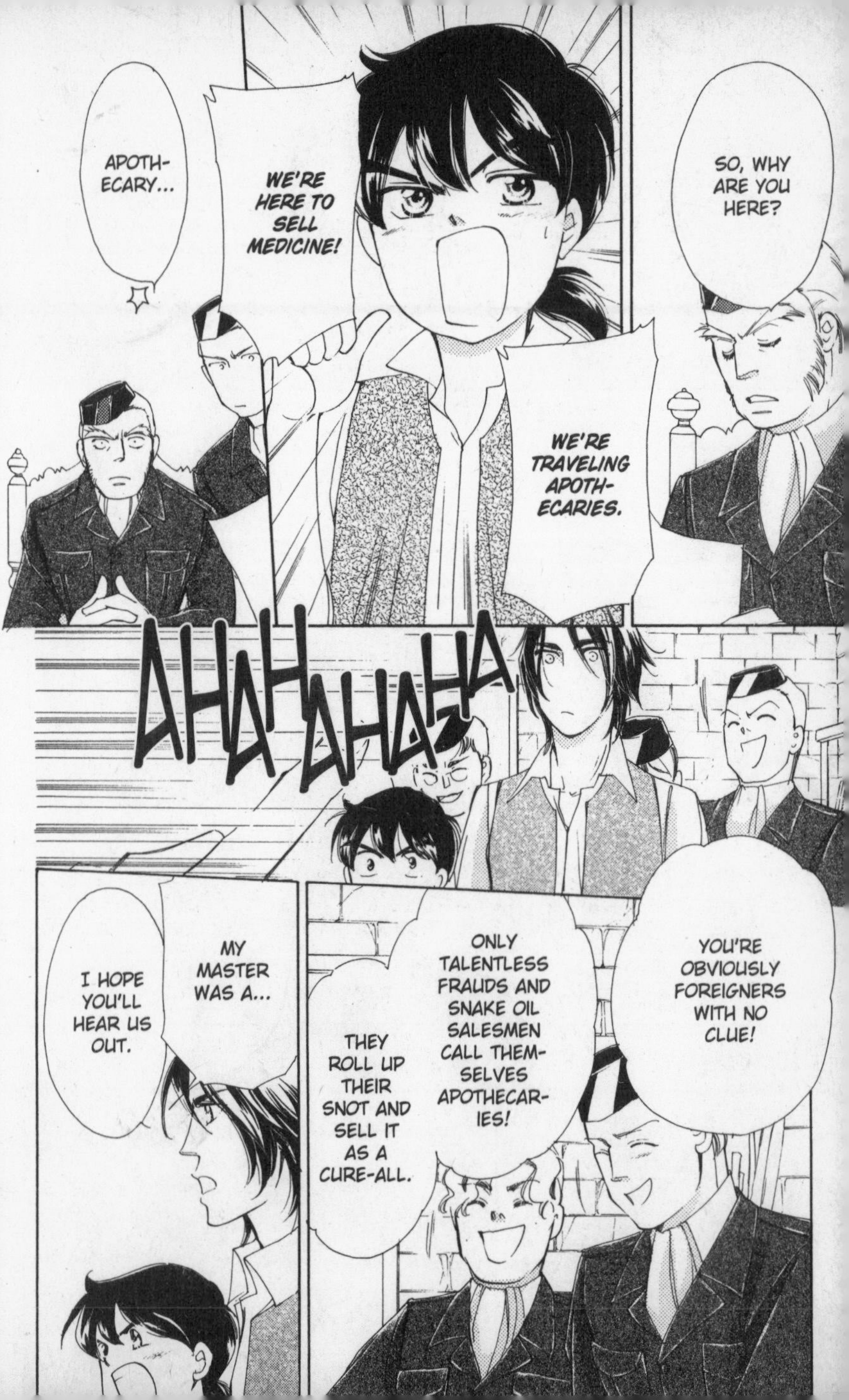
SO, WHY ARE YOU HERE?
WE'RE TRAVELING APOTH-ECARIES.
WE'RE HERE TO SELL MEDICINE!
APOTH-ECARY...
AHAHAHAHAHA
YOU'RE OBVIOUSLY FOREIGNERS WITH NO CLUE!
ONLY TALENTLESS FRAUDS AND SNAKE OIL SALESMEN CALL THEM-SELVES APOTHECAR-IES!
THEY ROLL UP THEIR SNOT AND SELL IT AS A CURE-ALL.
MY MASTER WAS A...
I HOPE YOU'LL HEAR US OUT.

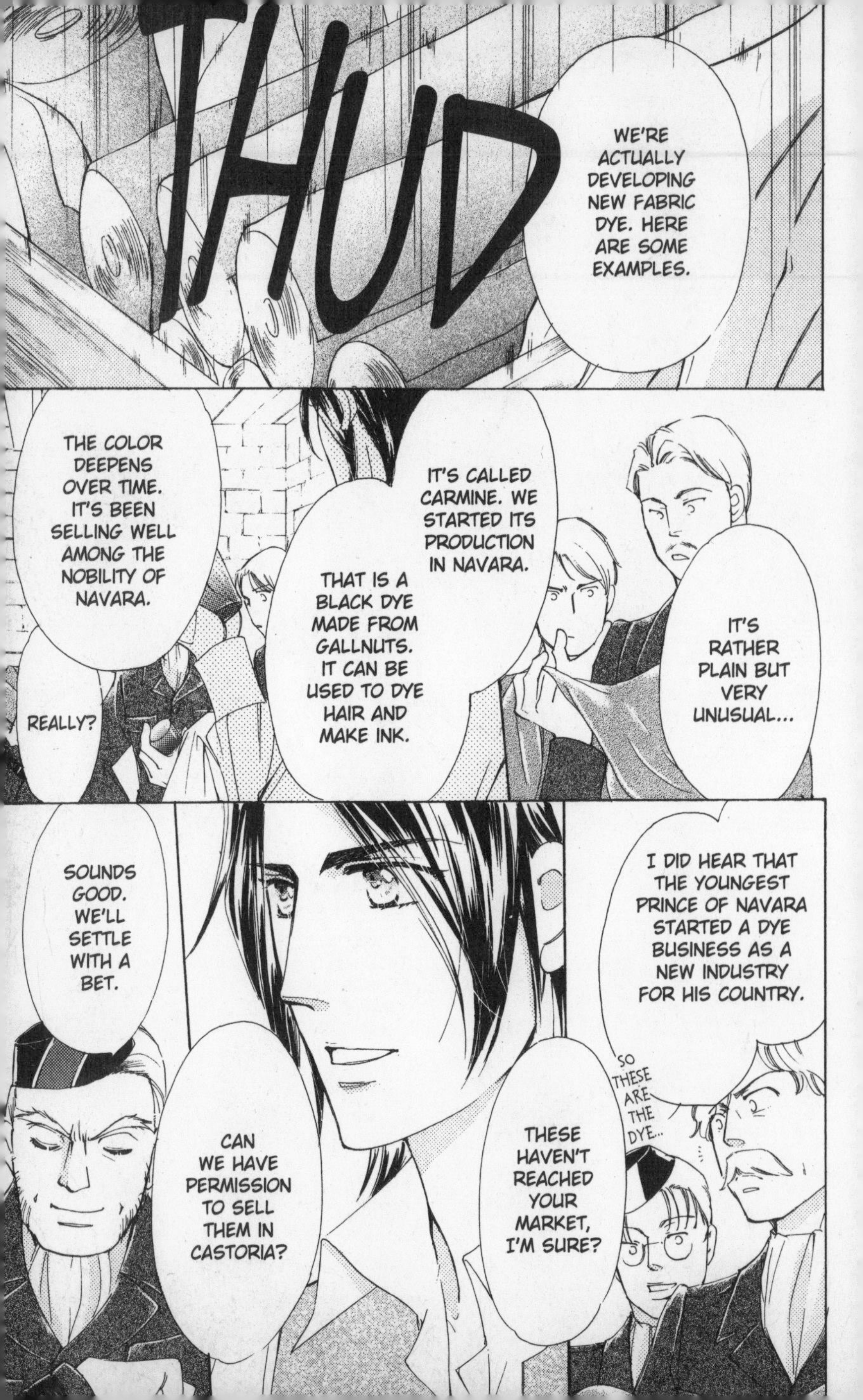
WE'RE ACTUALLY DEVELOPING NEW FABRIC DYE. HERE ARE SOME EXAMPLES.
THUD
IT'S CALLED CARMINE. WE STARTED ITS PRODUCTION IN NAVARA.
IT'S RATHER PLAIN BUT VERY UNUSUAL...
THAT IS A BLACK DYE MADE FROM GALLNUTS. IT CAN BE USED TO DYE HAIR AND MAKE INK.
THE COLOR DEEPENS OVER TIME. IT'S BEEN SELLING WELL AMONG THE NOBILITY OF NAVARA.
REALLY?
I DID HEAR THAT THE YOUNGEST PRINCE OF NAVARA STARTED A DYE BUSINESS AS A NEW INDUSTRY FOR HIS COUNTRY.
SO THESE ARE THE DYE...
THESE HAVEN'T REACHED YOUR MARKET, I'M SURE?
CAN WE HAVE PERMISSION TO SELL THEM IN CASTORIA?
SOUNDS GOOD. WE'LL SETTLE WITH A BET.

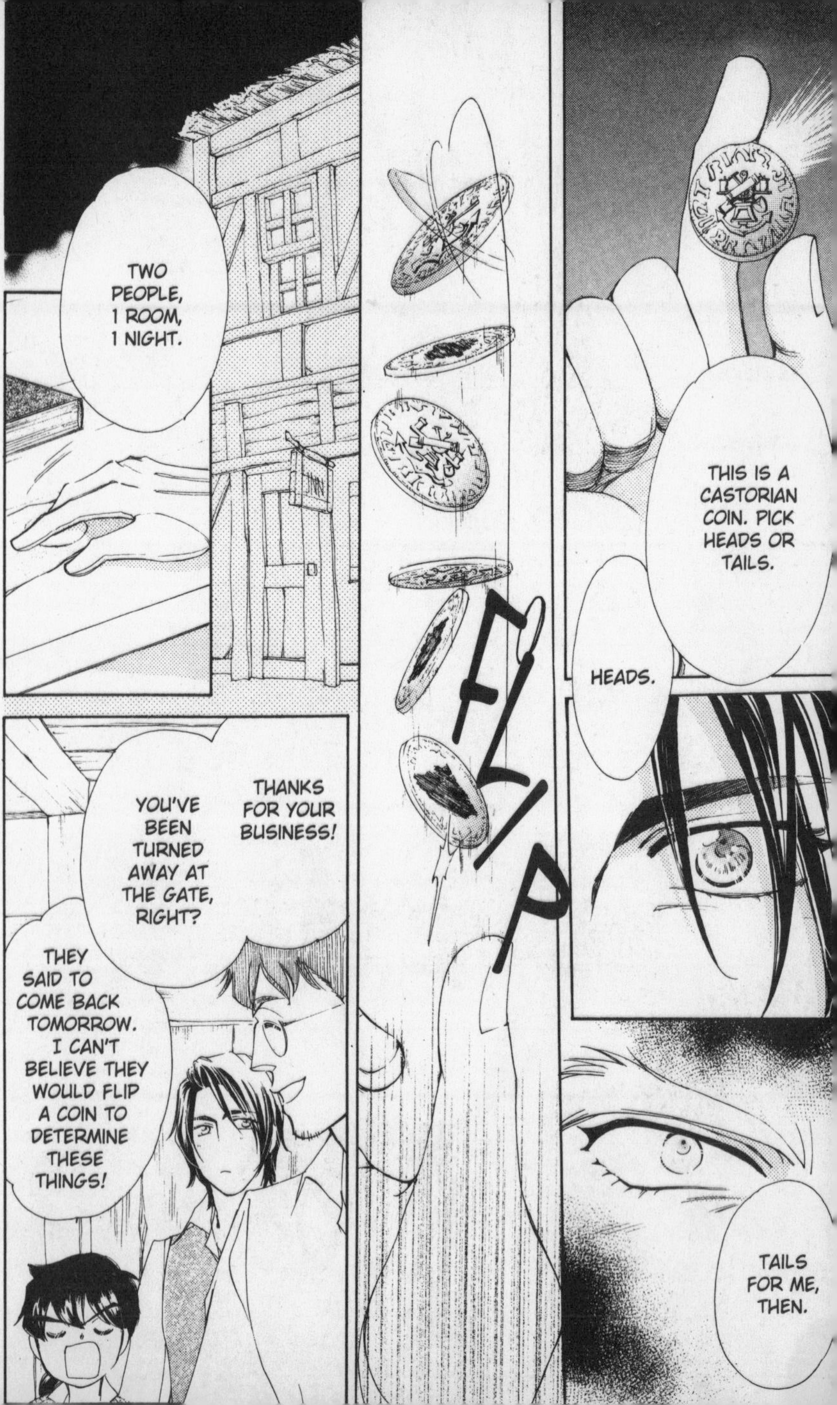
THIS IS A CASTORIAN COIN. PICK HEADS OR TAILS.
HEADS.
TAILS FOR ME, THEN.
FLIP
TWO PEOPLE, 1 ROOM, 1 NIGHT.
THANKS FOR YOUR BUSINESS!
YOU'VE BEEN TURNED AWAY AT THE GATE, RIGHT?
THEY SAID TO COME BACK TOMORROW. I CAN'T BELIEVE THEY WOULD FLIP A COIN TO DETERMINE THESE THINGS!

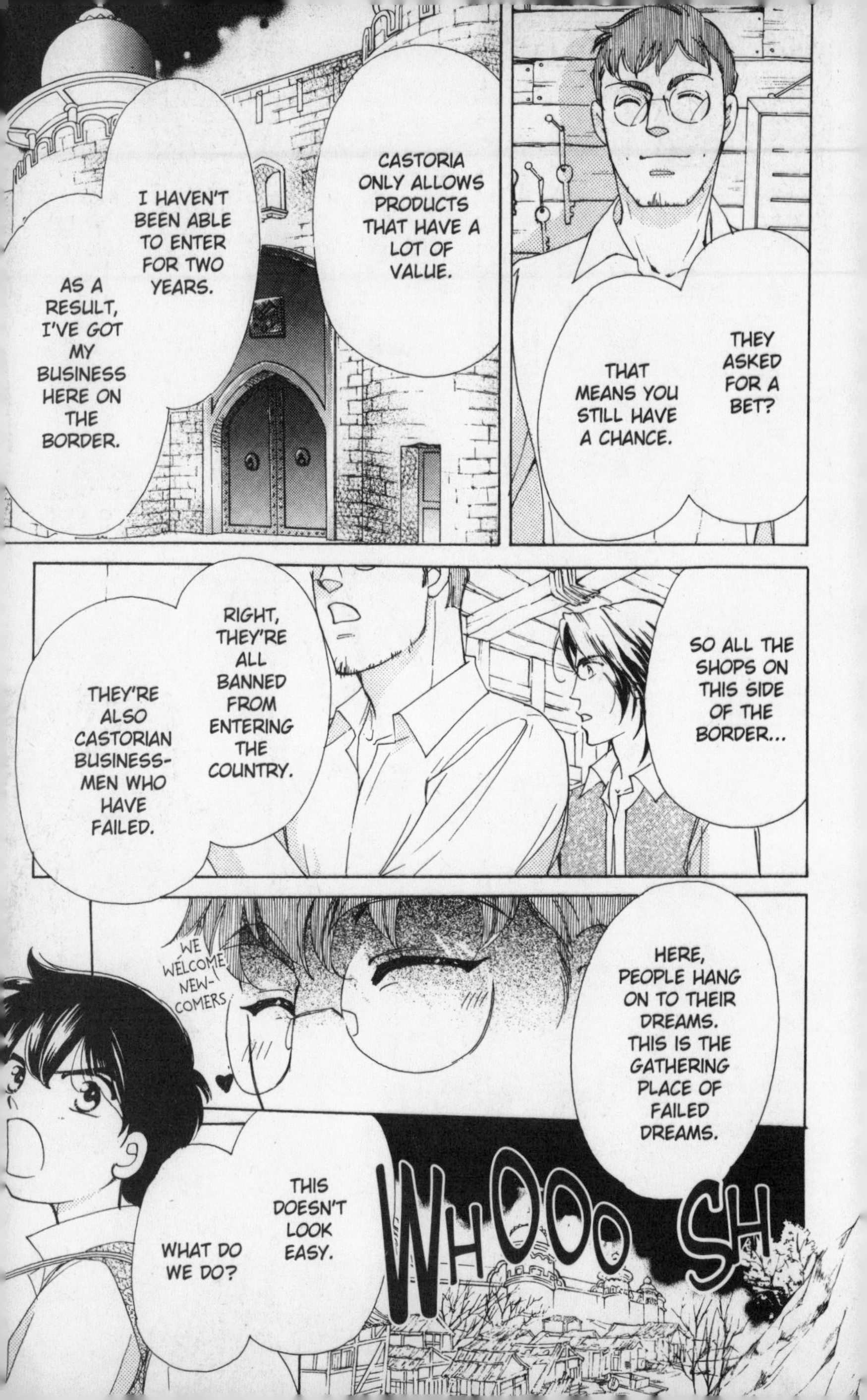
THEY ASKED FOR A BET?
THAT MEANS YOU STILL HAVE A CHANCE.
CASTORIA ONLY ALLOWS PRODUCTS THAT HAVE A LOT OF VALUE.
I HAVEN'T BEEN ABLE TO ENTER FOR TWO YEARS.
AS A RESULT, I'VE GOT MY BUSINESS HERE ON THE BORDER.
SO ALL THE SHOPS ON THIS SIDE OF THE BORDER...
RIGHT, THEY'RE ALL BANNED FROM ENTERING THE COUNTRY.
THEY'RE ALSO CASTORIAN BUSINESS-MEN WHO HAVE FAILED.
HERE, PEOPLE HANG ON TO THEIR DREAMS. THIS IS THE GATHERING PLACE OF FAILED DREAMS.
WE WELCOME NEW-COMERS
WHOOO SH
THIS DOESN'T LOOK EASY.
WHAT DO WE DO?

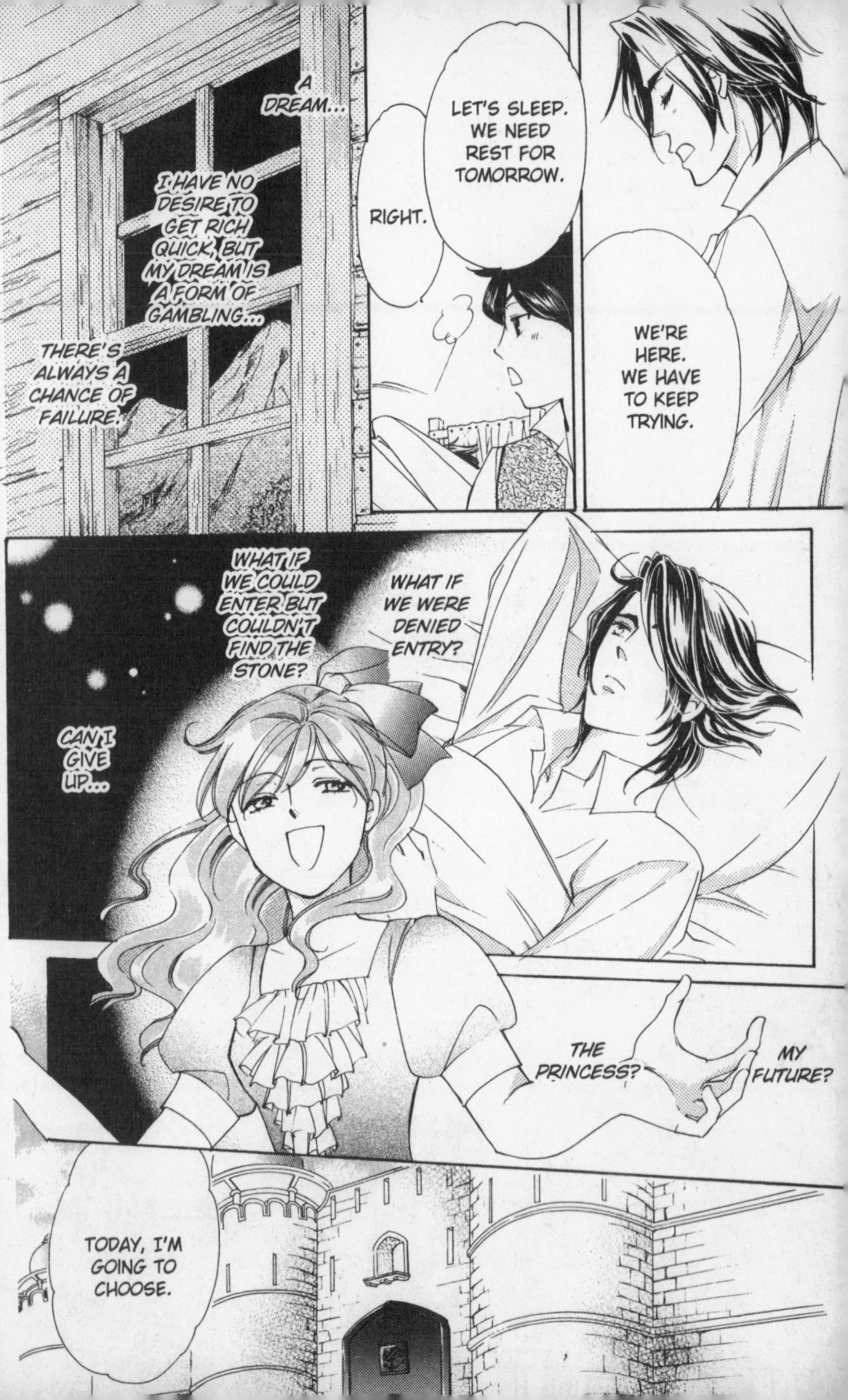

WE'RE HERE. WE HAVE TO KEEP TRYING.
LET'S SLEEP. WE NEED REST FOR TOMORROW.
RIGHT.
A DREAM...
I HAVE NO DESIRE TO GET RICH QUICK, BUT MY DREAM IS A FORM OF GAMBLING...
THERE'S ALWAYS A CHANCE OF FAILURE.
WHAT IF WE WERE DENIED ENTRY?
WHAT IF WE COULD ENTER BUT COULDN'T FIND THE STONE?
CAN I GIVE UP...
MY FUTURE?
THE PRINCESS?
TODAY, I'M GOING TO CHOOSE.

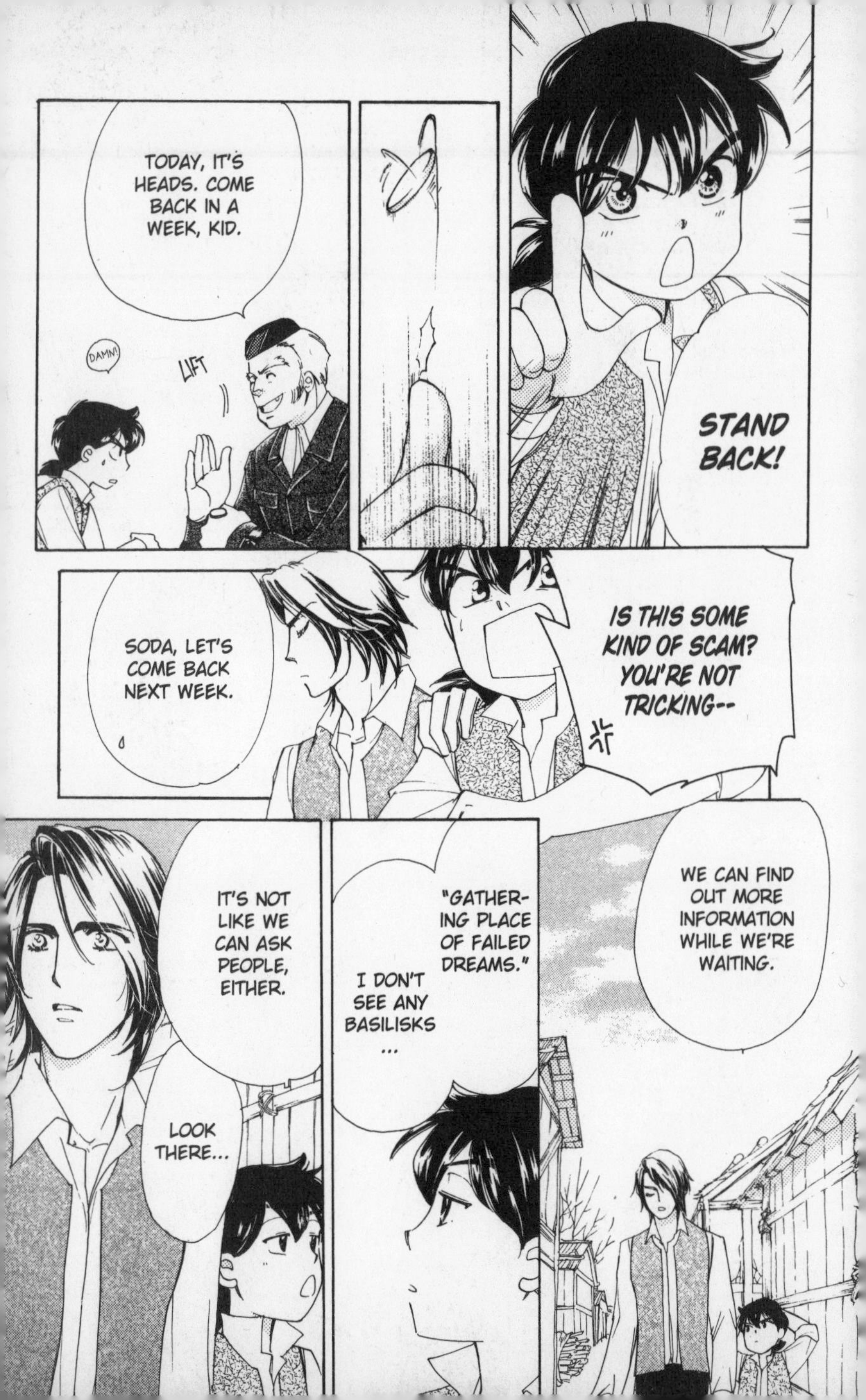
STAND BACK!
TODAY, IT'S HEADS. COME BACK IN A WEEK, KID.
LIFT
DAMN!
IS THIS SOME KIND OF SCAM? YOU'RE NOT TRICKING--
SODA, LET'S COME BACK NEXT WEEK.
WE CAN FIND OUT MORE INFORMATION WHILE WE'RE WAITING.
"GATHERING PLACE OF FAILED DREAMS."
I DON'T SEE ANY BASILISKS ...
IT'S NOT LIKE WE CAN ASK PEOPLE, EITHER.
LOOK THERE...

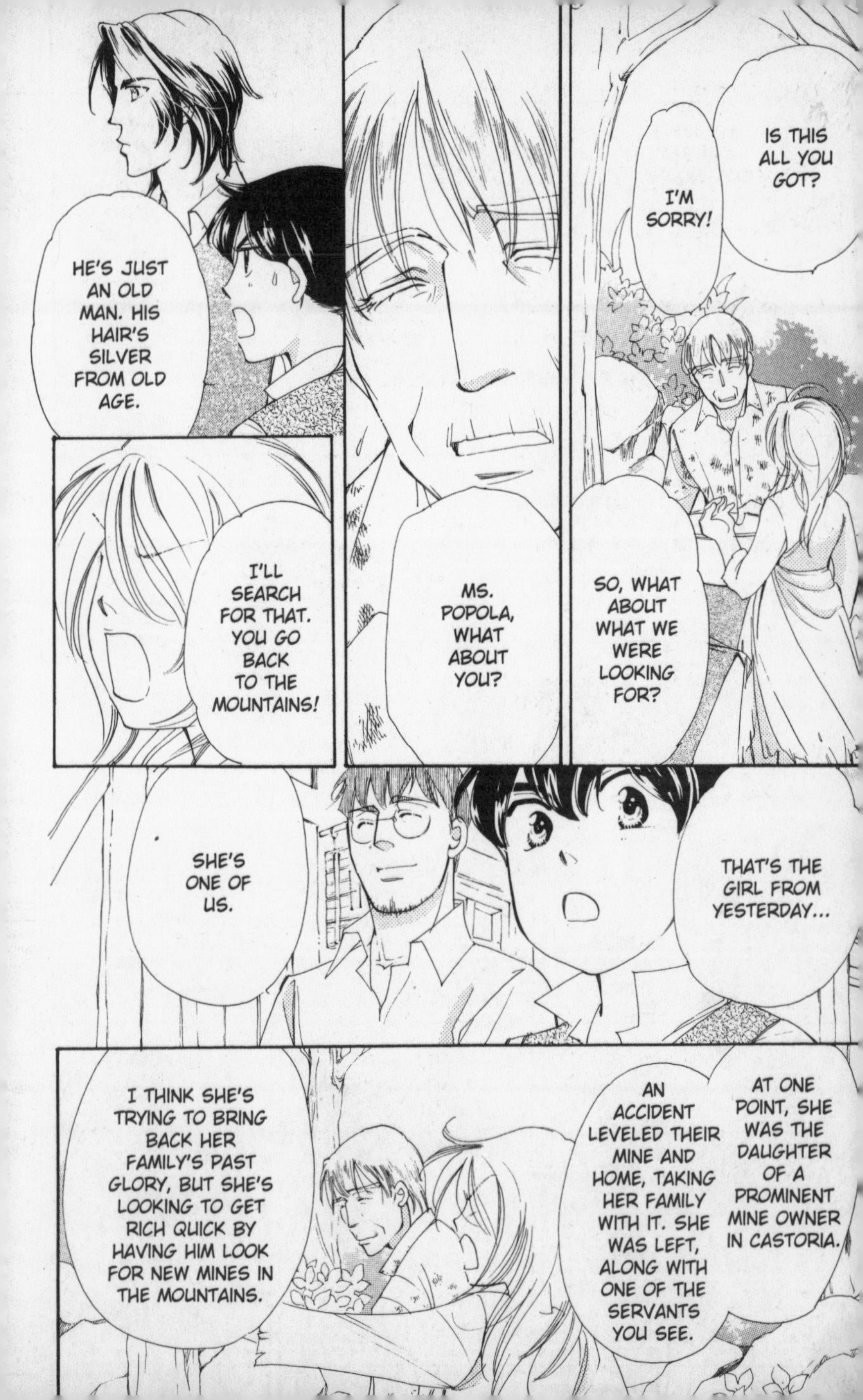
IS THIS ALL YOU GOT?
I'M SORRY!
SO, WHAT ABOUT WHAT WE WERE LOOKING FOR?
MS. POPOLA, WHAT ABOUT YOU?
HE'S JUST AN OLD MAN. HIS HAIR'S SILVER FROM OLD AGE.
I'LL SEARCH FOR THAT. YOU GO BACK TO THE MOUNTAINS!
THAT'S THE GIRL FROM YESTERDAY...
SHE'S ONE OF US.
AT ONE POINT, SHE WAS THE DAUGHTER OF A PROMINENT MINE OWNER IN CASTORIA.
AN ACCIDENT LEVELED THEIR MINE AND HOME, TAKING HER FAMILY WITH IT. SHE WAS LEFT, ALONG WITH ONE OF THE SERVANTS YOU SEE.
I THINK SHE'S TRYING TO BRING BACK HER FAMILY'S PAST GLORY, BUT SHE'S LOOKING TO GET RICH QUICK BY HAVING HIM LOOK FOR NEW MINES IN THE MOUNTAINS.

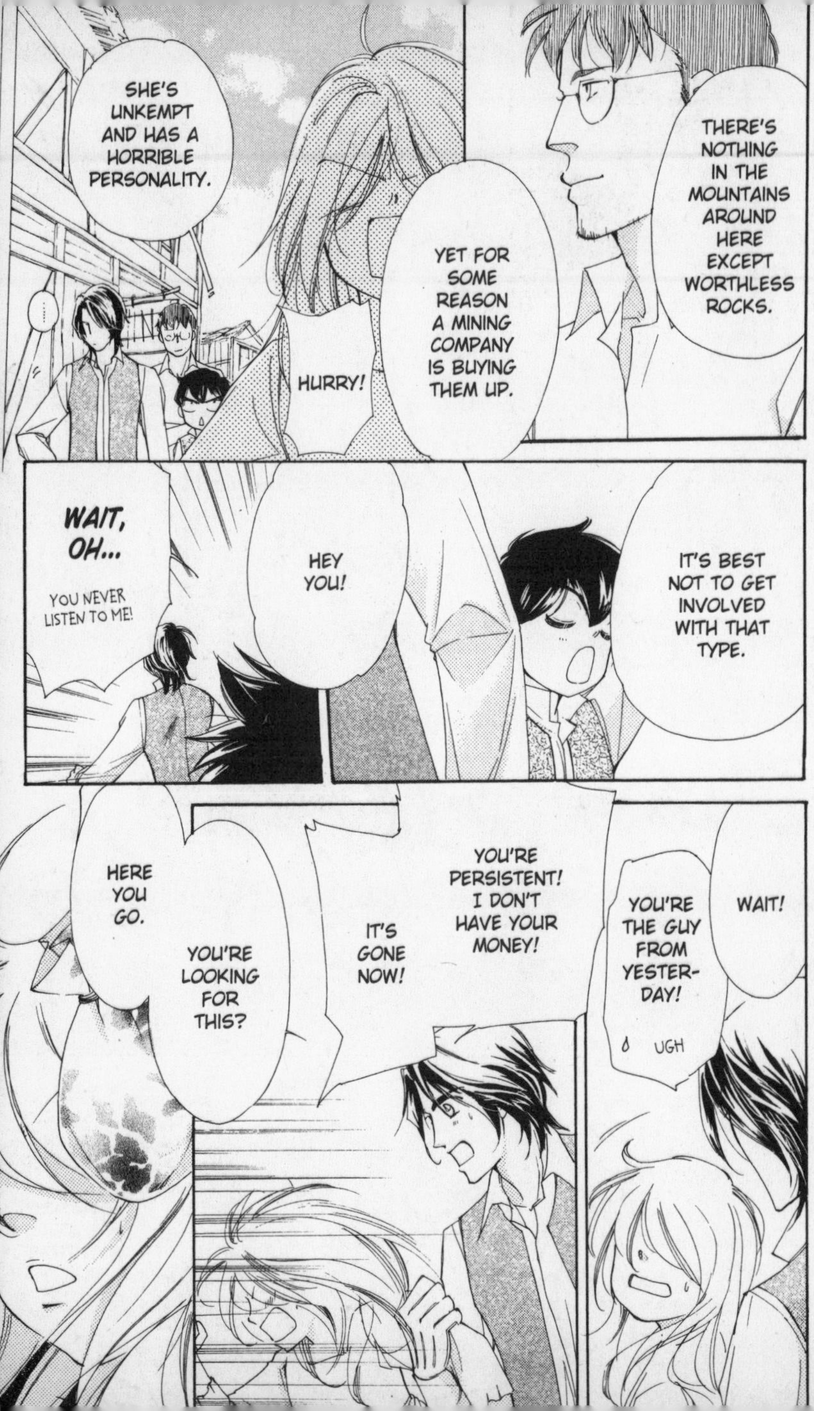
THERE'S NOTHING IN THE MOUNTAINS AROUND HERE EXCEPT WORTHLESS ROCKS.
YET FOR SOME REASON A MINING COMPANY IS BUYING THEM UP.
HURRY!
SHE'S UNKEMPT AND HAS A HORRIBLE PERSONALITY.
...
IT'S BEST NOT TO GET INVOLVED WITH THAT TYPE.
HEY YOU!
WAIT, OH...
YOU NEVER LISTEN TO ME!
WAIT!
YOU'RE THE GUY FROM YESTERDAY!
UGH
YOU'RE PERSISTENT! I DON'T HAVE YOUR MONEY!
IT'S GONE NOW!
HERE YOU GO.
YOU'RE LOOKING FOR THIS?

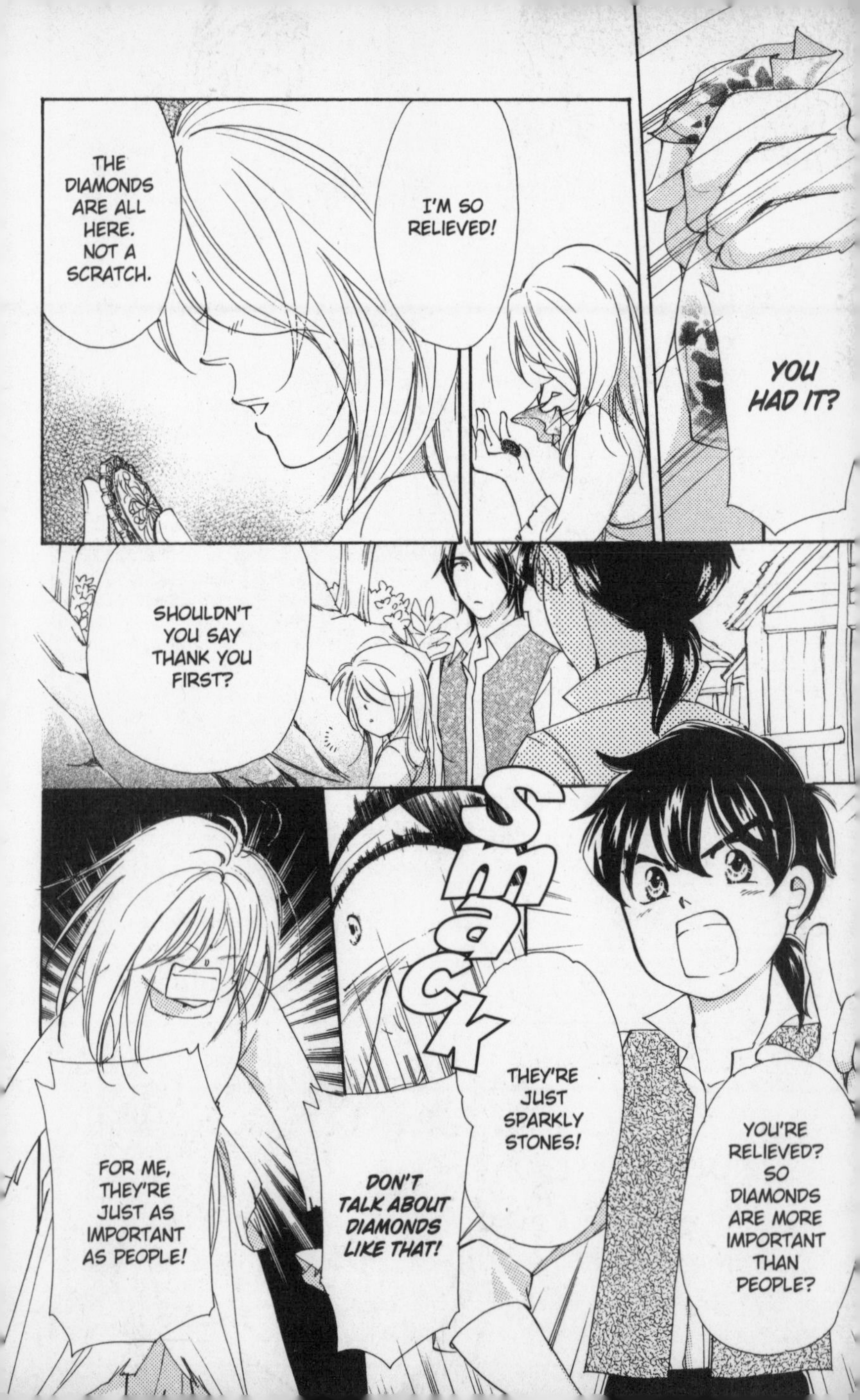
YOU HAD IT?
I'M SO RELIEVED!
THE DIAMONDS ARE ALL HERE. NOT A SCRATCH.
SHOULDN'T YOU SAY THANK YOU FIRST?
SMACK
YOU'RE RELIEVED? SO DIAMONDS ARE MORE IMPORTANT THAN PEOPLE?
THEY'RE JUST SPARKLY STONES!
DON'T TALK ABOUT DIAMONDS LIKE THAT!
FOR ME, THEY'RE JUST AS IMPORTANT AS PEOPLE!

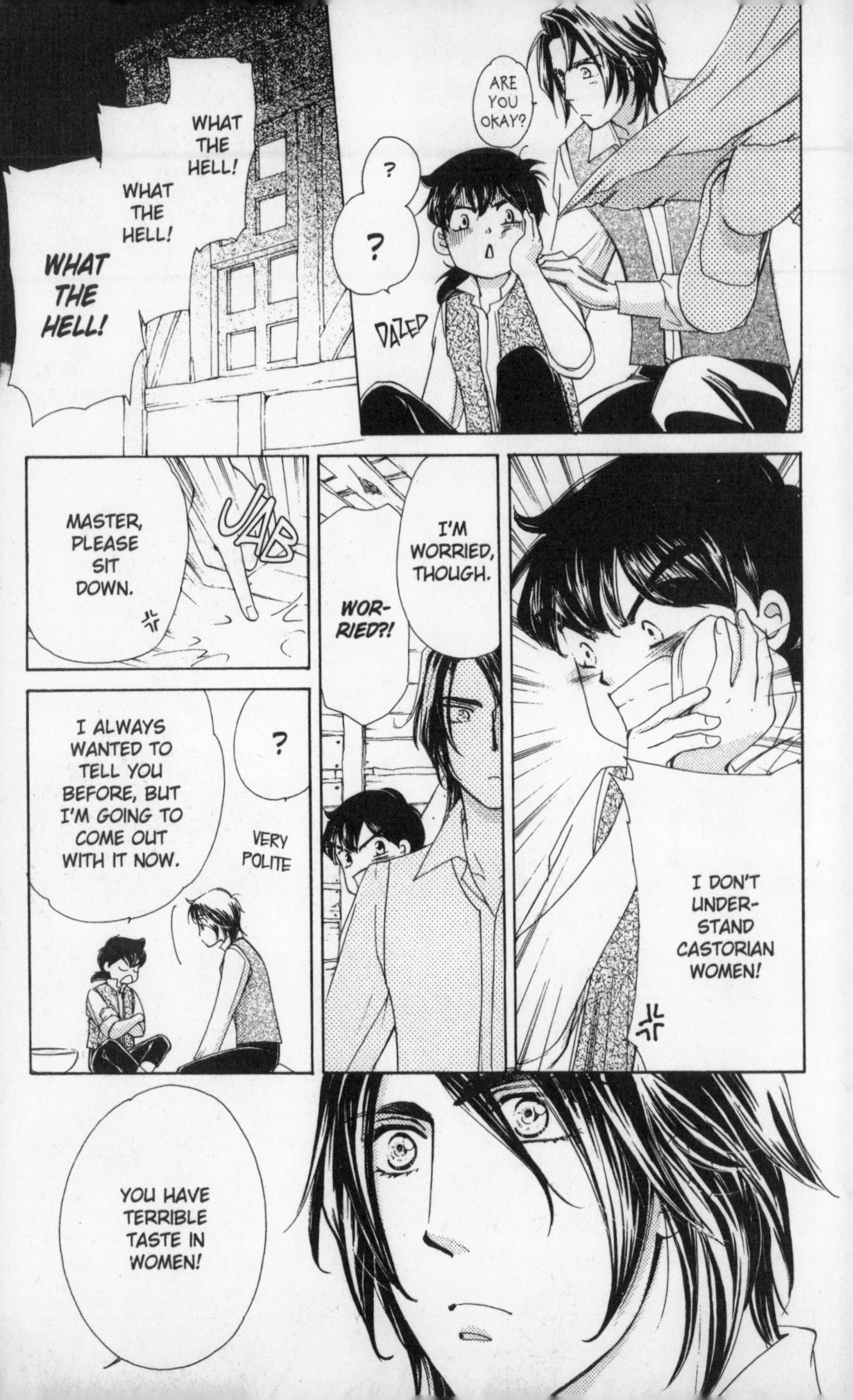
ARE YOU OKAY?
?
?
DAZED
WHAT THE HELL!
WHAT THE HELL!
WHAT THE HELL!
I DON'T UNDER-STAND CASTORIAN WOMEN!
I'M WORRIED, THOUGH.
WOR-RIED?!
JAB
MASTER, PLEASE SIT DOWN.
?
VERY POLITE
I ALWAYS WANTED TO TELL YOU BEFORE, BUT I'M GOING TO COME OUT WITH IT NOW.
YOU HAVE TERRIBLE TASTE IN WOMEN!

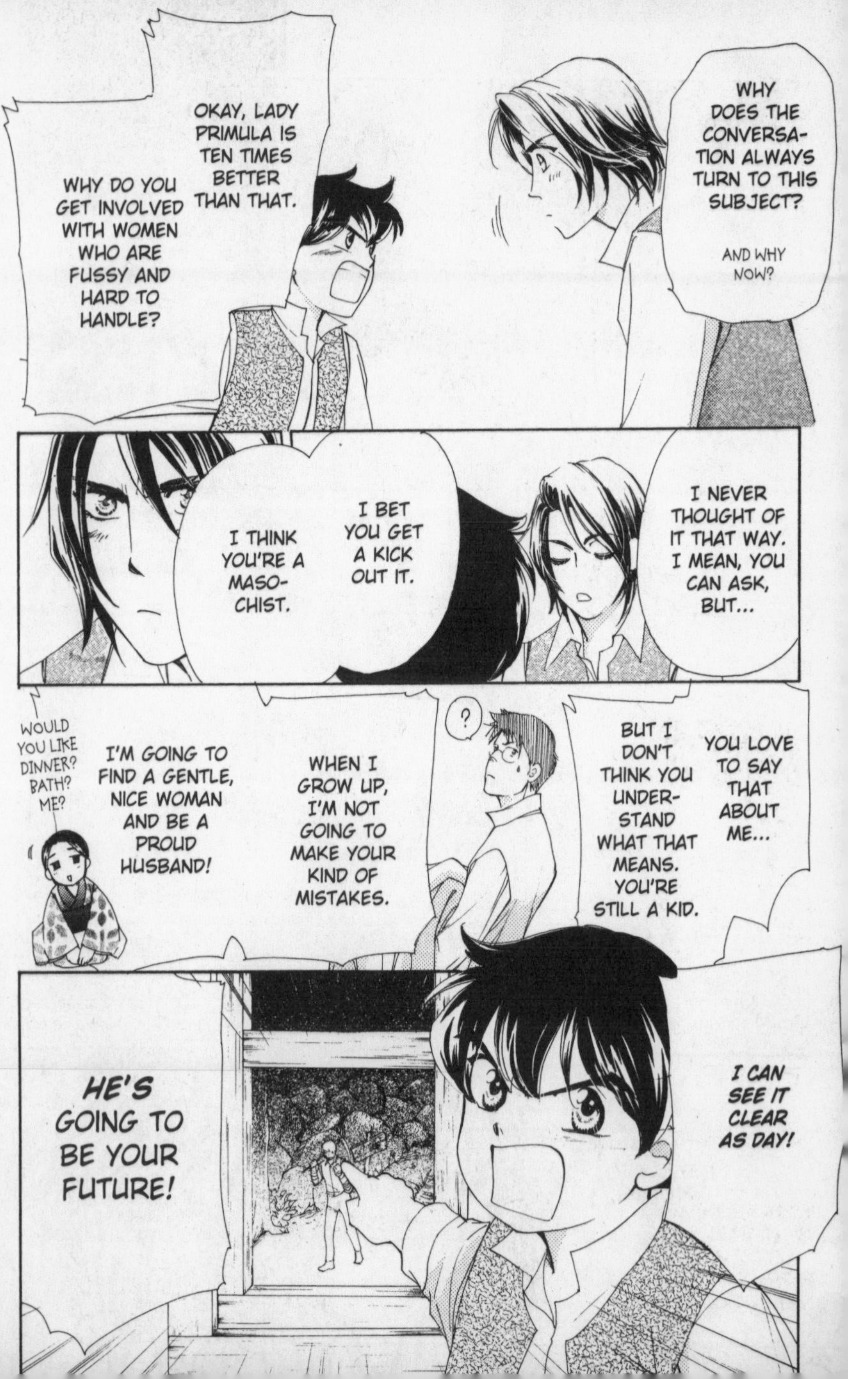
WHY DOES THE CONVERSATION ALWAYS TURN TO THIS SUBJECT?
AND WHY NOW?
OKAY, LADY PRIMULA IS TEN TIMES BETTER THAN THAT.
WHY DO YOU GET INVOLVED WITH WOMEN WHO ARE FUSSY AND HARD TO HANDLE?
I NEVER THOUGHT OF IT THAT WAY. I MEAN, YOU CAN ASK, BUT...
I BET YOU GET A KICK OUT IT.
I THINK YOU'RE A MASOCHIST.
YOU LOVE TO SAY THAT ABOUT ME...
BUT I DON'T THINK YOU UNDERSTAND WHAT THAT MEANS. YOU'RE STILL A KID.
?
WHEN I GROW UP, I'M NOT GOING TO MAKE YOUR KIND OF MISTAKES.
I'M GOING TO FIND A GENTLE, NICE WOMAN AND BE A PROUD HUSBAND!
WOULD YOU LIKE DINNER? BATH? ME?
I CAN SEE IT CLEAR AS DAY!
HE'S GOING TO BE YOUR FUTURE!

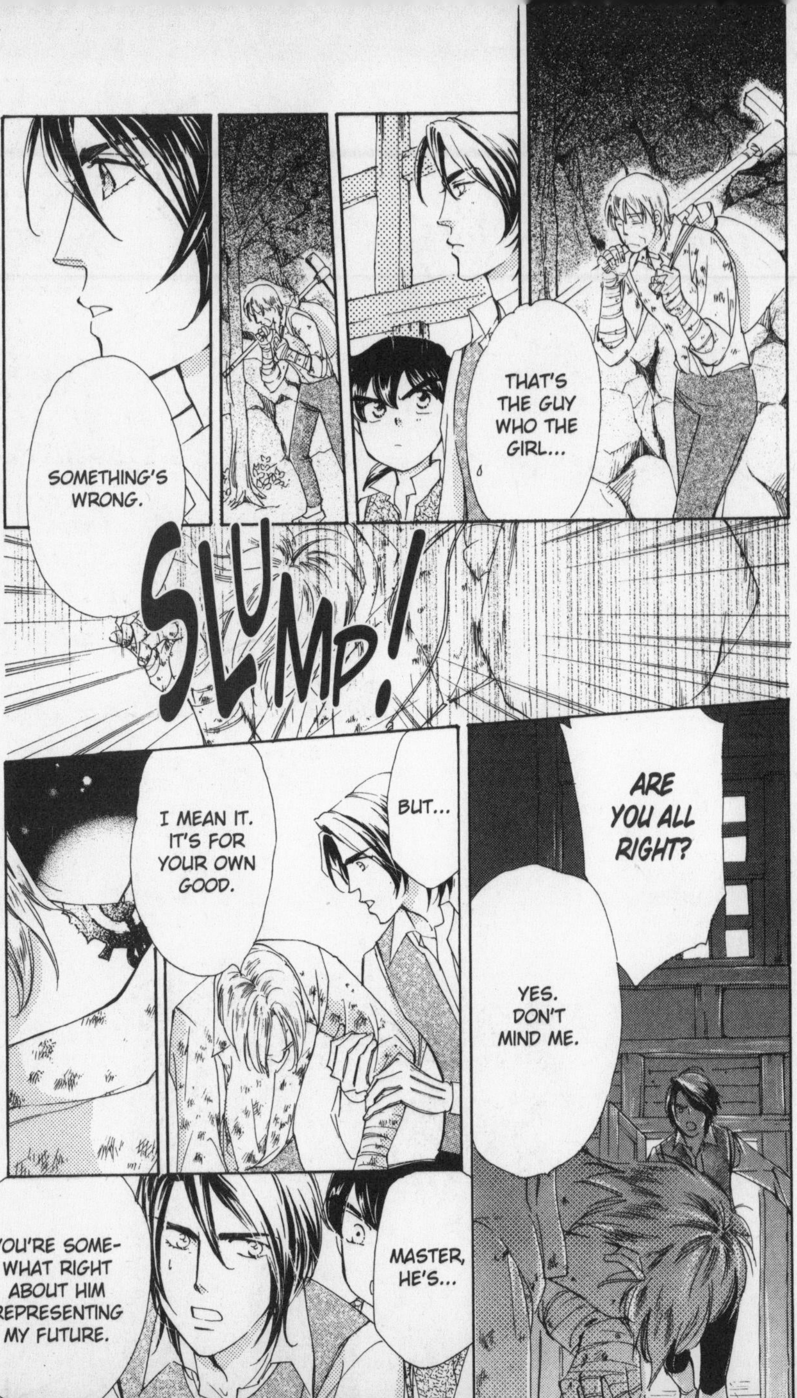
THAT'S THE GUY WHO THE GIRL...
SOMETHING'S WRONG.
SLUMP!
ARE YOU ALL RIGHT?
YES. DON'T MIND ME.
BUT...
I MEAN IT. IT'S FOR YOUR OWN GOOD.
MASTER, HE'S...
YOU'RE SOME-WHAT RIGHT ABOUT HIM REPRESENTING MY FUTURE.

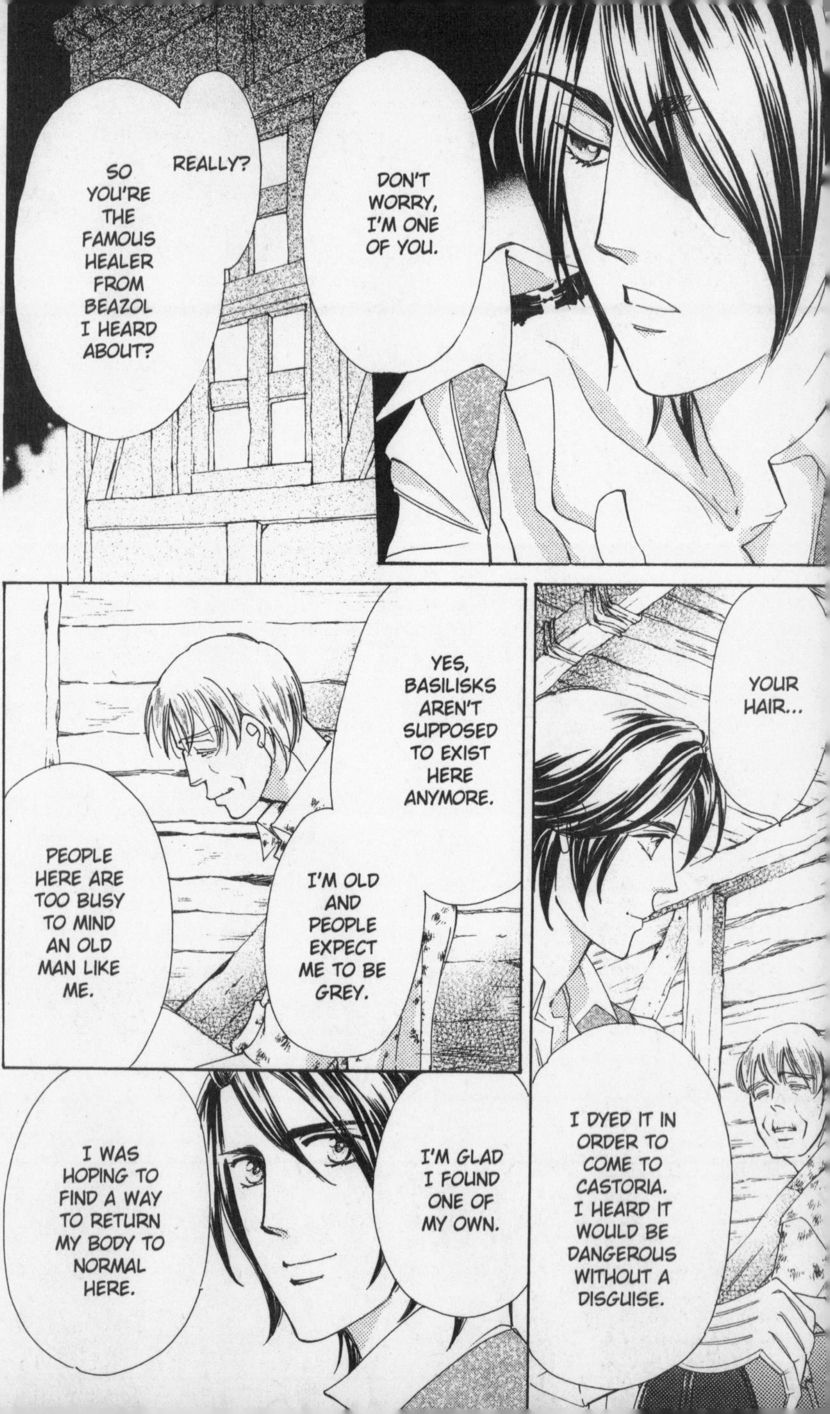
DON'T WORRY, I'M ONE OF YOU.
REALLY?
SO YOU'RE THE FAMOUS HEALER FROM BEAZOL I HEARD ABOUT?
YOUR HAIR...
I DYED IT IN ORDER TO COME TO CASTORIA. I HEARD IT WOULD BE DANGEROUS WITHOUT A DISGUISE.
YES, BASILISKS AREN'T SUPPOSED TO EXIST HERE ANYMORE.
I'M OLD AND PEOPLE EXPECT ME TO BE GREY.
PEOPLE HERE ARE TOO BUSY TO MIND AN OLD MAN LIKE ME.
I'M GLAD I FOUND ONE OF MY OWN.
I WAS HOPING TO FIND A WAY TO RETURN MY BODY TO NORMAL HERE.

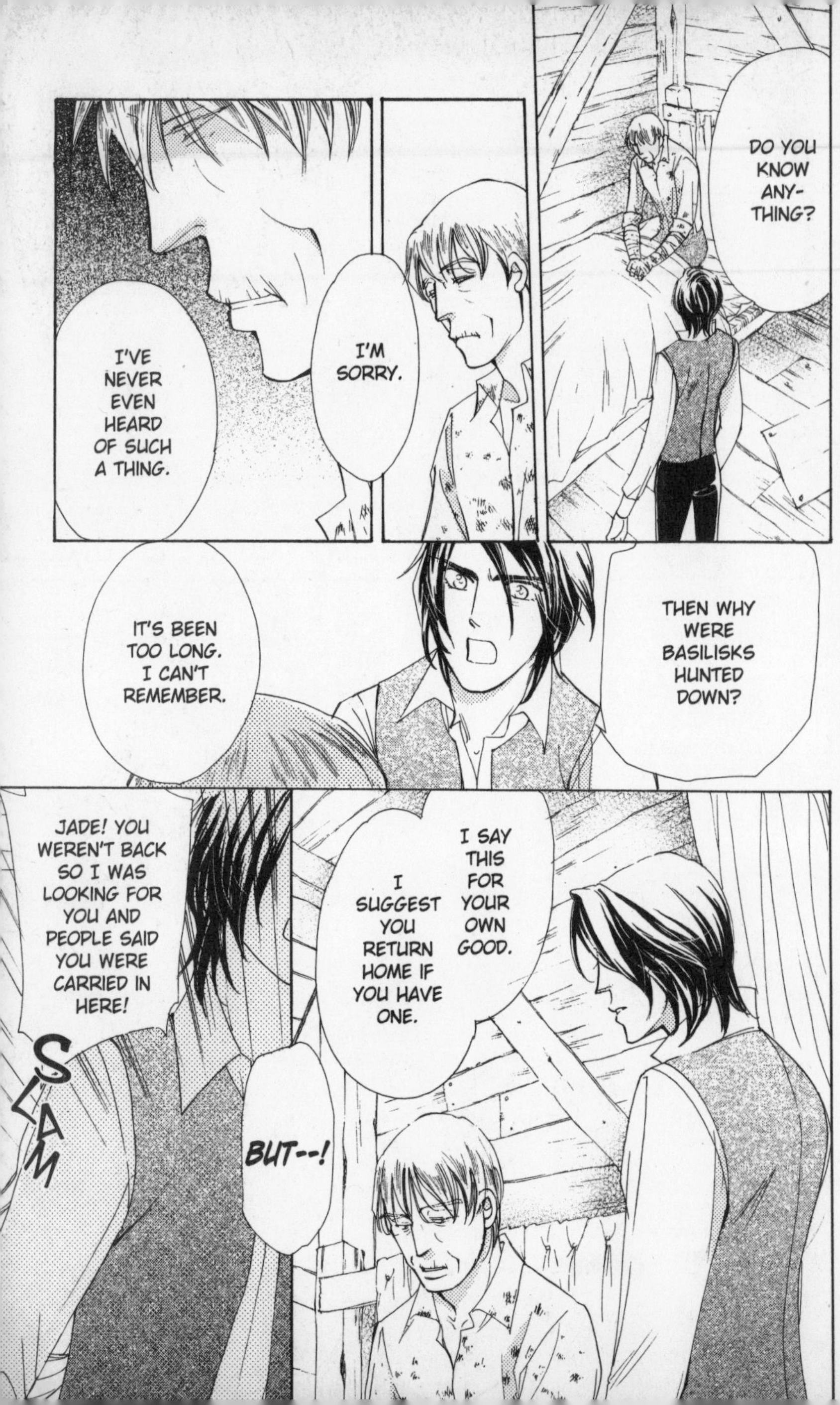
DO YOU KNOW ANY-THING?
I'M SORRY.
I'VE NEVER EVEN HEARD OF SUCH A THING.
THEN WHY WERE BASILISKS HUNTED DOWN?
IT'S BEEN TOO LONG. I CAN'T REMEMBER.
I SAY THIS FOR YOUR OWN GOOD.
I SUGGEST YOU RETURN HOME IF YOU HAVE ONE.
BUT--!
JADE! YOU WEREN'T BACK SO I WAS LOOKING FOR YOU AND PEOPLE SAID YOU WERE CARRIED IN HERE!
SLAM

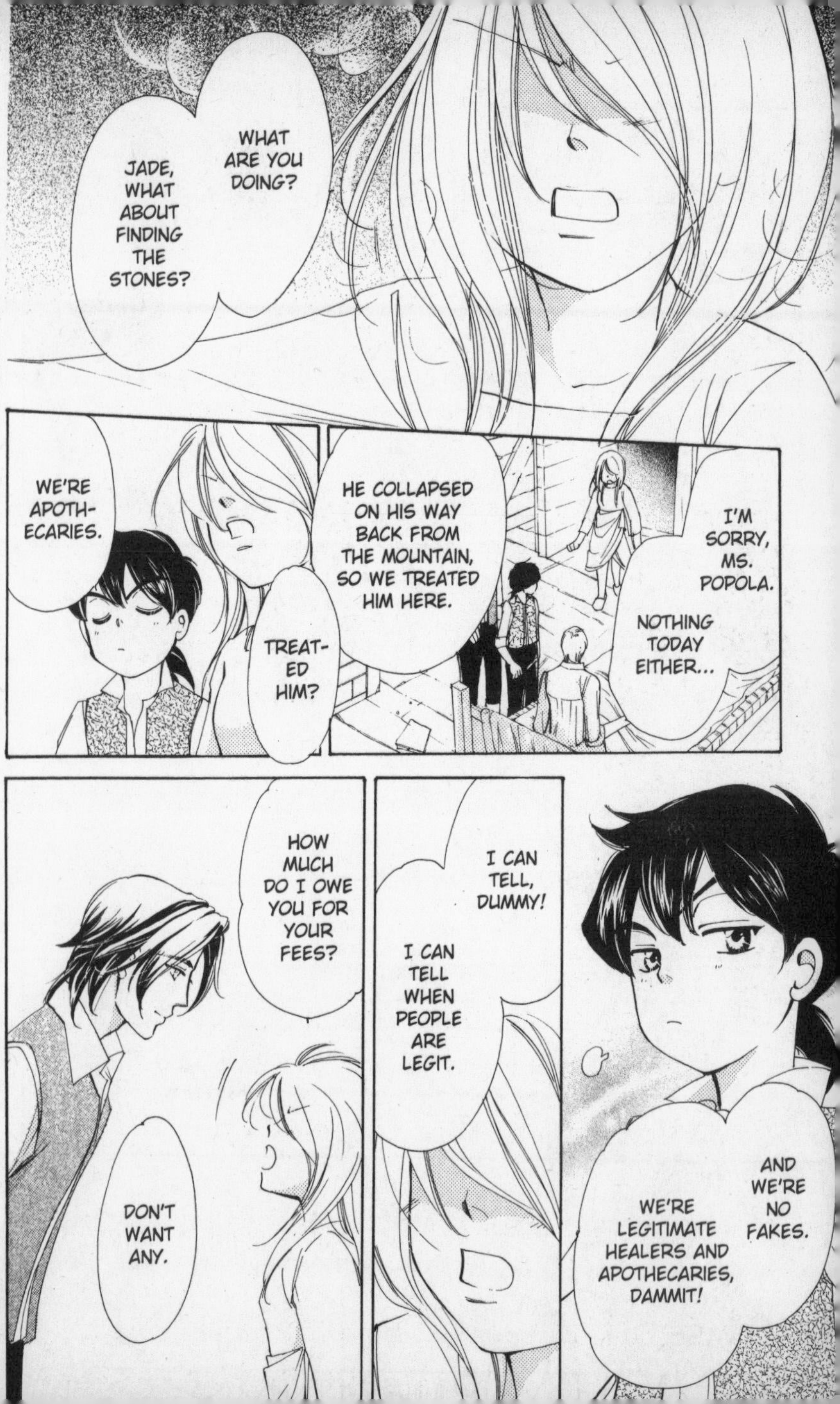
WHAT ARE YOU DOING?
JADE, WHAT ABOUT FINDING THE STONES?
I'M SORRY, MS. POPOLA.
NOTHING TODAY EITHER...
HE COLLAPSED ON HIS WAY BACK FROM THE MOUNTAIN, SO WE TREATED HIM HERE.
TREAT-ED HIM?
WE'RE APOTH-ECARIES.
AND WE'RE NO FAKES.
WE'RE LEGITIMATE HEALERS AND APOTHECARIES, DAMMIT!
I CAN TELL, DUMMY!
I CAN TELL WHEN PEOPLE ARE LEGIT.
HOW MUCH DO I OWE YOU FOR YOUR FEES?
DON'T WANT ANY.

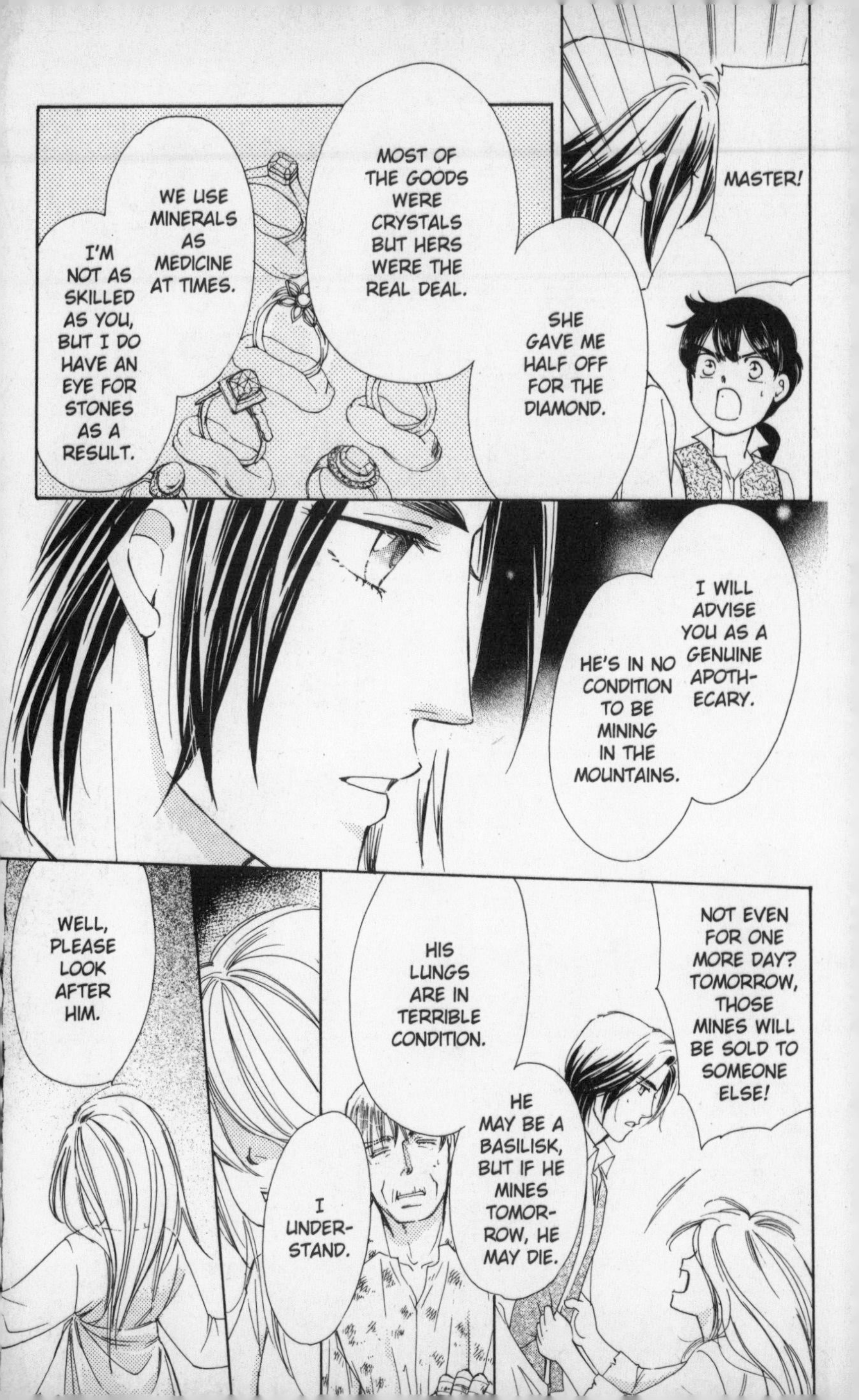
MASTER!
SHE GAVE ME HALF OFF FOR THE DIAMOND.
MOST OF THE GOODS WERE CRYSTALS BUT HERS WERE THE REAL DEAL.
WE USE MINERALS AS MEDICINE AT TIMES.
I'M NOT AS SKILLED AS YOU, BUT I DO HAVE AN EYE FOR STONES AS A RESULT.
I WILL ADVISE YOU AS A GENUINE APOTH-ECARY.
HE'S IN NO CONDITION TO BE MINING IN THE MOUNTAINS.
NOT EVEN FOR ONE MORE DAY? TOMORROW, THOSE MINES WILL BE SOLD TO SOMEONE ELSE!
HIS LUNGS ARE IN TERRIBLE CONDITION.
HE MAY BE A BASILISK, BUT IF HE MINES TOMOR-ROW, HE MAY DIE.
I UNDER-STAND.
WELL, PLEASE LOOK AFTER HIM.

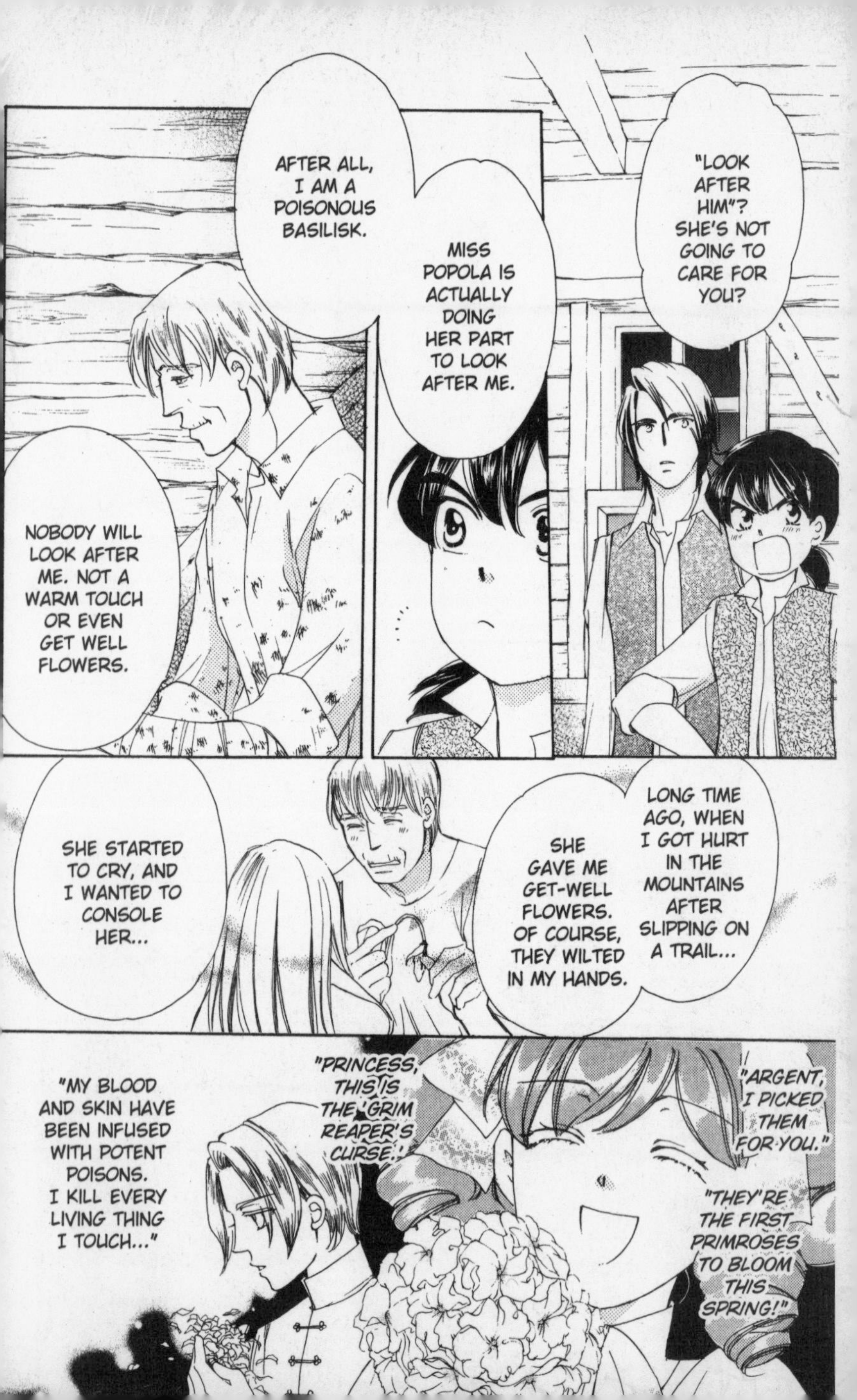
"LOOK AFTER HIM"? SHE'S NOT GOING TO CARE FOR YOU?
MISS POPOLA IS ACTUALLY DOING HER PART TO LOOK AFTER ME.
AFTER ALL, I AM A POISONOUS BASILISK.
NOBODY WILL LOOK AFTER ME. NOT A WARM TOUCH OR EVEN GET WELL FLOWERS.
LONG TIME AGO, WHEN I GOT HURT IN THE MOUNTAINS AFTER SLIPPING ON A TRAIL...
SHE GAVE ME GET-WELL FLOWERS. OF COURSE, THEY WILTED IN MY HANDS.
SHE STARTED TO CRY, AND I WANTED TO CONSOLE HER...
"ARGENT, I PICKED THEM FOR YOU."
"THEY'RE THE FIRST PRIMROSES TO BLOOM THIS SPRING!"
"PRINCESS, THIS IS THE GRIM REAPER'S CURSE."
"MY BLOOD AND SKIN HAVE BEEN INFUSED WITH POTENT POISONS. I KILL EVERY LIVING THING I TOUCH..."

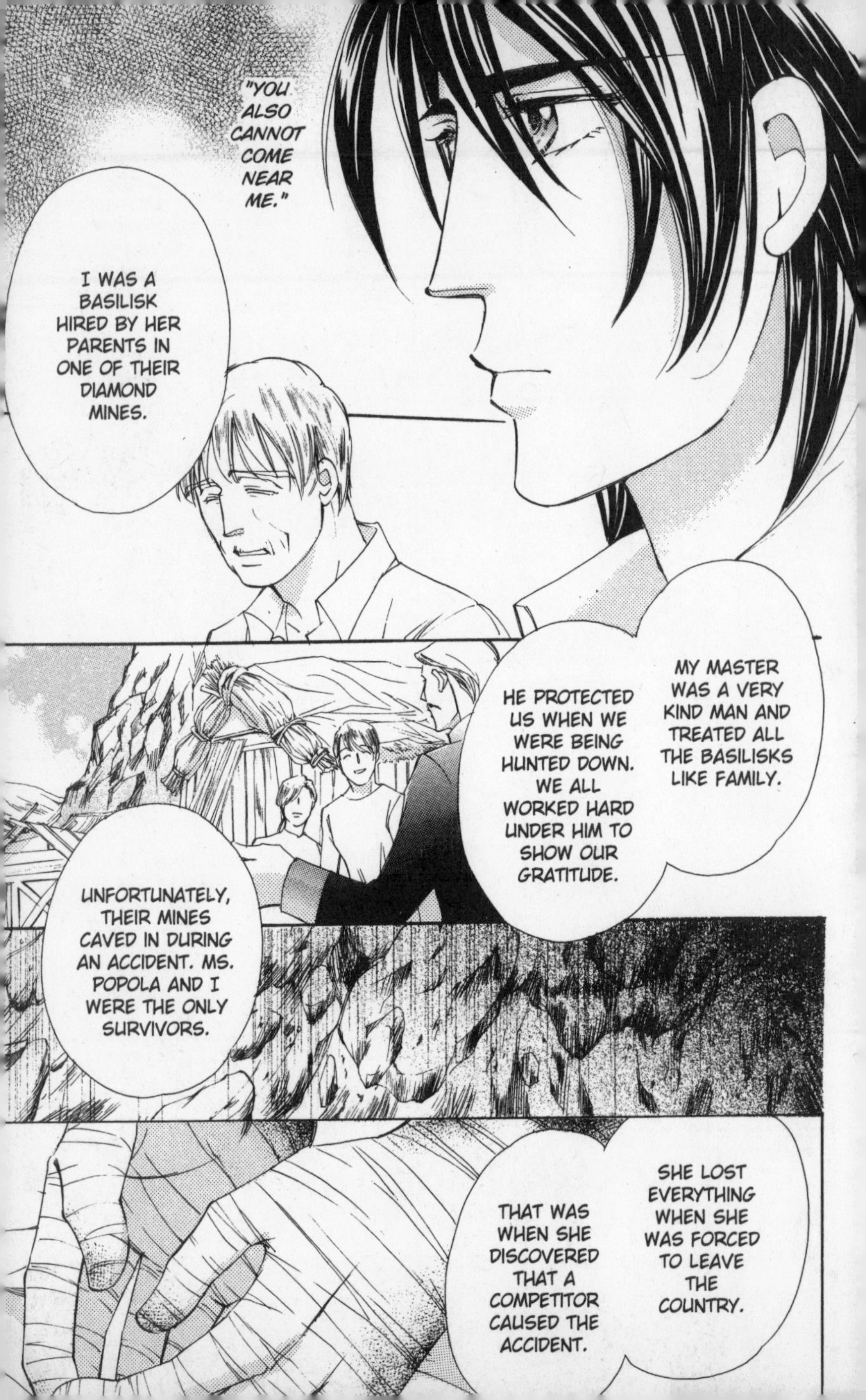
"YOU ALSO CANNOT COME NEAR ME."
I WAS A BASILISK HIRED BY HER PARENTS IN ONE OF THEIR DIAMOND MINES.
MY MASTER WAS A VERY KIND MAN AND TREATED ALL THE BASILISKS LIKE FAMILY.
HE PROTECTED US WHEN WE WERE BEING HUNTED DOWN. WE ALL WORKED HARD UNDER HIM TO SHOW OUR GRATITUDE.
UNFORTUNATELY, THEIR MINES CAVED IN DURING AN ACCIDENT. MS. POPOLA AND I WERE THE ONLY SURVIVORS.
SHE LOST EVERYTHING WHEN SHE WAS FORCED TO LEAVE THE COUNTRY.
THAT WAS WHEN SHE DISCOVERED THAT A COMPETITOR CAUSED THE ACCIDENT.

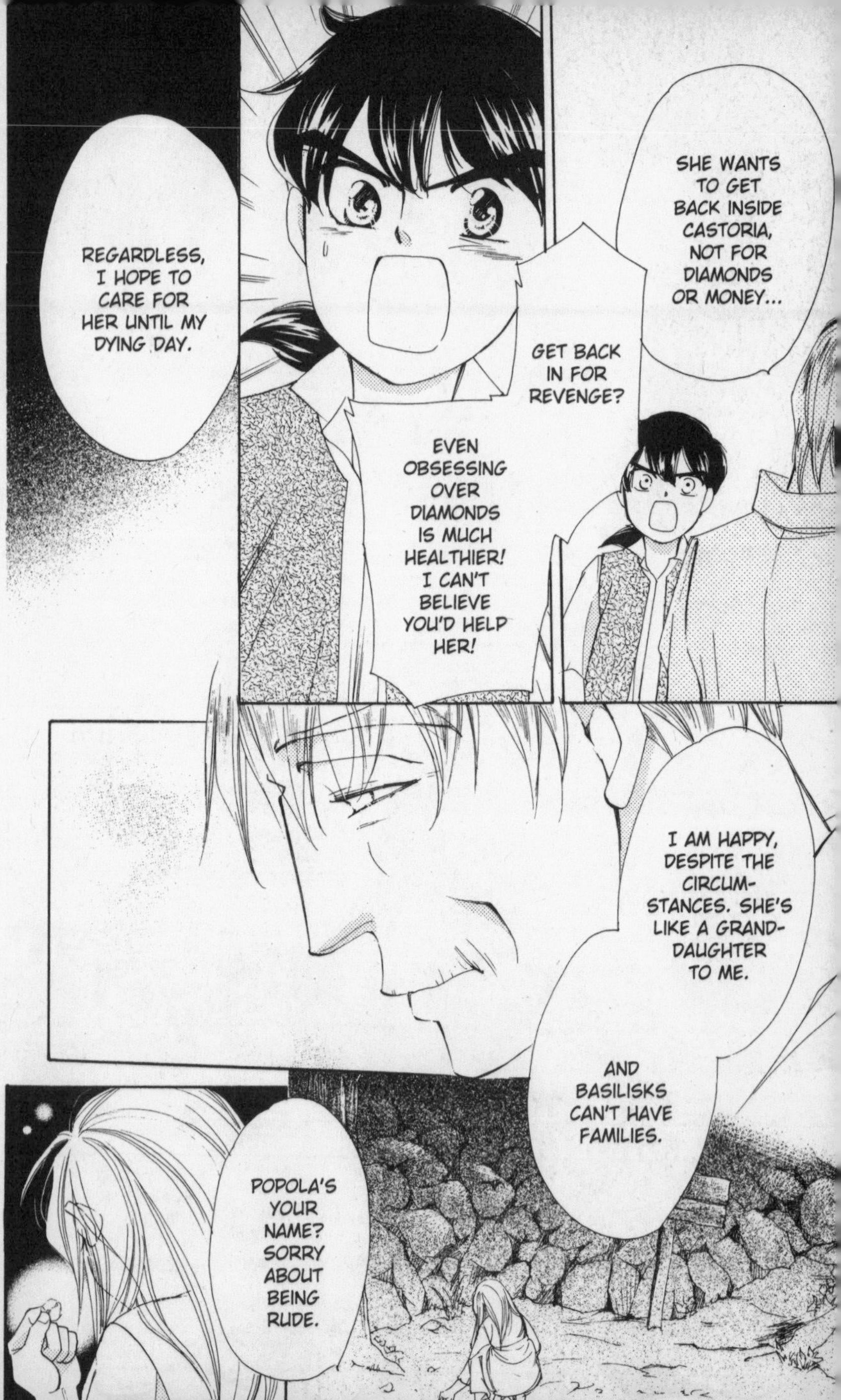
SHE WANTS TO GET BACK INSIDE CASTORIA, NOT FOR DIAMONDS OR MONEY...
GET BACK IN FOR REVENGE?
EVEN OBSESSING OVER DIAMONDS IS MUCH HEALTHIER! I CAN'T BELIEVE YOU'D HELP HER!
REGARDLESS, I HOPE TO CARE FOR HER UNTIL MY DYING DAY.
I AM HAPPY, DESPITE THE CIRCUM-STANCES. SHE'S LIKE A GRAND-DAUGHTER TO ME.
AND BASILISKS CAN'T HAVE FAMILIES.
POPOLA'S YOUR NAME? SORRY ABOUT BEING RUDE.

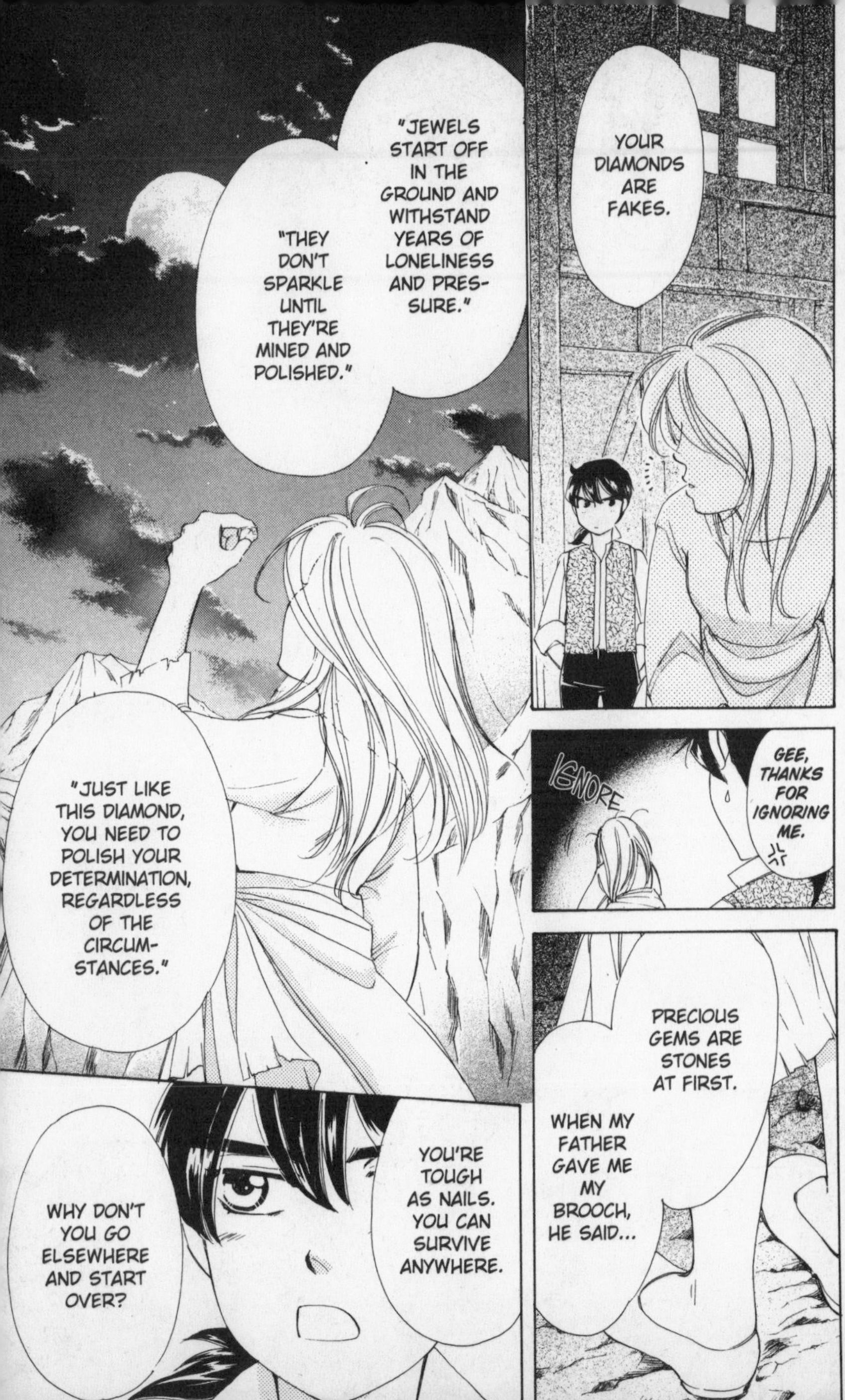
YOUR DIAMONDS ARE FAKES.
IGNORE
GEE, THANKS FOR IGNORING ME.
PRECIOUS GEMS ARE STONES AT FIRST.
WHEN MY FATHER GAVE ME MY BROOCH, HE SAID...
"JEWELS START OFF IN THE GROUND AND WITHSTAND YEARS OF LONELINESS AND PRES-SURE."
"THEY DON'T SPARKLE UNTIL THEY'RE MINED AND POLISHED."
"JUST LIKE THIS DIAMOND, YOU NEED TO POLISH YOUR DETERMINATION, REGARDLESS OF THE CIRCUM-STANCES."
YOU'RE TOUGH AS NAILS. YOU CAN SURVIVE ANYWHERE.
WHY DON'T YOU GO ELSEWHERE AND START OVER?

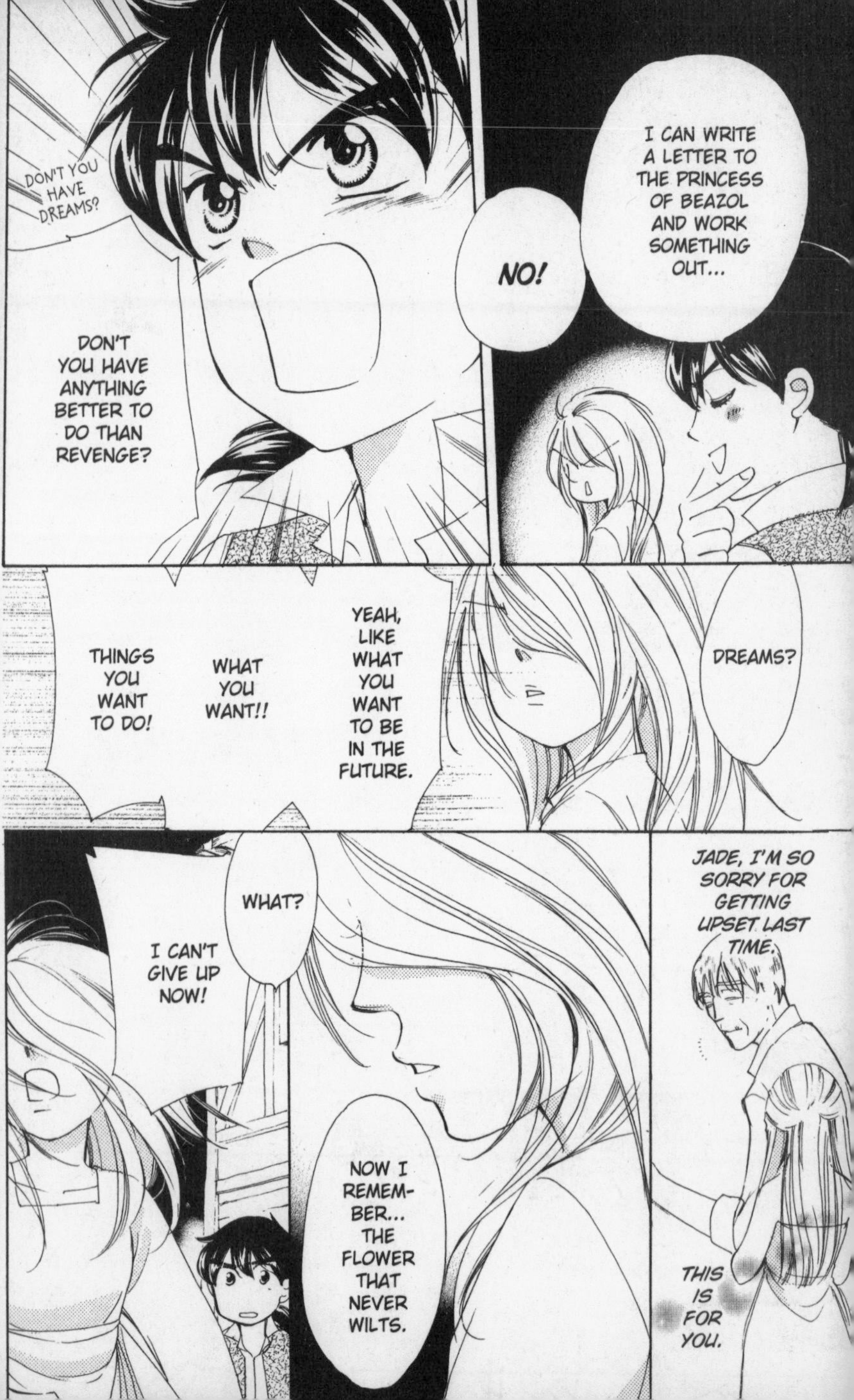
I CAN WRITE A LETTER TO THE PRINCESS OF BEAZOL AND WORK SOMETHING OUT...
NO!
DON'T YOU HAVE DREAMS?
DON'T YOU HAVE ANYTHING BETTER TO DO THAN REVENGE?
DREAMS?
YEAH, LIKE WHAT YOU WANT TO BE IN THE FUTURE.
WHAT YOU WANT!!
THINGS YOU WANT TO DO!
JADE, I'M SO SORRY FOR GETTING UPSET LAST TIME.
THIS IS FOR YOU.
NOW I REMEMBER... THE FLOWER THAT NEVER WILTS.
WHAT?
I CAN'T GIVE UP NOW!

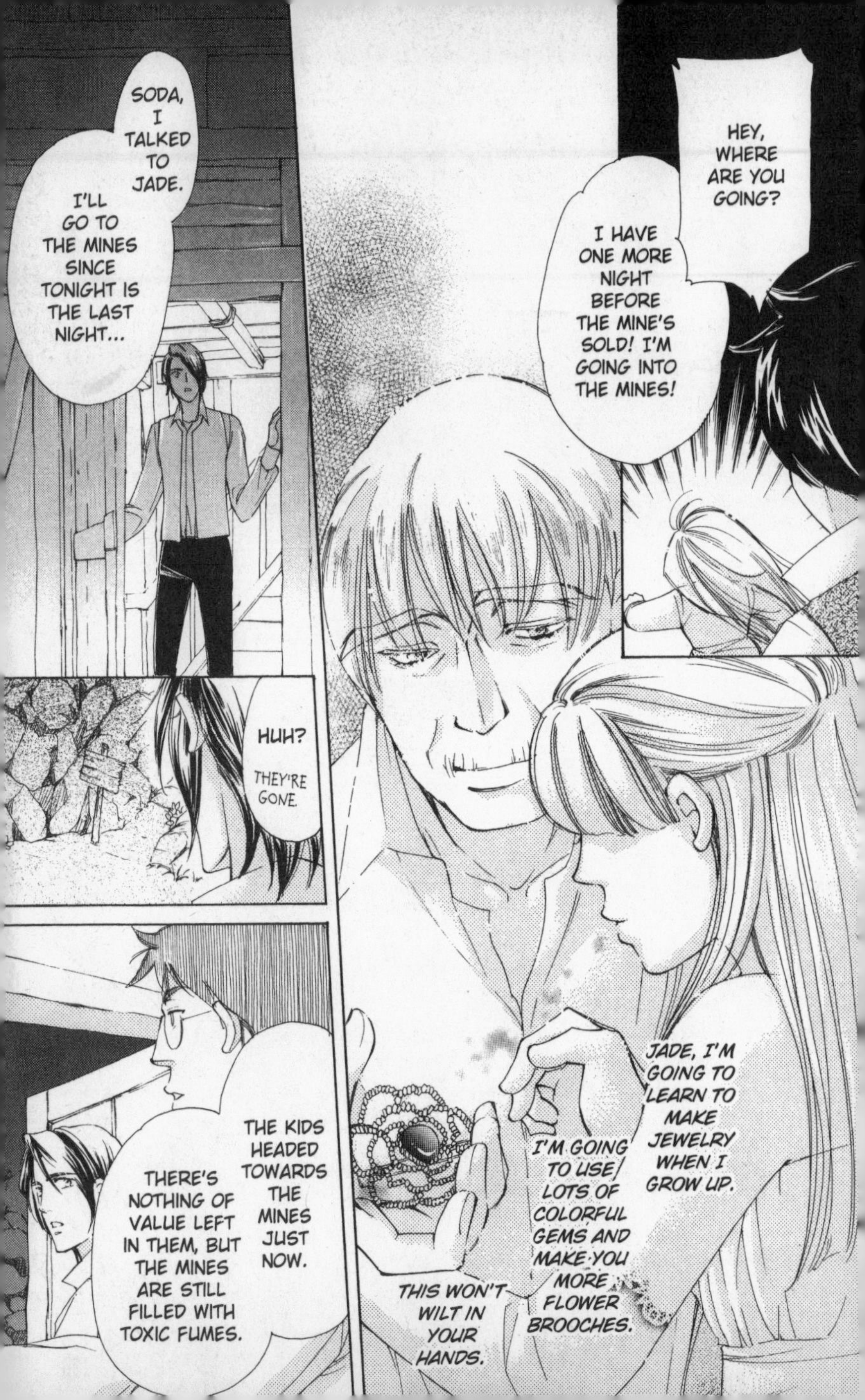
HEY, WHERE ARE YOU GOING?
I HAVE ONE MORE NIGHT BEFORE THE MINE'S SOLD! I'M GOING INTO THE MINES!
JADE, I'M GOING TO LEARN TO MAKE JEWELRY WHEN I GROW UP.
I'M GOING TO USE LOTS OF COLORFUL GEMS AND MAKE YOU MORE FLOWER BROOCHES.
THIS WON'T WILT IN YOUR HANDS.
SODA, I TALKED TO JADE.
I'LL GO TO THE MINES SINCE TONIGHT IS THE LAST NIGHT...
HUH?
THEY'RE GONE.
THE KIDS HEADED TOWARDS THE MINES JUST NOW.
THERE'S NOTHING OF VALUE LEFT IN THEM, BUT THE MINES ARE STILL FILLED WITH TOXIC FUMES.

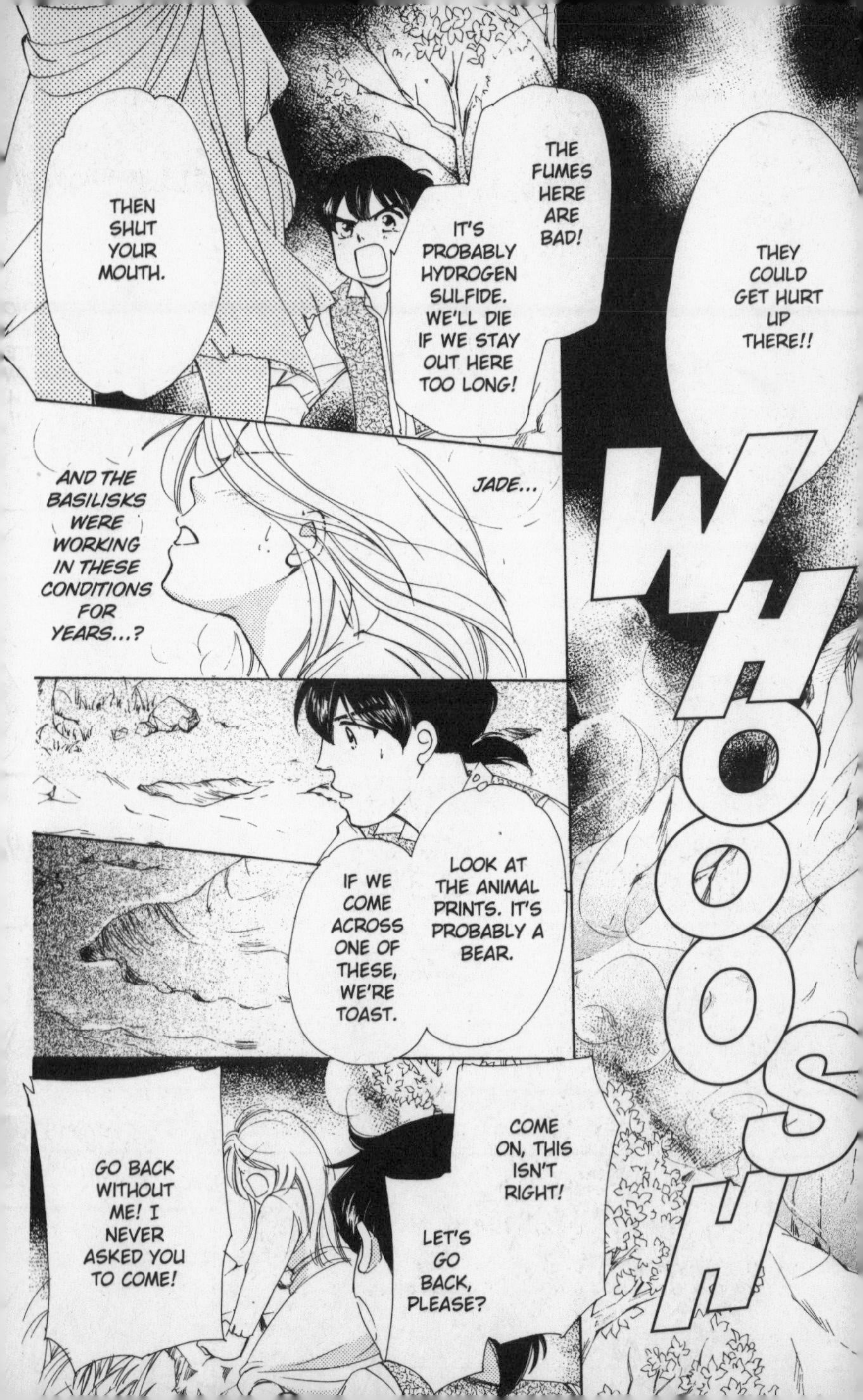
THEY COULD GET HURT UP THERE!!
WHOOOSH
THE FUMES HERE ARE BAD!
IT'S PROBABLY HYDROGEN SULFIDE. WE'LL DIE IF WE STAY OUT HERE TOO LONG!
THEN SHUT YOUR MOUTH.
JADE...
AND THE BASILISKS WERE WORKING IN THESE CONDITIONS FOR YEARS...?
LOOK AT THE ANIMAL PRINTS. IT'S PROBABLY A BEAR.
IF WE COME ACROSS ONE OF THESE, WE'RE TOAST.
COME ON, THIS ISN'T RIGHT!
LET'S GO BACK, PLEASE?
GO BACK WITHOUT ME! I NEVER ASKED YOU TO COME!

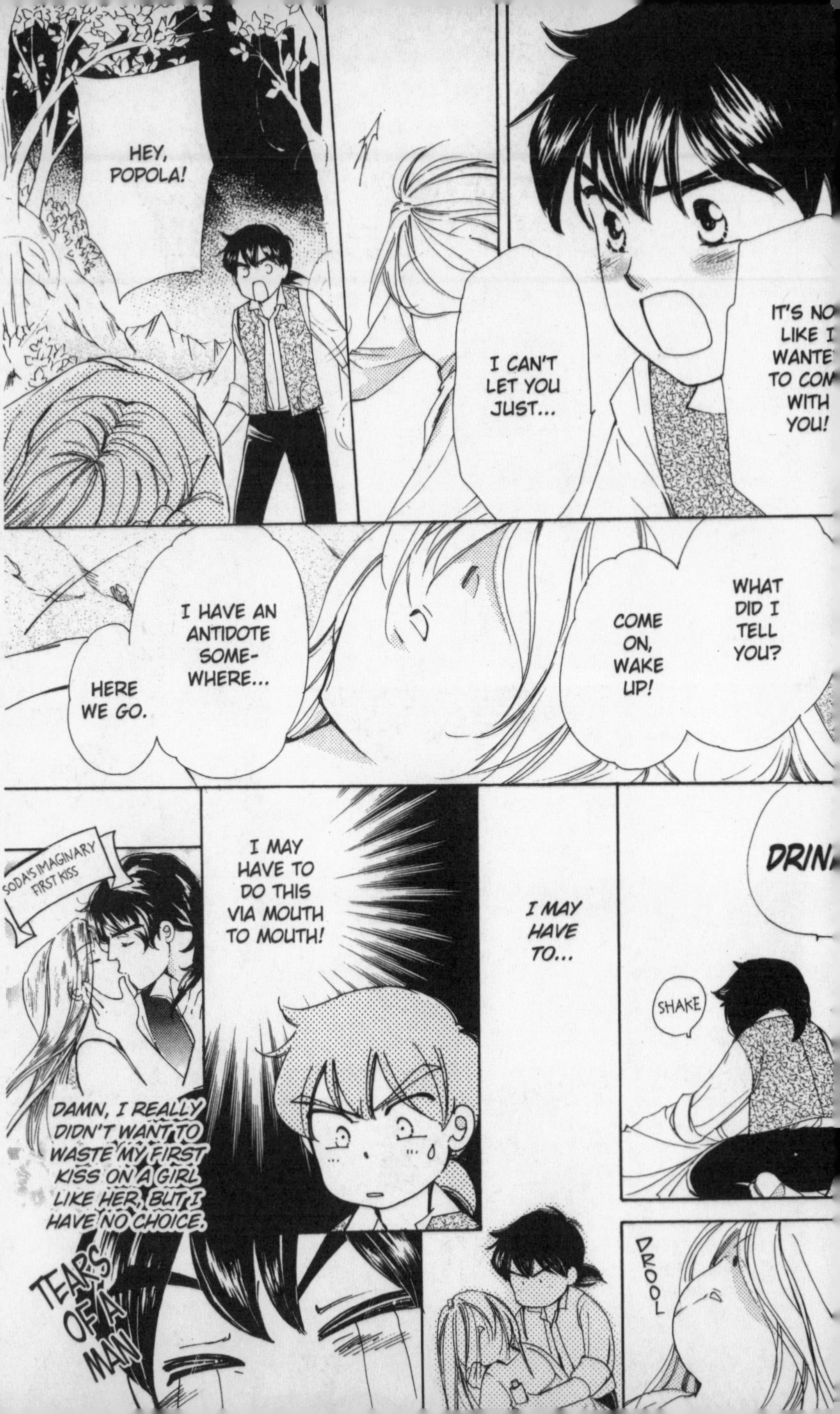
IT'S NO LIKE I WANTE TO COM WITH YOU!
I CAN'T LET YOU JUST...
HEY, POPOLA!
WHAT DID I TELL YOU?
COME ON, WAKE UP!
I HAVE AN ANTIDOTE SOME-WHERE...
HERE WE GO.
DRIN
SHAKE
I MAY HAVE TO...
I MAY HAVE TO DO THIS VIA MOUTH TO MOUTH!
SODA'S IMAGINARY FIRST KISS
DAMN, I REALLY DIDN'T WANT TO WASTE MY FIRST KISS ON A GIRL LIKE HER, BUT I HAVE NO CHOICE.
DROOL
TEARS OF A MAN

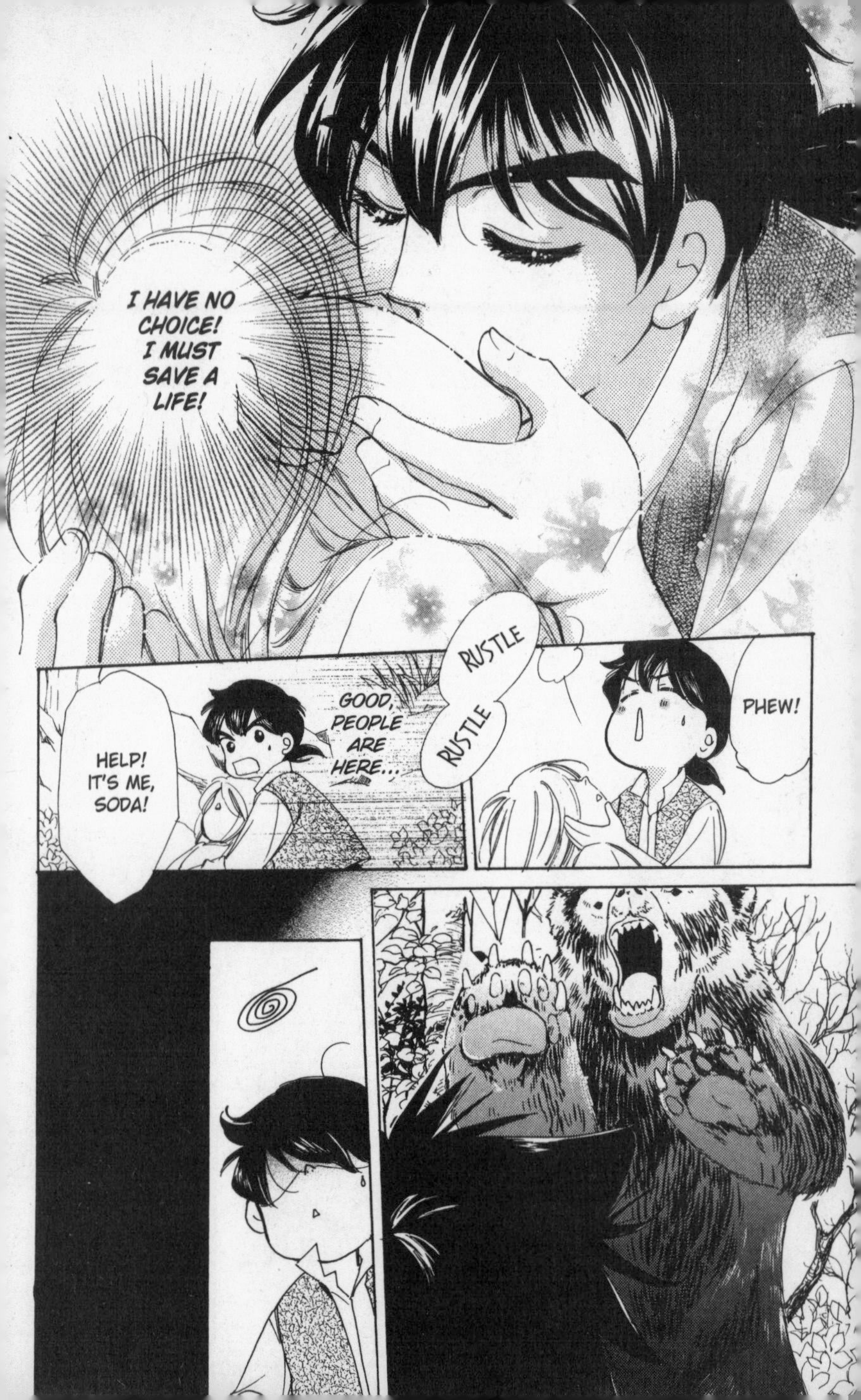
I HAVE NO CHOICE! I MUST SAVE A LIFE!
PHEW!
RUSTLE
RUSTLE
GOOD, PEOPLE ARE HERE...
HELP! IT'S ME, SODA!

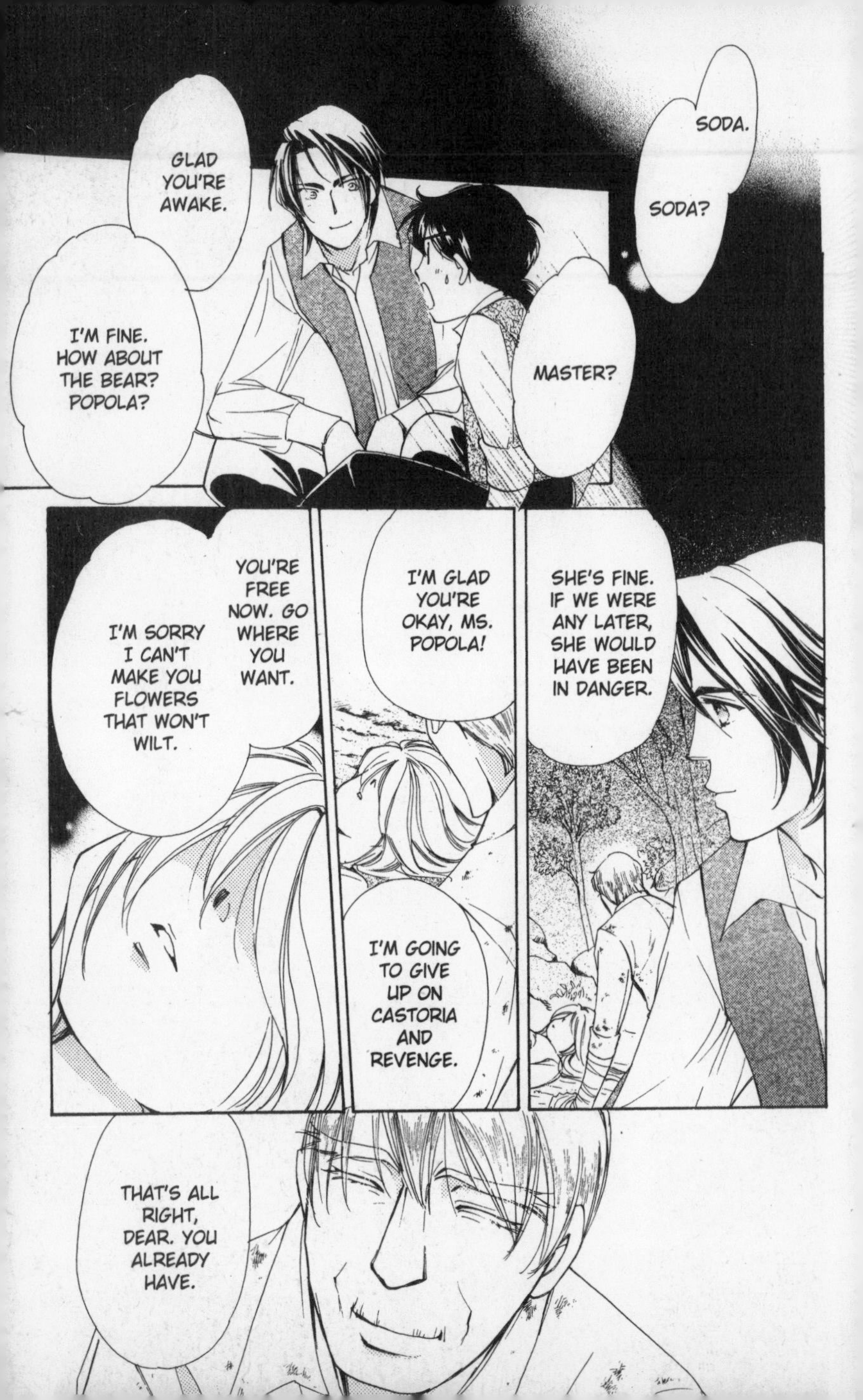
SODA.
SODA?
MASTER?
GLAD YOU'RE AWAKE.
I'M FINE. HOW ABOUT THE BEAR? POPOLA?
SHE'S FINE. IF WE WERE ANY LATER, SHE WOULD HAVE BEEN IN DANGER.
I'M GLAD YOU'RE OKAY, MS. POPOLA!
I'M GOING TO GIVE UP ON CASTORIA AND REVENGE.
YOU'RE FREE NOW. GO WHERE YOU WANT.
I'M SORRY I CAN'T MAKE YOU FLOWERS THAT WON'T WILT.
THAT'S ALL RIGHT, DEAR. YOU ALREADY HAVE.

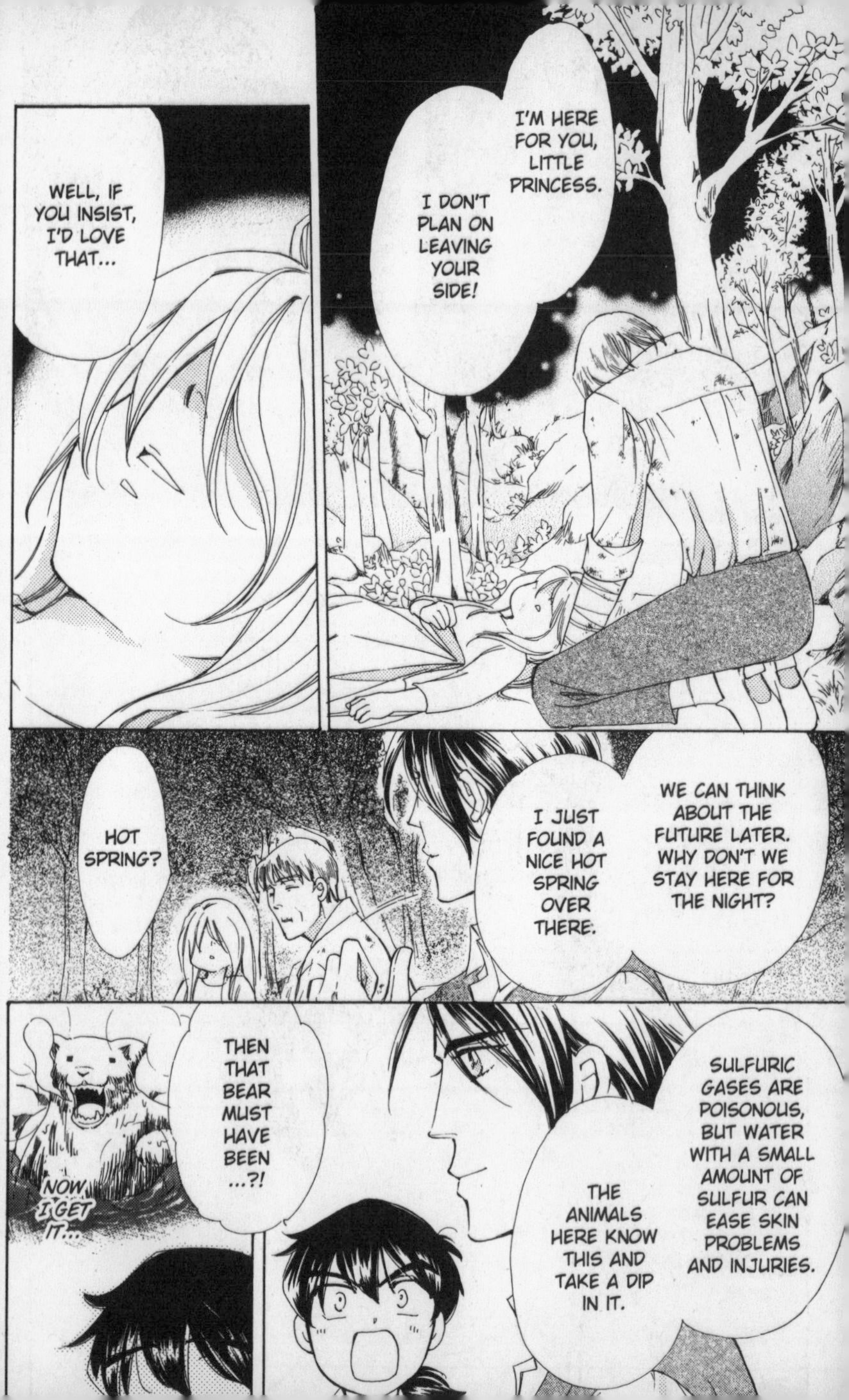
I'M HERE FOR YOU, LITTLE PRINCESS.
I DON'T PLAN ON LEAVING YOUR SIDE!
WELL, IF YOU INSIST, I'D LOVE THAT...
WE CAN THINK ABOUT THE FUTURE LATER. WHY DON'T WE STAY HERE FOR THE NIGHT?
I JUST FOUND A NICE HOT SPRING OVER THERE.
HOT SPRING?
SULFURIC GASES ARE POISONOUS, BUT WATER WITH A SMALL AMOUNT OF SULFUR CAN EASE SKIN PROBLEMS AND INJURIES.
THE ANIMALS HERE KNOW THIS AND TAKE A DIP IN IT.
THEN THAT BEAR MUST HAVE BEEN ...?!
NOW I GET IT...

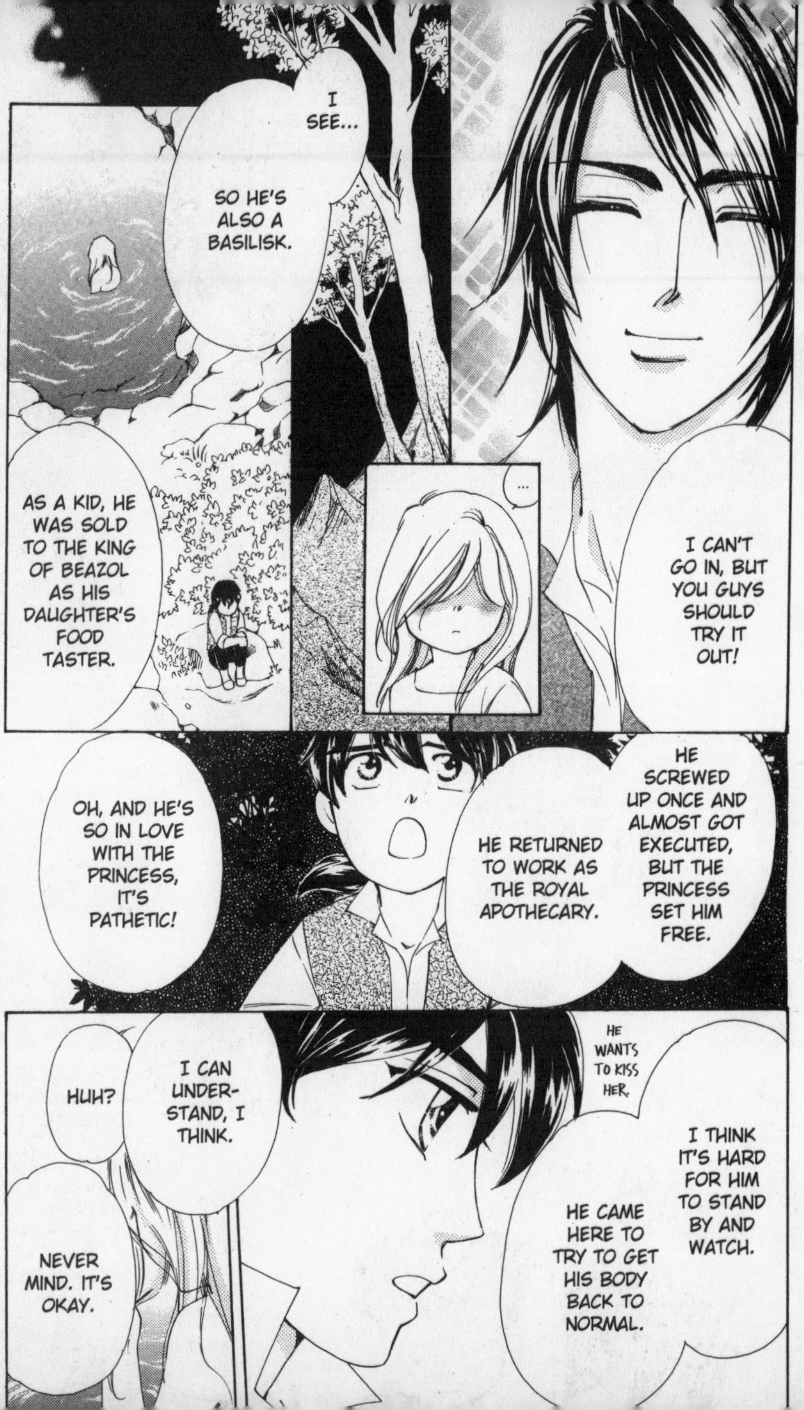
I CAN'T GO IN, BUT YOU GUYS SHOULD TRY IT OUT!
...
I SEE...
SO HE'S ALSO A BASILISK.
AS A KID, HE WAS SOLD TO THE KING OF BEAZOL AS HIS DAUGHTER'S FOOD TASTER.
HE SCREWED UP ONCE AND ALMOST GOT EXECUTED, BUT THE PRINCESS SET HIM FREE.
HE RETURNED TO WORK AS THE ROYAL APOTHECARY.
OH, AND HE'S SO IN LOVE WITH THE PRINCESS, IT'S PATHETIC!
HE WANTS TO KISS HER.
I THINK IT'S HARD FOR HIM TO STAND BY AND WATCH.
HE CAME HERE TO TRY TO GET HIS BODY BACK TO NORMAL.
I CAN UNDER-STAND, I THINK.
HUH?
NEVER MIND. IT'S OKAY.

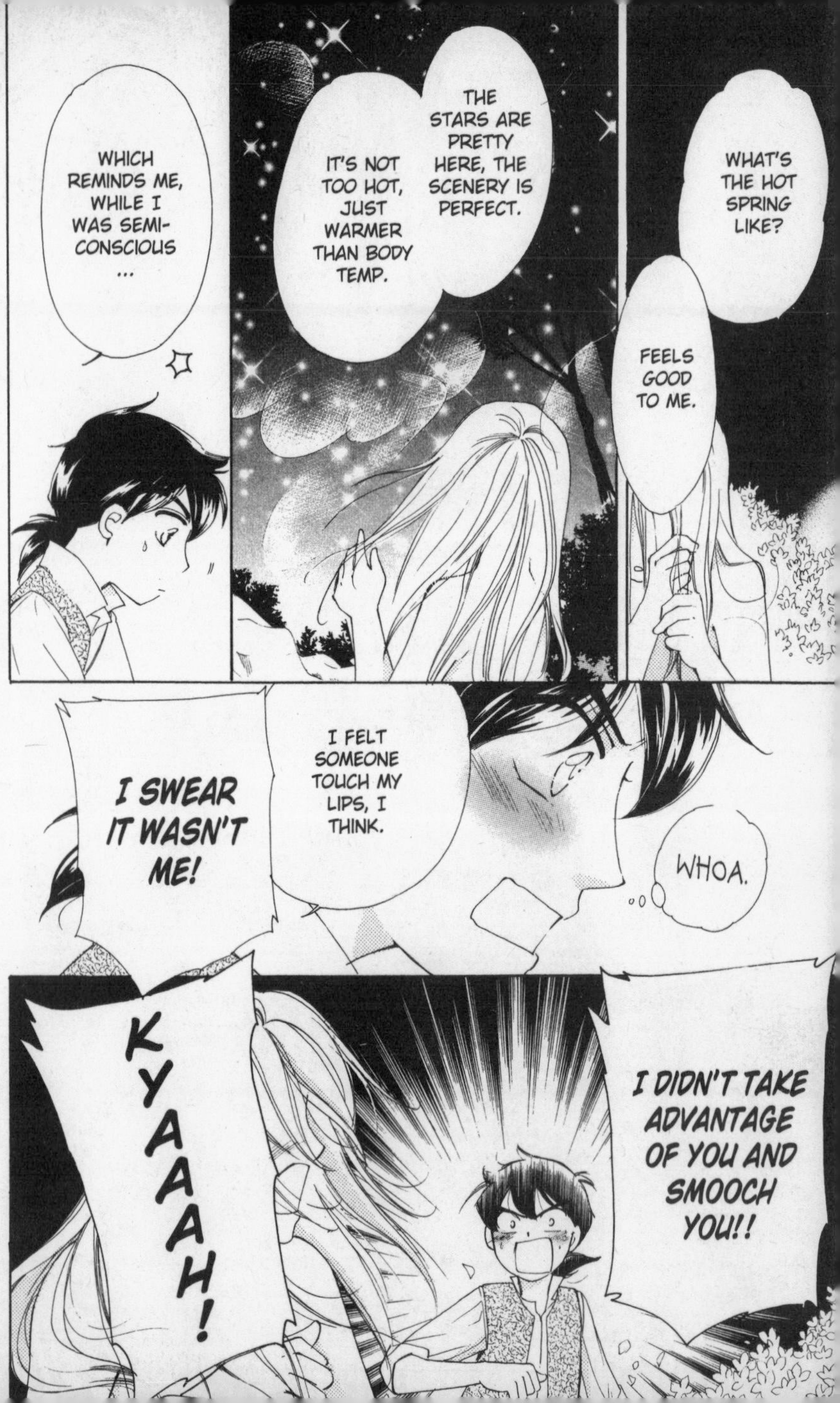
WHAT'S THE HOT SPRING LIKE?
FEELS GOOD TO ME.
THE STARS ARE PRETTY HERE, THE SCENERY IS PERFECT.
IT'S NOT TOO HOT, JUST WARMER THAN BODY TEMP.
WHICH REMINDS ME, WHILE I WAS SEMI-CONSCIOUS ...
I FELT SOMEONE TOUCH MY LIPS, I THINK.
WHOA.
I SWEAR IT WASN'T ME!
I DIDN'T TAKE ADVANTAGE OF YOU AND SMOOCH YOU!!
KYAAAH!

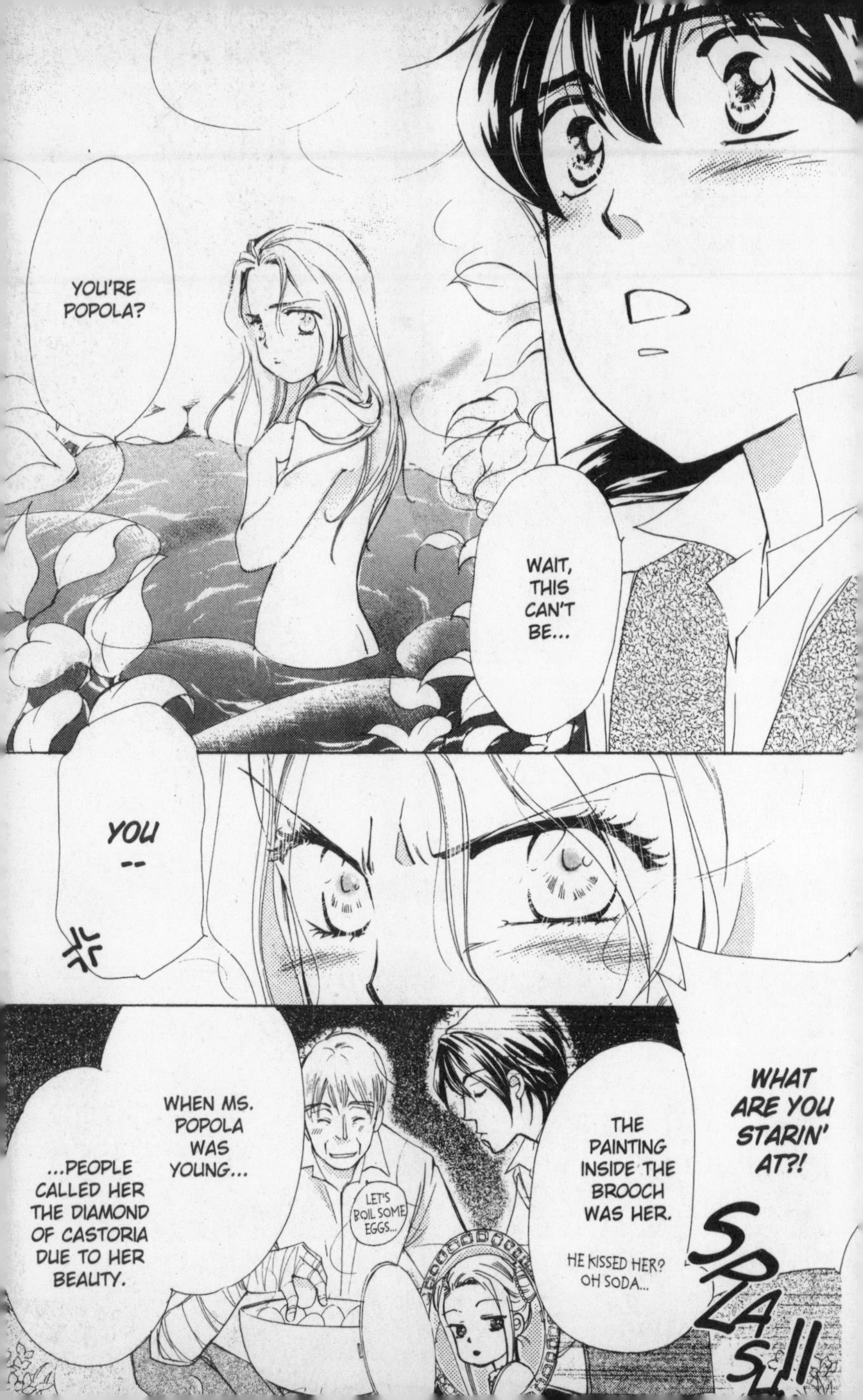
WAIT, THIS CAN'T BE...
YOU'RE POPOLA?
YOU --
WHAT ARE YOU STARIN' AT?!
SPLASH!!
THE PAINTING INSIDE THE BROOCH WAS HER.
HE KISSED HER? OH SODA...
WHEN MS. POPOLA WAS YOUNG...
LET'S BOIL SOME EGGS...
...PEOPLE CALLED HER THE DIAMOND OF CASTORIA DUE TO HER BEAUTY.

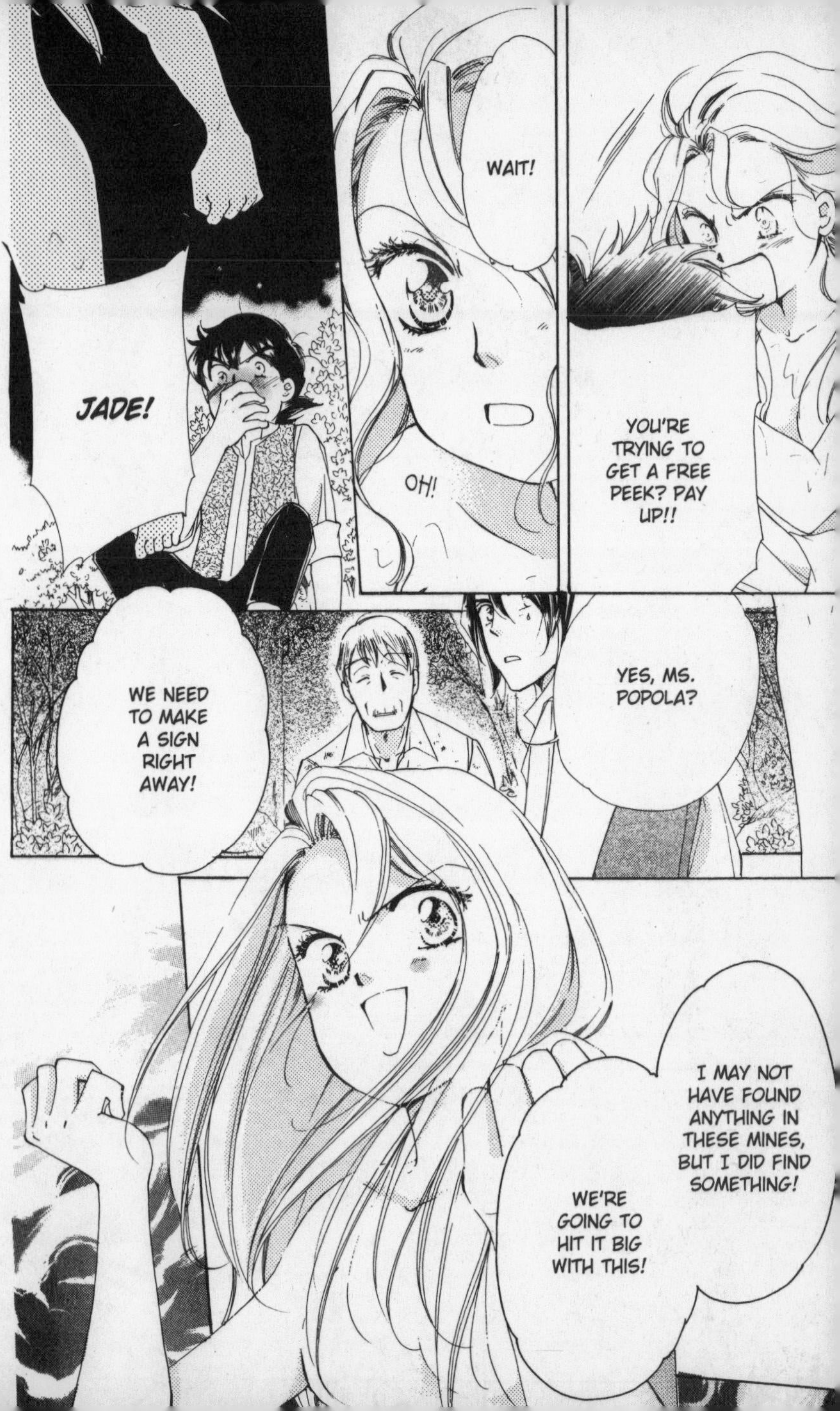
YOU'RE TRYING TO GET A FREE PEEK? PAY UP!!
WAIT!
OH!
JADE!
YES, MS. POPOLA?
WE NEED TO MAKE A SIGN RIGHT AWAY!
I MAY NOT HAVE FOUND ANYTHING IN THESE MINES, BUT I DID FIND SOMETHING!
WE'RE GOING TO HIT IT BIG WITH THIS!

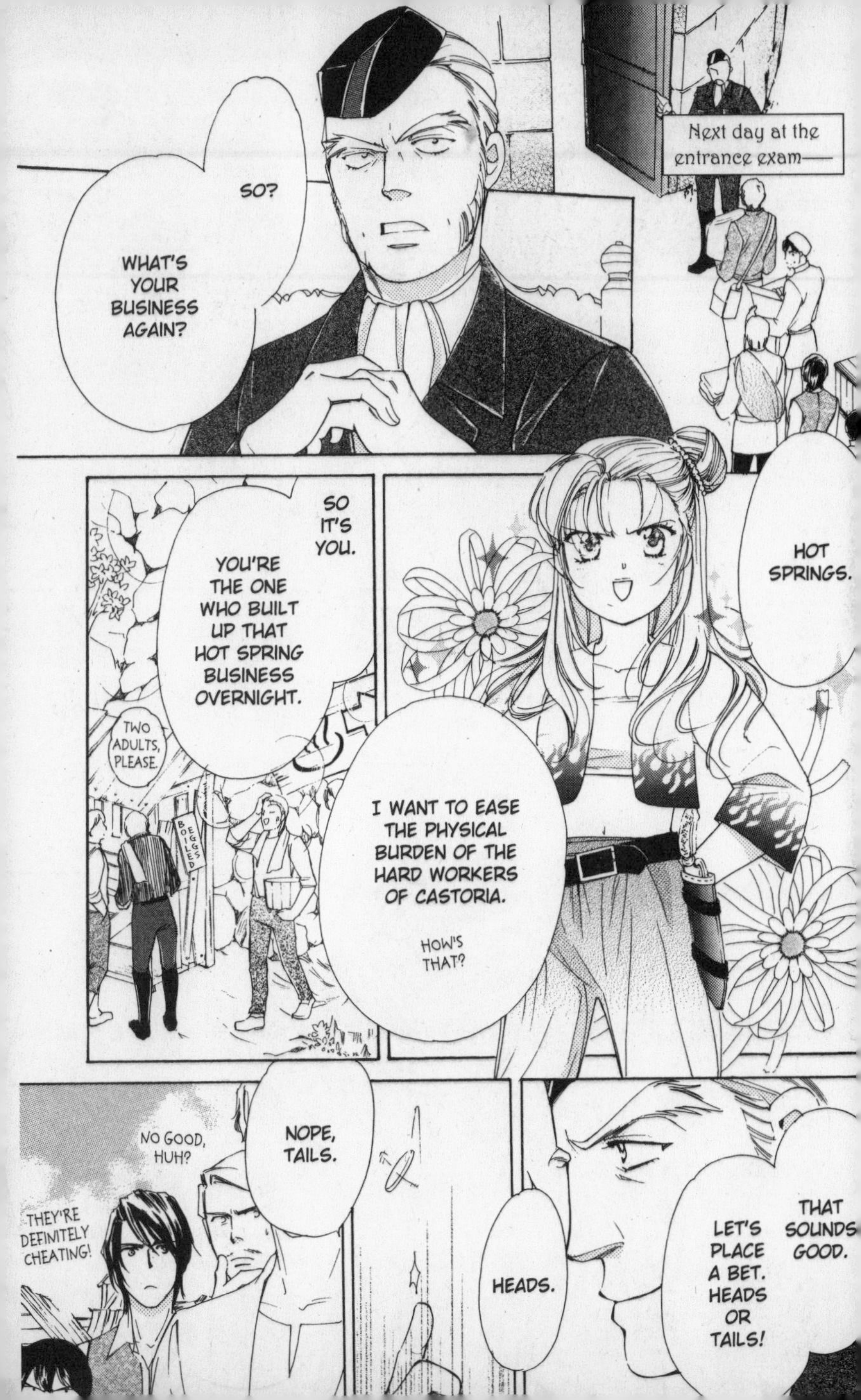
Next day at the entrance exam——
SO?
WHAT'S YOUR BUSINESS AGAIN?
HOT SPRINGS.
I WANT TO EASE THE PHYSICAL BURDEN OF THE HARD WORKERS OF CASTORIA.
HOW'S THAT?
SO IT'S YOU.
YOU'RE THE ONE WHO BUILT UP THAT HOT SPRING BUSINESS OVERNIGHT.
TWO ADULTS, PLEASE.
BOILED EGGS
THAT SOUNDS GOOD.
LET'S PLACE A BET. HEADS OR TAILS!
HEADS.
NOPE, TAILS.
NO GOOD, HUH?
THEY'RE DEFINITELY CHEATING!

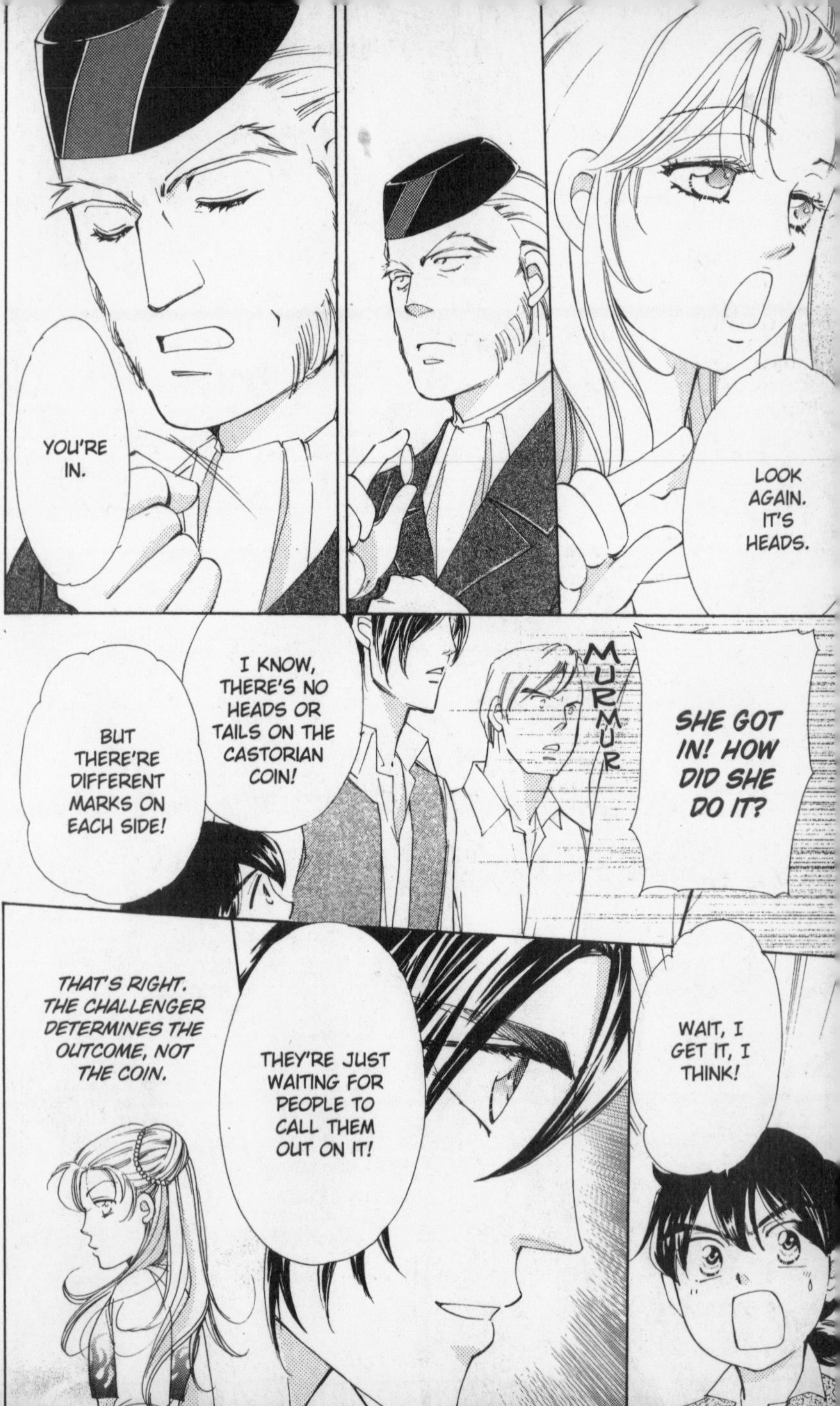
LOOK AGAIN. IT'S HEADS.
YOU'RE IN.
SHE GOT IN! HOW DID SHE DO IT?
MURMUR
I KNOW, THERE'S NO HEADS OR TAILS ON THE CASTORIAN COIN!
BUT THERE'RE DIFFERENT MARKS ON EACH SIDE!
WAIT, I GET IT, I THINK!
THEY'RE JUST WAITING FOR PEOPLE TO CALL THEM OUT ON IT!
THAT'S RIGHT. THE CHALLENGER DETERMINES THE OUTCOME, NOT THE COIN.

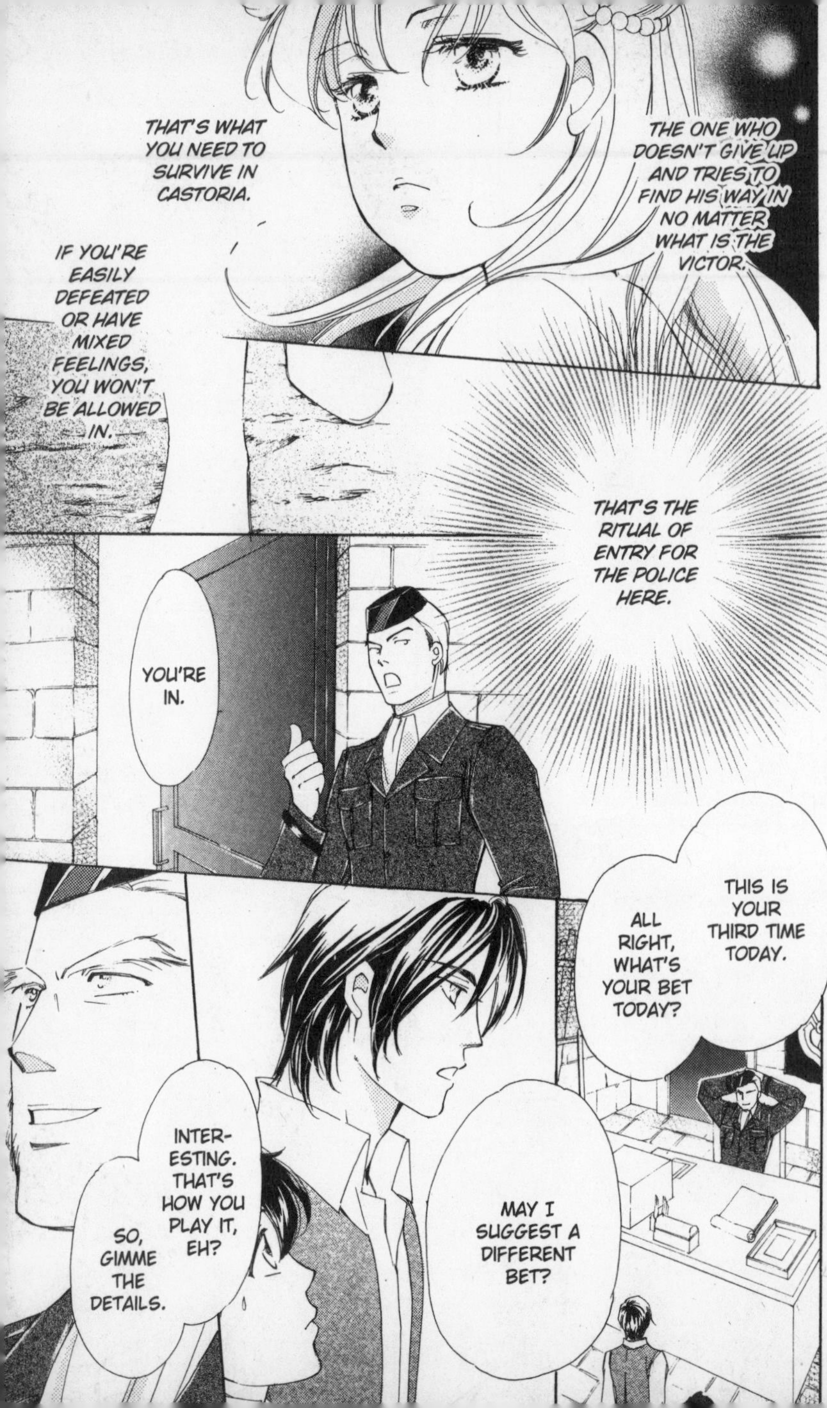
THE ONE WHO DOESN'T GIVE UP AND TRIES TO FIND HIS WAY IN NO MATTER WHAT IS THE VICTOR.
THAT'S WHAT YOU NEED TO SURVIVE IN CASTORIA.
IF YOU'RE EASILY DEFEATED OR HAVE MIXED FEELINGS, YOU WON'T BE ALLOWED IN.
THAT'S THE RITUAL OF ENTRY FOR THE POLICE HERE.
YOU'RE IN.
THIS IS YOUR THIRD TIME TODAY.
ALL RIGHT, WHAT'S YOUR BET TODAY?
MAY I SUGGEST A DIFFERENT BET?
INTER-ESTING. THAT'S HOW YOU PLAY IT, EH?
SO, GIMME THE DETAILS.

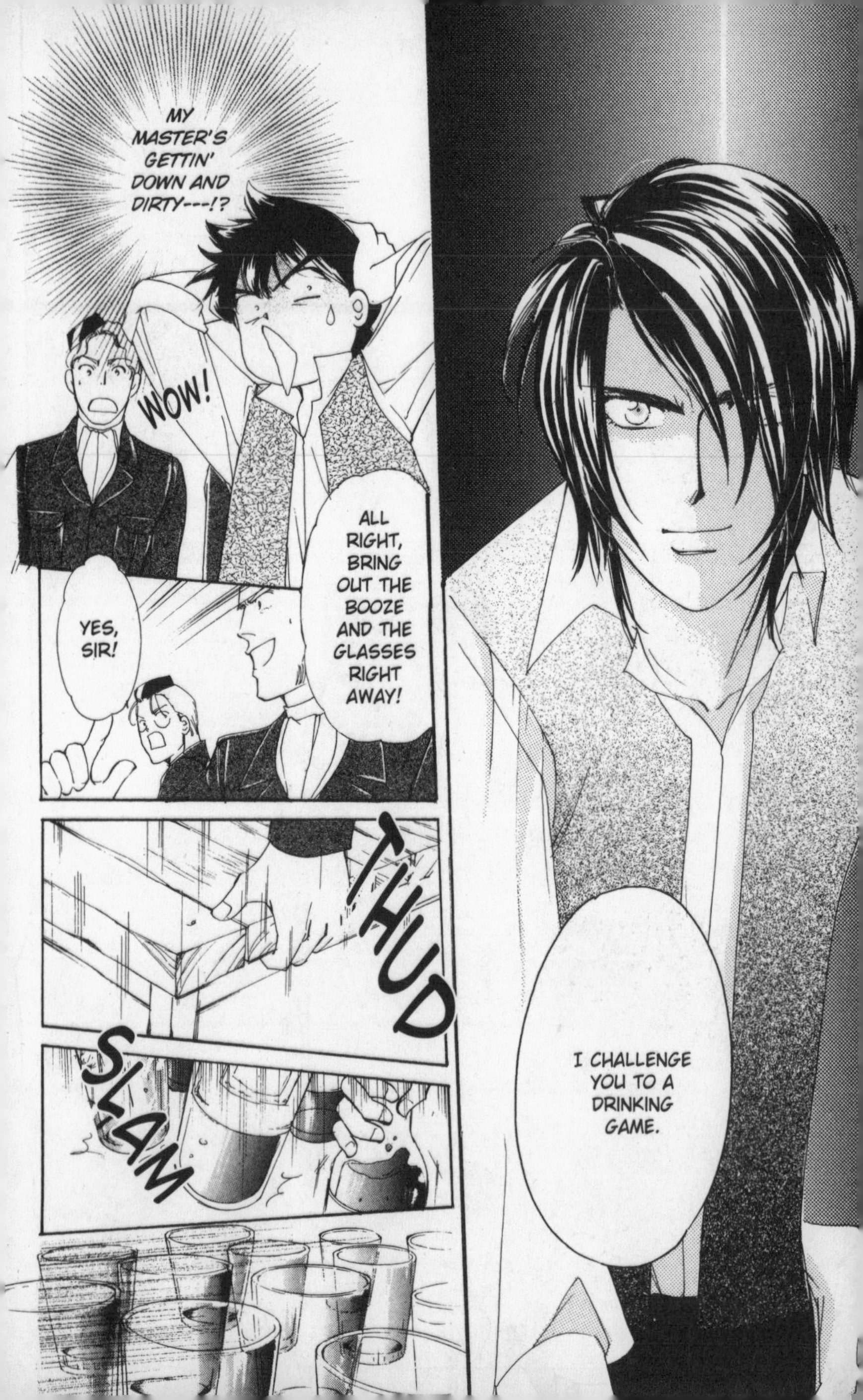
I CHALLENGE YOU TO A DRINKING GAME.
MY MASTER'S GETTIN' DOWN AND DIRTY---!?
WOW!
ALL RIGHT, BRING OUT THE BOOZE AND THE GLASSES RIGHT AWAY!
YES, SIR!
THUD
SLAM

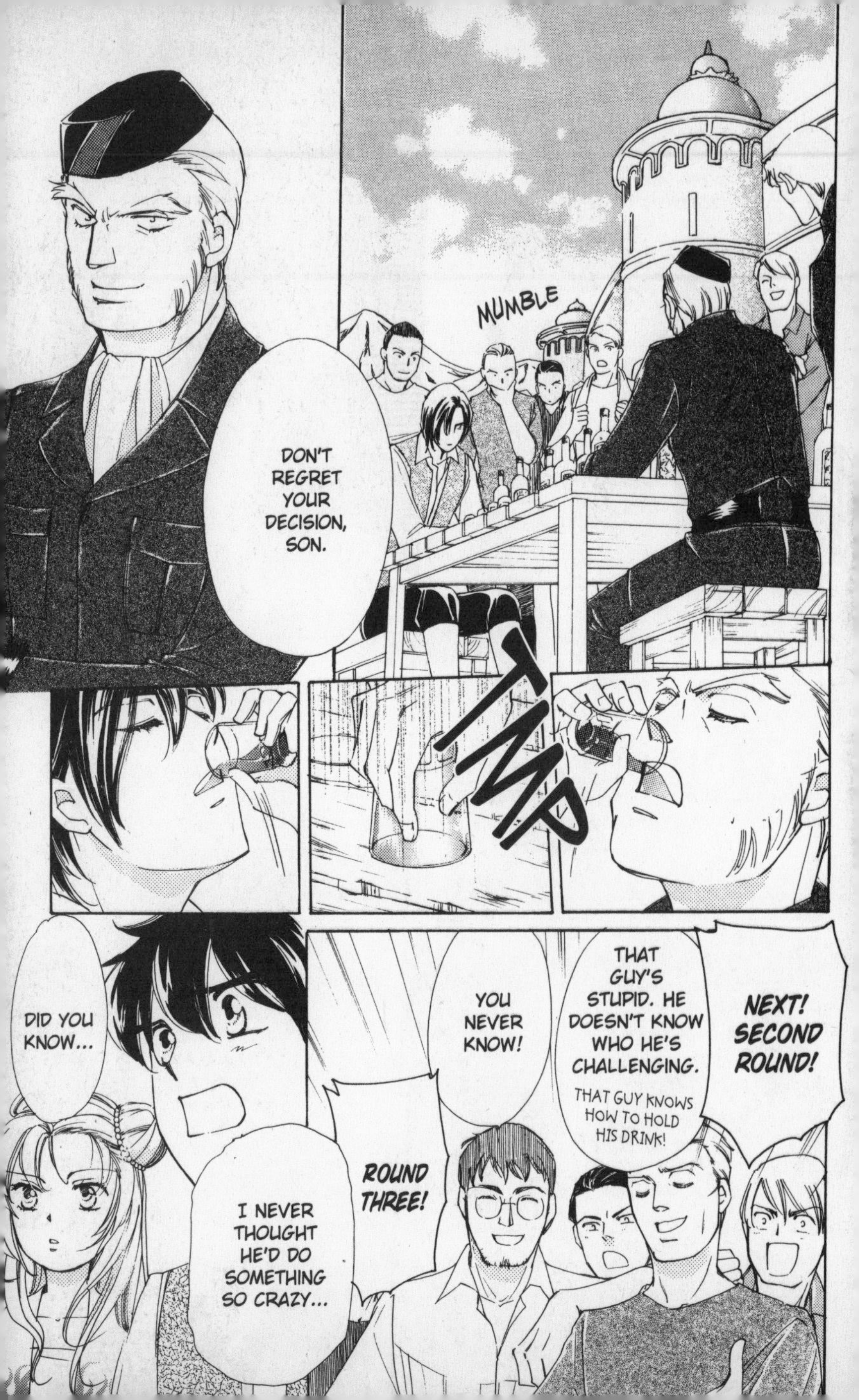
MUMBLE
DON'T REGRET YOUR DECISION, SON.
TMP
NEXT! SECOND ROUND!
THAT GUY'S STUPID. HE DOESN'T KNOW WHO HE'S CHALLENGING.
THAT GUY KNOWS HOW TO HOLD HIS DRINK!
YOU NEVER KNOW!
ROUND THREE!
DID YOU KNOW...
I NEVER THOUGHT HE'D DO SOMETHING SO CRAZY...

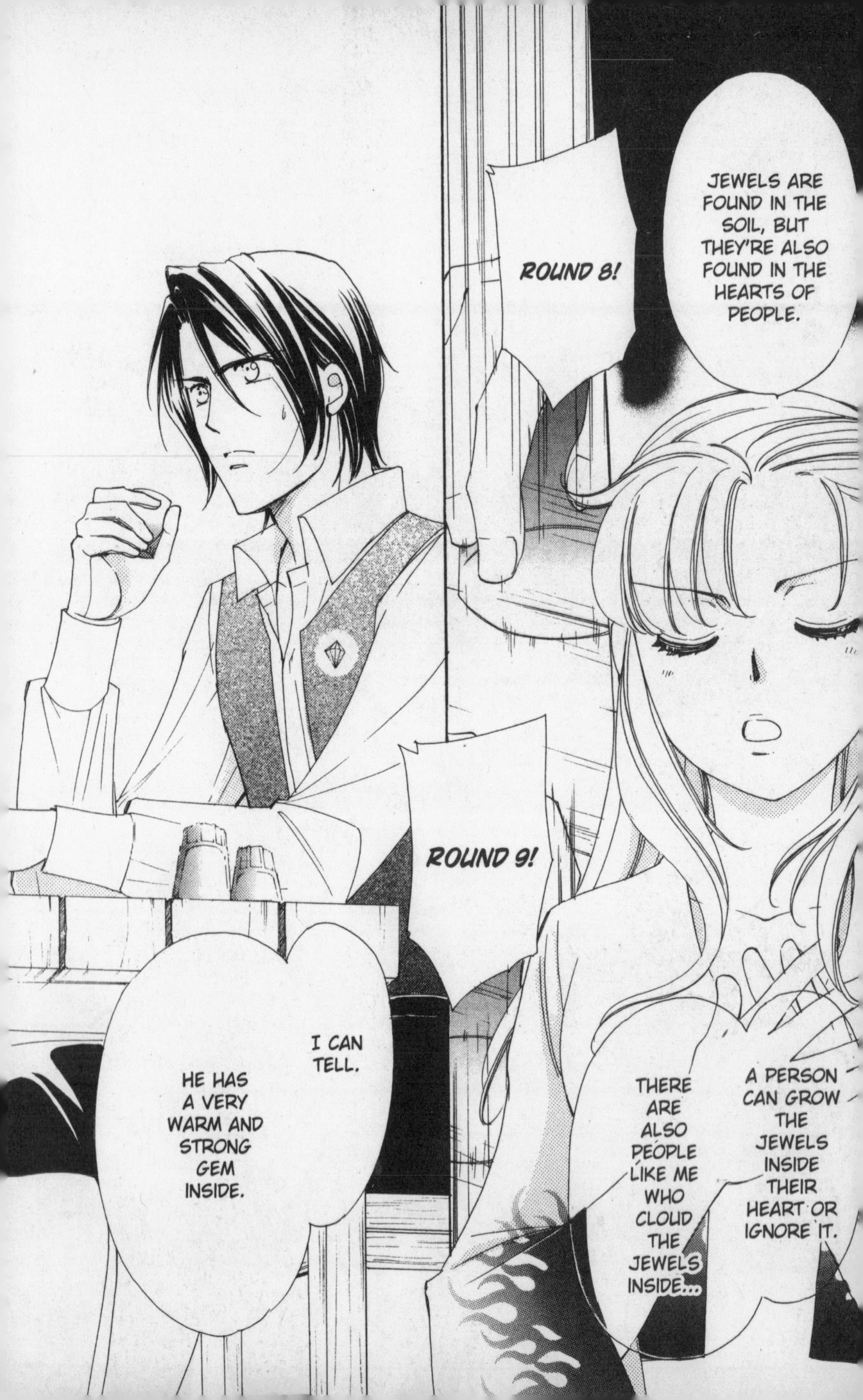
JEWELS ARE FOUND IN THE SOIL, BUT THEY'RE ALSO FOUND IN THE HEARTS OF PEOPLE.
ROUND 8!
ROUND 9!
A PERSON CAN GROW THE JEWELS INSIDE THEIR HEART OR IGNORE IT.
THERE ARE ALSO PEOPLE LIKE ME WHO CLOUD THE JEWELS INSIDE...
I CAN TELL.
HE HAS A VERY WARM AND STRONG GEM INSIDE.

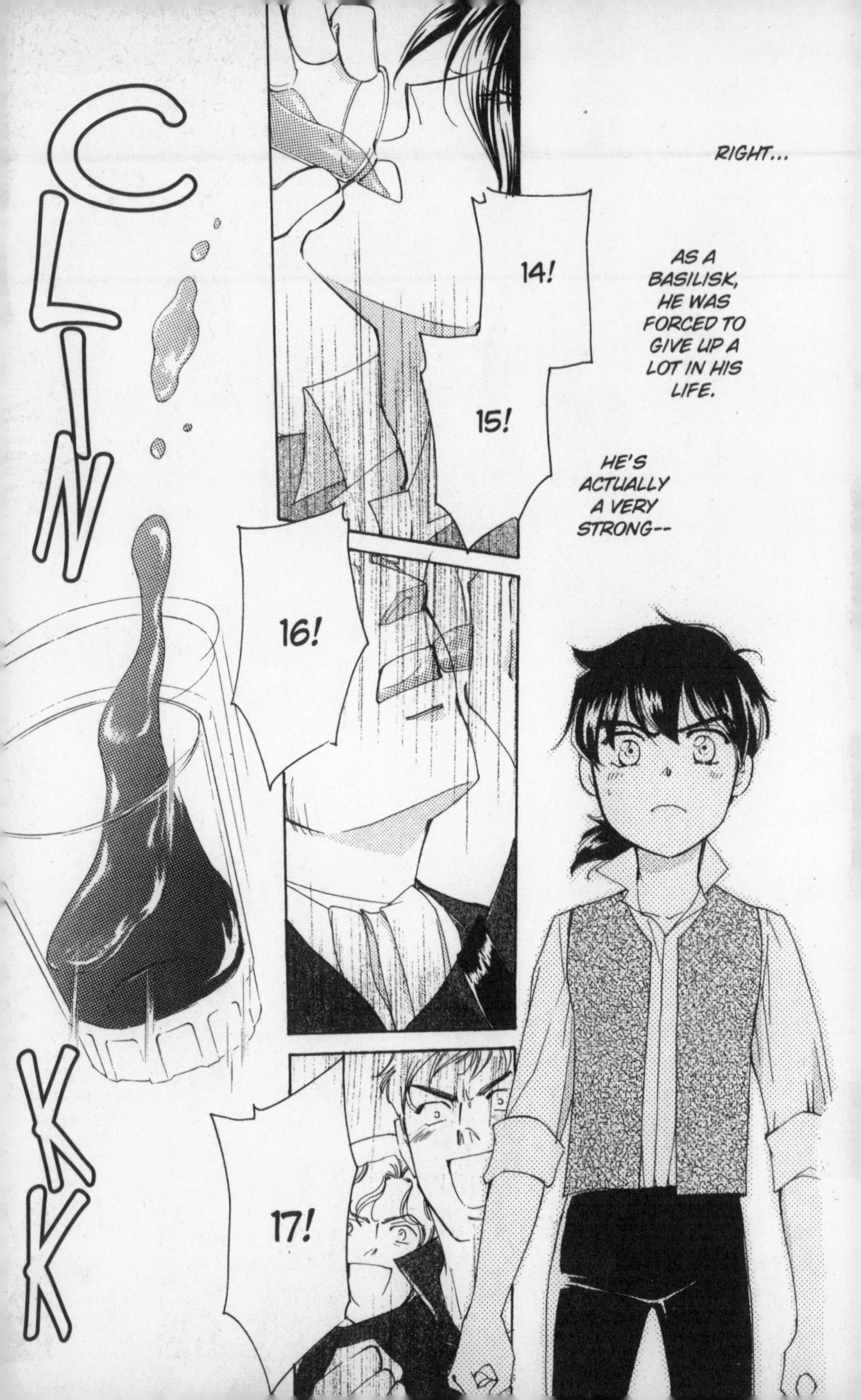
RIGHT...
AS A BASILISK, HE WAS FORCED TO GIVE UP A LOT IN HIS LIFE.
HE'S ACTUALLY A VERY STRONG--
14!
15!
16!
17!
CLINKKK

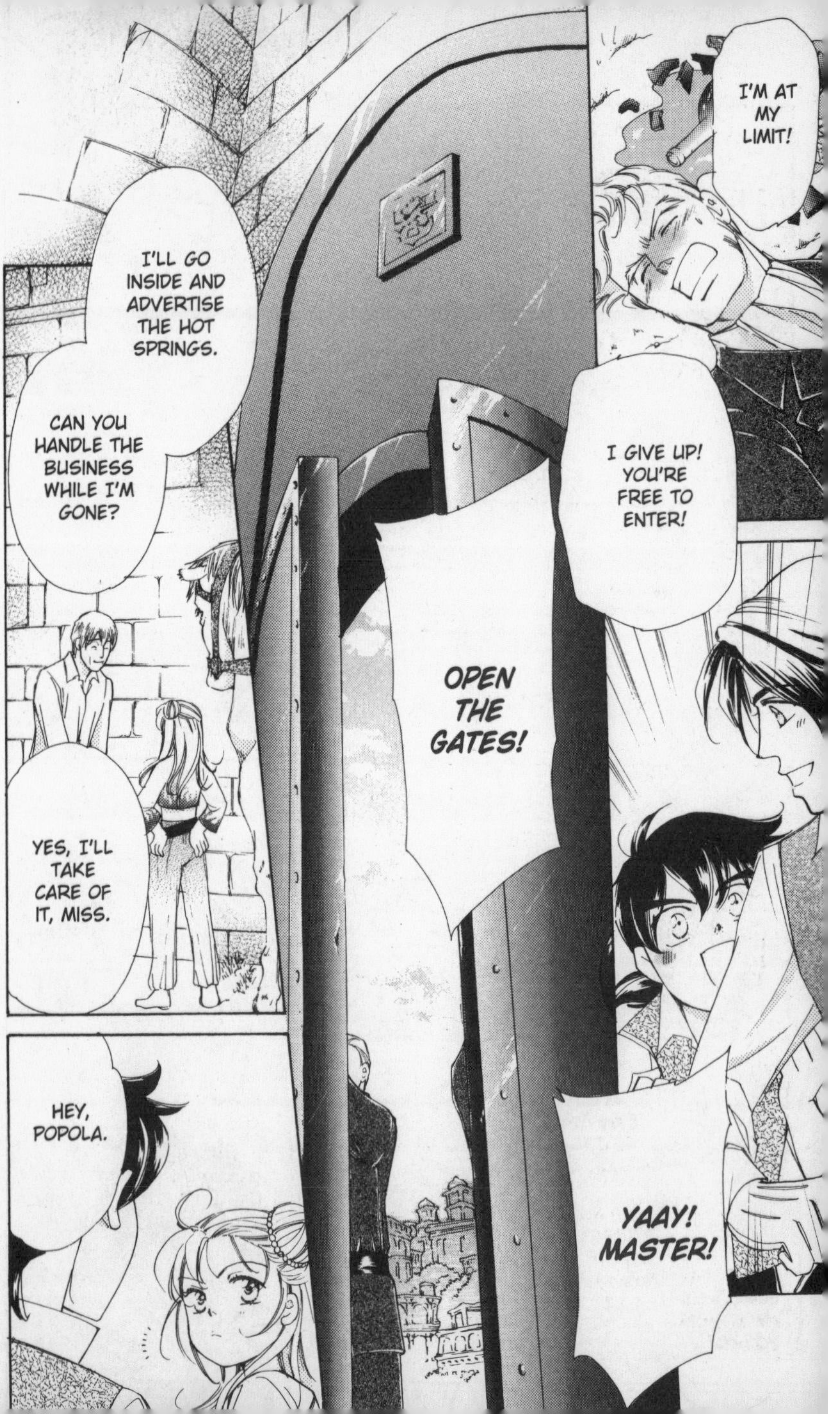
I'M AT MY LIMIT!
I GIVE UP! YOU'RE FREE TO ENTER!
OPEN THE GATES!
YAAY! MASTER!
I'LL GO INSIDE AND ADVERTISE THE HOT SPRINGS.
CAN YOU HANDLE THE BUSINESS WHILE I'M GONE?
YES, I'LL TAKE CARE OF IT, MISS.
HEY, POPOLA.

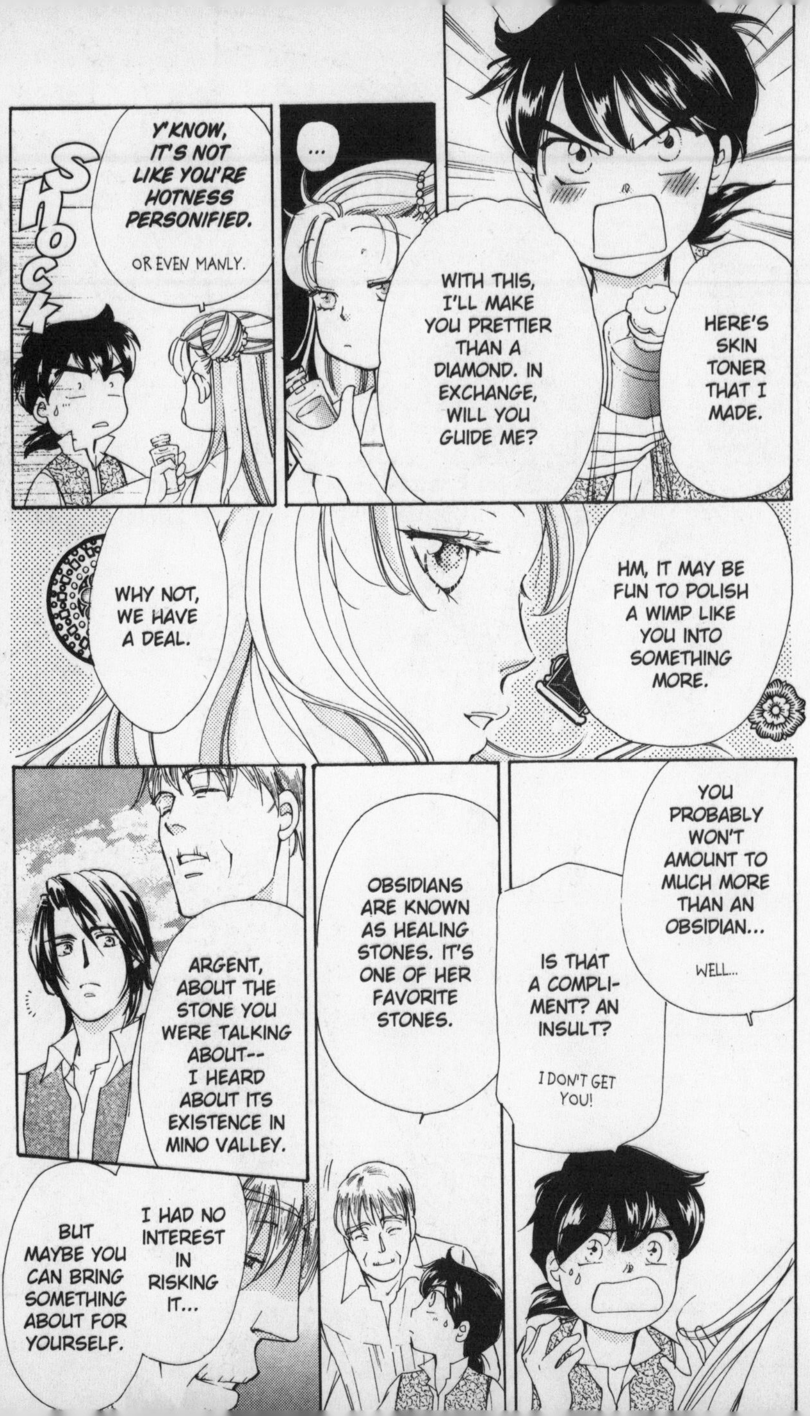

HERE'S SKIN TONER THAT I MADE.
WITH THIS, I'LL MAKE YOU PRETTIER THAN A DIAMOND. IN EXCHANGE, WILL YOU GUIDE ME?
...
SHOCK
Y'KNOW, IT'S NOT LIKE YOU'RE HOTNESS PERSONIFIED.
OR EVEN MANLY.
HM, IT MAY BE FUN TO POLISH A WIMP LIKE YOU INTO SOMETHING MORE.
WHY NOT, WE HAVE A DEAL.
YOU PROBABLY WON'T AMOUNT TO MUCH MORE THAN AN OBSIDIAN...
WELL...
IS THAT A COMPLI-MENT? AN INSULT?
I DON'T GET YOU!
OBSIDIANS ARE KNOWN AS HEALING STONES. IT'S ONE OF HER FAVORITE STONES.
ARGENT, ABOUT THE STONE YOU WERE TALKING ABOUT-- I HEARD ABOUT ITS EXISTENCE IN MINO VALLEY.
I HAD NO INTEREST IN RISKING IT...
BUT MAYBE YOU CAN BRING SOMETHING ABOUT FOR YOURSELF.

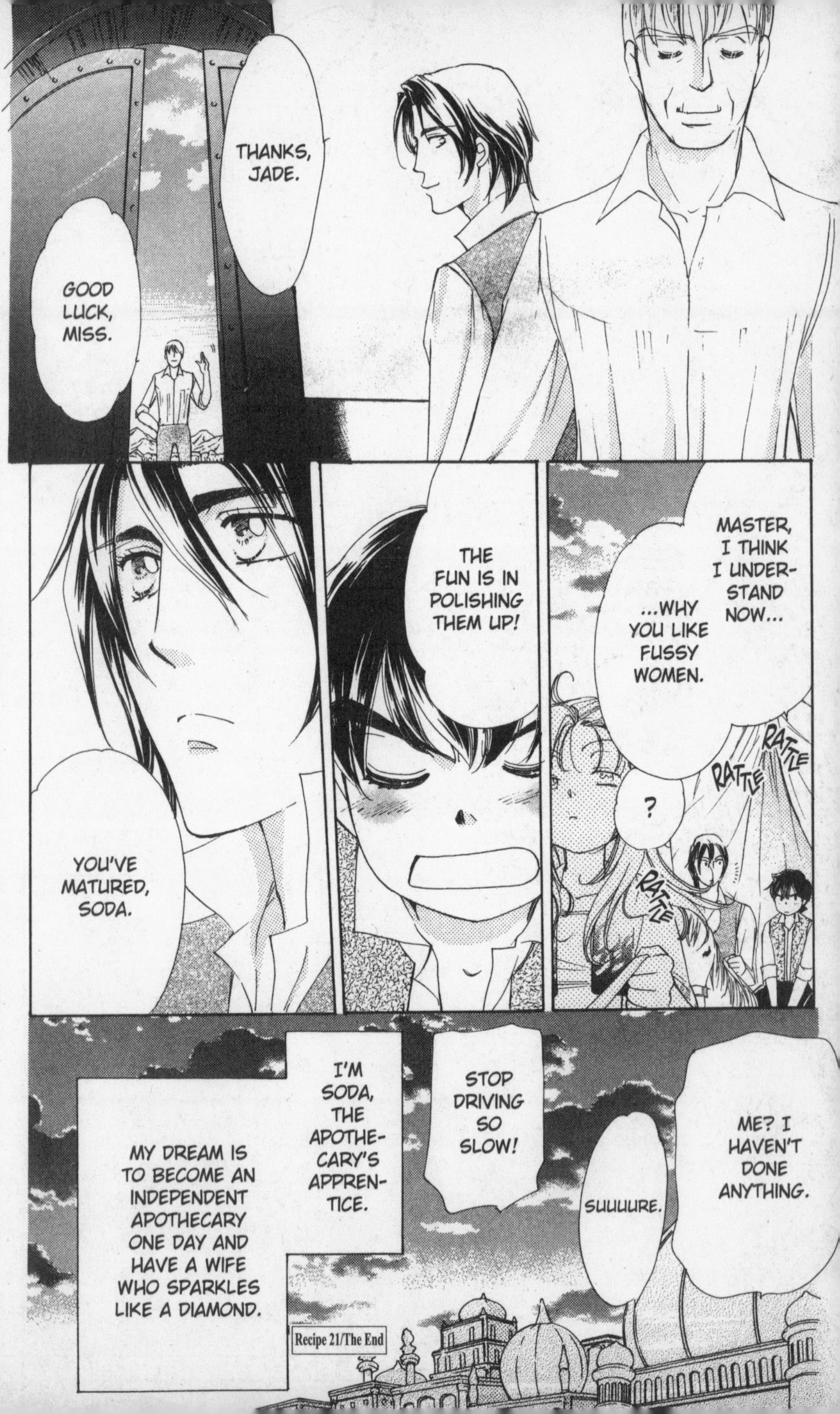
THANKS, JADE.
GOOD LUCK, MISS.
MASTER, I THINK I UNDER-STAND NOW...
...WHY YOU LIKE FUSSY WOMEN.
RATTLE RATTLE
?
RATTLE
THE FUN IS IN POLISHING THEM UP!
YOU'VE MATURED, SODA.
ME? I HAVEN'T DONE ANYTHING.
SUUUURE.
STOP DRIVING SO SLOW!
I'M SODA, THE APOTHE-CARY'S APPREN-TICE.
MY DREAM IS TO BECOME AN INDEPENDENT APOTHECARY ONE DAY AND HAVE A WIFE WHO SPARKLES LIKE A DIAMOND.
Recipe 21/The End

Apothecarius Argentum

Recipe 22 • Mino Valley

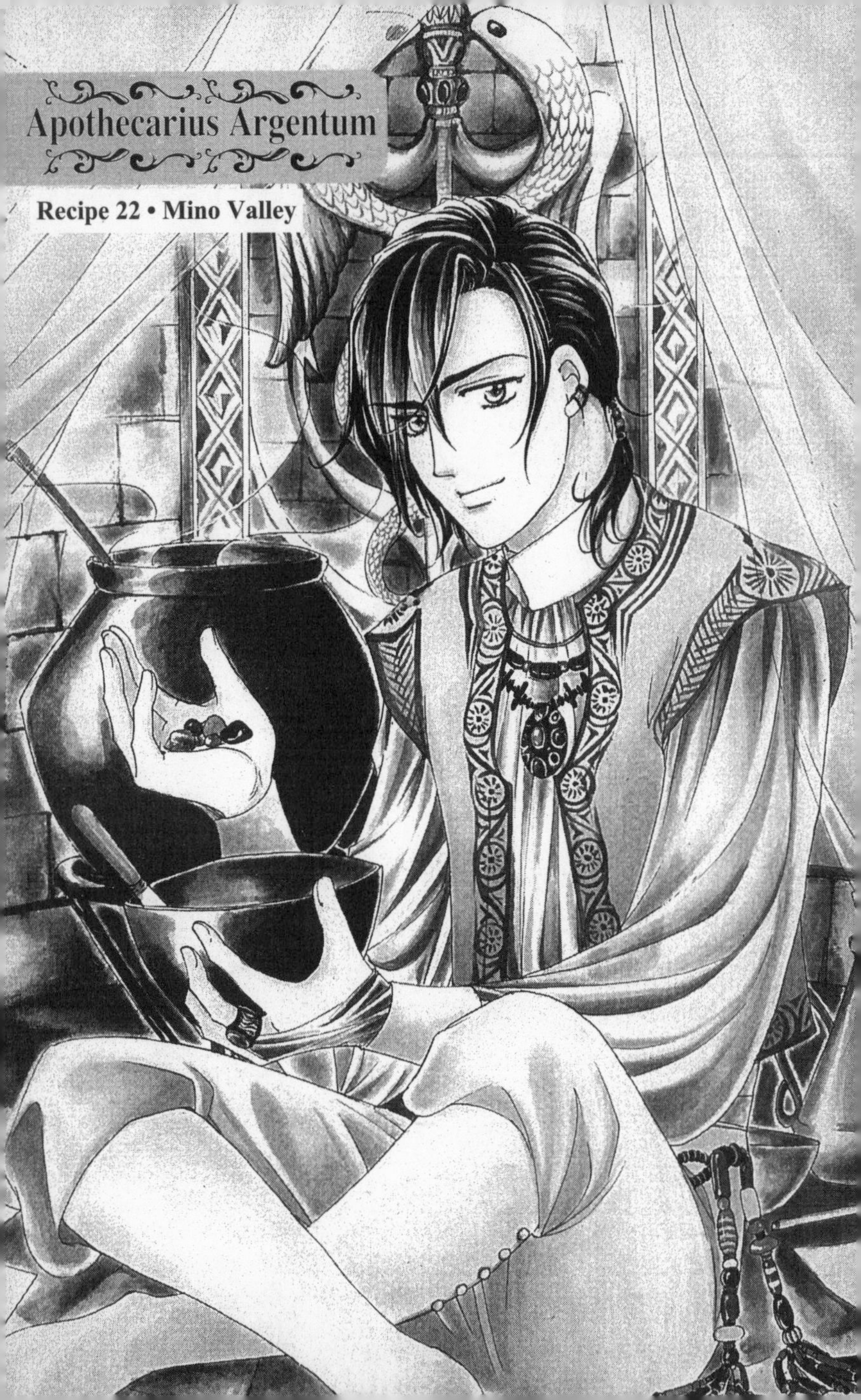

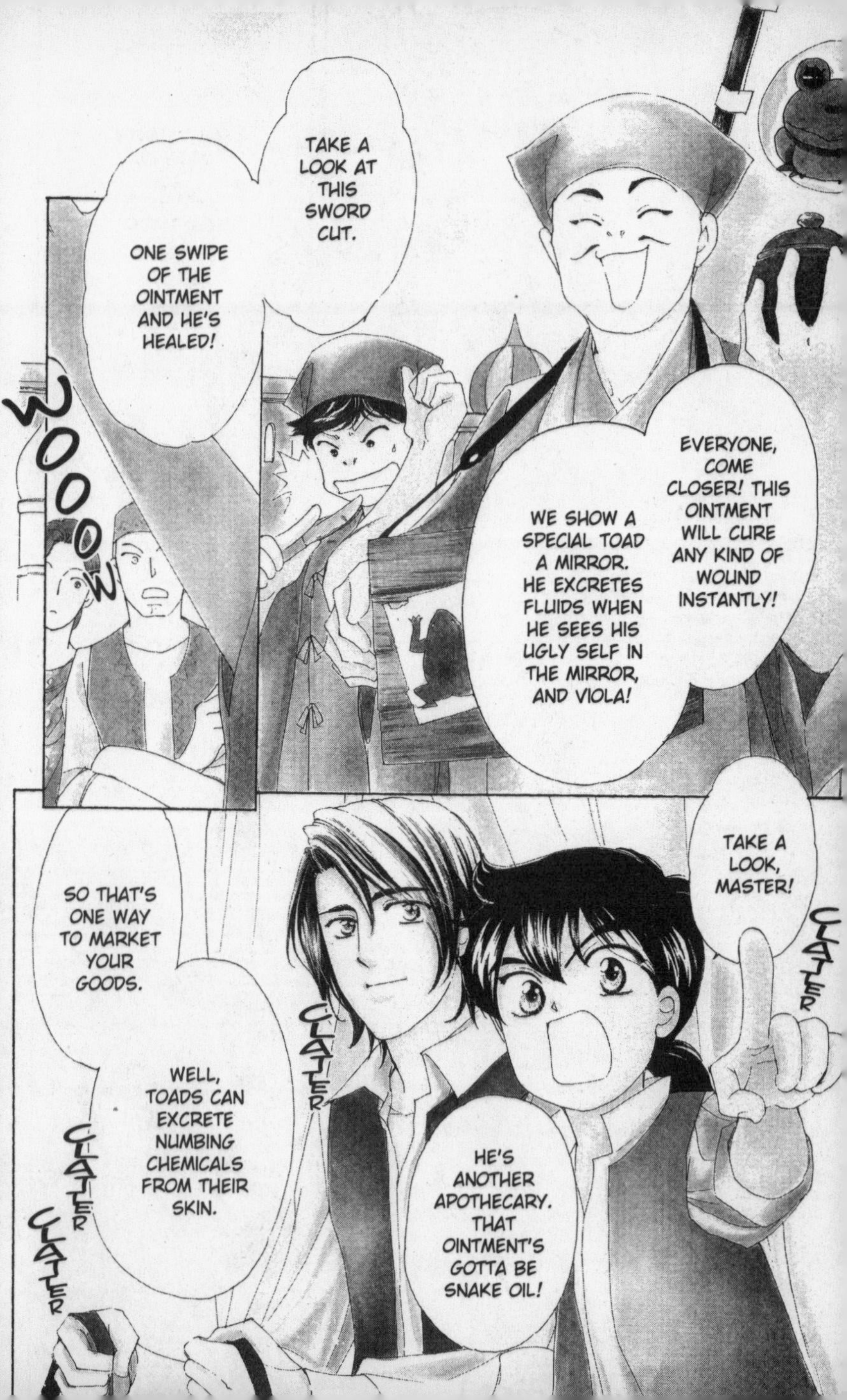
EVERYONE, COME CLOSER! THIS OINTMENT WILL CURE ANY KIND OF WOUND INSTANTLY!
WE SHOW A SPECIAL TOAD A MIRROR. HE EXCRETES FLUIDS WHEN HE SEES HIS UGLY SELF IN THE MIRROR, AND VIOLA!
TAKE A LOOK AT THIS SWORD CUT.
ONE SWIPE OF THE OINTMENT AND HE'S HEALED!
WOOOOW
TAKE A LOOK, MASTER!
CLATTER
HE'S ANOTHER APOTHECARY. THAT OINTMENT'S GOTTA BE SNAKE OIL!
CLATTER
SO THAT'S ONE WAY TO MARKET YOUR GOODS.
WELL, TOADS CAN EXCRETE NUMBING CHEMICALS FROM THEIR SKIN.
CLATTER
CLATTER

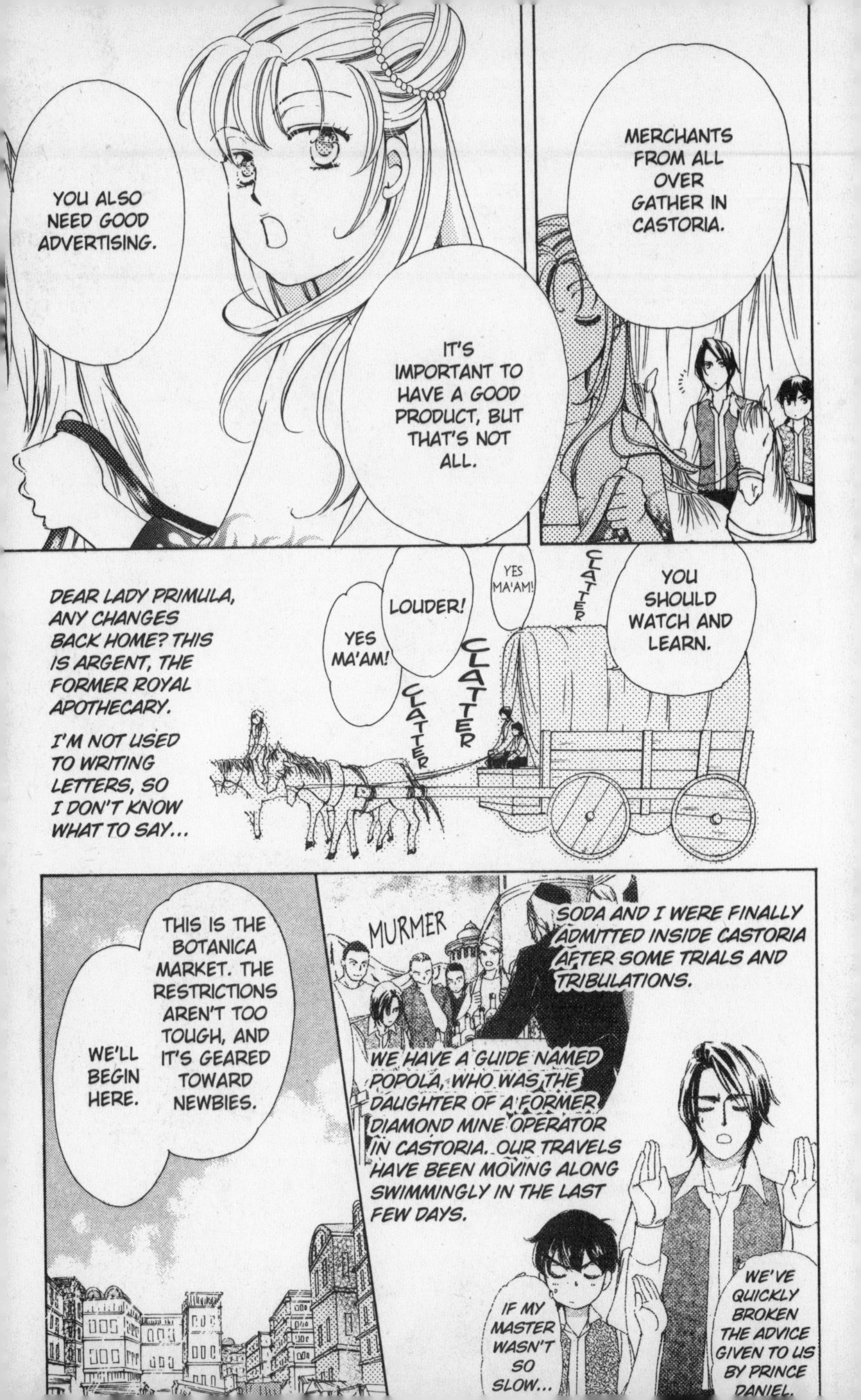
MERCHANTS FROM ALL OVER GATHER IN CASTORIA.
IT'S IMPORTANT TO HAVE A GOOD PRODUCT, BUT THAT'S NOT ALL.
YOU ALSO NEED GOOD ADVERTISING.
YOU SHOULD WATCH AND LEARN.
CLATTER
YES MA'AM!
LOUDER!
CLATTER
YES MA'AM!
CLATTER
DEAR LADY PRIMULA, ANY CHANGES BACK HOME? THIS IS ARGENT, THE FORMER ROYAL APOTHECARY.
I'M NOT USED TO WRITING LETTERS, SO I DON'T KNOW WHAT TO SAY...
SODA AND I WERE FINALLY ADMITTED INSIDE CASTORIA AFTER SOME TRIALS AND TRIBULATIONS.
MURMER
WE HAVE A GUIDE NAMED POPOLA, WHO WAS THE DAUGHTER OF A FORMER DIAMOND MINE OPERATOR IN CASTORIA. OUR TRAVELS HAVE BEEN MOVING ALONG SWIMMINGLY IN THE LAST FEW DAYS.
WE'VE QUICKLY BROKEN THE ADVICE GIVEN TO US BY PRINCE DANIEL.
IF MY MASTER WASN'T SO SLOW...
THIS IS THE BOTANICA MARKET. THE RESTRICTIONS AREN'T TOO TOUGH, AND IT'S GEARED TOWARD NEWBIES.
WE'LL BEGIN HERE.

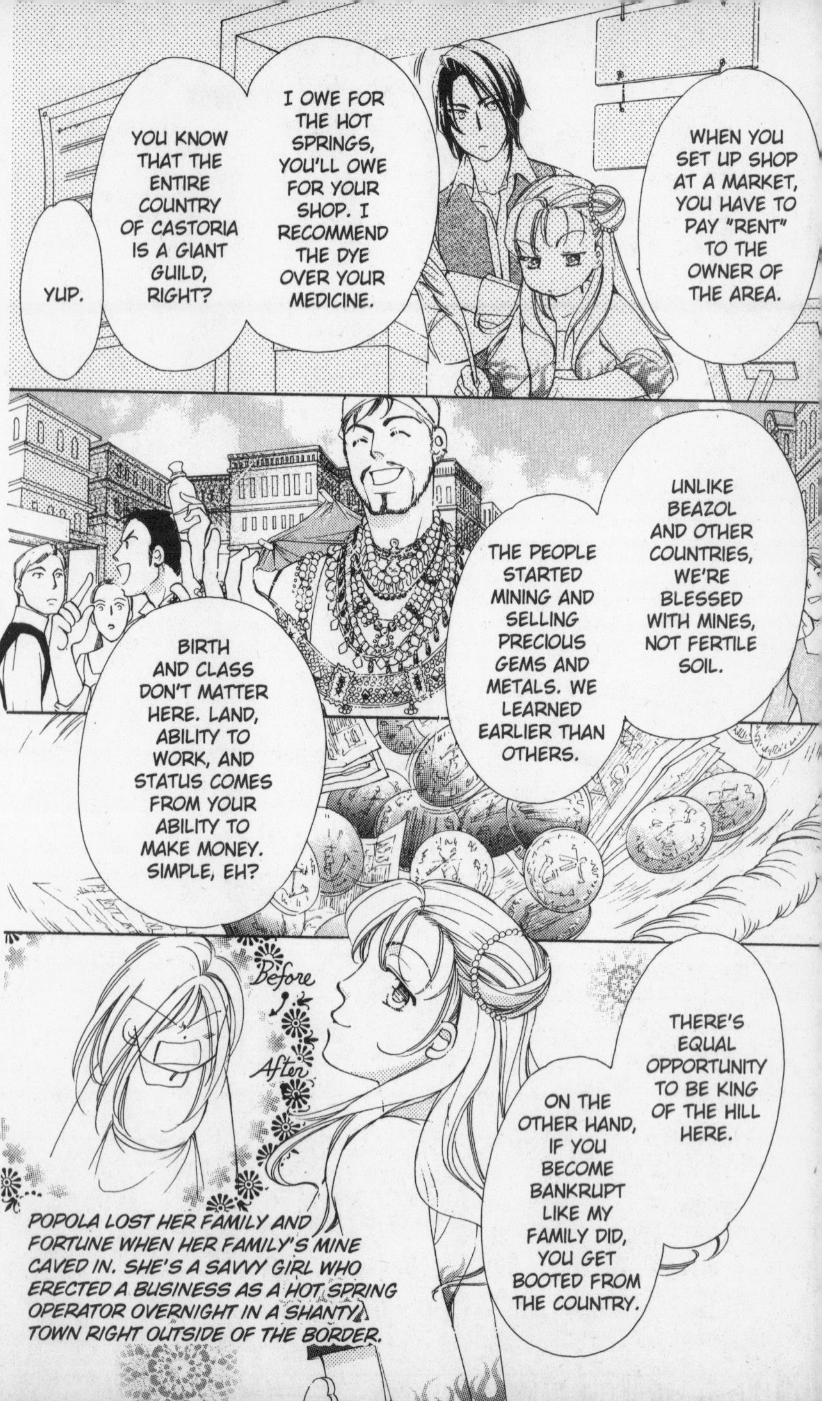
WHEN YOU SET UP SHOP AT A MARKET, YOU HAVE TO PAY "RENT" TO THE OWNER OF THE AREA.
I OWE FOR THE HOT SPRINGS, YOU'LL OWE FOR YOUR SHOP. I RECOMMEND THE DYE OVER YOUR MEDICINE.
YOU KNOW THAT THE ENTIRE COUNTRY OF CASTORIA IS A GIANT GUILD, RIGHT?
YUP.
UNLIKE BEAZOL AND OTHER COUNTRIES, WE'RE BLESSED WITH MINES, NOT FERTILE SOIL.
THE PEOPLE STARTED MINING AND SELLING PRECIOUS GEMS AND METALS. WE LEARNED EARLIER THAN OTHERS.
BIRTH AND CLASS DON'T MATTER HERE. LAND, ABILITY TO WORK, AND STATUS COMES FROM YOUR ABILITY TO MAKE MONEY. SIMPLE, EH?
THERE'S EQUAL OPPORTUNITY TO BE KING OF THE HILL HERE.
ON THE OTHER HAND, IF YOU BECOME BANKRUPT LIKE MY FAMILY DID, YOU GET BOOTED FROM THE COUNTRY.
Before
After
POPOLA LOST HER FAMILY AND FORTUNE WHEN HER FAMILY'S MINE CAVED IN. SHE'S A SAVVY GIRL WHO ERECTED A BUSINESS AS A HOT SPRING OPERATOR OVERNIGHT IN A SHANTY TOWN RIGHT OUTSIDE OF THE BORDER.

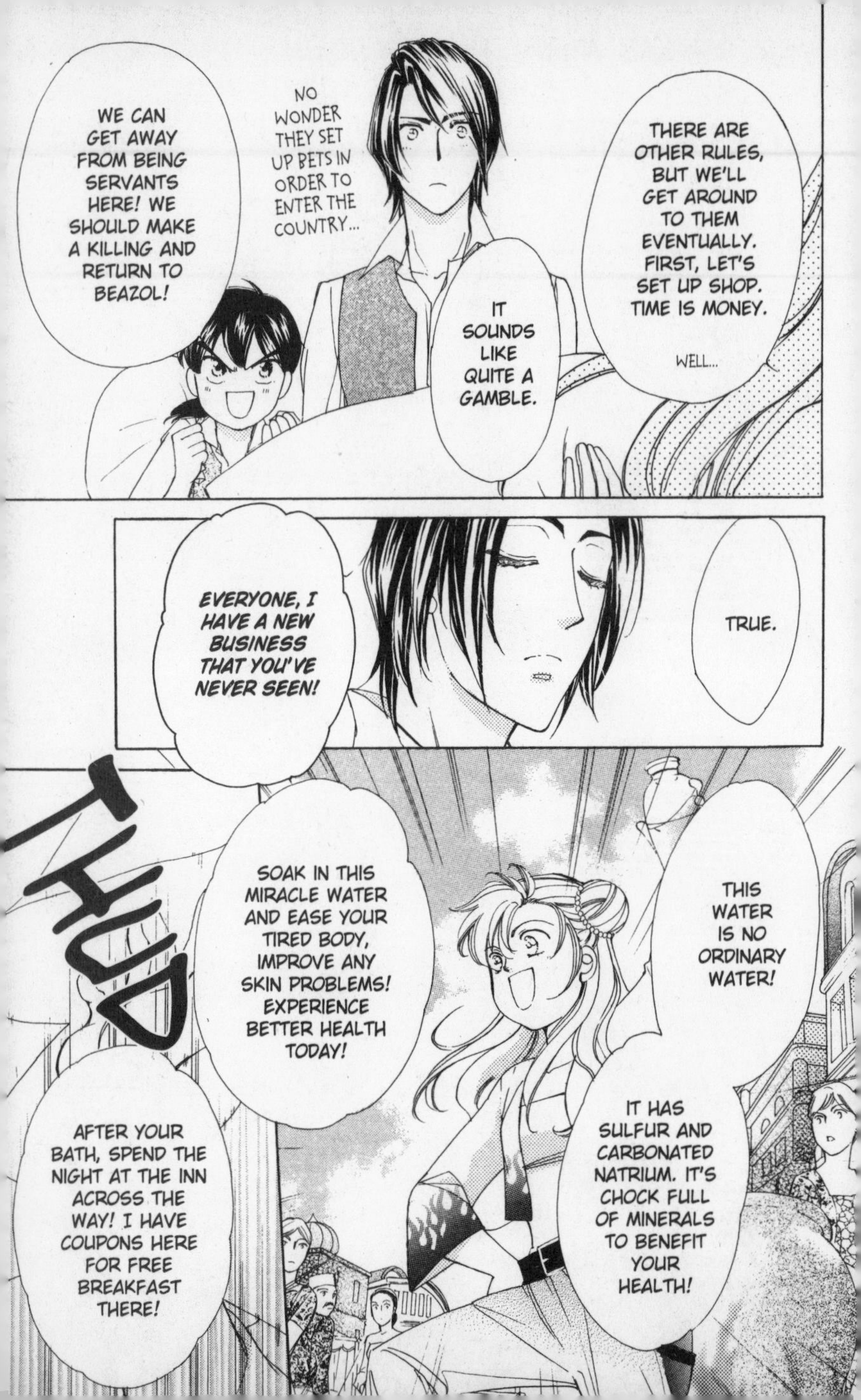
THERE ARE OTHER RULES, BUT WE'LL GET AROUND TO THEM EVENTUALLY. FIRST, LET'S SET UP SHOP. TIME IS MONEY.
WELL...
IT SOUNDS LIKE QUITE A GAMBLE.
NO WONDER THEY SET UP BETS IN ORDER TO ENTER THE COUNTRY...
WE CAN GET AWAY FROM BEING SERVANTS HERE! WE SHOULD MAKE A KILLING AND RETURN TO BEAZOL!
TRUE.
EVERYONE, I HAVE A NEW BUSINESS THAT YOU'VE NEVER SEEN!
THIS WATER IS NO ORDINARY WATER!
THUD
SOAK IN THIS MIRACLE WATER AND EASE YOUR TIRED BODY, IMPROVE ANY SKIN PROBLEMS! EXPERIENCE BETTER HEALTH TODAY!
IT HAS SULFUR AND CARBONATED NATRIUM. IT'S CHOCK FULL OF MINERALS TO BENEFIT YOUR HEALTH!
AFTER YOUR BATH, SPEND THE NIGHT AT THE INN ACROSS THE WAY! I HAVE COUPONS HERE FOR FREE BREAKFAST THERE!

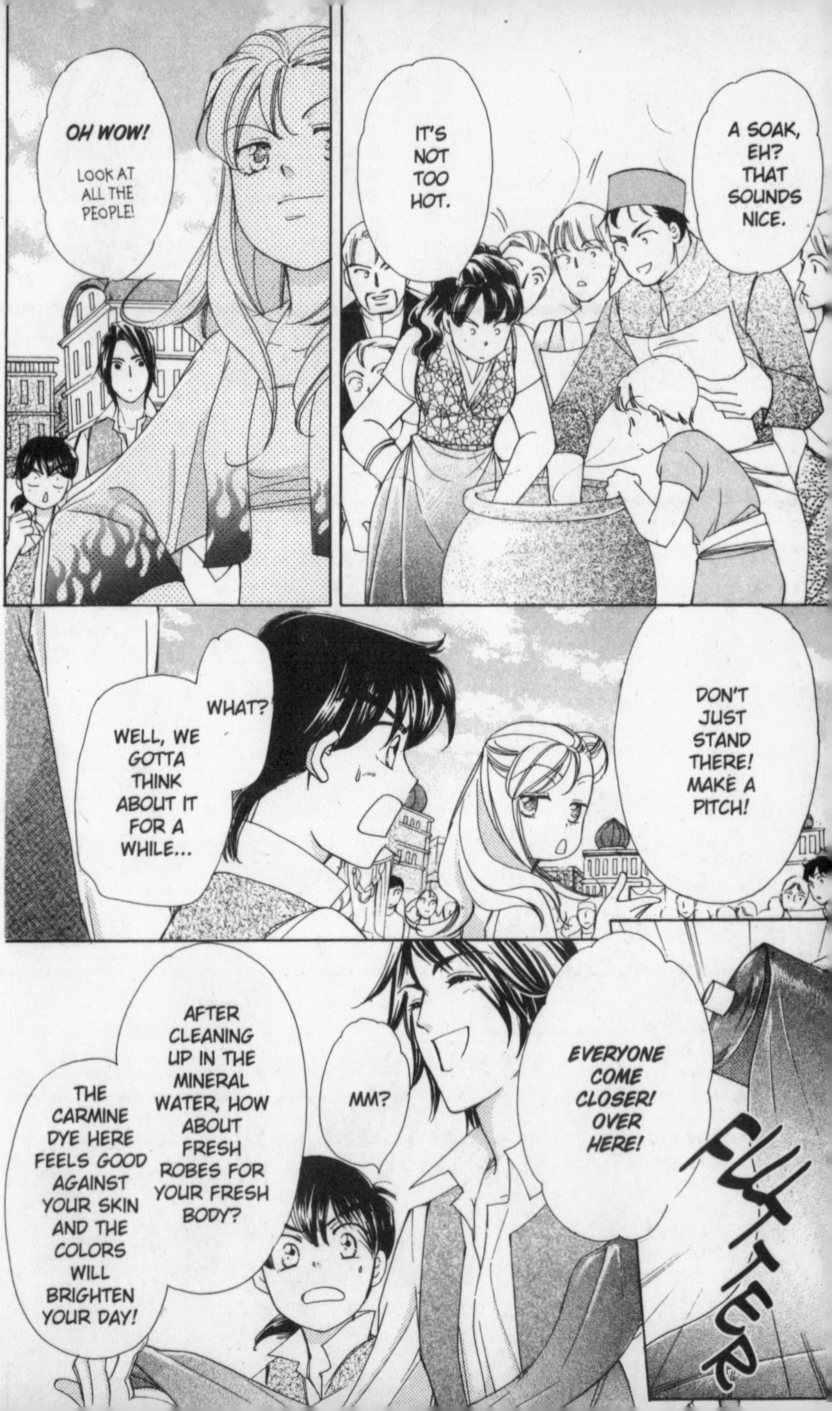
A SOAK, EH? THAT SOUNDS NICE.
IT'S NOT TOO HOT.
OH WOW! LOOK AT ALL THE PEOPLE!
DON'T JUST STAND THERE! MAKE A PITCH!
WHAT?
WELL, WE GOTTA THINK ABOUT IT FOR A WHILE...
FLUTTER
EVERYONE COME CLOSER! OVER HERE!
MM?
AFTER CLEANING UP IN THE MINERAL WATER, HOW ABOUT FRESH ROBES FOR YOUR FRESH BODY?
THE CARMINE DYE HERE FEELS GOOD AGAINST YOUR SKIN AND THE COLORS WILL BRIGHTEN YOUR DAY!

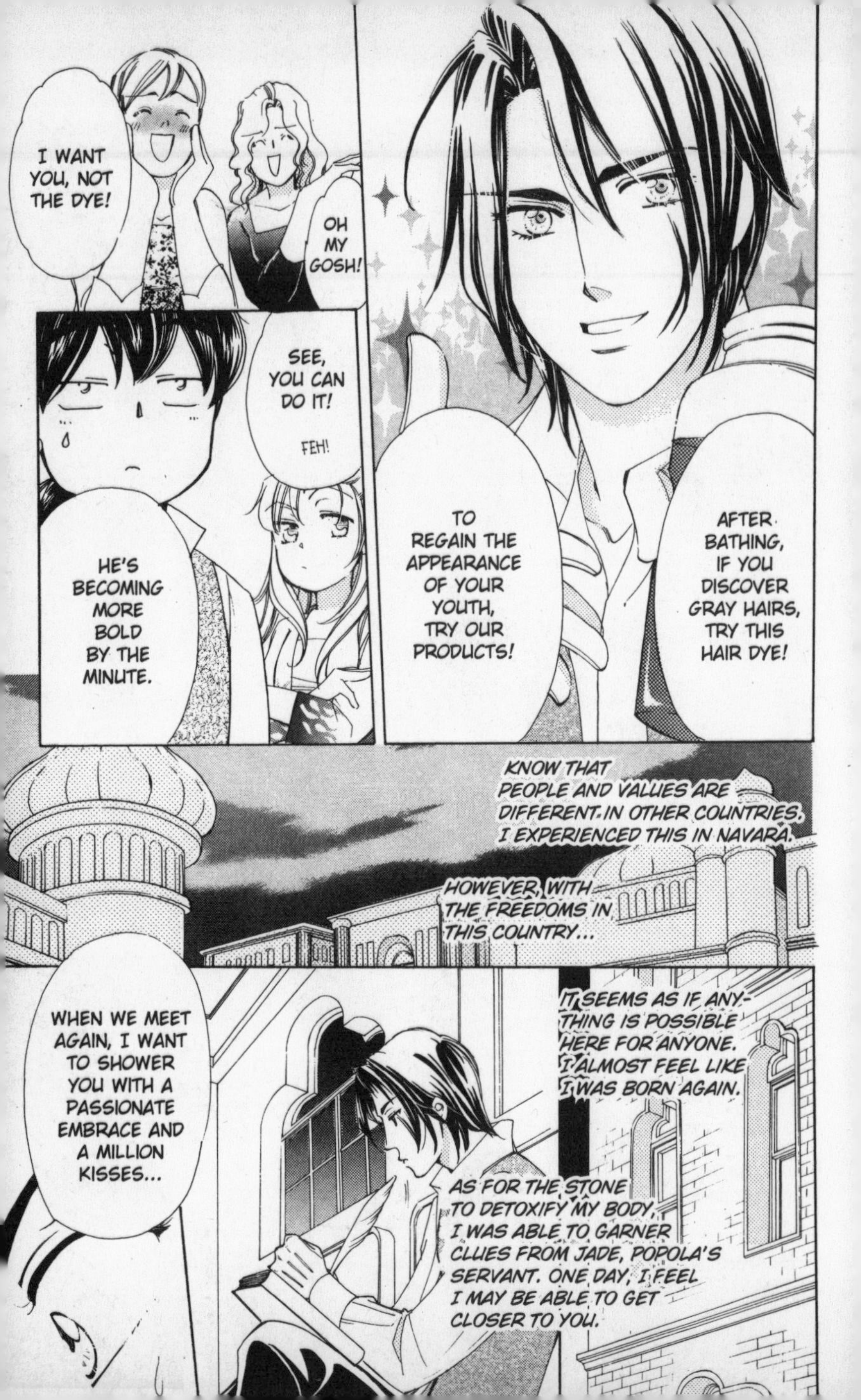
AFTER BATHING, IF YOU DISCOVER GRAY HAIRS, TRY THIS HAIR DYE!
TO REGAIN THE APPEARANCE OF YOUR YOUTH, TRY OUR PRODUCTS!
OH MY GOSH!
I WANT YOU, NOT THE DYE!
SEE, YOU CAN DO IT!
FEH!
HE'S BECOMING MORE BOLD BY THE MINUTE.
KNOW THAT PEOPLE AND VALUES ARE DIFFERENT IN OTHER COUNTRIES. I EXPERIENCED THIS IN NAVARA.
HOWEVER, WITH THE FREEDOMS IN THIS COUNTRY...
IT SEEMS AS IF ANYTHING IS POSSIBLE HERE FOR ANYONE. I ALMOST FEEL LIKE I WAS BORN AGAIN.
AS FOR THE STONE TO DETOXIFY MY BODY, I WAS ABLE TO GARNER CLUES FROM JADE, POPOLA'S SERVANT. ONE DAY, I FEEL I MAY BE ABLE TO GET CLOSER TO YOU.
WHEN WE MEET AGAIN, I WANT TO SHOWER YOU WITH A PASSIONATE EMBRACE AND A MILLION KISSES...

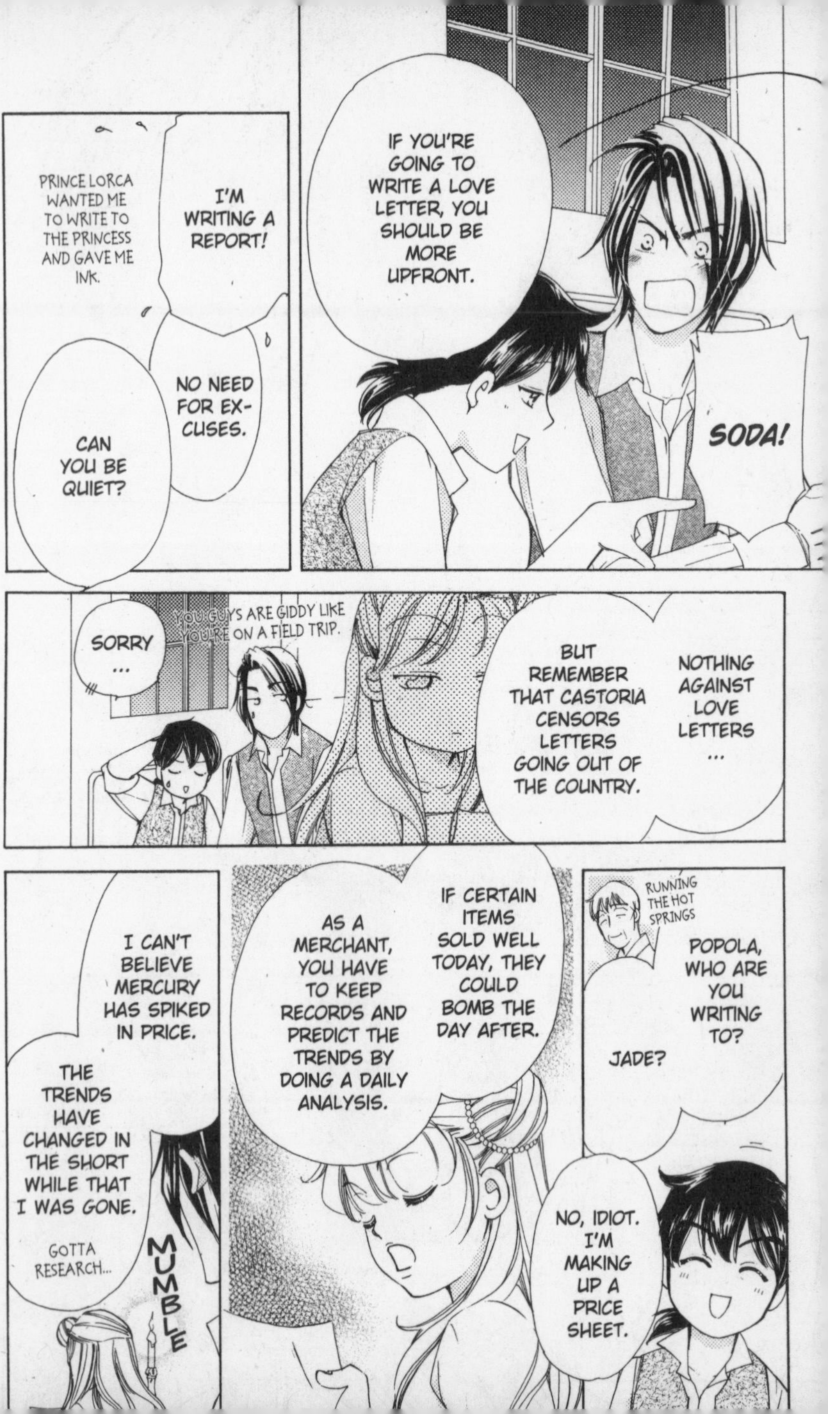
IF YOU'RE GOING TO WRITE A LOVE LETTER, YOU SHOULD BE MORE UPFRONT.
SODA!
I'M WRITING A REPORT!
PRINCE LORCA WANTED ME TO WRITE TO THE PRINCESS AND GAVE ME INK.
NO NEED FOR EX-CUSES.
CAN YOU BE QUIET?
NOTHING AGAINST LOVE LETTERS...
BUT REMEMBER THAT CASTORIA CENSORS LETTERS GOING OUT OF THE COUNTRY.
YOU GUYS ARE GIDDY LIKE YOU'RE ON A FIELD TRIP.
SORRY...
RUNNING THE HOT SPRINGS
POPOLA, WHO ARE YOU WRITING TO?
JADE?
NO, IDIOT. I'M MAKING UP A PRICE SHEET.
IF CERTAIN ITEMS SOLD WELL TODAY, THEY COULD BOMB THE DAY AFTER.
AS A MERCHANT, YOU HAVE TO KEEP RECORDS AND PREDICT THE TRENDS BY DOING A DAILY ANALYSIS.
I CAN'T BELIEVE MERCURY HAS SPIKED IN PRICE.
THE TRENDS HAVE CHANGED IN THE SHORT WHILE THAT I WAS GONE.
GOTTA RESEARCH...
MUMBLE

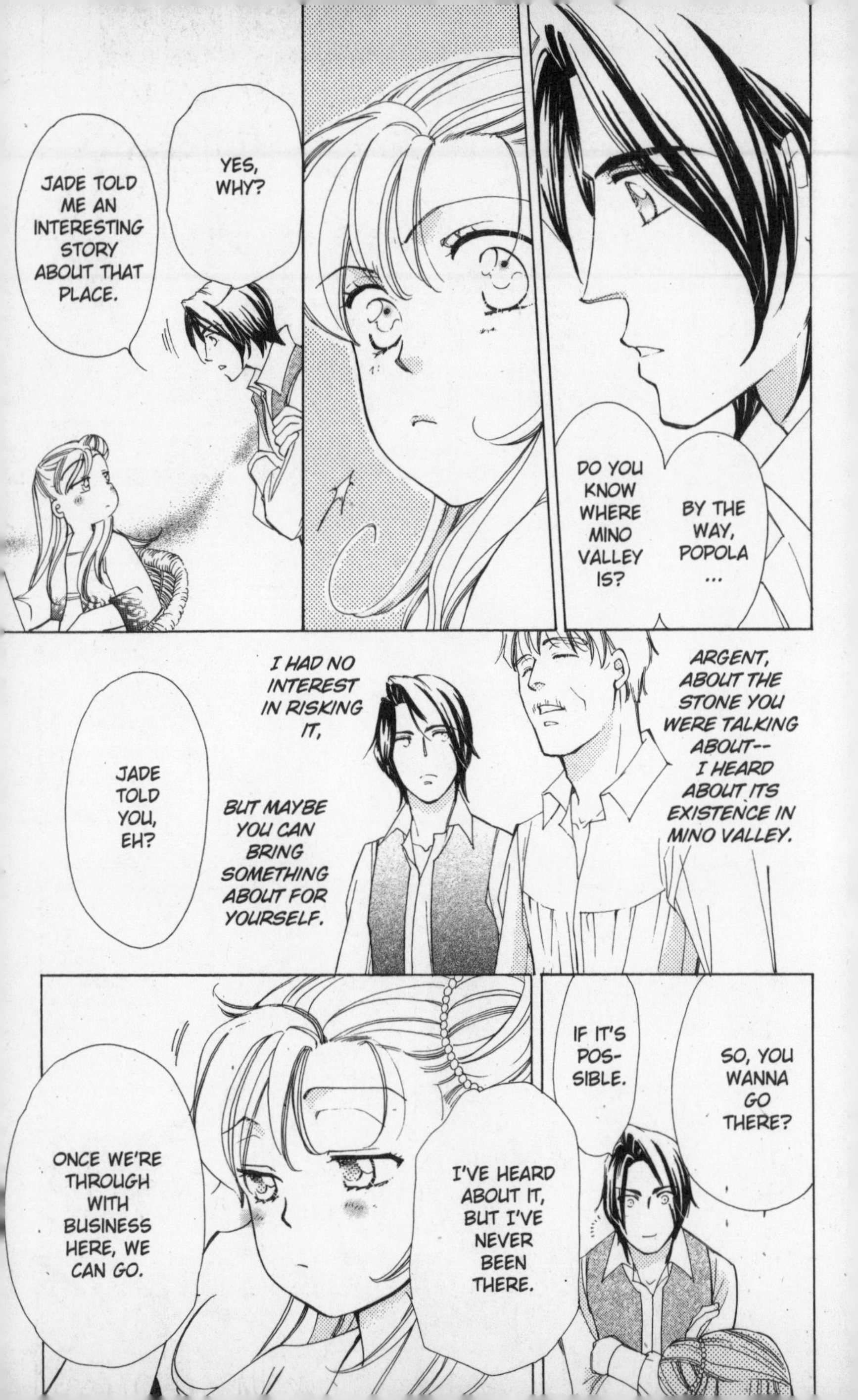
BY THE WAY, POPOLA...
DO YOU KNOW WHERE MINO VALLEY IS?
YES, WHY?
JADE TOLD ME AN INTERESTING STORY ABOUT THAT PLACE.
ARGENT, ABOUT THE STONE YOU WERE TALKING ABOUT-- I HEARD ABOUT ITS EXISTENCE IN MINO VALLEY.
I HAD NO INTEREST IN RISKING IT,
BUT MAYBE YOU CAN BRING SOMETHING ABOUT FOR YOURSELF.
JADE TOLD YOU, EH?
SO, YOU WANNA GO THERE?
IF IT'S POS-SIBLE.
I'VE HEARD ABOUT IT, BUT I'VE NEVER BEEN THERE.
ONCE WE'RE THROUGH WITH BUSINESS HERE, WE CAN GO.

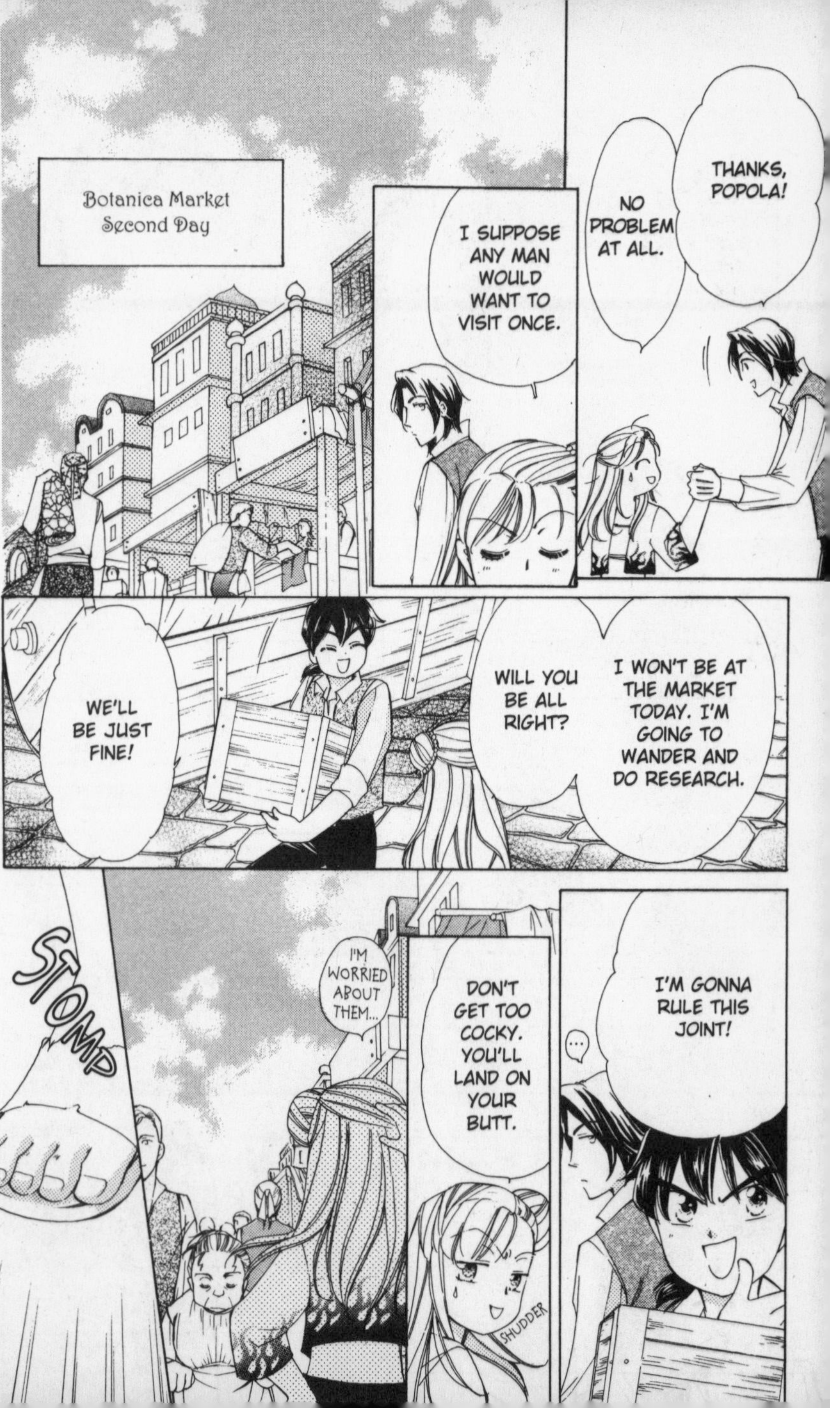
THANKS, POPOLA!
NO PROBLEM AT ALL.
I SUPPOSE ANY MAN WOULD WANT TO VISIT ONCE.
Botanica Market
Second Day
I WON'T BE AT THE MARKET TODAY. I'M GOING TO WANDER AND DO RESEARCH.
WILL YOU BE ALL RIGHT?
WE'LL BE JUST FINE!
I'M GONNA RULE THIS JOINT!
...
DON'T GET TOO COCKY. YOU'LL LAND ON YOUR BUTT.
SHUDDER
I'M WORRIED ABOUT THEM...
STOMP

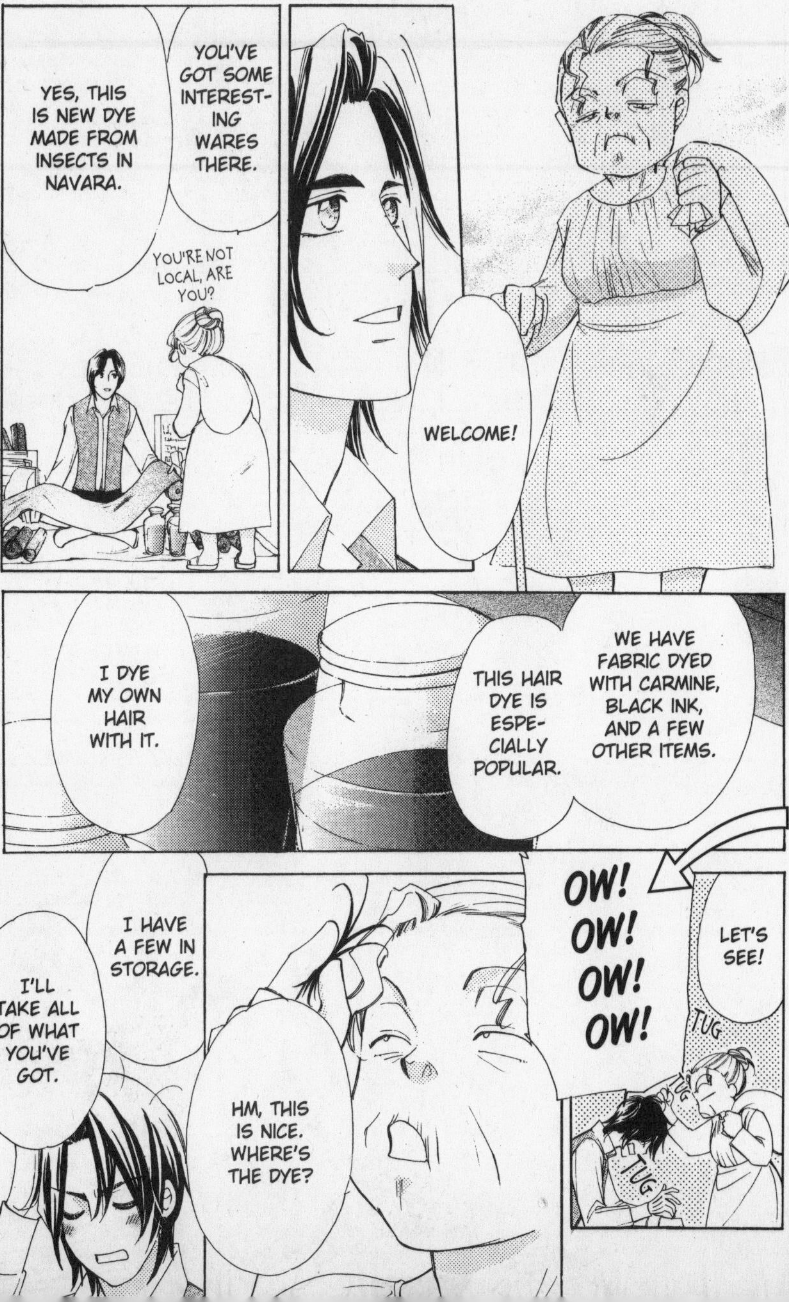
WELCOME!
YOU'VE GOT SOME INTEREST-ING WARES THERE.
YES, THIS IS NEW DYE MADE FROM INSECTS IN NAVARA.
YOU'RE NOT LOCAL, ARE YOU?
WE HAVE FABRIC DYED WITH CARMINE, BLACK INK, AND A FEW OTHER ITEMS.
THIS HAIR DYE IS ESPE-CIALLY POPULAR.
I DYE MY OWN HAIR WITH IT.
LET'S SEE!
TUG
OW! OW! OW! OW!
TUG
TUG
HM, THIS IS NICE. WHERE'S THE DYE?
I HAVE A FEW IN STORAGE.
I'LL TAKE ALL OF WHAT YOU'VE GOT.

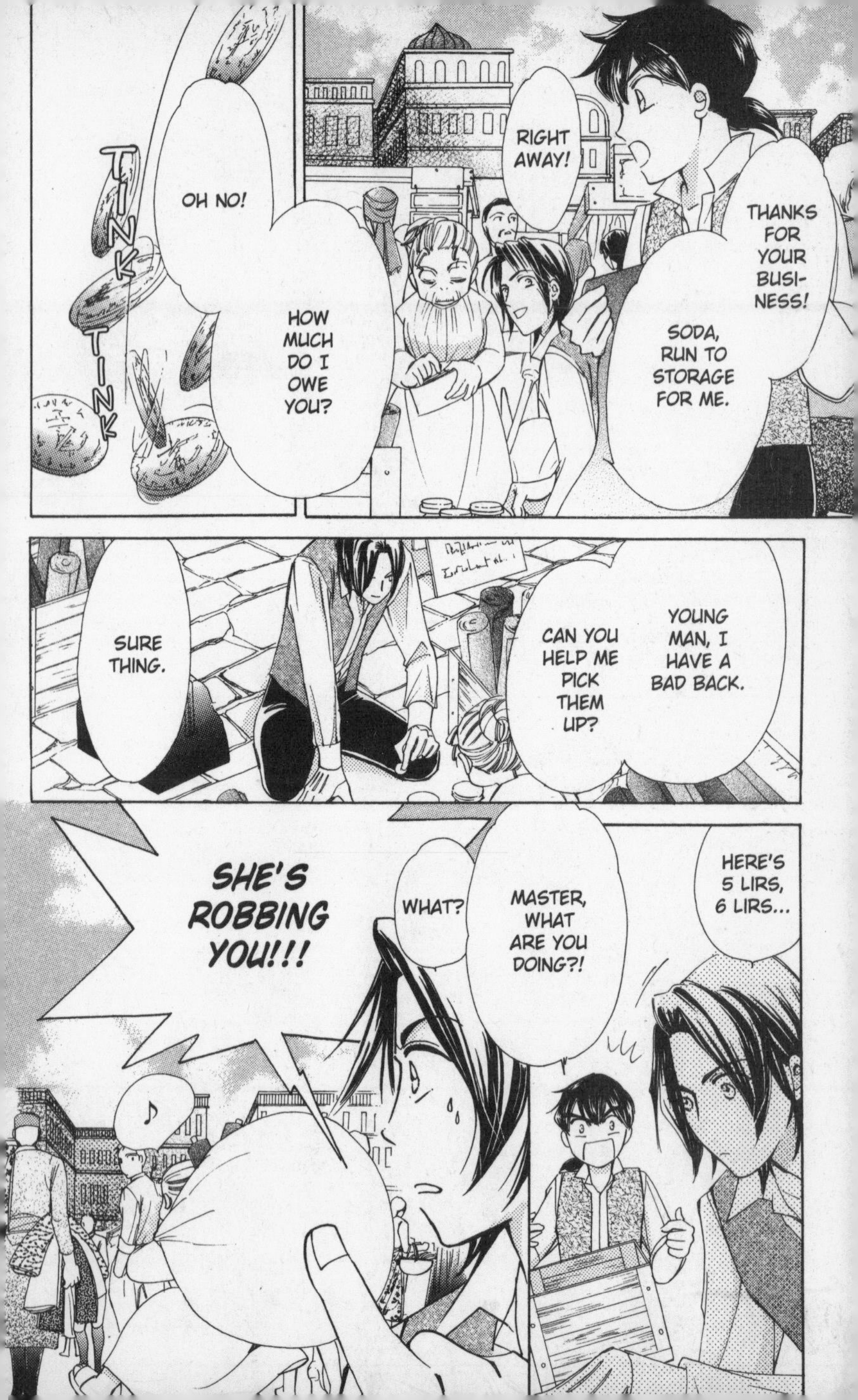
THANKS FOR YOUR BUSI-NESS!
RIGHT AWAY!
SODA, RUN TO STORAGE FOR ME.
HOW MUCH DO I OWE YOU?
OH NO!
TINK
TINK
YOUNG MAN, I HAVE A BAD BACK.
CAN YOU HELP ME PICK THEM UP?
SURE THING.
HERE'S 5 LIRS, 6 LIRS...
MASTER, WHAT ARE YOU DOING?!
WHAT?
SHE'S ROBBING YOU!!!

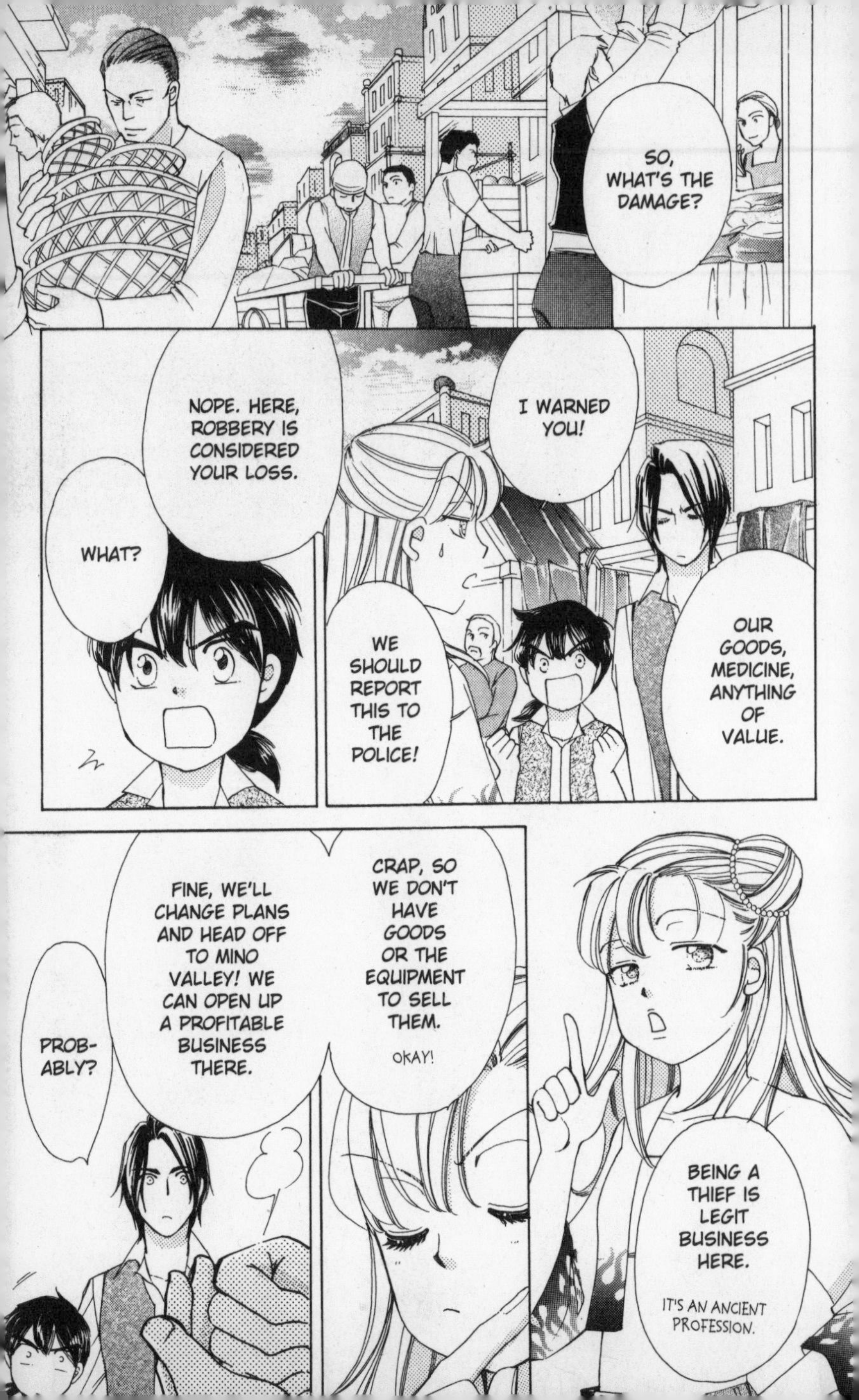
SO, WHAT'S THE DAMAGE?
OUR GOODS, MEDICINE, ANYTHING OF VALUE.
I WARNED YOU!
WE SHOULD REPORT THIS TO THE POLICE!
NOPE. HERE, ROBBERY IS CONSIDERED YOUR LOSS.
WHAT?
BEING A THIEF IS LEGIT BUSINESS HERE.
IT'S AN ANCIENT PROFESSION.
CRAP, SO WE DON'T HAVE GOODS OR THE EQUIPMENT TO SELL THEM.
OKAY!
FINE, WE'LL CHANGE PLANS AND HEAD OFF TO MINO VALLEY! WE CAN OPEN UP A PROFITABLE BUSINESS THERE.
PROB-ABLY?

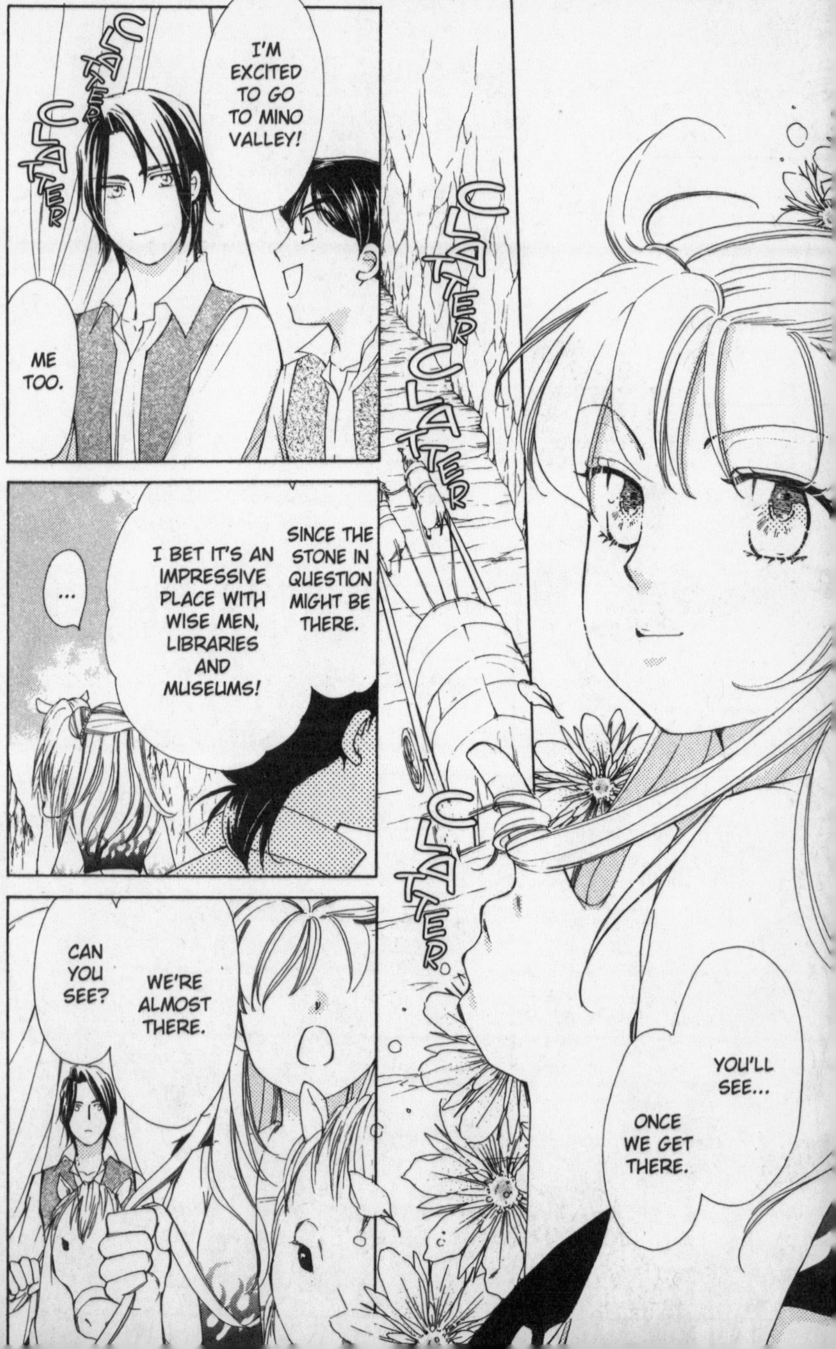
CLATTER CLATTER
CLATTER.
YOU'LL SEE...
ONCE WE GET THERE.
I'M EXCITED TO GO TO MINO VALLEY!
CLATTER CLATTER
ME TOO.
SINCE THE STONE IN QUESTION MIGHT BE THERE.
I BET IT'S AN IMPRESSIVE PLACE WITH WISE MEN, LIBRARIES AND MUSEUMS!
...
WE'RE ALMOST THERE.
CAN YOU SEE?

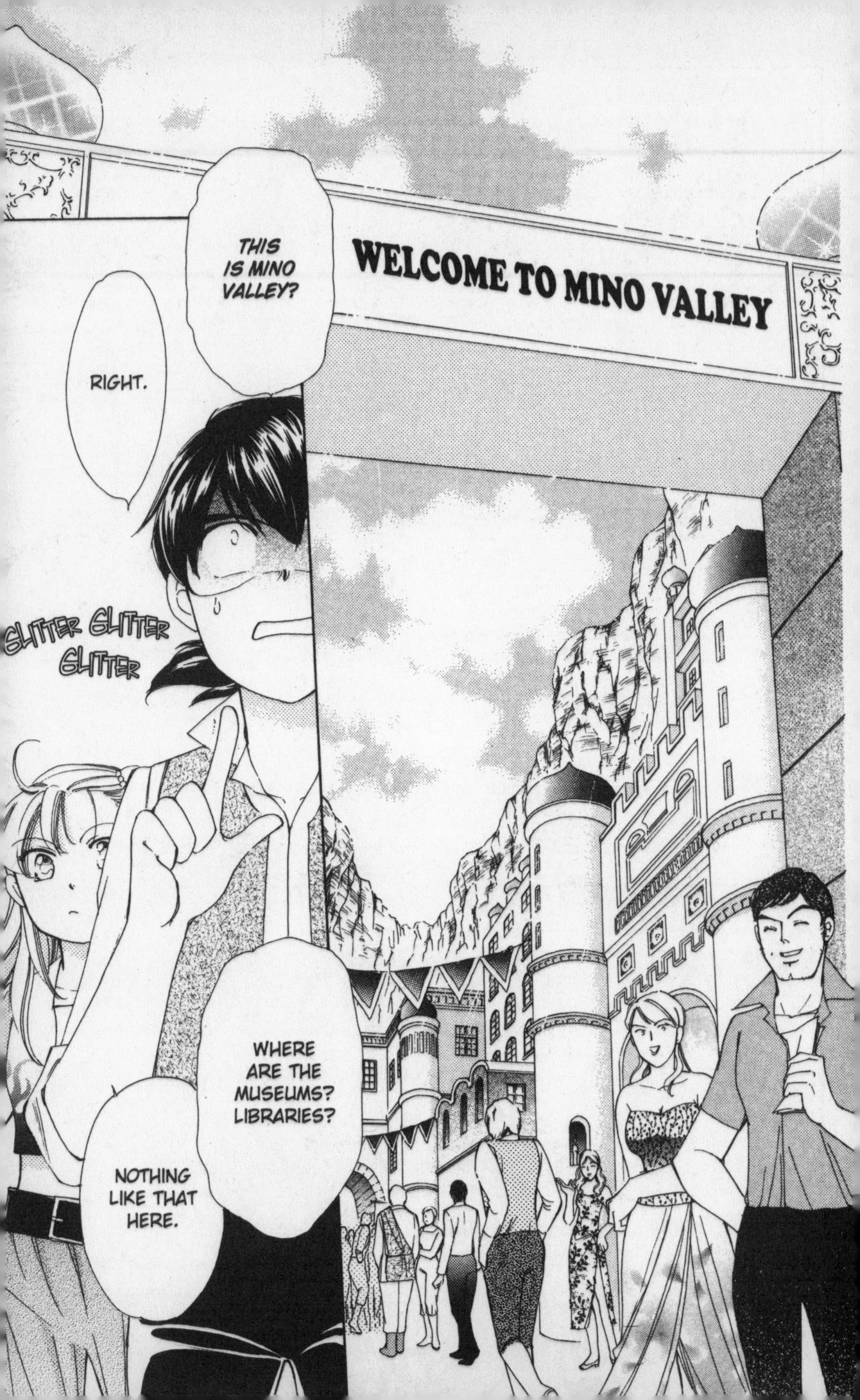

WELCOME TO MINO VALLEY
THIS IS MINO VALLEY?
RIGHT.
GLITTER GLITTER GLITTER
WHERE ARE THE MUSEUMS? LIBRARIES?
NOTHING LIKE THAT HERE.

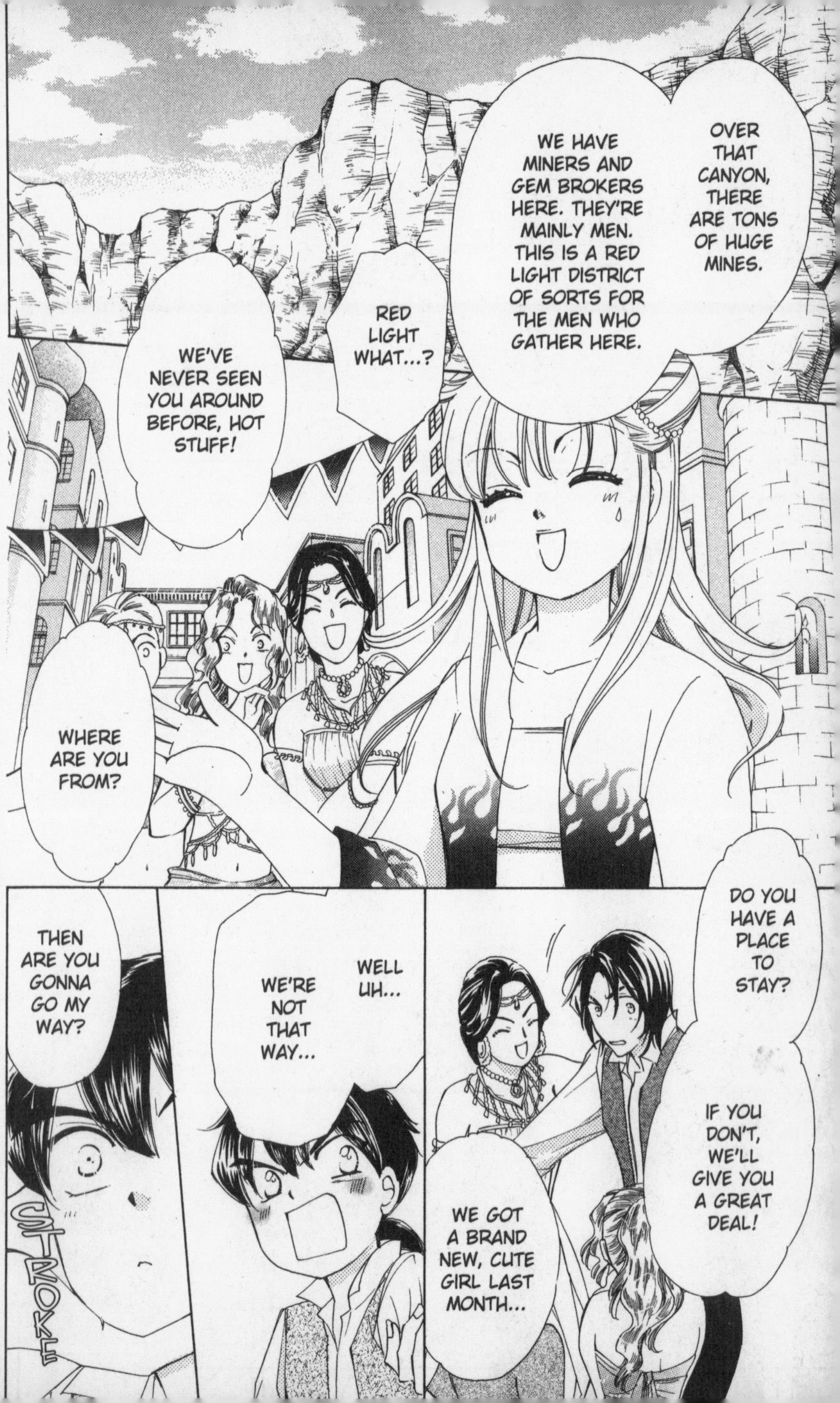
OVER THAT CANYON, THERE ARE TONS OF HUGE MINES.
WE HAVE MINERS AND GEM BROKERS HERE. THEY'RE MAINLY MEN. THIS IS A RED LIGHT DISTRICT OF SORTS FOR THE MEN WHO GATHER HERE.
RED LIGHT WHAT...?
WE'VE NEVER SEEN YOU AROUND BEFORE, HOT STUFF!
WHERE ARE YOU FROM?
DO YOU HAVE A PLACE TO STAY?
IF YOU DON'T, WE'LL GIVE YOU A GREAT DEAL!
WE GOT A BRAND NEW, CUTE GIRL LAST MONTH...
WELL UH...
WE'RE NOT THAT WAY...
THEN ARE YOU GONNA GO MY WAY?
STROKE

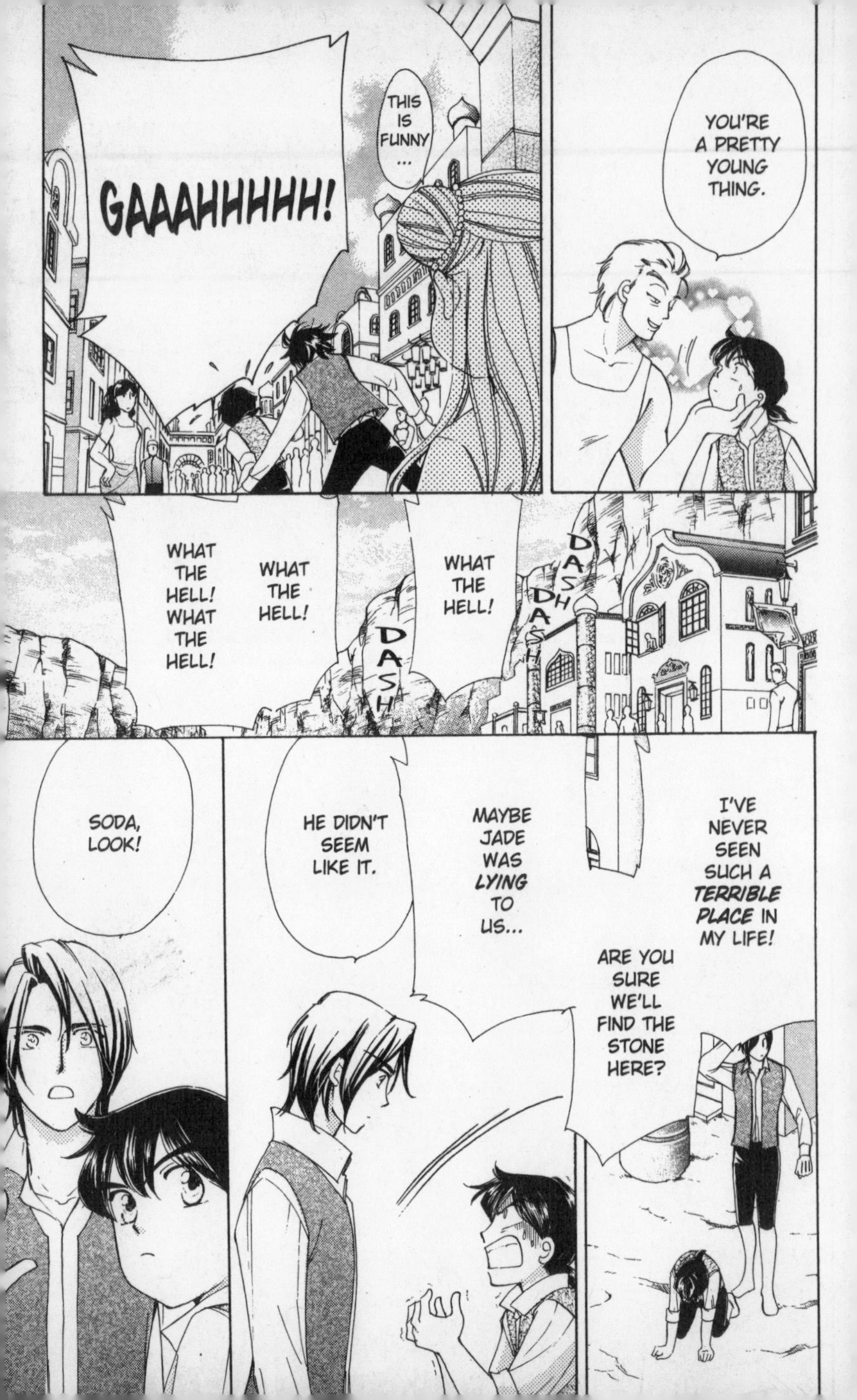
YOU'RE A PRETTY YOUNG THING.
THIS IS FUNNY...
GAAAHHHHH!
DASH
DASH
WHAT THE HELL!
DASH
WHAT THE HELL!
WHAT THE HELL! WHAT THE HELL!
I'VE NEVER SEEN SUCH A *TERRIBLE PLACE* IN MY LIFE!
ARE YOU SURE WE'LL FIND THE STONE HERE?
MAYBE JADE WAS *LYING* TO US...
HE DIDN'T SEEM LIKE IT.
SODA, LOOK!

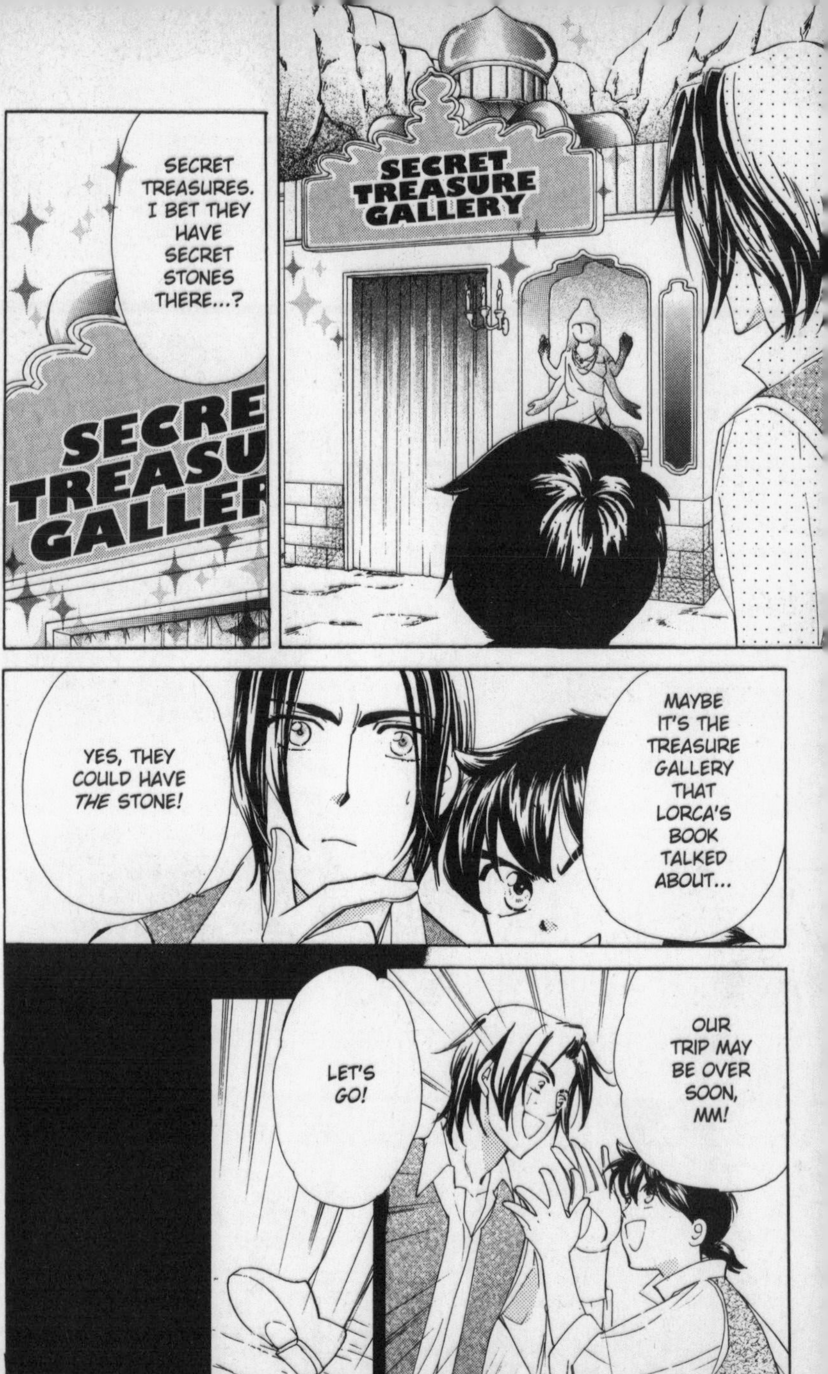
SECRET TREASURE GALLERY
SECRET TREASURES. I BET THEY HAVE SECRET STONES THERE...?
SECRE TREASU GALLER
MAYBE IT'S THE TREASURE GALLERY THAT LORCA'S BOOK TALKED ABOUT...
YES, THEY COULD HAVE *THE* STONE!
OUR TRIP MAY BE OVER SOON, MM!
LET'S GO!

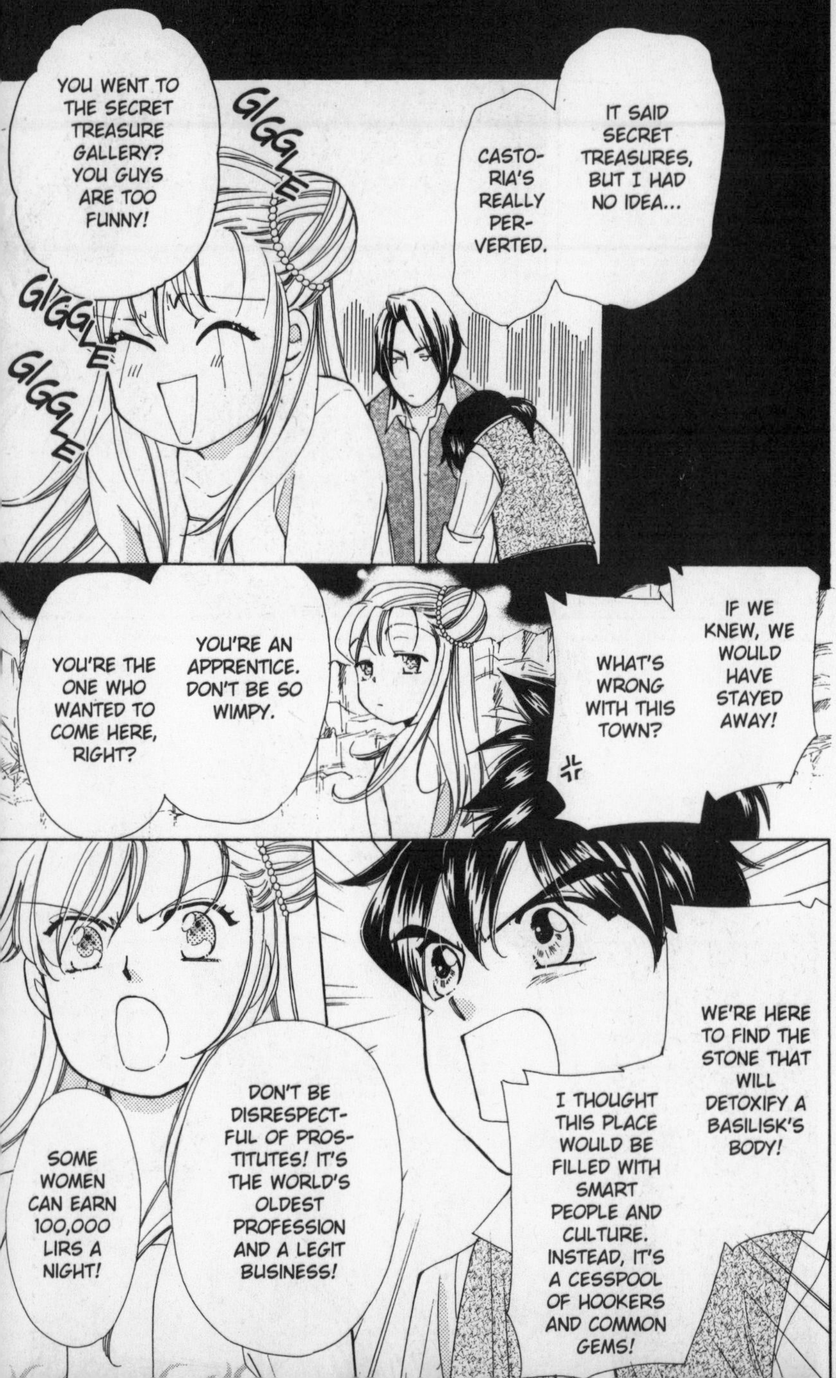
IT SAID SECRET TREASURES, BUT I HAD NO IDEA...
CASTO-RIA'S REALLY PER-VERTED.
YOU WENT TO THE SECRET TREASURE GALLERY? YOU GUYS ARE TOO FUNNY!
GIGGLE
GIGGLE
GIGGLE
IF WE KNEW, WE WOULD HAVE STAYED AWAY!
WHAT'S WRONG WITH THIS TOWN?
YOU'RE AN APPRENTICE. DON'T BE SO WIMPY.
YOU'RE THE ONE WHO WANTED TO COME HERE, RIGHT?
WE'RE HERE TO FIND THE STONE THAT WILL DETOXIFY A BASILISK'S BODY!
I THOUGHT THIS PLACE WOULD BE FILLED WITH SMART PEOPLE AND CULTURE. INSTEAD, IT'S A CESSPOOL OF HOOKERS AND COMMON GEMS!
DON'T BE DISRESPECT-FUL OF PROS-TITUTES! IT'S THE WORLD'S OLDEST PROFESSION AND A LEGIT BUSINESS!
SOME WOMEN CAN EARN 100,000 LIRS A NIGHT!

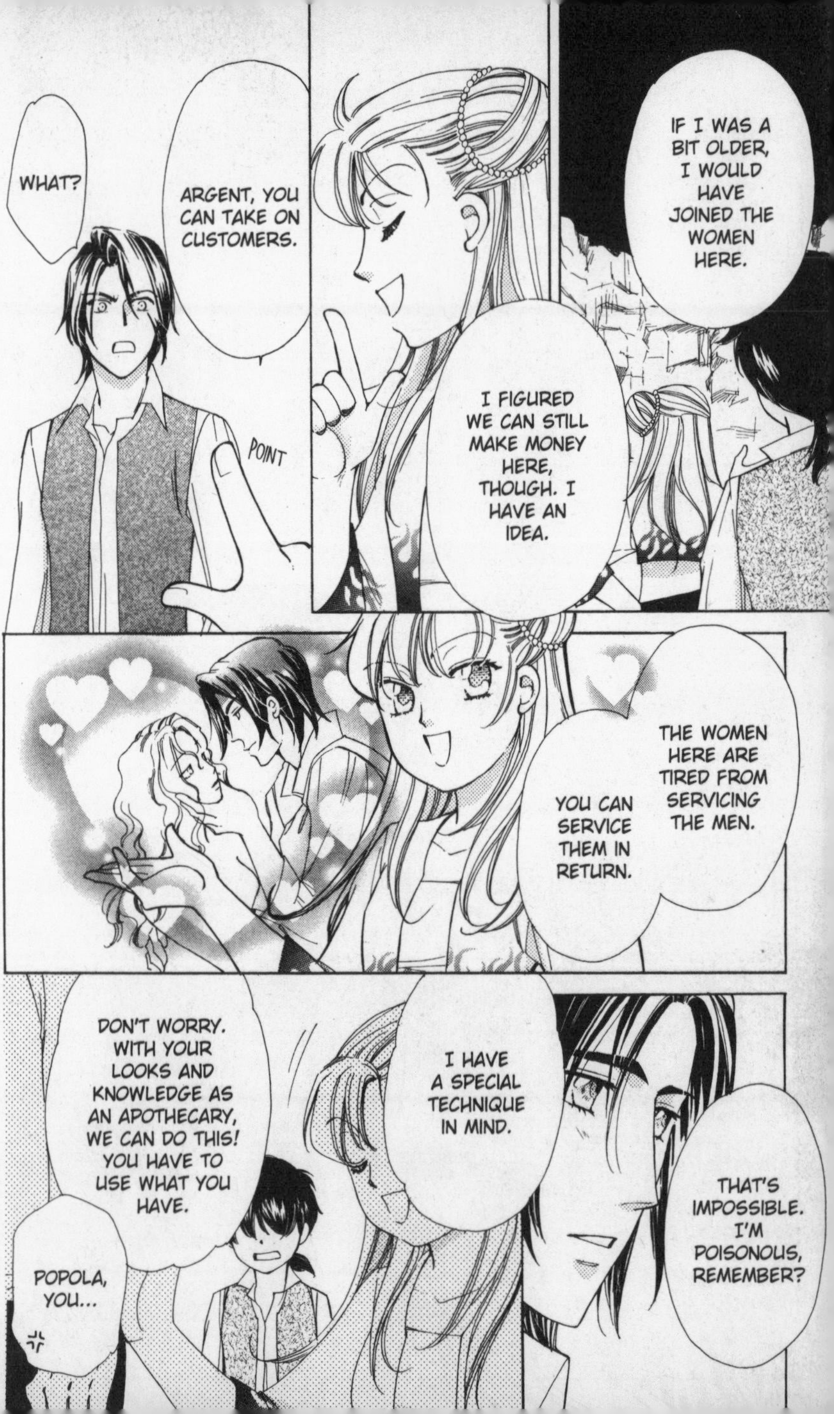
IF I WAS A BIT OLDER, I WOULD HAVE JOINED THE WOMEN HERE.
I FIGURED WE CAN STILL MAKE MONEY HERE, THOUGH. I HAVE AN IDEA.
ARGENT, YOU CAN TAKE ON CUSTOMERS.
POINT
WHAT?
THE WOMEN HERE ARE TIRED FROM SERVICING THE MEN.
YOU CAN SERVICE THEM IN RETURN.
THAT'S IMPOSSIBLE. I'M POISONOUS, REMEMBER?
I HAVE A SPECIAL TECHNIQUE IN MIND.
DON'T WORRY. WITH YOUR LOOKS AND KNOWLEDGE AS AN APOTHECARY, WE CAN DO THIS! YOU HAVE TO USE WHAT YOU HAVE.
POPOLA, YOU...

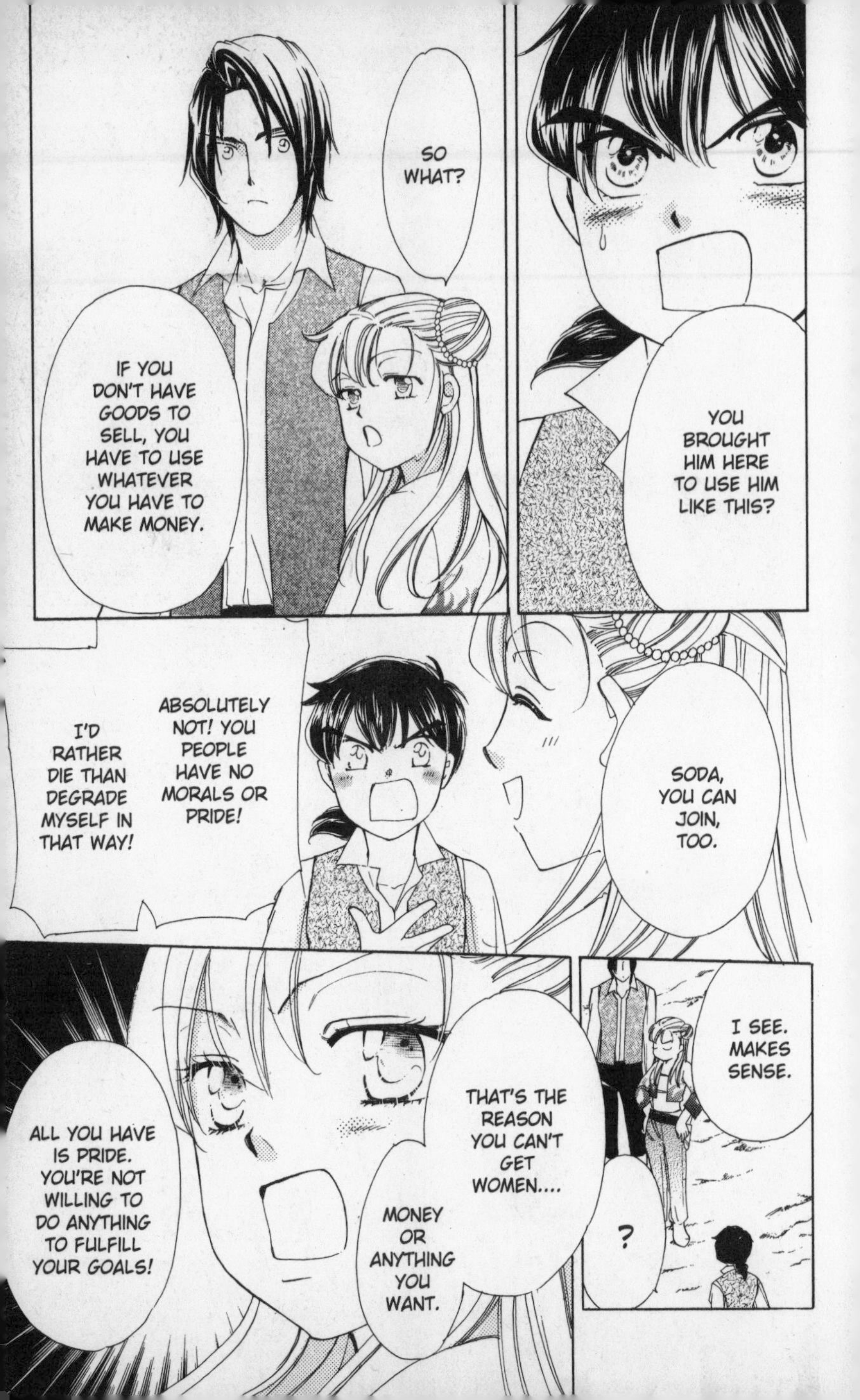
YOU BROUGHT HIM HERE TO USE HIM LIKE THIS?
SO WHAT?
IF YOU DON'T HAVE GOODS TO SELL, YOU HAVE TO USE WHATEVER YOU HAVE TO MAKE MONEY.
SODA, YOU CAN JOIN, TOO.
ABSOLUTELY NOT! YOU PEOPLE HAVE NO MORALS OR PRIDE!
I'D RATHER DIE THAN DEGRADE MYSELF IN THAT WAY!
I SEE. MAKES SENSE.
?
THAT'S THE REASON YOU CAN'T GET WOMEN....
MONEY OR ANYTHING YOU WANT.
ALL YOU HAVE IS PRIDE. YOU'RE NOT WILLING TO DO ANYTHING TO FULFILL YOUR GOALS!

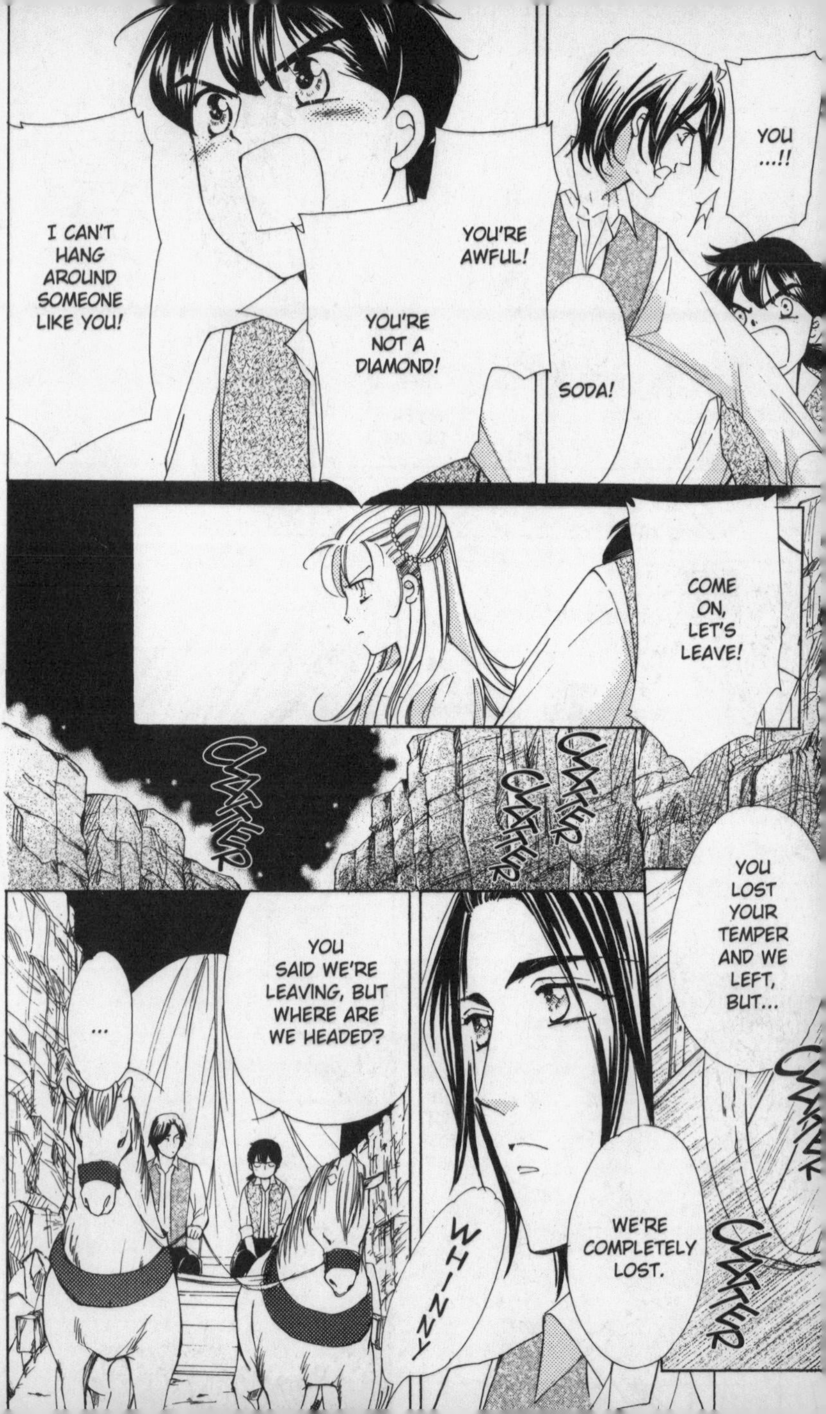
YOU ...!!
SODA!
YOU'RE AWFUL!
YOU'RE NOT A DIAMOND!
I CAN'T HANG AROUND SOMEONE LIKE YOU!
COME ON, LET'S LEAVE!
CLATTER CLATTER
CLATTER
YOU LOST YOUR TEMPER AND WE LEFT, BUT...
CLATTER
CLATTER
WE'RE COMPLETELY LOST.
WHINNY
YOU SAID WE'RE LEAVING, BUT WHERE ARE WE HEADED?
...

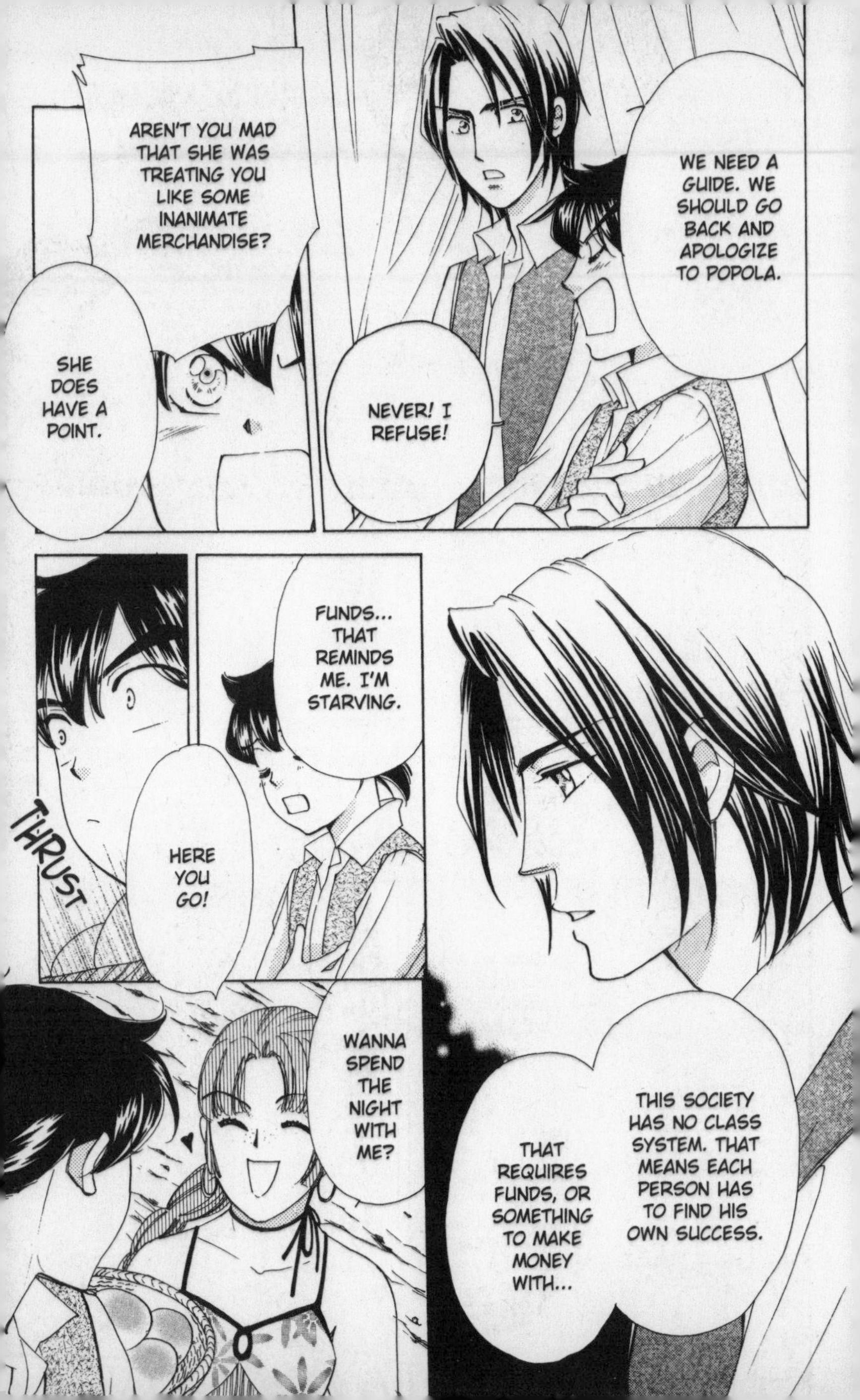
WE NEED A GUIDE. WE SHOULD GO BACK AND APOLOGIZE TO POPOLA.
NEVER! I REFUSE!
AREN'T YOU MAD THAT SHE WAS TREATING YOU LIKE SOME INANIMATE MERCHANDISE?
SHE DOES HAVE A POINT.
THIS SOCIETY HAS NO CLASS SYSTEM. THAT MEANS EACH PERSON HAS TO FIND HIS OWN SUCCESS.
THAT REQUIRES FUNDS, OR SOMETHING TO MAKE MONEY WITH...
FUNDS... THAT REMINDS ME. I'M STARVING.
THRUST
HERE YOU GO!
WANNA SPEND THE NIGHT WITH ME?

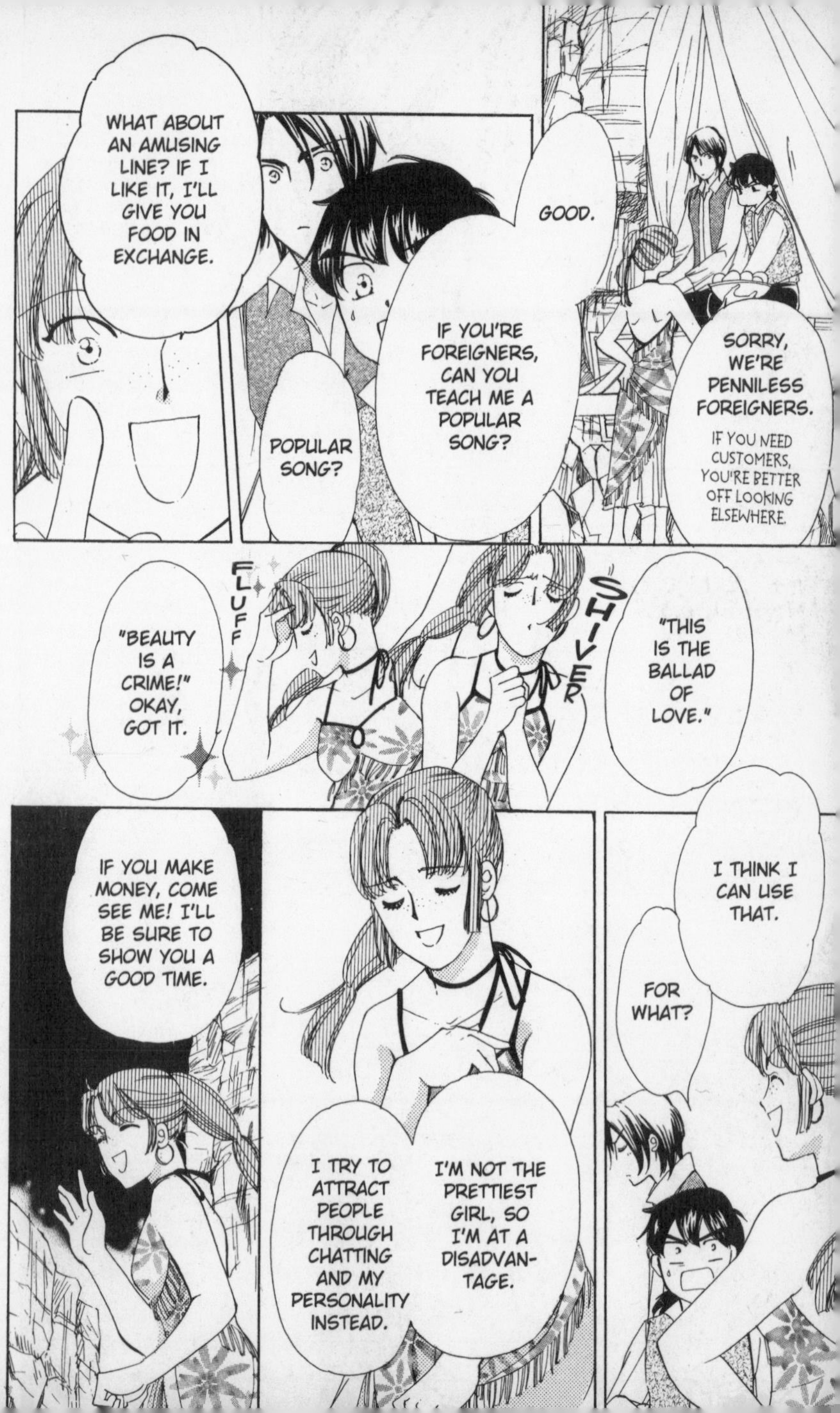
SORRY, WE'RE PENNILESS FOREIGNERS.
IF YOU NEED CUSTOMERS, YOU'RE BETTER OFF LOOKING ELSEWHERE.
GOOD.
IF YOU'RE FOREIGNERS, CAN YOU TEACH ME A POPULAR SONG?
POPULAR SONG?
WHAT ABOUT AN AMUSING LINE? IF I LIKE IT, I'LL GIVE YOU FOOD IN EXCHANGE.
"THIS IS THE BALLAD OF LOVE."
SHIVER
FLUFF
"BEAUTY IS A CRIME!" OKAY, GOT IT.
I THINK I CAN USE THAT.
FOR WHAT?
I'M NOT THE PRETTIEST GIRL, SO I'M AT A DISADVAN-TAGE.
I TRY TO ATTRACT PEOPLE THROUGH CHATTING AND MY PERSONALITY INSTEAD.
IF YOU MAKE MONEY, COME SEE ME! I'LL BE SURE TO SHOW YOU A GOOD TIME.

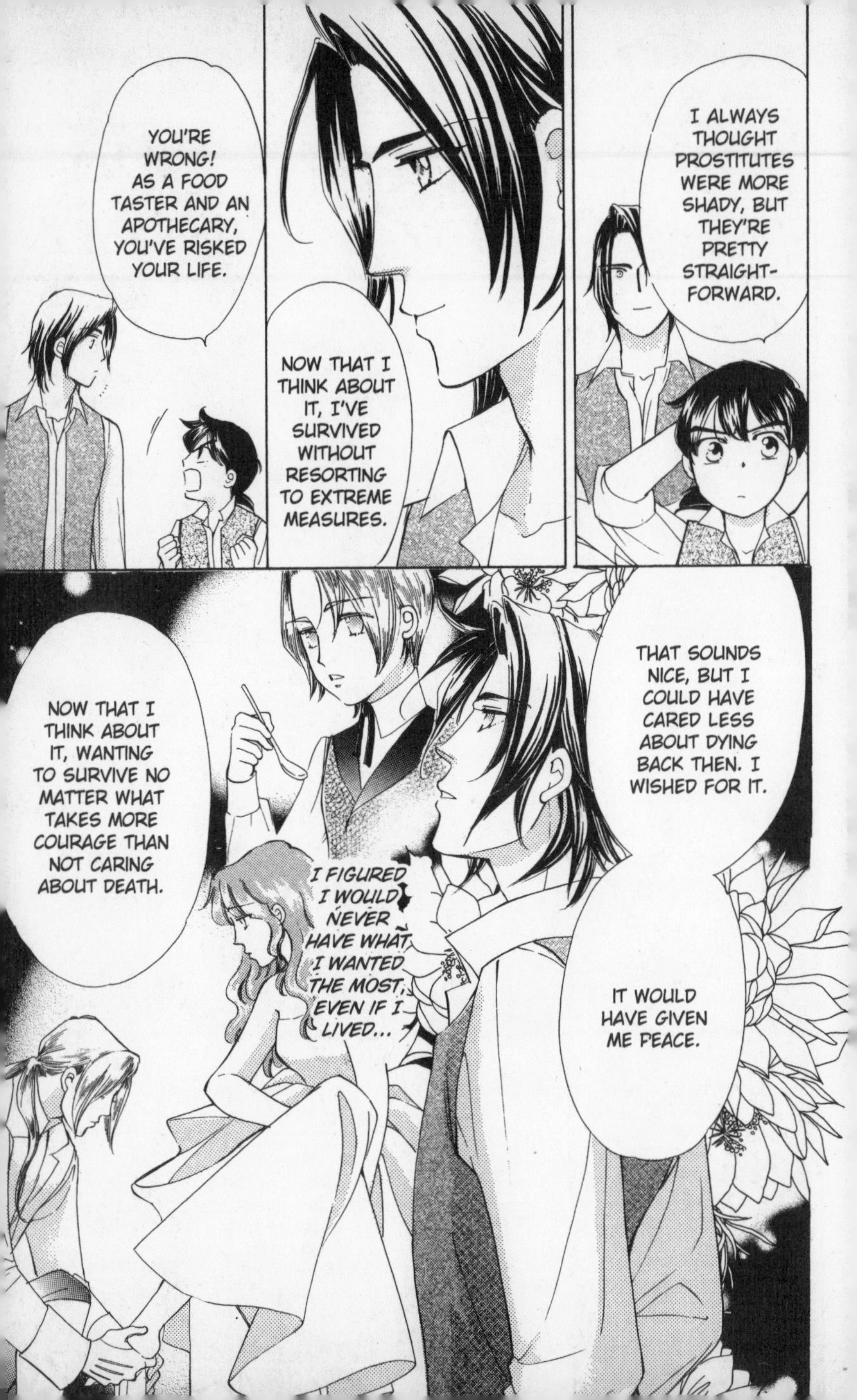
I ALWAYS THOUGHT PROSTITUTES WERE MORE SHADY, BUT THEY'RE PRETTY STRAIGHT-FORWARD.
NOW THAT I THINK ABOUT IT, I'VE SURVIVED WITHOUT RESORTING TO EXTREME MEASURES.
YOU'RE WRONG! AS A FOOD TASTER AND AN APOTHECARY, YOU'VE RISKED YOUR LIFE.
THAT SOUNDS NICE, BUT I COULD HAVE CARED LESS ABOUT DYING BACK THEN. I WISHED FOR IT.
IT WOULD HAVE GIVEN ME PEACE.
I FIGURED I WOULD NEVER HAVE WHAT I WANTED THE MOST, EVEN IF I LIVED...
NOW THAT I THINK ABOUT IT, WANTING TO SURVIVE NO MATTER WHAT TAKES MORE COURAGE THAN NOT CARING ABOUT DEATH.

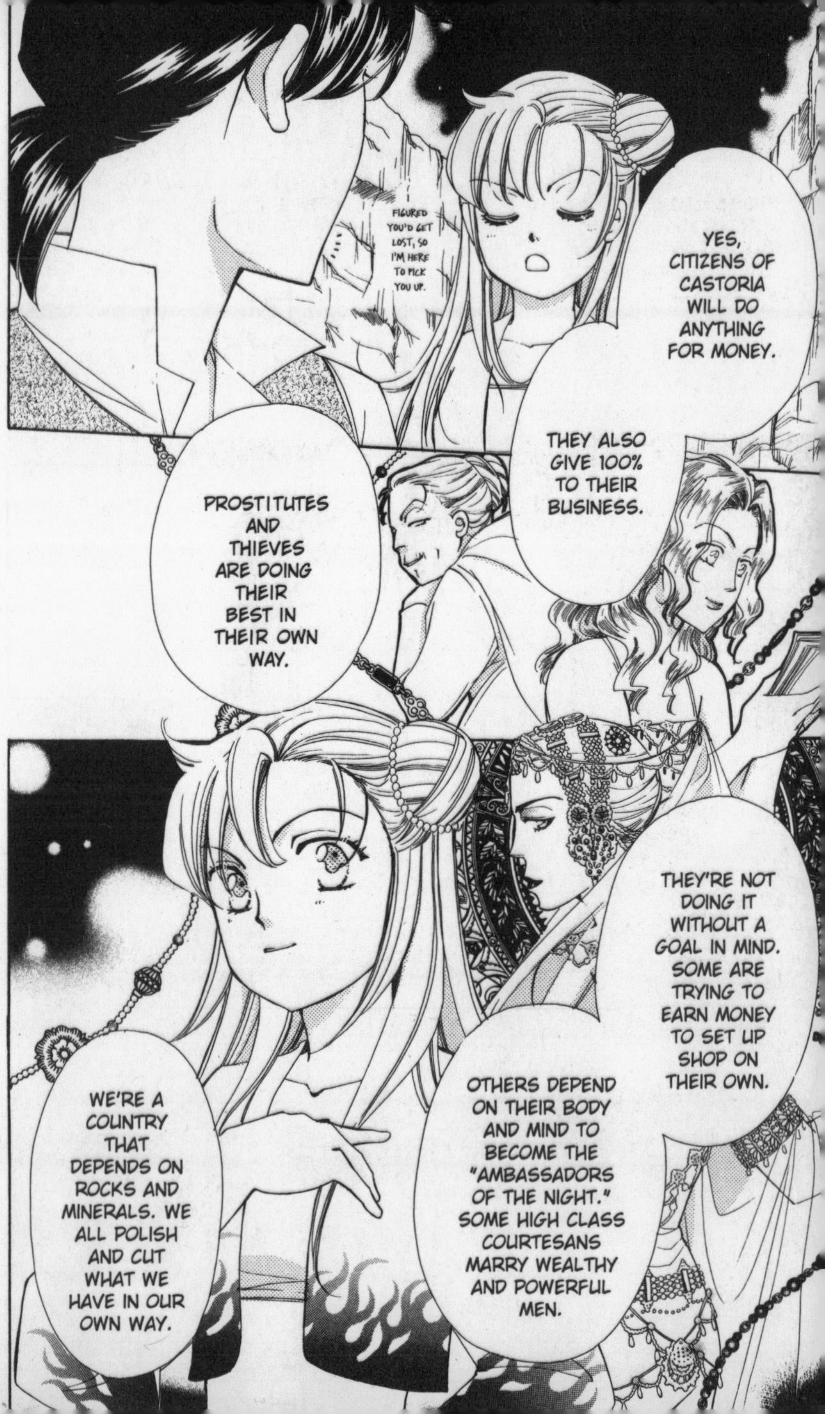
YES, CITIZENS OF CASTORIA WILL DO ANYTHING FOR MONEY.
FIGURED YOU'D GET LOST, SO I'M HERE TO PICK YOU UP.
THEY ALSO GIVE 100% TO THEIR BUSINESS.
PROSTITUTES AND THIEVES ARE DOING THEIR BEST IN THEIR OWN WAY.
THEY'RE NOT DOING IT WITHOUT A GOAL IN MIND. SOME ARE TRYING TO EARN MONEY TO SET UP SHOP ON THEIR OWN.
OTHERS DEPEND ON THEIR BODY AND MIND TO BECOME THE "AMBASSADORS OF THE NIGHT." SOME HIGH CLASS COURTESANS MARRY WEALTHY AND POWERFUL MEN.
WE'RE A COUNTRY THAT DEPENDS ON ROCKS AND MINERALS. WE ALL POLISH AND CUT WHAT WE HAVE IN OUR OWN WAY.

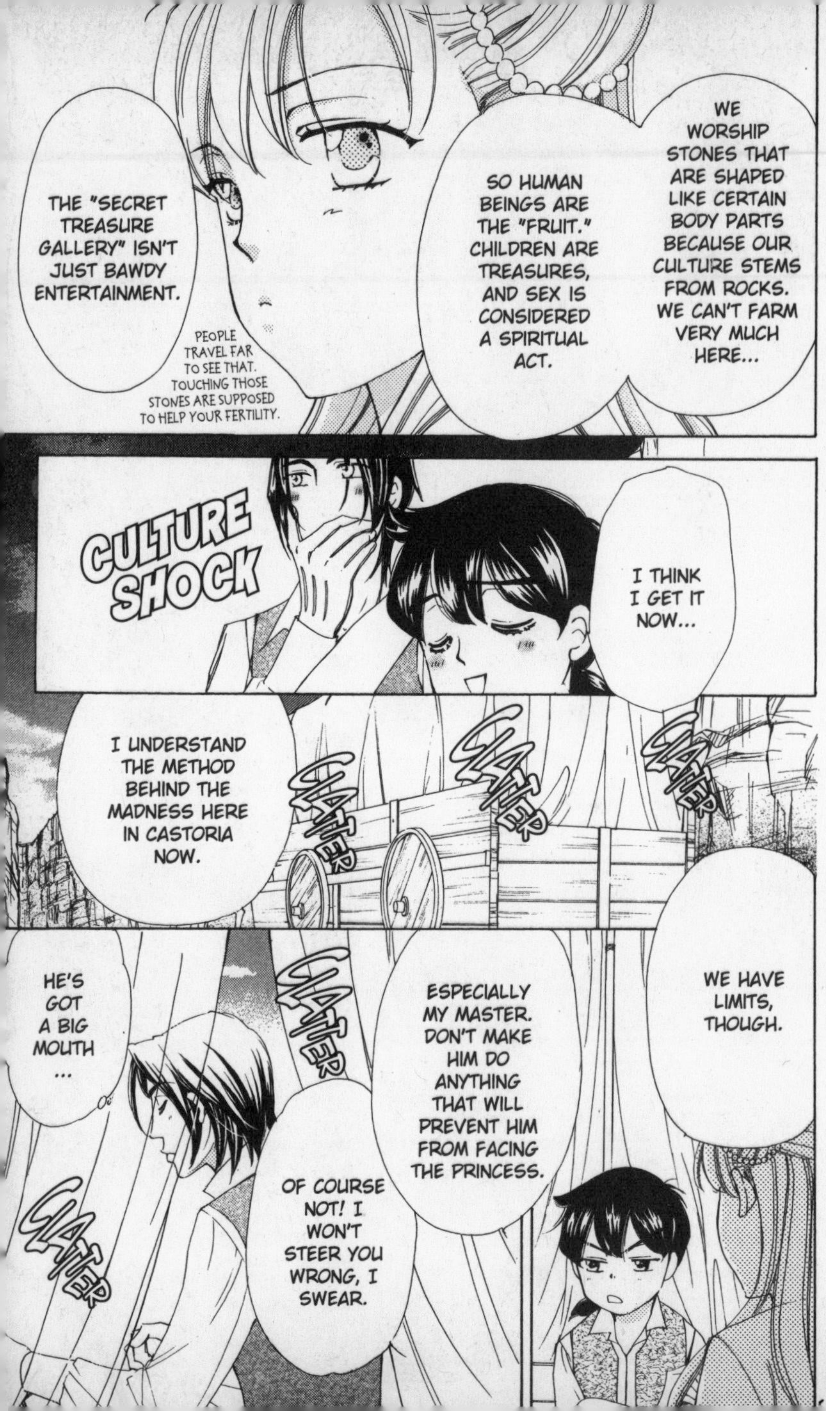
WE WORSHIP STONES THAT ARE SHAPED LIKE CERTAIN BODY PARTS BECAUSE OUR CULTURE STEMS FROM ROCKS. WE CAN'T FARM VERY MUCH HERE...
SO HUMAN BEINGS ARE THE "FRUIT." CHILDREN ARE TREASURES, AND SEX IS CONSIDERED A SPIRITUAL ACT.
THE "SECRET TREASURE GALLERY" ISN'T JUST BAWDY ENTERTAINMENT.
PEOPLE TRAVEL FAR TO SEE THAT. TOUCHING THOSE STONES ARE SUPPOSED TO HELP YOUR FERTILITY.
I THINK I GET IT NOW...
CULTURE SHOCK
CLATTER
CLATTER
CLATTER
I UNDERSTAND THE METHOD BEHIND THE MADNESS HERE IN CASTORIA NOW.
WE HAVE LIMITS, THOUGH.
ESPECIALLY MY MASTER. DON'T MAKE HIM DO ANYTHING THAT WILL PREVENT HIM FROM FACING THE PRINCESS.
CLATTER
OF COURSE NOT! I WON'T STEER YOU WRONG, I SWEAR.
HE'S GOT A BIG MOUTH ...
CLATTER

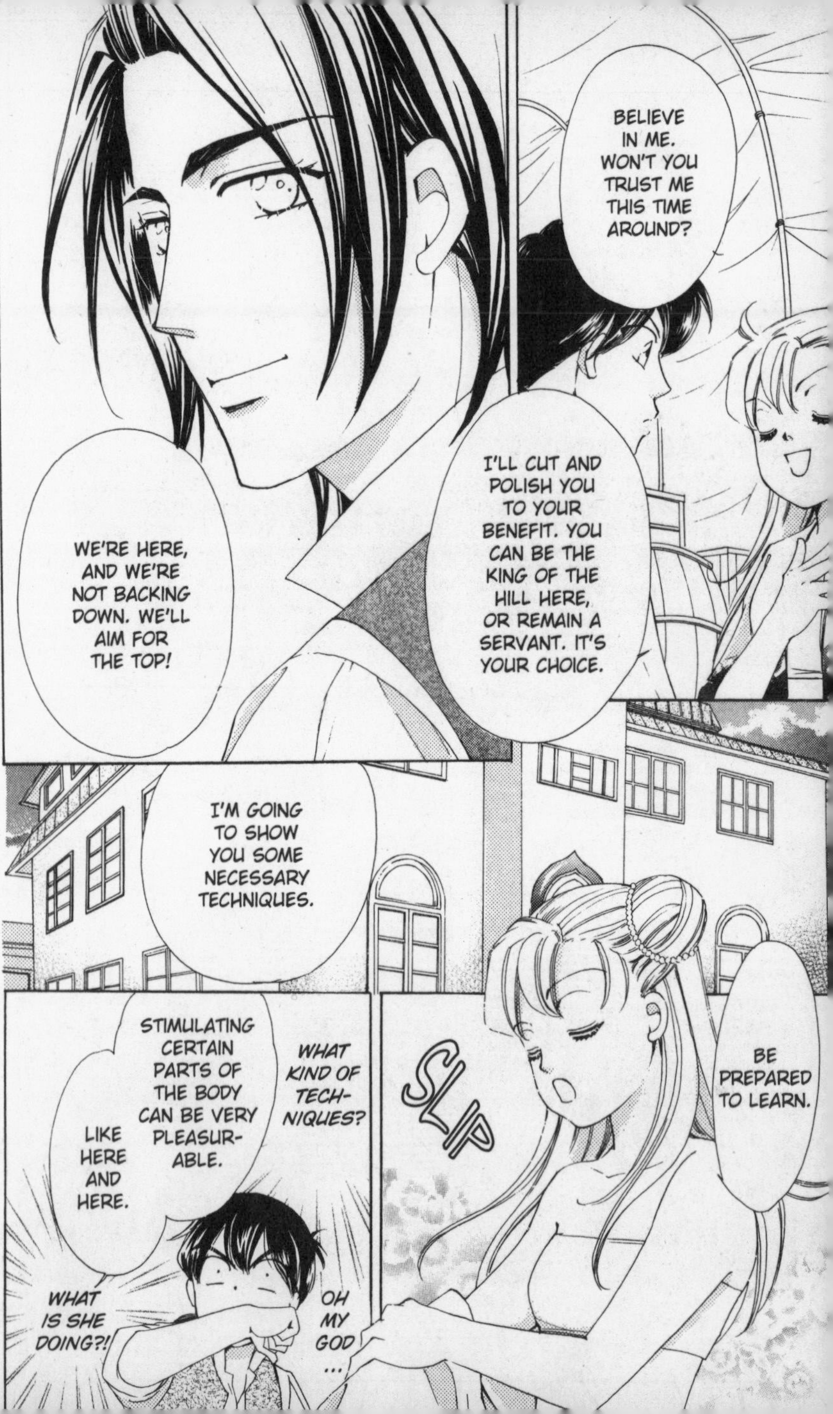
BELIEVE IN ME. WON'T YOU TRUST ME THIS TIME AROUND?
I'LL CUT AND POLISH YOU TO YOUR BENEFIT. YOU CAN BE THE KING OF THE HILL HERE, OR REMAIN A SERVANT. IT'S YOUR CHOICE.
WE'RE HERE, AND WE'RE NOT BACKING DOWN. WE'LL AIM FOR THE TOP!
I'M GOING TO SHOW YOU SOME NECESSARY TECHNIQUES.
BE PREPARED TO LEARN.
SLIP
WHAT KIND OF TECH-NIQUES?
STIMULATING CERTAIN PARTS OF THE BODY CAN BE VERY PLEASUR-ABLE.
LIKE HERE AND HERE.
OH MY GOD ...
WHAT IS SHE DOING?!

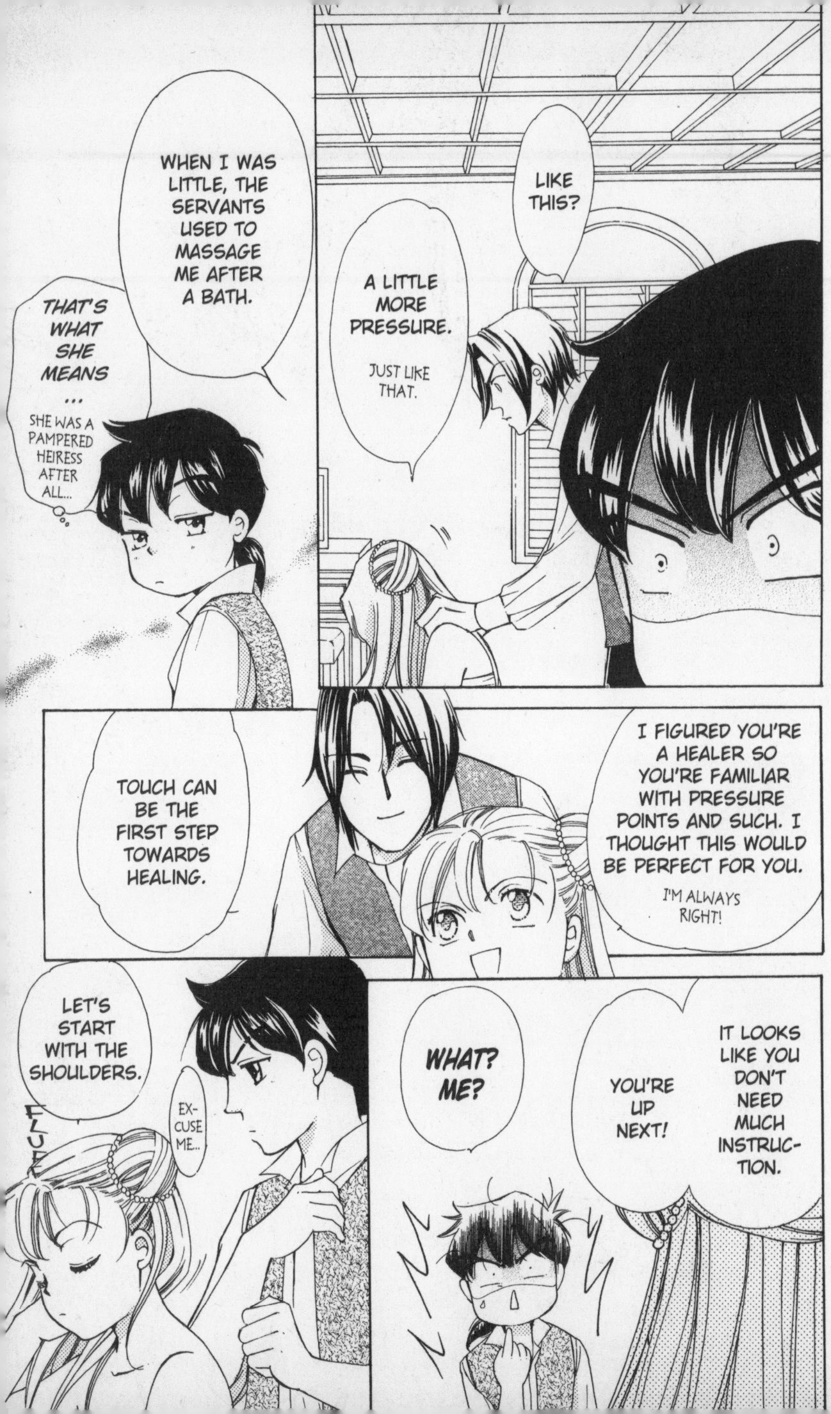
LIKE THIS?
A LITTLE MORE PRESSURE.
JUST LIKE THAT.
WHEN I WAS LITTLE, THE SERVANTS USED TO MASSAGE ME AFTER A BATH.
THAT'S WHAT SHE MEANS...
SHE WAS A PAMPERED HEIRESS AFTER ALL...
I FIGURED YOU'RE A HEALER SO YOU'RE FAMILIAR WITH PRESSURE POINTS AND SUCH. I THOUGHT THIS WOULD BE PERFECT FOR YOU.
I'M ALWAYS RIGHT!
TOUCH CAN BE THE FIRST STEP TOWARDS HEALING.
IT LOOKS LIKE YOU DON'T NEED MUCH INSTRUC-TION.
YOU'RE UP NEXT!
WHAT? ME?
LET'S START WITH THE SHOULDERS.
EX-CUSE ME...
FLUF

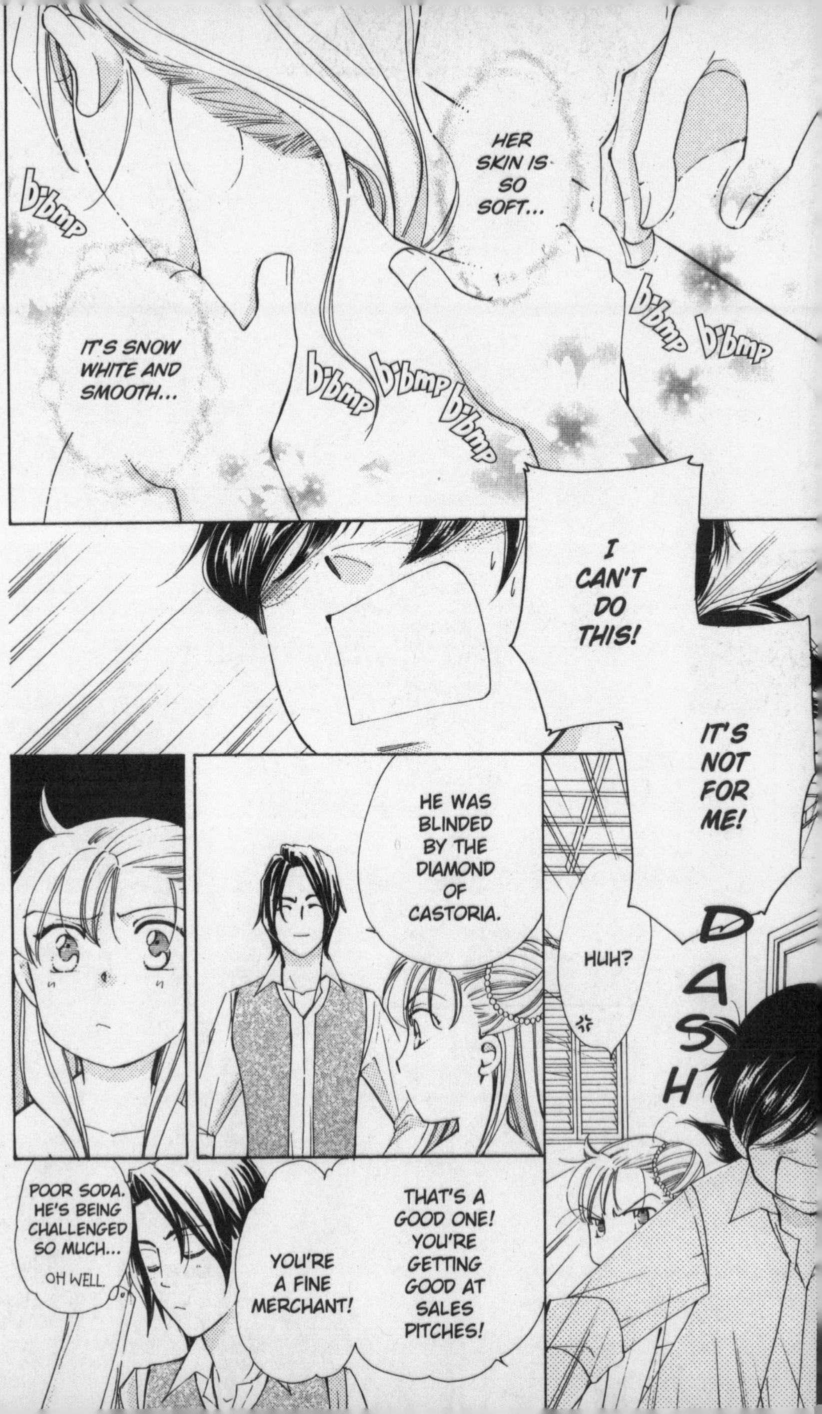
HER SKIN IS SO SOFT...
B'BMP
B'BMP
B'BMP
B'BMP
B'BMP
B'BMP
IT'S SNOW WHITE AND SMOOTH...
I CAN'T DO THIS!
IT'S NOT FOR ME!
DASH
HUH?
HE WAS BLINDED BY THE DIAMOND OF CASTORIA.
THAT'S A GOOD ONE! YOU'RE GETTING GOOD AT SALES PITCHES!
YOU'RE A FINE MERCHANT!
POOR SODA. HE'S BEING CHALLENGED SO MUCH...
OH WELL.

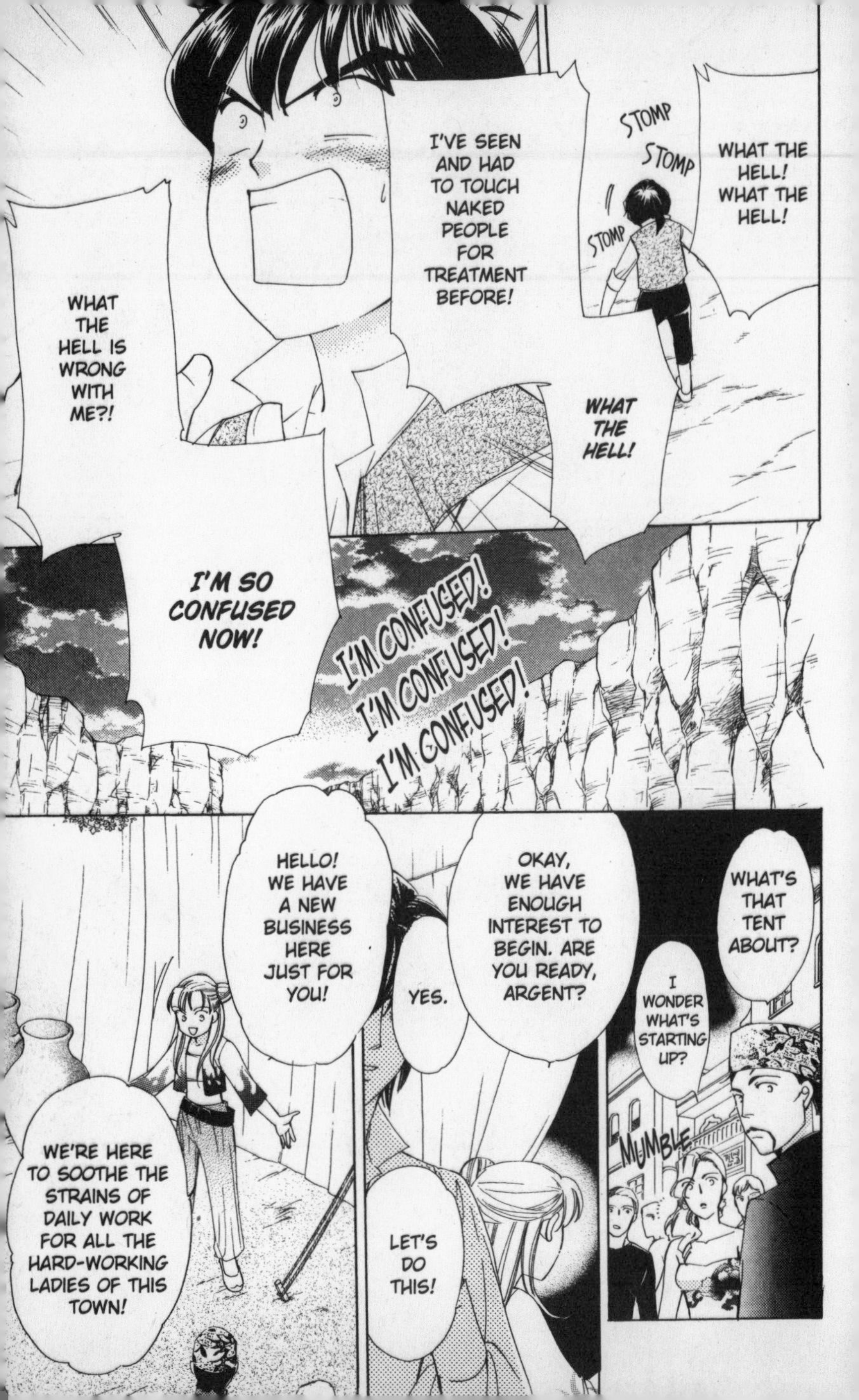
WHAT THE HELL! WHAT THE HELL!
STOMP
STOMP
STOMP
WHAT THE HELL!
I'VE SEEN AND HAD TO TOUCH NAKED PEOPLE FOR TREATMENT BEFORE!
WHAT THE HELL IS WRONG WITH ME?!
I'M CONFUSED! I'M CONFUSED! I'M CONFUSED!
I'M SO CONFUSED NOW!
WHAT'S THAT TENT ABOUT?
I WONDER WHAT'S STARTING UP?
MUMBLE
OKAY, WE HAVE ENOUGH INTEREST TO BEGIN. ARE YOU READY, ARGENT?
YES.
LET'S DO THIS!
HELLO! WE HAVE A NEW BUSINESS HERE JUST FOR YOU!
WE'RE HERE TO SOOTHE THE STRAINS OF DAILY WORK FOR ALL THE HARD-WORKING LADIES OF THIS TOWN!

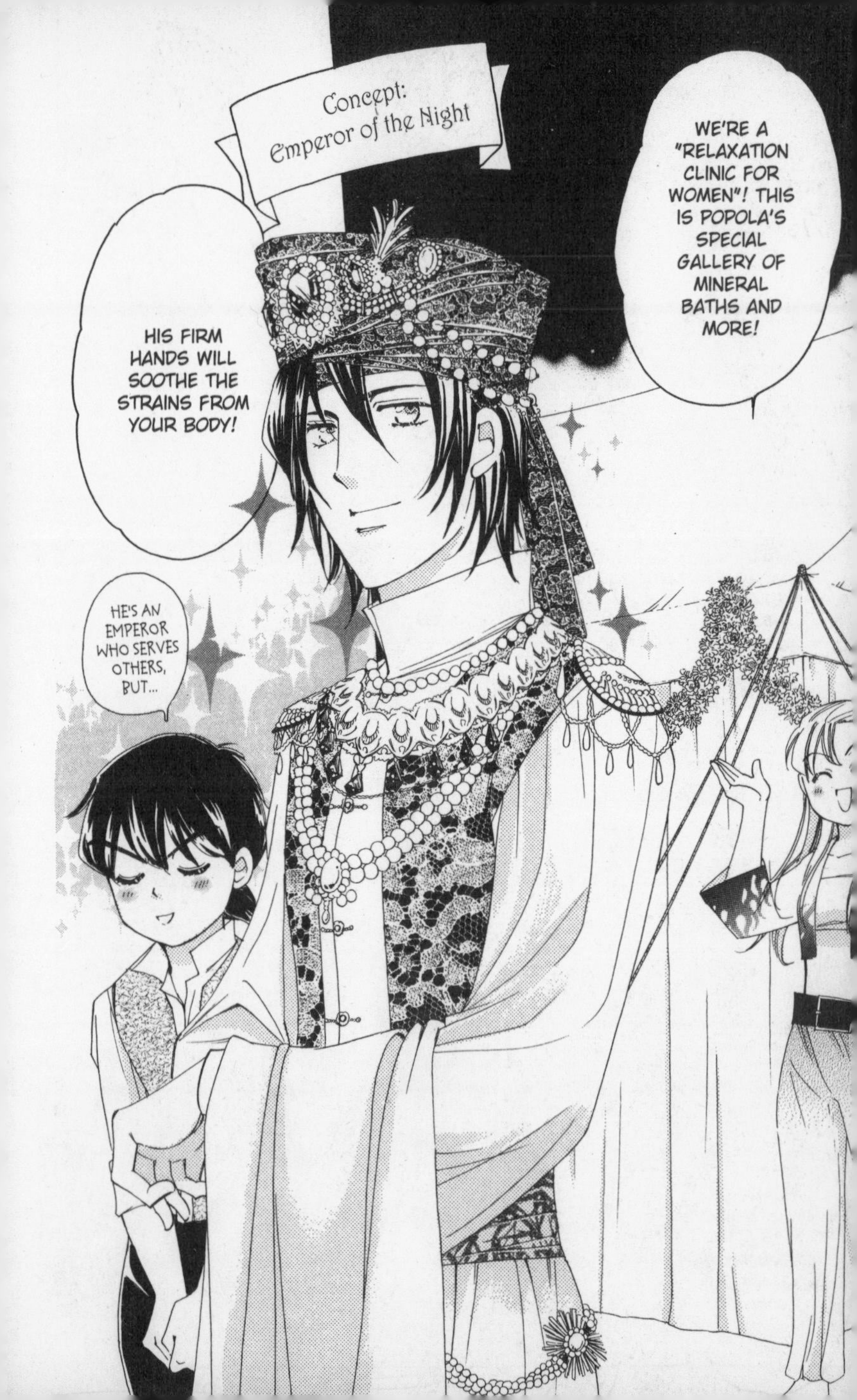
Concept: Emperor of the Night
WE'RE A "RELAXATION CLINIC FOR WOMEN"! THIS IS POPOLA'S SPECIAL GALLERY OF MINERAL BATHS AND MORE!
HIS FIRM HANDS WILL SOOTHE THE STRAINS FROM YOUR BODY!
HE'S AN EMPEROR WHO SERVES OTHERS, BUT...

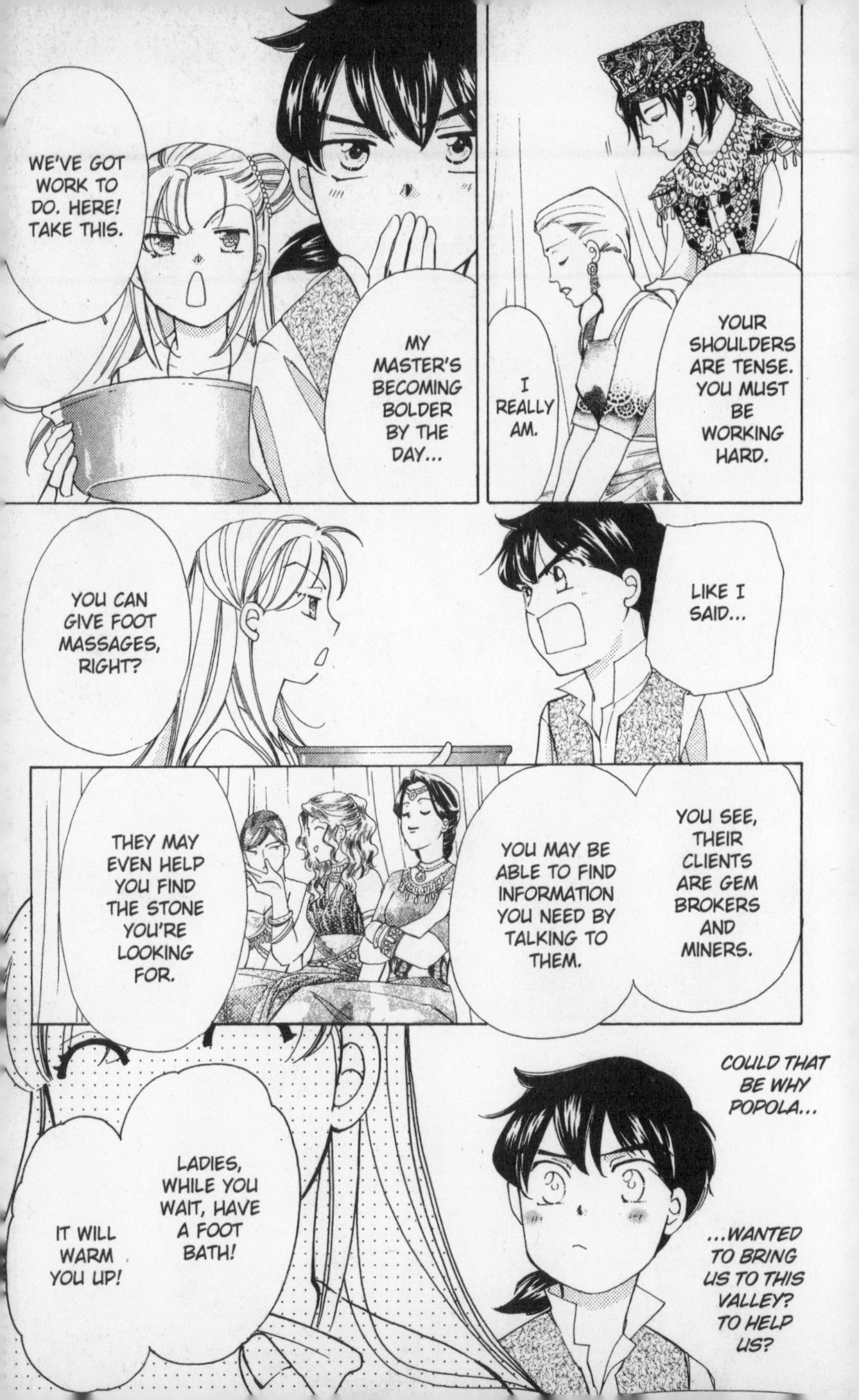
YOUR SHOULDERS ARE TENSE. YOU MUST BE WORKING HARD.
I REALLY AM.
MY MASTER'S BECOMING BOLDER BY THE DAY...
WE'VE GOT WORK TO DO. HERE! TAKE THIS.
LIKE I SAID...
YOU CAN GIVE FOOT MASSAGES, RIGHT?
YOU SEE, THEIR CLIENTS ARE GEM BROKERS AND MINERS.
YOU MAY BE ABLE TO FIND INFORMATION YOU NEED BY TALKING TO THEM.
THEY MAY EVEN HELP YOU FIND THE STONE YOU'RE LOOKING FOR.
COULD THAT BE WHY POPOLA...
...WANTED TO BRING US TO THIS VALLEY? TO HELP US?
LADIES, WHILE YOU WAIT, HAVE A FOOT BATH!
IT WILL WARM YOU UP!

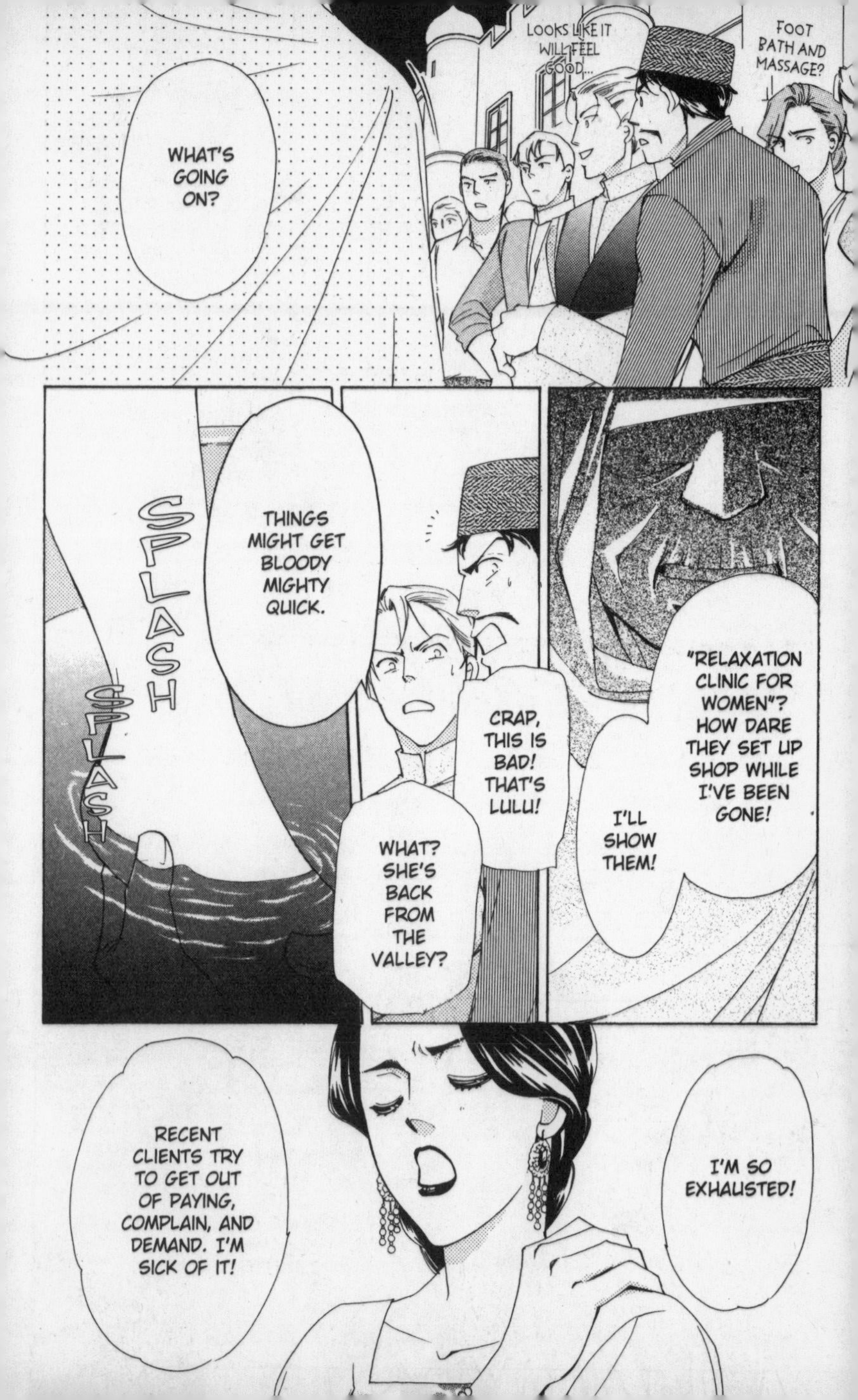
FOOT BATH AND MASSAGE?
LOOKS LIKE IT WILL FEEL GOOD...
WHAT'S GOING ON?
"RELAXATION CLINIC FOR WOMEN"? HOW DARE THEY SET UP SHOP WHILE I'VE BEEN GONE!
I'LL SHOW THEM!
CRAP, THIS IS BAD! THAT'S LULU!
WHAT? SHE'S BACK FROM THE VALLEY?
THINGS MIGHT GET BLOODY MIGHTY QUICK.
SPLASH
SPLASH
I'M SO EXHAUSTED!
RECENT CLIENTS TRY TO GET OUT OF PAYING, COMPLAIN, AND DEMAND. I'M SICK OF IT!

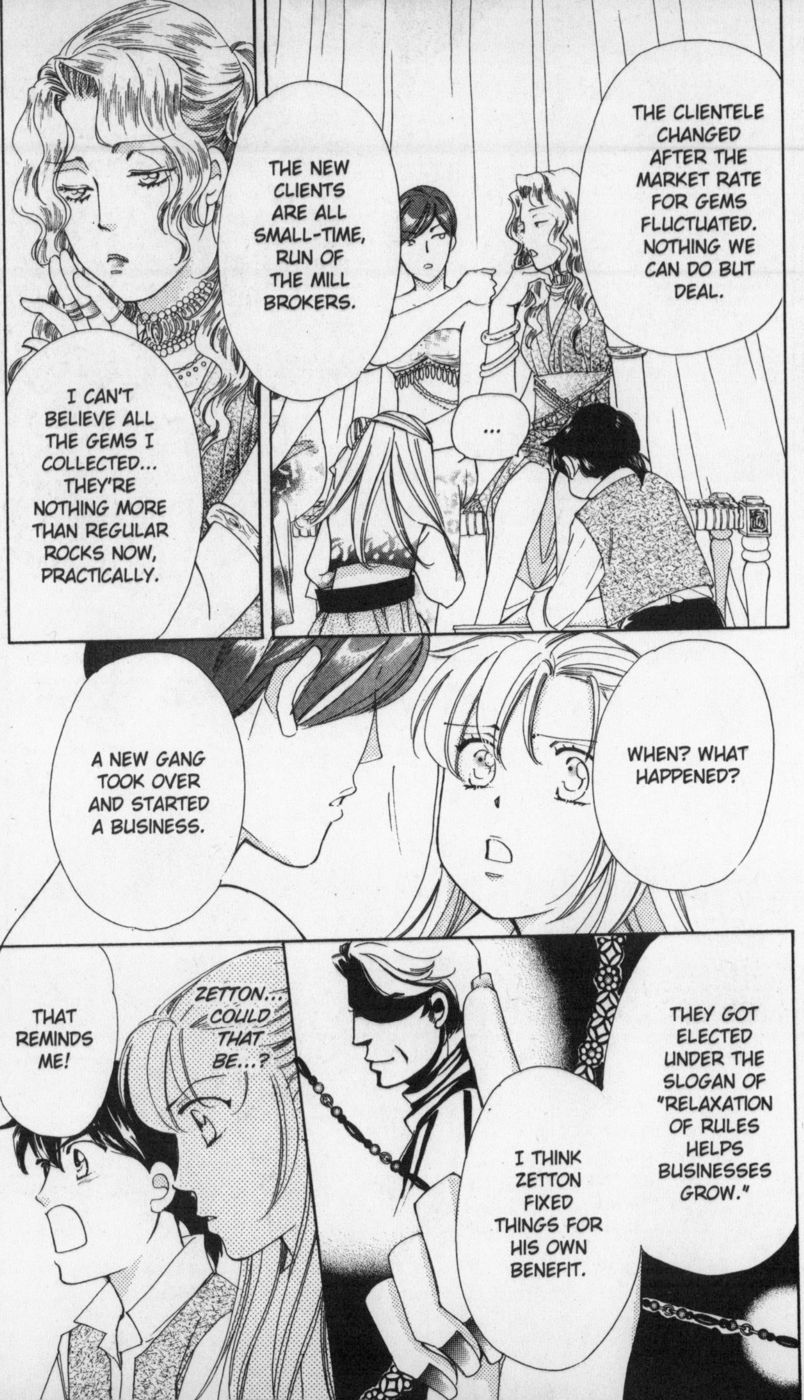
THE CLIENTELE CHANGED AFTER THE MARKET RATE FOR GEMS FLUCTUATED. NOTHING WE CAN DO BUT DEAL.
THE NEW CLIENTS ARE ALL SMALL-TIME, RUN OF THE MILL BROKERS.
...
I CAN'T BELIEVE ALL THE GEMS I COLLECTED... THEY'RE NOTHING MORE THAN REGULAR ROCKS NOW, PRACTICALLY.
WHEN? WHAT HAPPENED?
A NEW GANG TOOK OVER AND STARTED A BUSINESS.
THEY GOT ELECTED UNDER THE SLOGAN OF "RELAXATION OF RULES HELPS BUSINESSES GROW."
I THINK ZETTON FIXED THINGS FOR HIS OWN BENEFIT.
ZETTON... COULD THAT BE...?
THAT REMINDS ME!

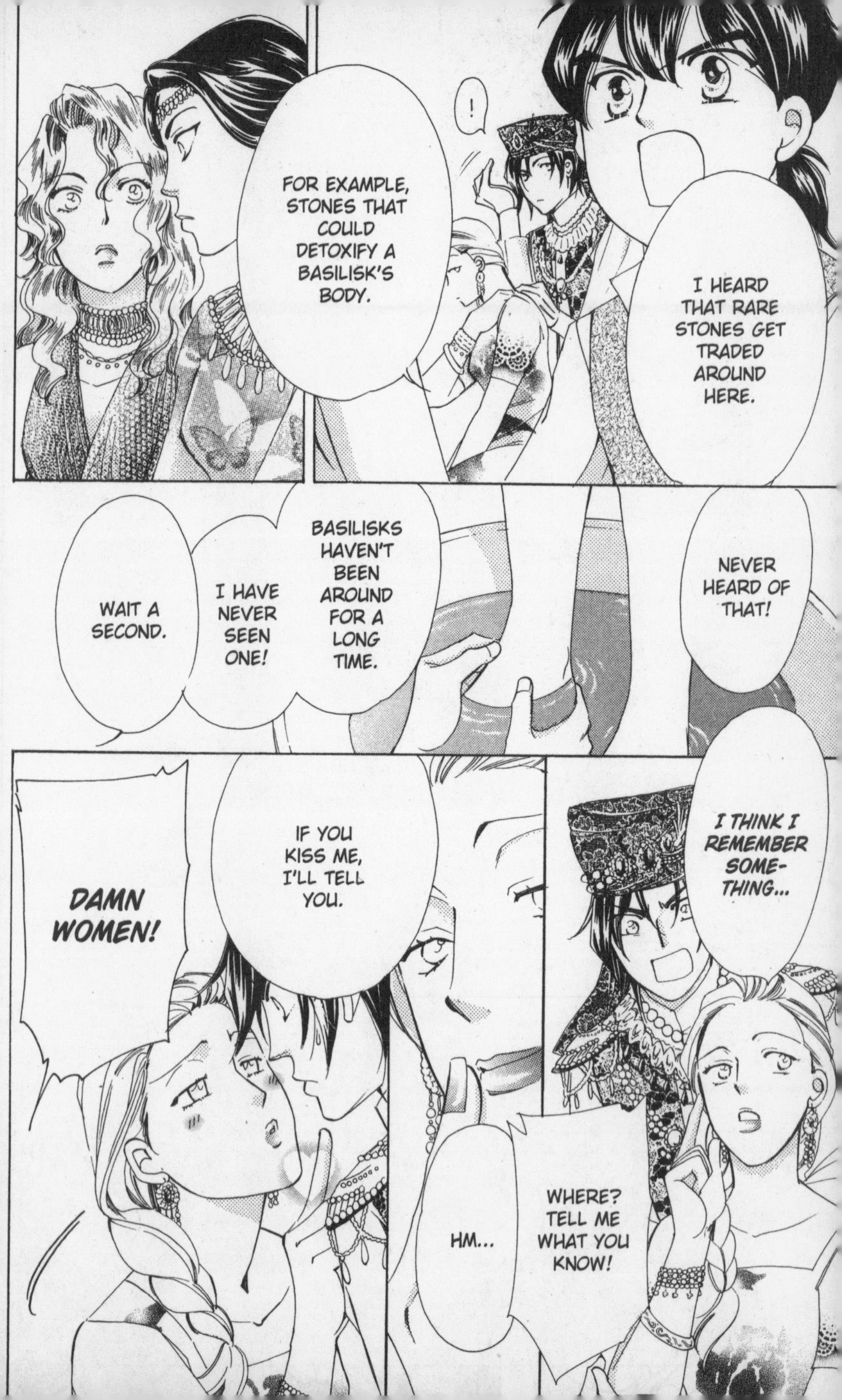
I HEARD THAT RARE STONES GET TRADED AROUND HERE.
!
FOR EXAMPLE, STONES THAT COULD DETOXIFY A BASILISK'S BODY.
NEVER HEARD OF THAT!
BASILISKS HAVEN'T BEEN AROUND FOR A LONG TIME.
I HAVE NEVER SEEN ONE!
WAIT A SECOND.
I THINK I REMEMBER SOME-THING...
WHERE? TELL ME WHAT YOU KNOW!
HM...
IF YOU KISS ME, I'LL TELL YOU.
DAMN WOMEN!

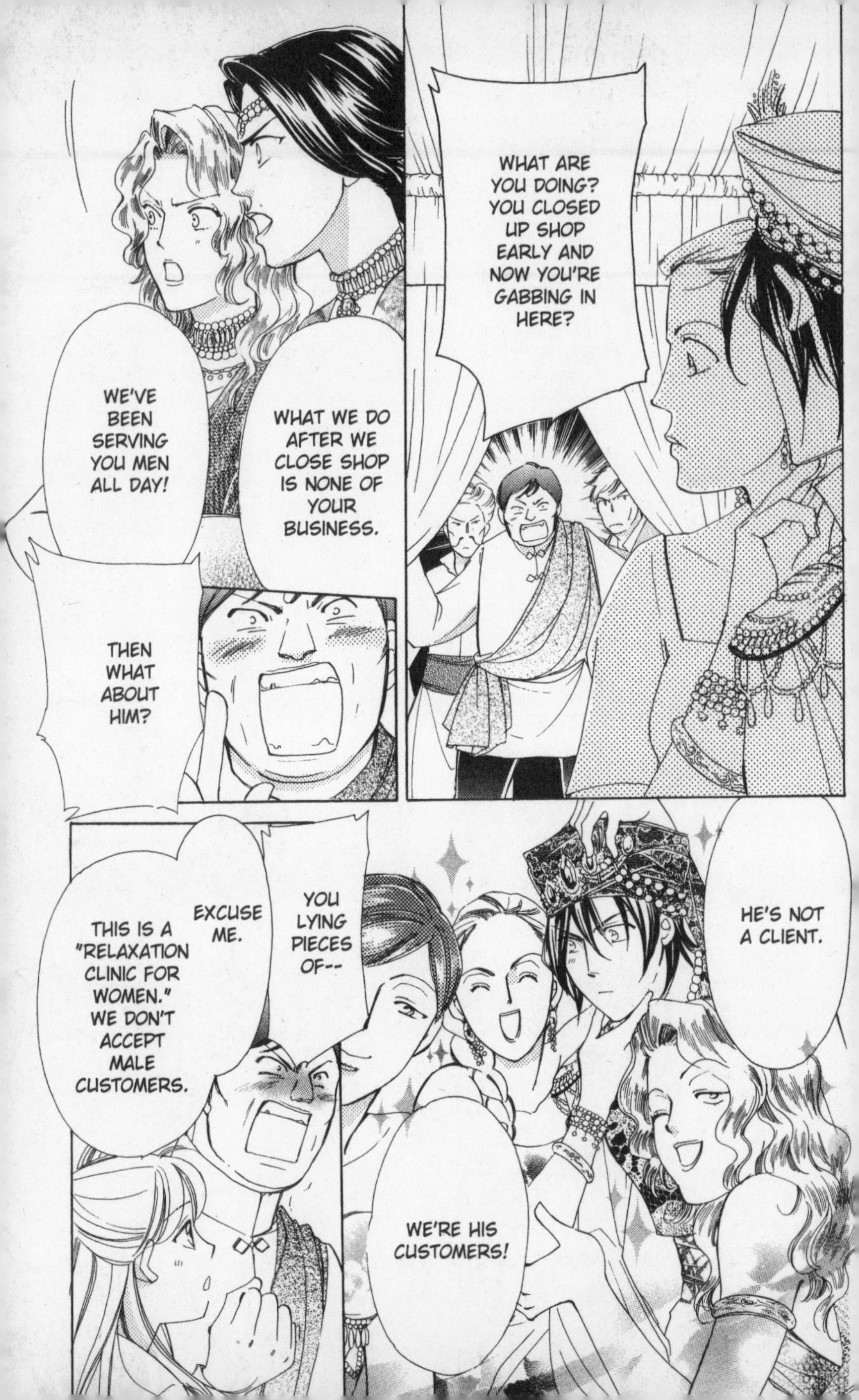
WHAT ARE YOU DOING? YOU CLOSED UP SHOP EARLY AND NOW YOU'RE GABBING IN HERE?
WHAT WE DO AFTER WE CLOSE SHOP IS NONE OF YOUR BUSINESS.
WE'VE BEEN SERVING YOU MEN ALL DAY!
THEN WHAT ABOUT HIM?
HE'S NOT A CLIENT.
WE'RE HIS CUSTOMERS!
YOU LYING PIECES OF--
EXCUSE ME.
THIS IS A "RELAXATION CLINIC FOR WOMEN." WE DON'T ACCEPT MALE CUSTOMERS.

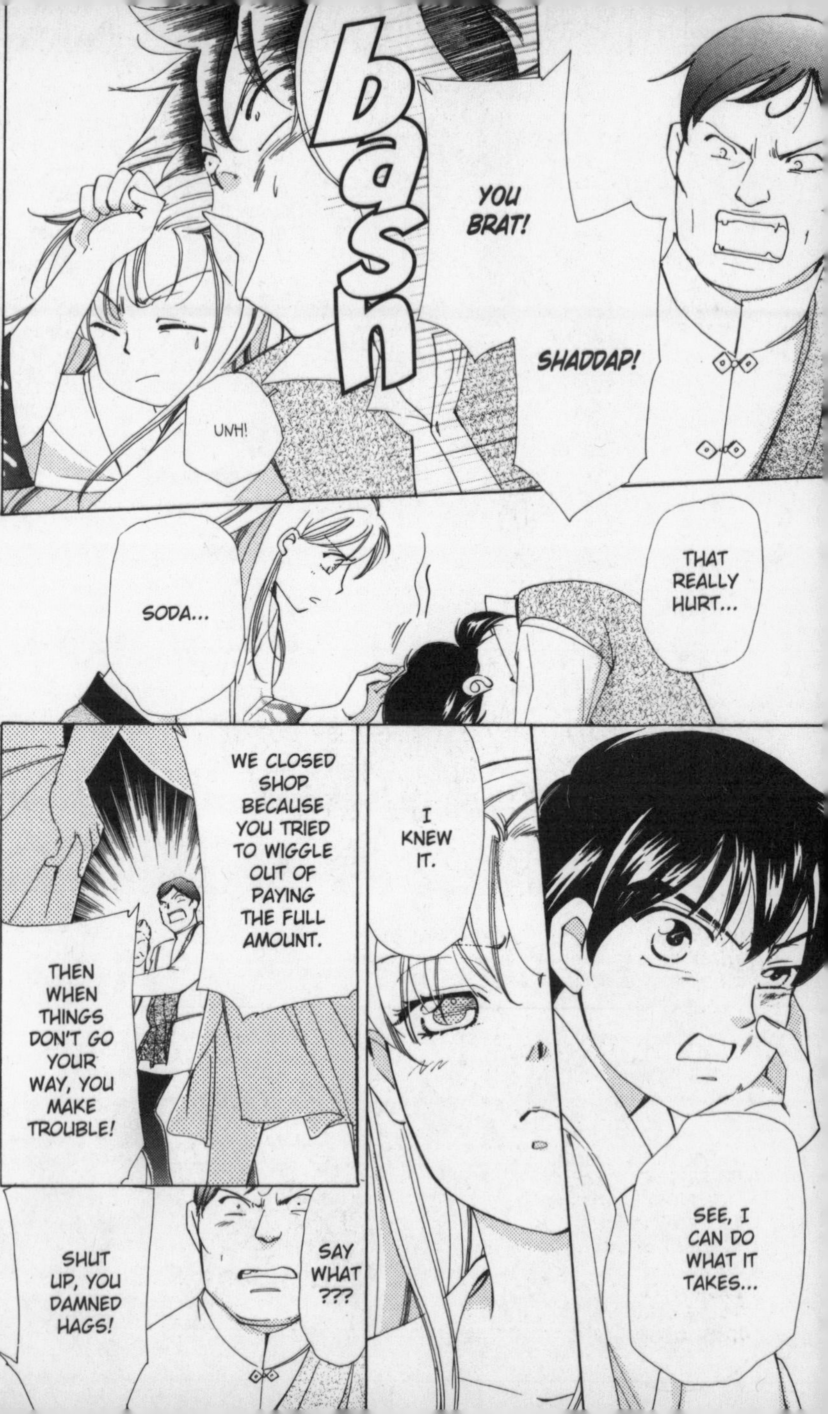
YOU BRAT!
SHADDAP!
bash
UNH!
THAT REALLY HURT...
SODA...
I KNEW IT.
SEE, I CAN DO WHAT IT TAKES...
WE CLOSED SHOP BECAUSE YOU TRIED TO WIGGLE OUT OF PAYING THE FULL AMOUNT.
THEN WHEN THINGS DON'T GO YOUR WAY, YOU MAKE TROUBLE!
SAY WHAT ???
SHUT UP, YOU DAMNED HAGS!

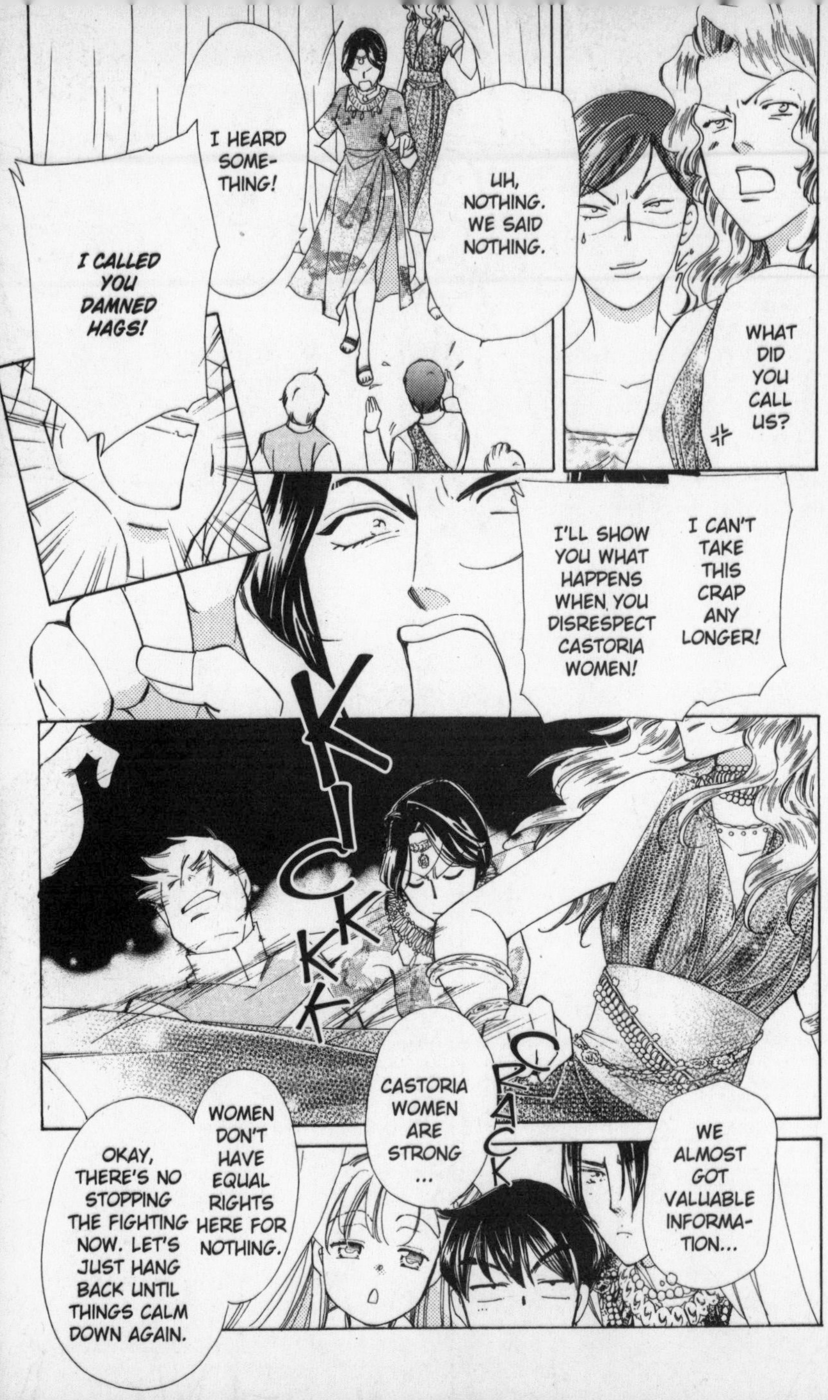
WHAT DID YOU CALL US?
I HEARD SOME-THING!
UH, NOTHING. WE SAID NOTHING.
I CALLED YOU DAMNED HAGS!
I CAN'T TAKE THIS CRAP ANY LONGER!
I'LL SHOW YOU WHAT HAPPENS WHEN YOU DISRESPECT CASTORIA WOMEN!
KLICKKKK
CRACK
WE ALMOST GOT VALUABLE INFORMA-TION...
...
CASTORIA WOMEN ARE STRONG...
WOMEN DON'T HAVE EQUAL RIGHTS HERE FOR NOTHING.
OKAY, THERE'S NO STOPPING THE FIGHTING NOW. LET'S JUST HANG BACK UNTIL THINGS CALM DOWN AGAIN.

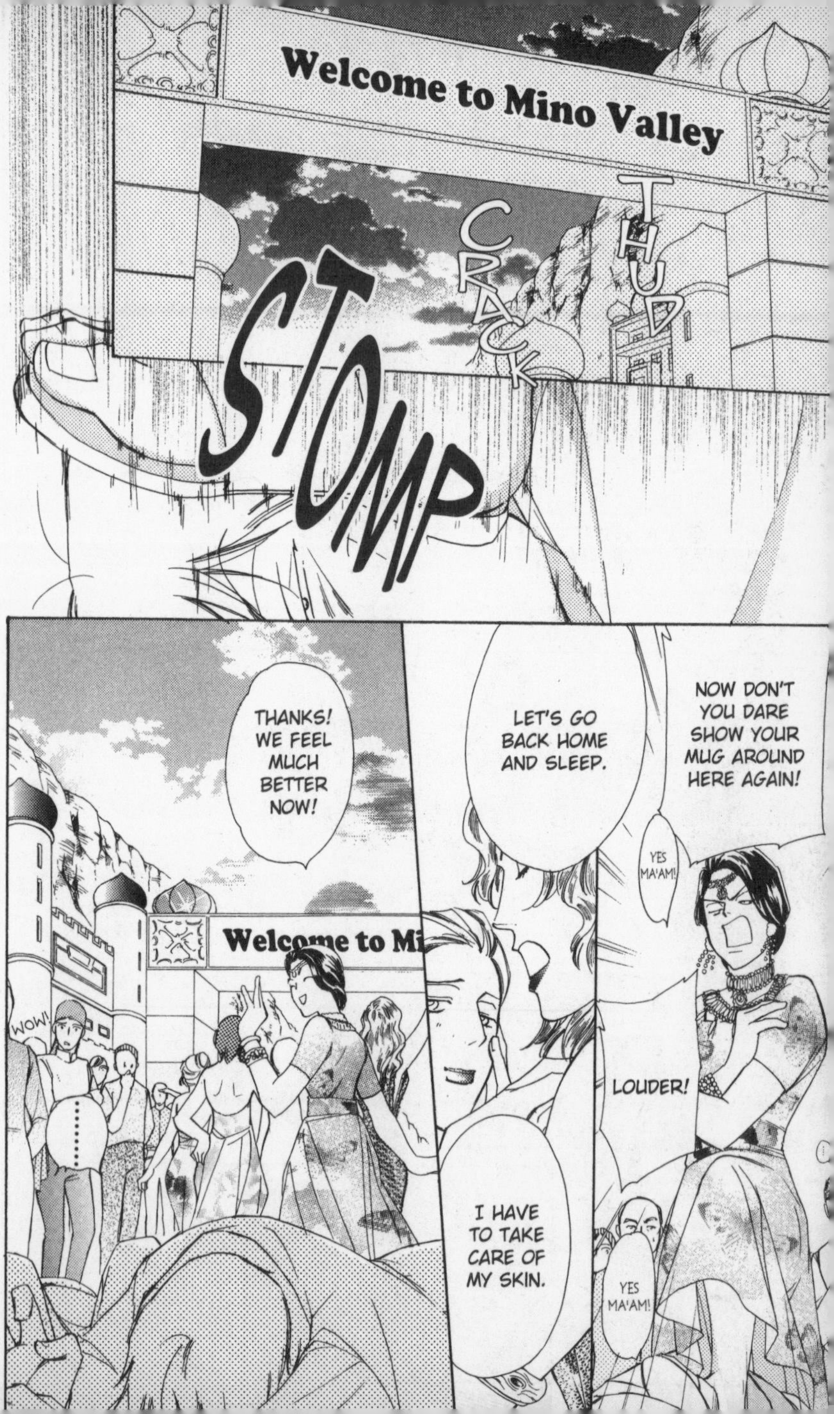
Welcome to Mino Valley
THUD
CRACK
STOMP
NOW DON'T YOU DARE SHOW YOUR MUG AROUND HERE AGAIN!
YES MA'AM!
LOUDER!
YES MA'AM!
LET'S GO BACK HOME AND SLEEP.
I HAVE TO TAKE CARE OF MY SKIN.
THANKS! WE FEEL MUCH BETTER NOW!
WOW!
......

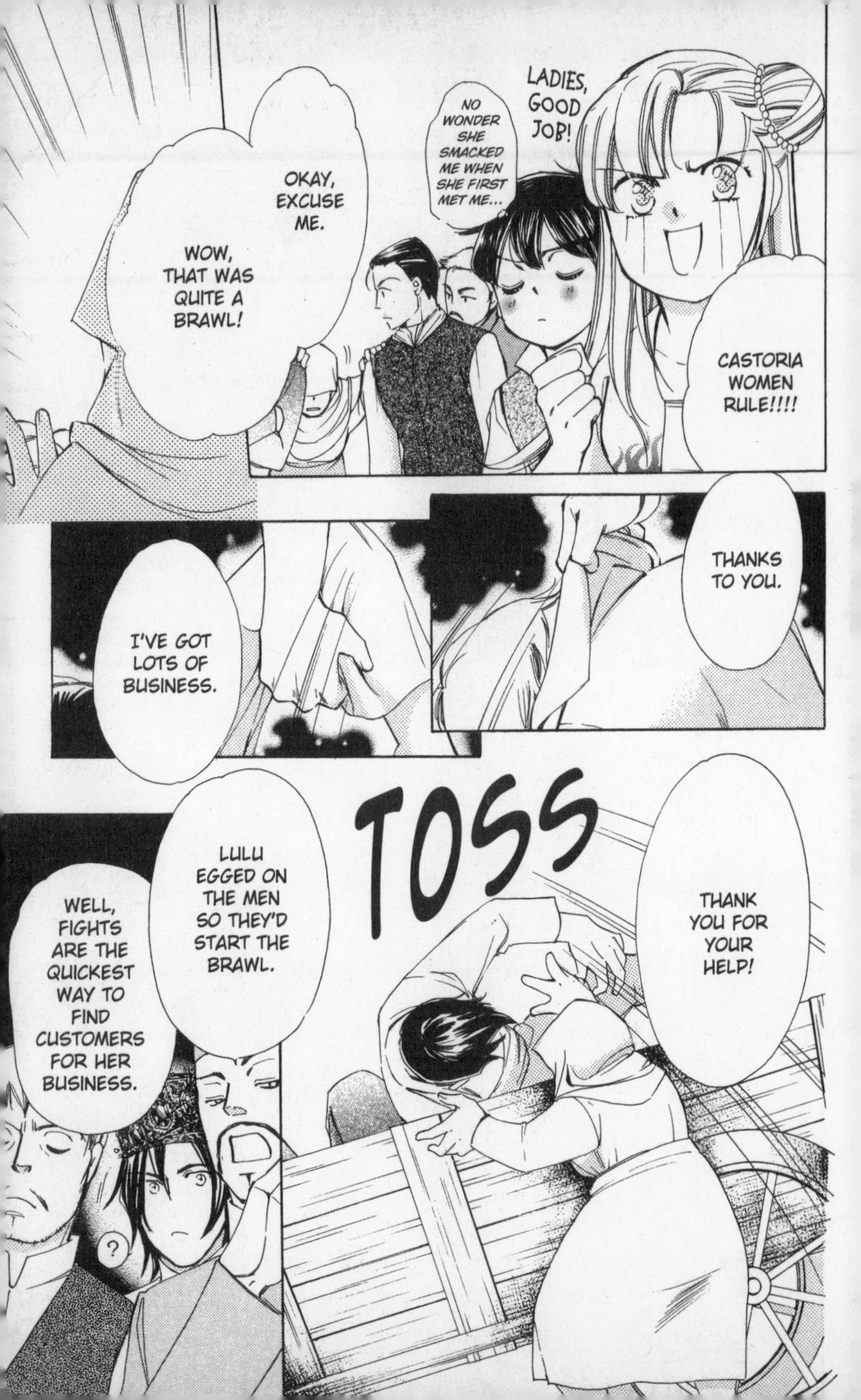
LADIES, GOOD JOB!
CASTORIA WOMEN RULE!!!!
NO WONDER SHE SMACKED ME WHEN SHE FIRST MET ME...
OKAY, EXCUSE ME.
WOW, THAT WAS QUITE A BRAWL!
THANKS TO YOU.
I'VE GOT LOTS OF BUSINESS.
THANK YOU FOR YOUR HELP!
TOSS
LULU EGGED ON THE MEN SO THEY'D START THE BRAWL.
WELL, FIGHTS ARE THE QUICKEST WAY TO FIND CUSTOMERS FOR HER BUSINESS.
?

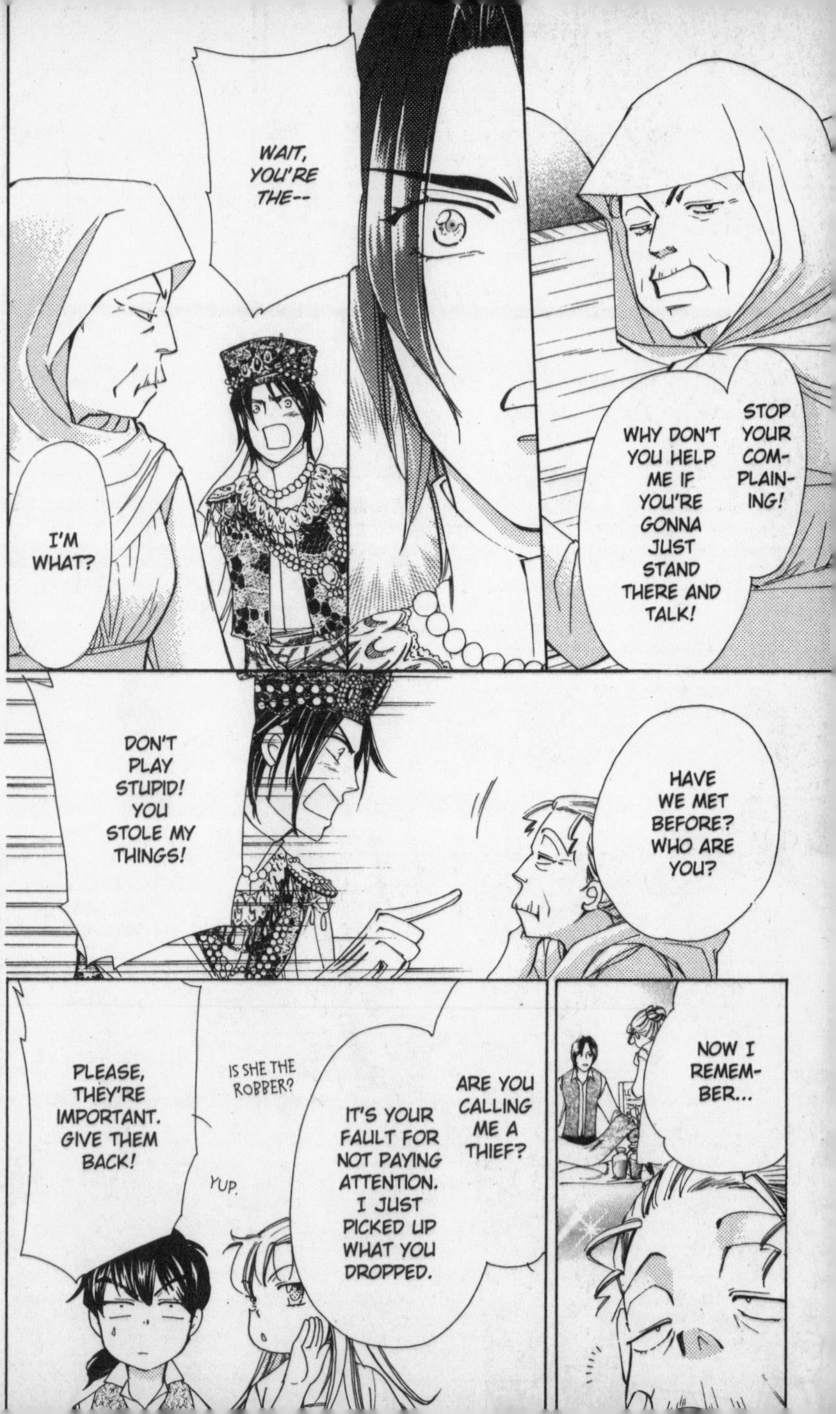
STOP YOUR COM-PLAIN-ING!
WHY DON'T YOU HELP ME IF YOU'RE GONNA JUST STAND THERE AND TALK!
WAIT, YOU'RE THE--
I'M WHAT?
HAVE WE MET BEFORE? WHO ARE YOU?
DON'T PLAY STUPID! YOU STOLE MY THINGS!
NOW I REMEM-BER...
ARE YOU CALLING ME A THIEF?
IT'S YOUR FAULT FOR NOT PAYING ATTENTION. I JUST PICKED UP WHAT YOU DROPPED.
IS SHE THE ROBBER?
YUP.
PLEASE, THEY'RE IMPORTANT. GIVE THEM BACK!

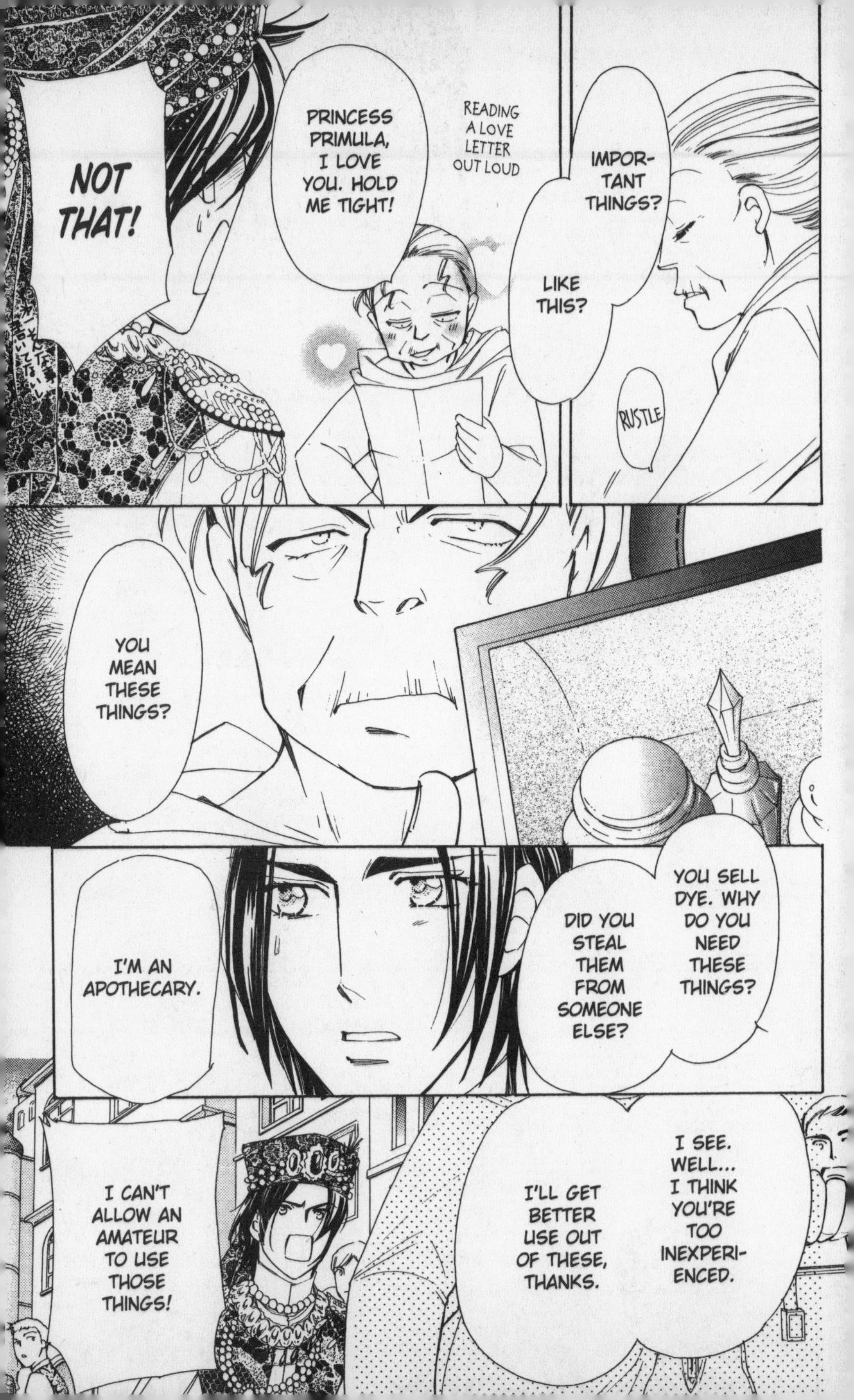
IMPORTANT THINGS?
LIKE THIS?
RUSTLE
PRINCESS PRIMULA, I LOVE YOU. HOLD ME TIGHT!
READING A LOVE LETTER OUT LOUD
NOT THAT!
YOU MEAN THESE THINGS?
YOU SELL DYE. WHY DO YOU NEED THESE THINGS?
DID YOU STEAL THEM FROM SOMEONE ELSE?
I'M AN APOTHECARY.
I SEE. WELL... I THINK YOU'RE TOO INEXPERIENCED.
I'LL GET BETTER USE OUT OF THESE, THANKS.
I CAN'T ALLOW AN AMATEUR TO USE THOSE THINGS!

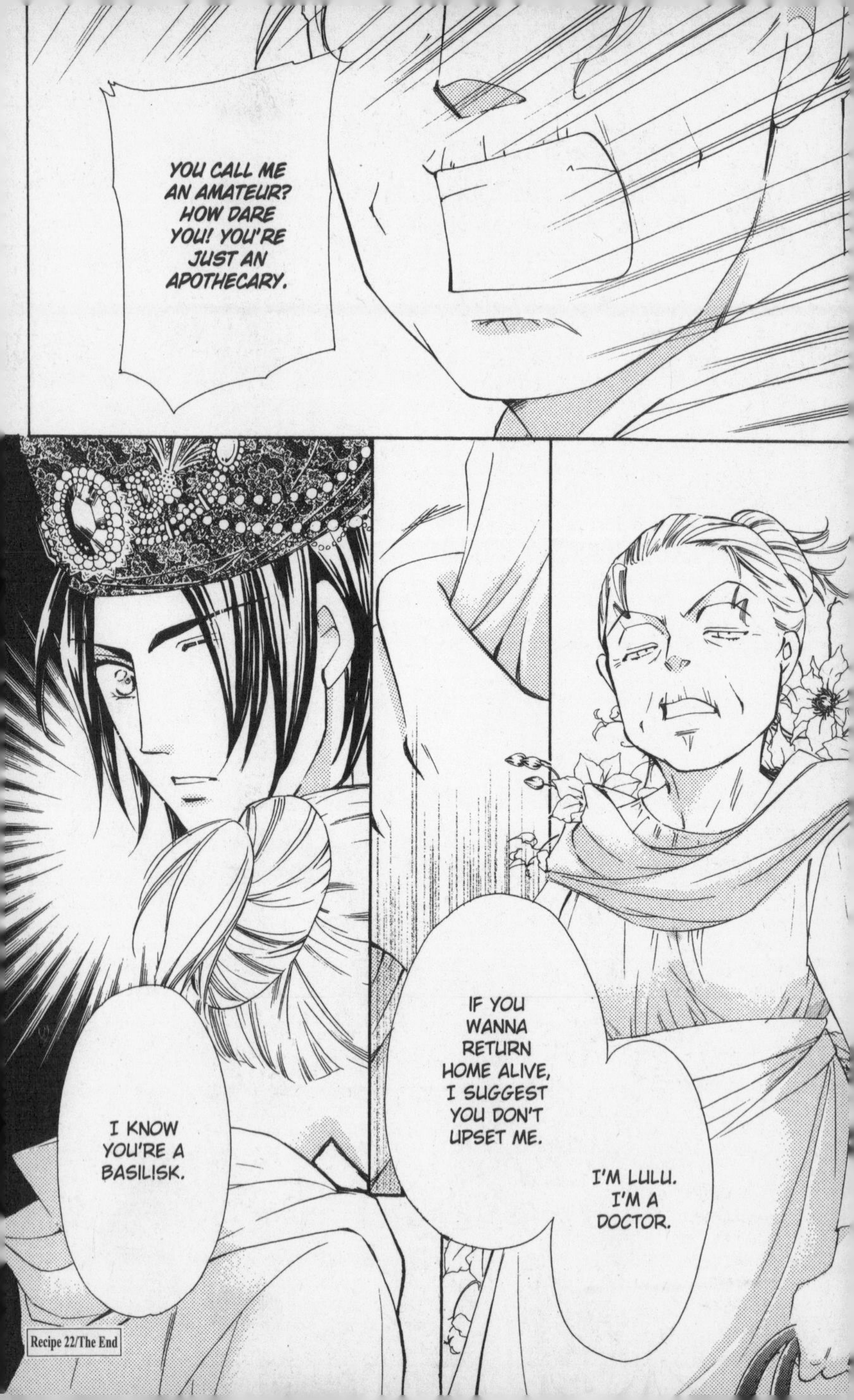
YOU CALL ME AN AMATEUR? HOW DARE YOU! YOU'RE JUST AN APOTHECARY.
I'M LULU. I'M A DOCTOR.
IF YOU WANNA RETURN HOME ALIVE, I SUGGEST YOU DON'T UPSET ME.
I KNOW YOU'RE A BASILISK.
Recipe 22/The End

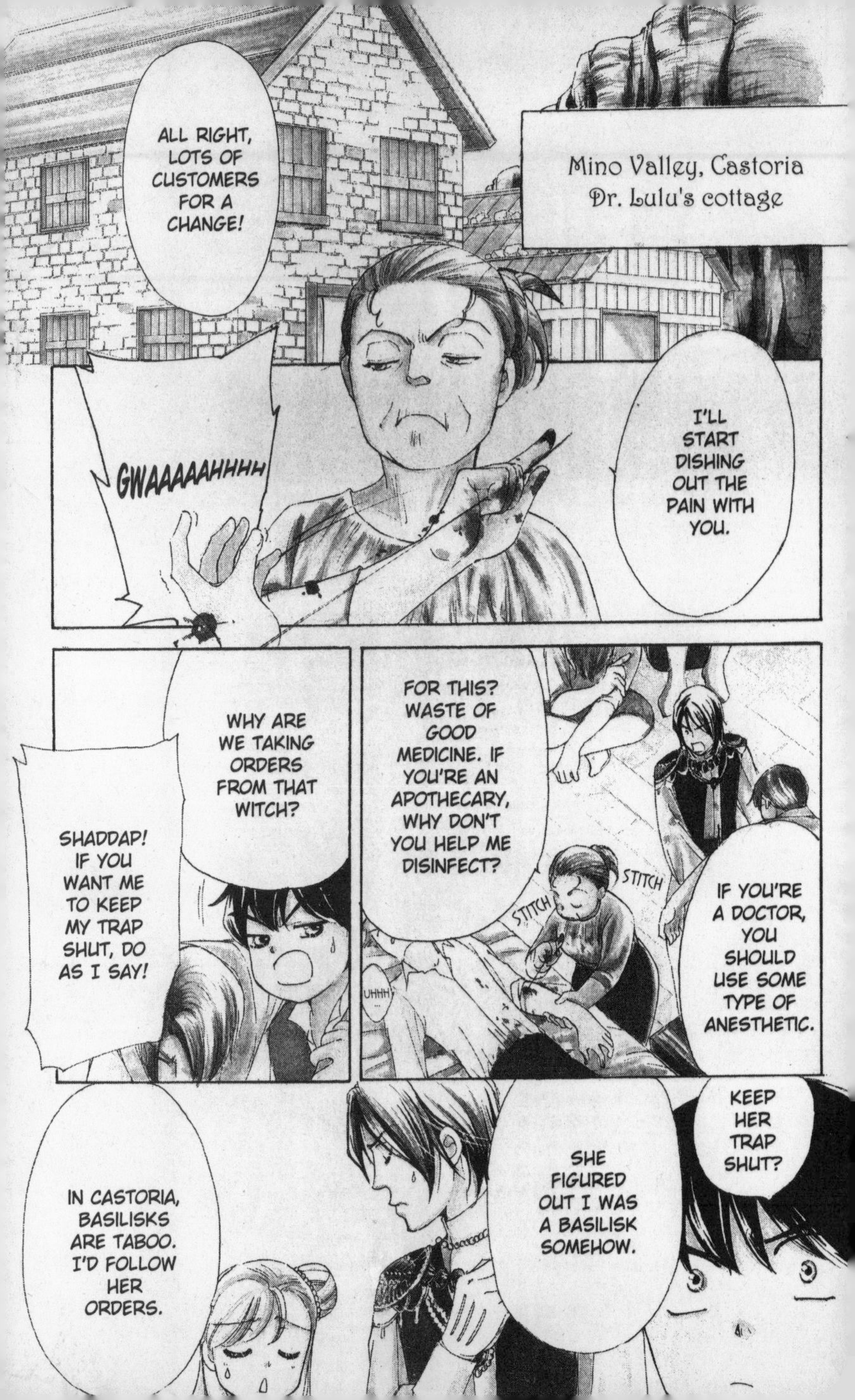
Mino Valley, Castoria
Dr. Lulu's cottage
ALL RIGHT, LOTS OF CUSTOMERS FOR A CHANGE!
I'LL START DISHING OUT THE PAIN WITH YOU.
GWAAAAAHHHH
IF YOU'RE A DOCTOR, YOU SHOULD USE SOME TYPE OF ANESTHETIC.
STITCH
STITCH
FOR THIS? WASTE OF GOOD MEDICINE. IF YOU'RE AN APOTHECARY, WHY DON'T YOU HELP ME DISINFECT?
UHHH...
WHY ARE WE TAKING ORDERS FROM THAT WITCH?
SHADDAP! IF YOU WANT ME TO KEEP MY TRAP SHUT, DO AS I SAY!
KEEP HER TRAP SHUT?
SHE FIGURED OUT I WAS A BASILISK SOMEHOW.
IN CASTORIA, BASILISKS ARE TABOO. I'D FOLLOW HER ORDERS.

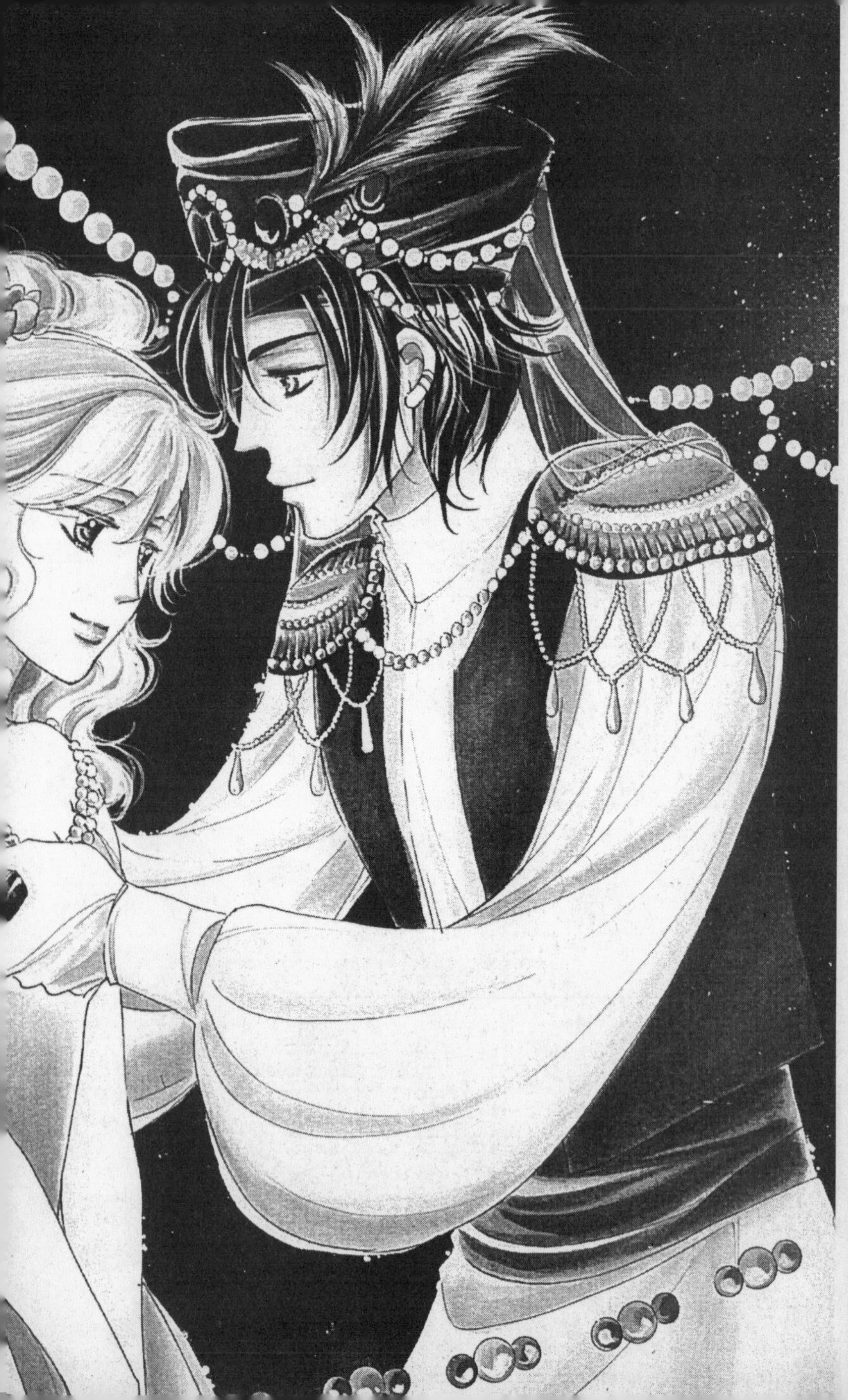

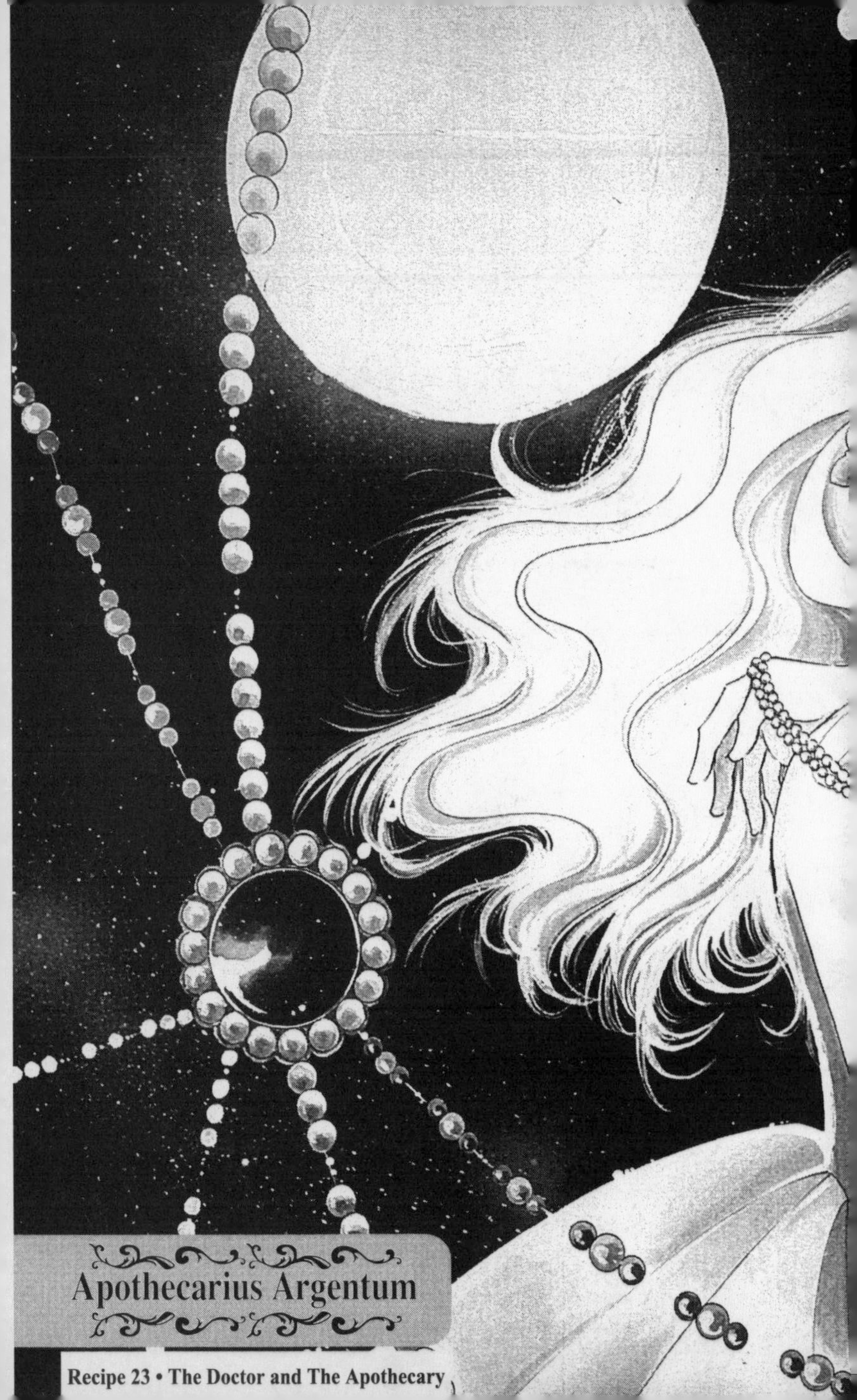
Apothecarius Argentum
Recipe 23 • The Doctor and The Apothecary

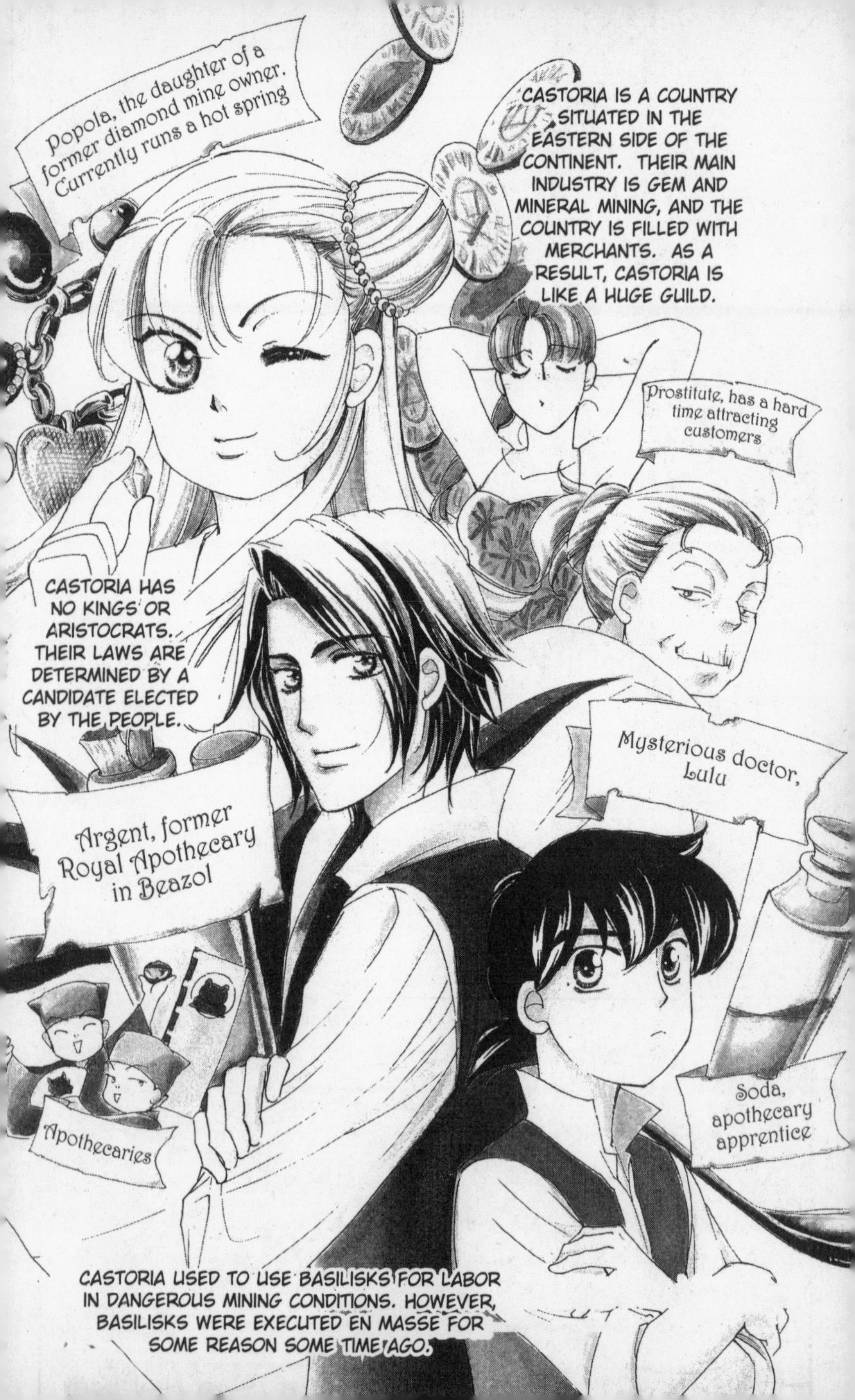
CASTORIA IS A COUNTRY SITUATED IN THE EASTERN SIDE OF THE CONTINENT. THEIR MAIN INDUSTRY IS GEM AND MINERAL MINING, AND THE COUNTRY IS FILLED WITH MERCHANTS. AS A RESULT, CASTORIA IS LIKE A HUGE GUILD.
Popola, the daughter of a former diamond mine owner. Currently runs a hot spring
Prostitute, has a hard time attracting customers
CASTORIA HAS NO KINGS OR ARISTOCRATS. THEIR LAWS ARE DETERMINED BY A CANDIDATE ELECTED BY THE PEOPLE.
Mysterious doctor, Lulu
Argent, former Royal Apothecary in Beazol
Soda, apothecary apprentice
Apothecaries
CASTORIA USED TO USE BASILISKS FOR LABOR IN DANGEROUS MINING CONDITIONS. HOWEVER, BASILISKS WERE EXECUTED EN MASSE FOR SOME REASON SOME TIME AGO.

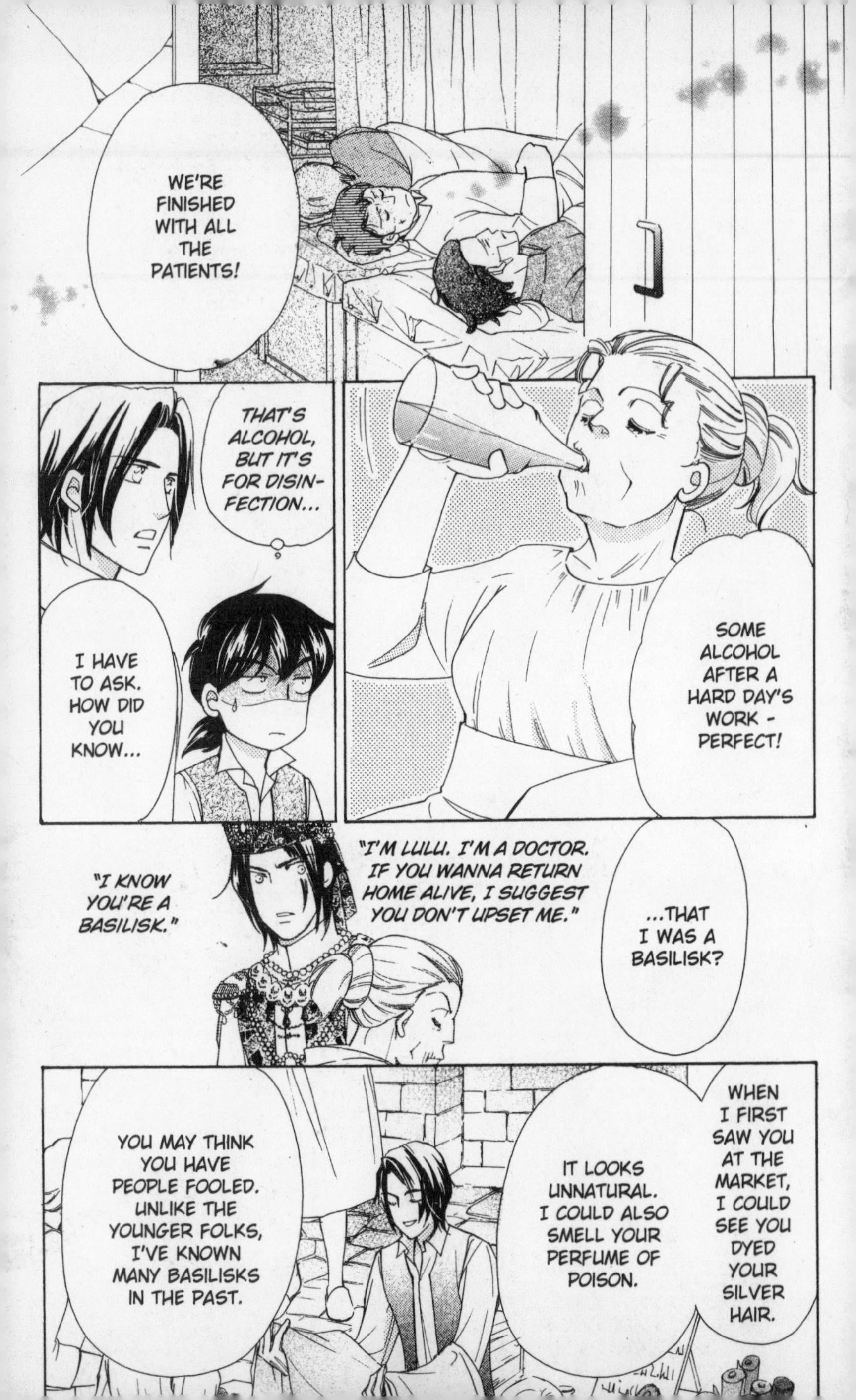
WE'RE FINISHED WITH ALL THE PATIENTS!
SOME ALCOHOL AFTER A HARD DAY'S WORK - PERFECT!
THAT'S ALCOHOL, BUT IT'S FOR DISIN-FECTION...
I HAVE TO ASK. HOW DID YOU KNOW...
...THAT I WAS A BASILISK?
"I'M LULU. I'M A DOCTOR. IF YOU WANNA RETURN HOME ALIVE, I SUGGEST YOU DON'T UPSET ME."
"I KNOW YOU'RE A BASILISK."
WHEN I FIRST SAW YOU AT THE MARKET, I COULD SEE YOU DYED YOUR SILVER HAIR.
IT LOOKS UNNATURAL. I COULD ALSO SMELL YOUR PERFUME OF POISON.
YOU MAY THINK YOU HAVE PEOPLE FOOLED. UNLIKE THE YOUNGER FOLKS, I'VE KNOWN MANY BASILISKS IN THE PAST.

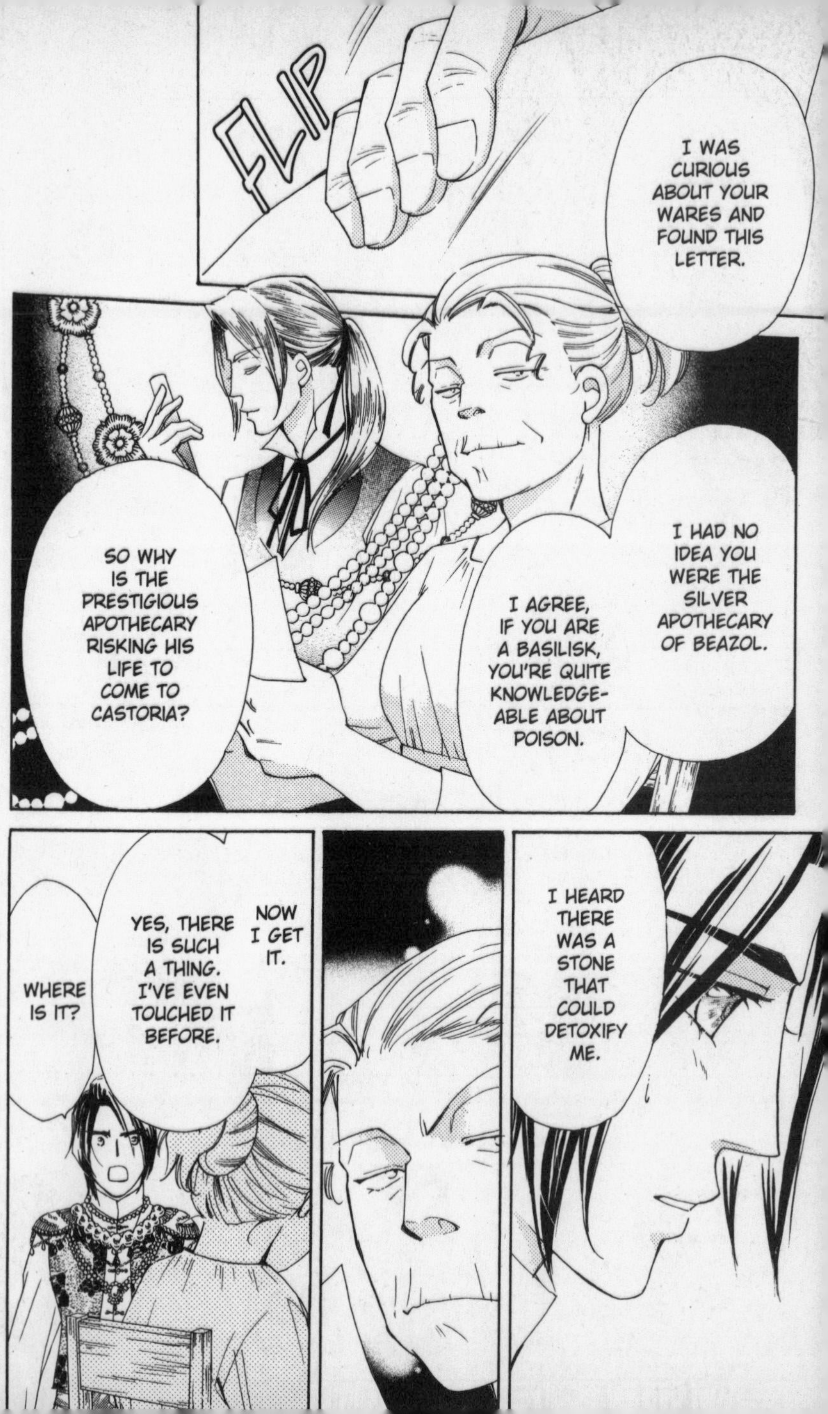
FLIP
I WAS CURIOUS ABOUT YOUR WARES AND FOUND THIS LETTER.
I HAD NO IDEA YOU WERE THE SILVER APOTHECARY OF BEAZOL.
I AGREE, IF YOU ARE A BASILISK, YOU'RE QUITE KNOWLEDGE-ABLE ABOUT POISON.
SO WHY IS THE PRESTIGIOUS APOTHECARY RISKING HIS LIFE TO COME TO CASTORIA?
I HEARD THERE WAS A STONE THAT COULD DETOXIFY ME.
NOW I GET IT.
YES, THERE IS SUCH A THING. I'VE EVEN TOUCHED IT BEFORE.
WHERE IS IT?

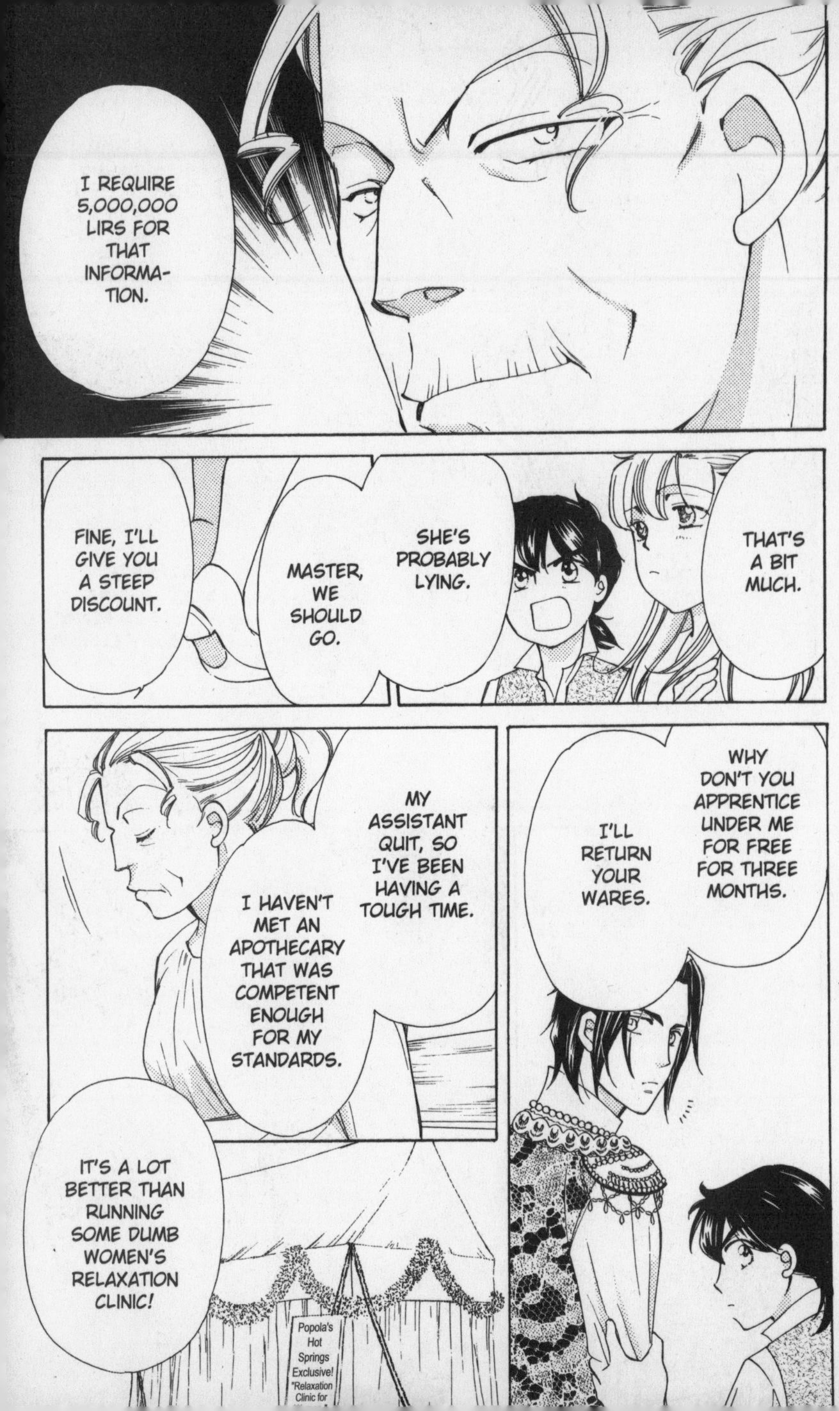
I REQUIRE 5,000,000 LIRS FOR THAT INFORMATION.
THAT'S A BIT MUCH.
SHE'S PROBABLY LYING.
MASTER, WE SHOULD GO.
FINE, I'LL GIVE YOU A STEEP DISCOUNT.
WHY DON'T YOU APPRENTICE UNDER ME FOR FREE FOR THREE MONTHS.
I'LL RETURN YOUR WARES.
MY ASSISTANT QUIT, SO I'VE BEEN HAVING A TOUGH TIME.
I HAVEN'T MET AN APOTHECARY THAT WAS COMPETENT ENOUGH FOR MY STANDARDS.
IT'S A LOT BETTER THAN RUNNING SOME DUMB WOMEN'S RELAXATION CLINIC!
Popola's Hot Springs Exclusive! "Relaxation Clinic for

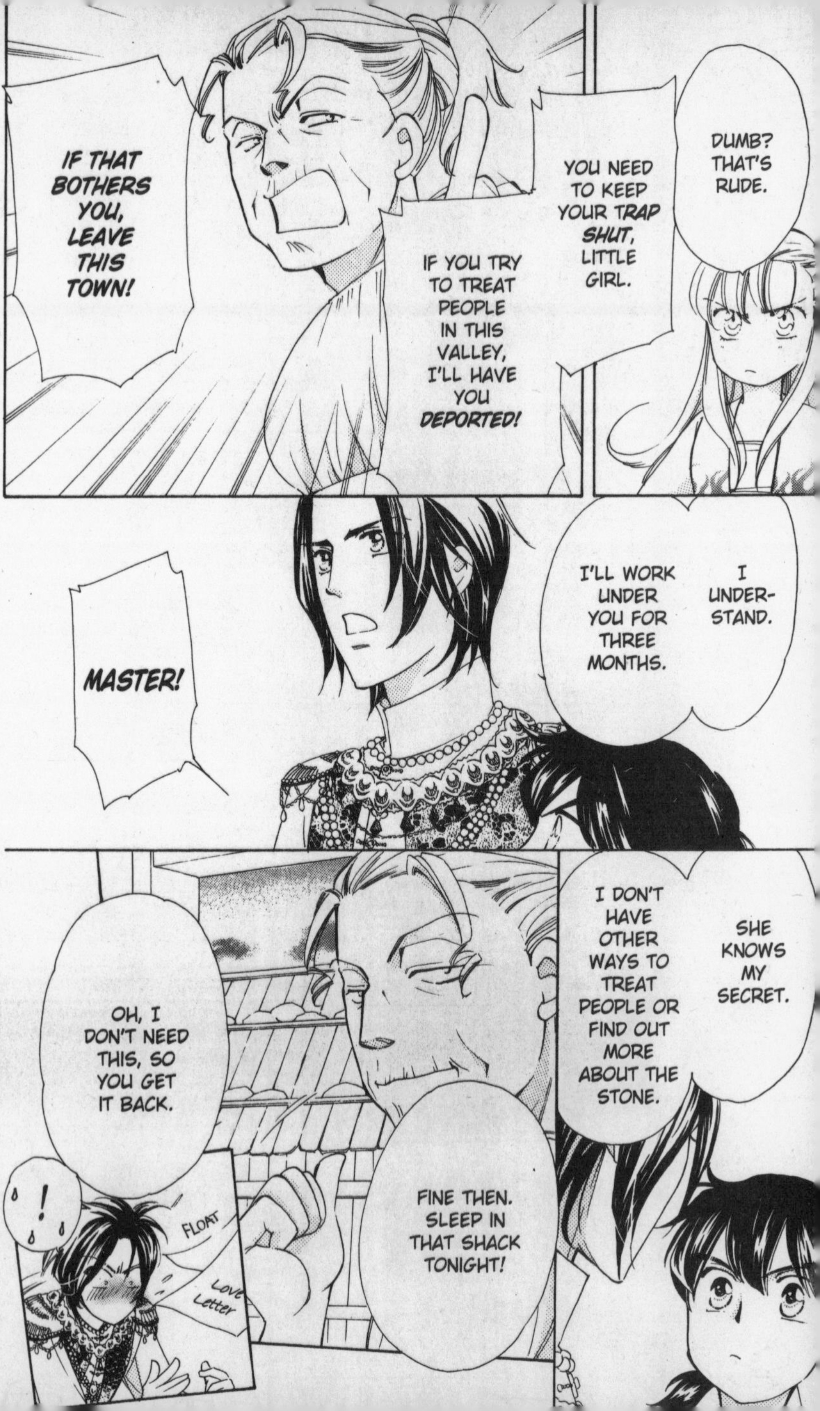
DUMB? THAT'S RUDE.
YOU NEED TO KEEP YOUR TRAP SHUT, LITTLE GIRL.
IF YOU TRY TO TREAT PEOPLE IN THIS VALLEY, I'LL HAVE YOU DEPORTED!
IF THAT BOTHERS YOU, LEAVE THIS TOWN!
I UNDERSTAND.
I'LL WORK UNDER YOU FOR THREE MONTHS.
MASTER!
SHE KNOWS MY SECRET.
I DON'T HAVE OTHER WAYS TO TREAT PEOPLE OR FIND OUT MORE ABOUT THE STONE.
FINE THEN. SLEEP IN THAT SHACK TONIGHT!
OH, I DON'T NEED THIS, SO YOU GET IT BACK.
!
FLOAT
Love Letter

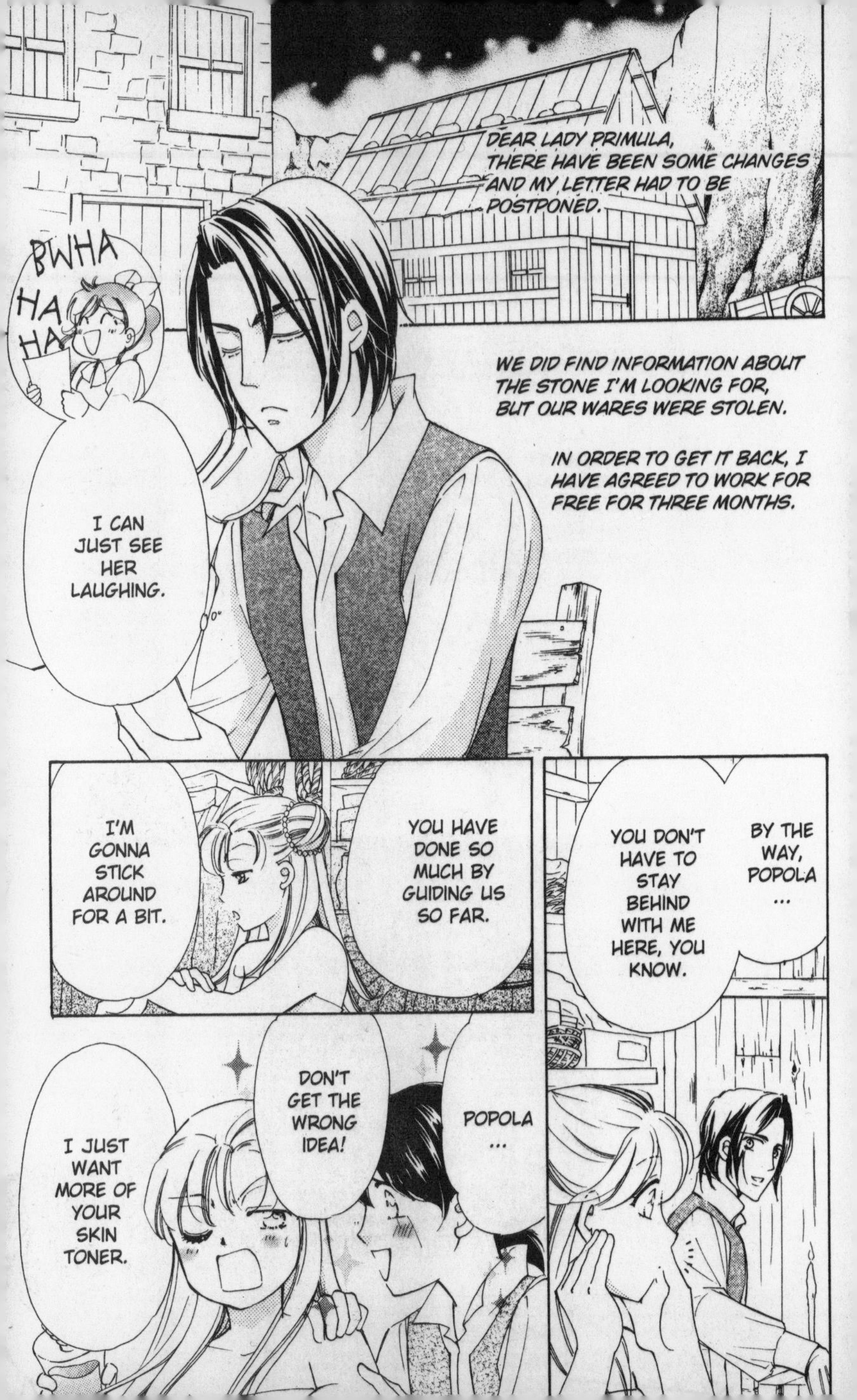
DEAR LADY PRIMULA, THERE HAVE BEEN SOME CHANGES AND MY LETTER HAD TO BE POSTPONED.
WE DID FIND INFORMATION ABOUT THE STONE I'M LOOKING FOR, BUT OUR WARES WERE STOLEN.
IN ORDER TO GET IT BACK, I HAVE AGREED TO WORK FOR FREE FOR THREE MONTHS.
BWHA HA HA
I CAN JUST SEE HER LAUGHING.
BY THE WAY, POPOLA ...
YOU DON'T HAVE TO STAY BEHIND WITH ME HERE, YOU KNOW.
YOU HAVE DONE SO MUCH BY GUIDING US SO FAR.
I'M GONNA STICK AROUND FOR A BIT.
POPOLA ...
DON'T GET THE WRONG IDEA!
I JUST WANT MORE OF YOUR SKIN TONER.

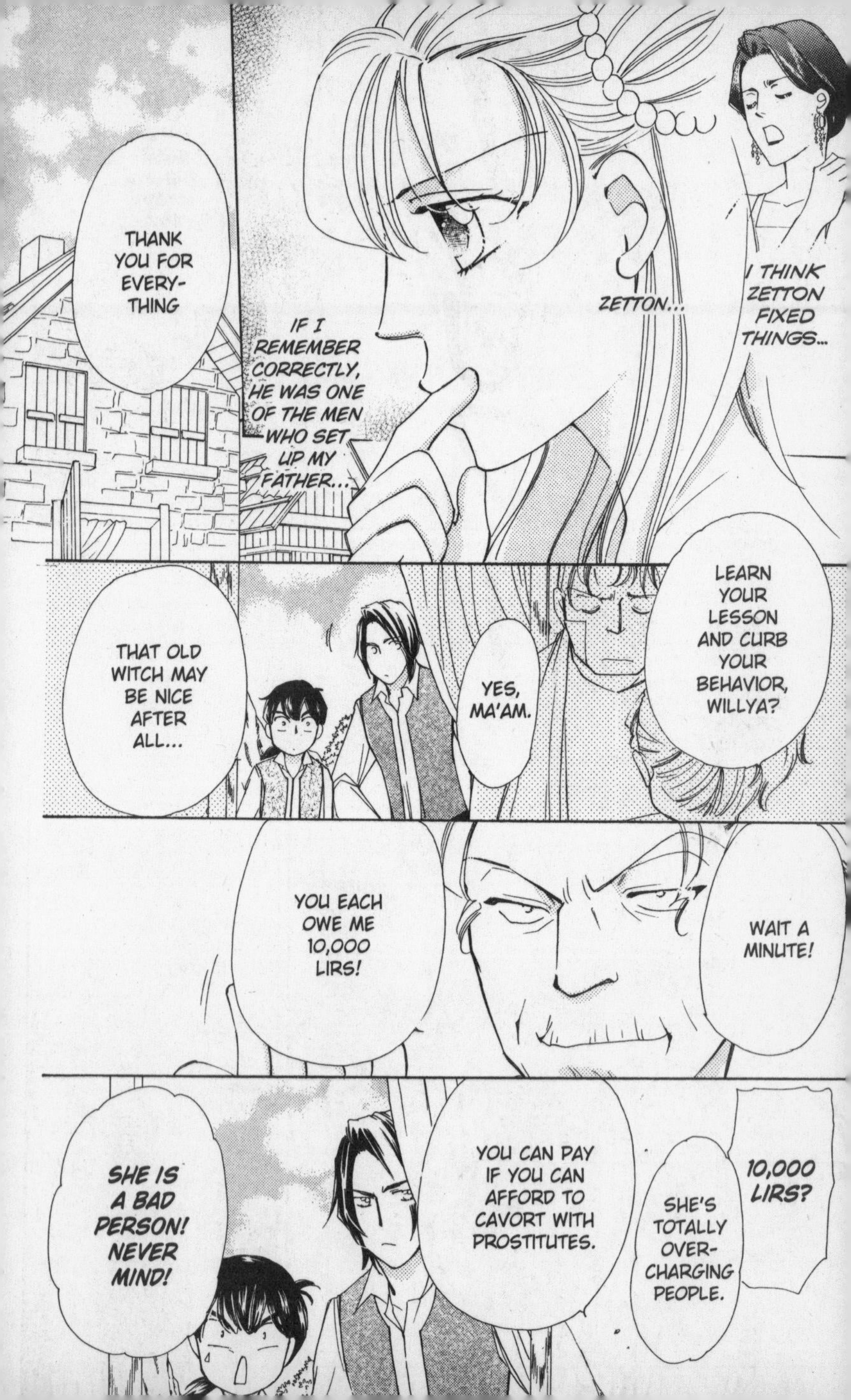
I THINK ZETTON FIXED THINGS...
ZETTON...
IF I REMEMBER CORRECTLY, HE WAS ONE OF THE MEN WHO SET UP MY FATHER...
THANK YOU FOR EVERY-THING
LEARN YOUR LESSON AND CURB YOUR BEHAVIOR, WILLYA?
YES, MA'AM.
THAT OLD WITCH MAY BE NICE AFTER ALL...
WAIT A MINUTE!
YOU EACH OWE ME 10,000 LIRS!
10,000 LIRS?
SHE'S TOTALLY OVER-CHARGING PEOPLE.
YOU CAN PAY IF YOU CAN AFFORD TO CAVORT WITH PROSTITUTES.
SHE IS A BAD PERSON! NEVER MIND!

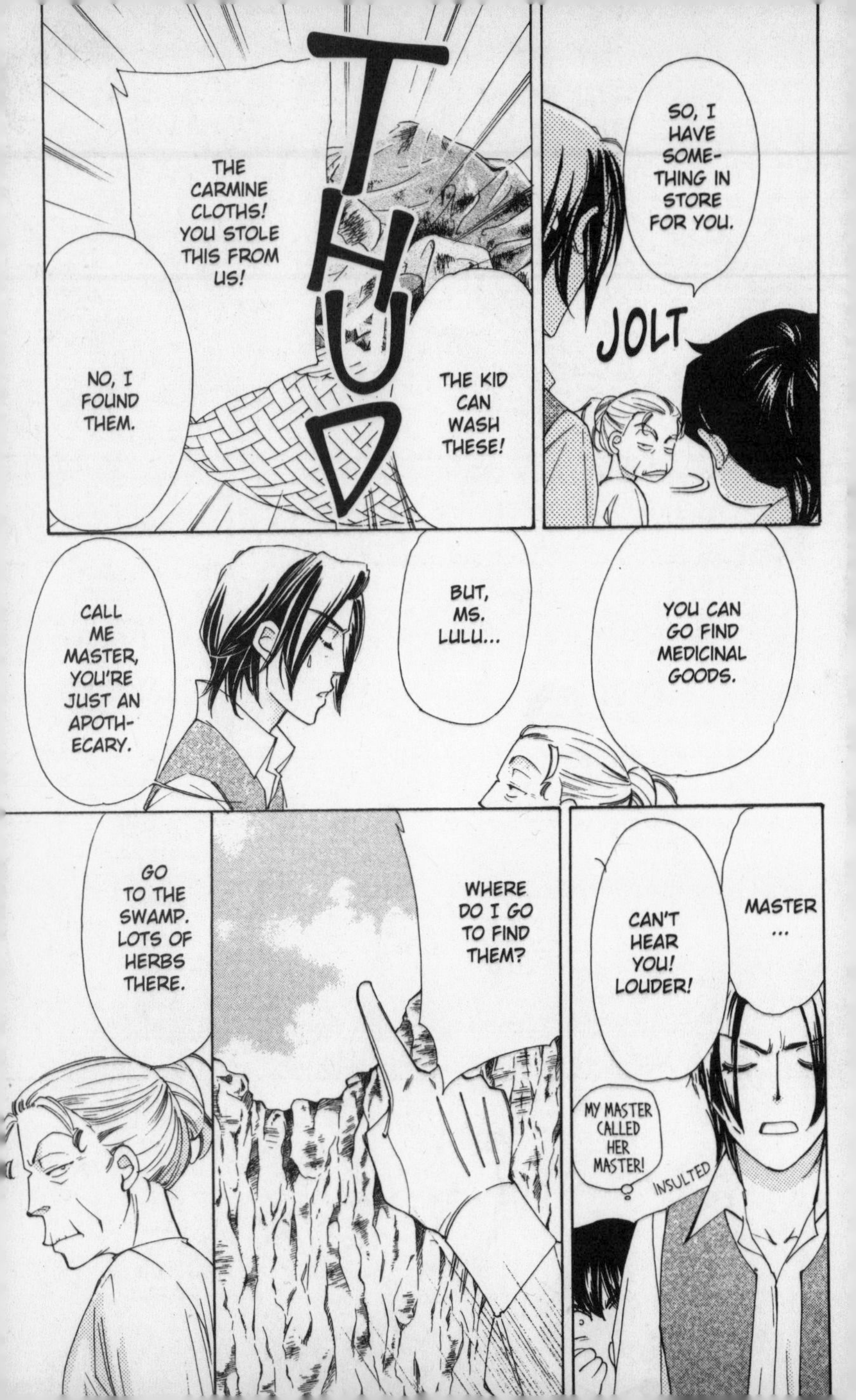
SO, I HAVE SOME-THING IN STORE FOR YOU.
JOLT
THE KID CAN WASH THESE!
THUD
THE CARMINE CLOTHS! YOU STOLE THIS FROM US!
NO, I FOUND THEM.
YOU CAN GO FIND MEDICINAL GOODS.
BUT, MS. LULU...
CALL ME MASTER, YOU'RE JUST AN APOTH-ECARY.
MASTER...
CAN'T HEAR YOU! LOUDER!
MY MASTER CALLED HER MASTER!
INSULTED
WHERE DO I GO TO FIND THEM?
GO TO THE SWAMP. LOTS OF HERBS THERE.

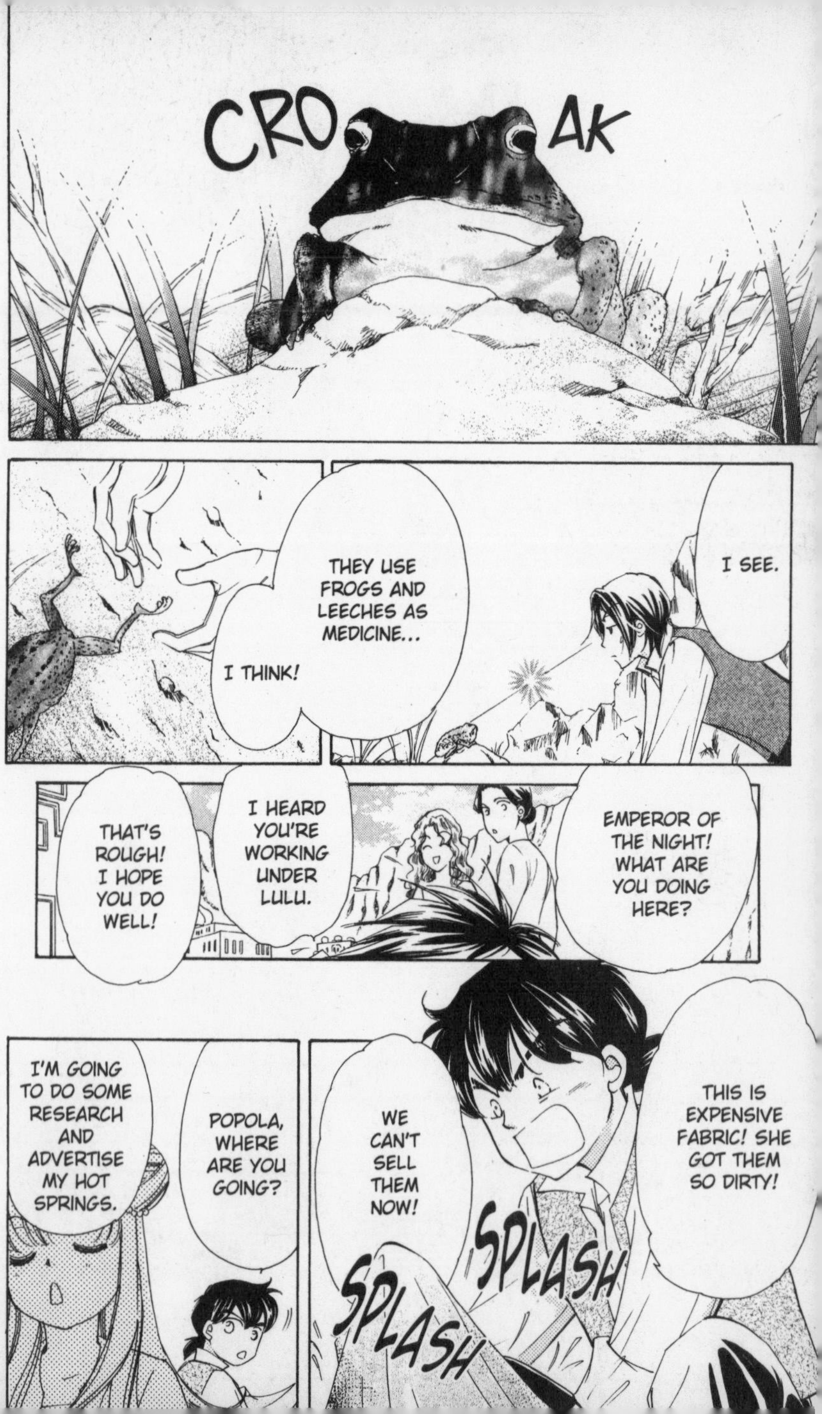
CROAK
I SEE.
THEY USE FROGS AND LEECHES AS MEDICINE... I THINK!
EMPEROR OF THE NIGHT! WHAT ARE YOU DOING HERE?
I HEARD YOU'RE WORKING UNDER LULU.
THAT'S ROUGH! I HOPE YOU DO WELL!
THIS IS EXPENSIVE FABRIC! SHE GOT THEM SO DIRTY!
WE CAN'T SELL THEM NOW!
SPLASH
SPLASH
POPOLA, WHERE ARE YOU GOING?
I'M GOING TO DO SOME RESEARCH AND ADVERTISE MY HOT SPRINGS.

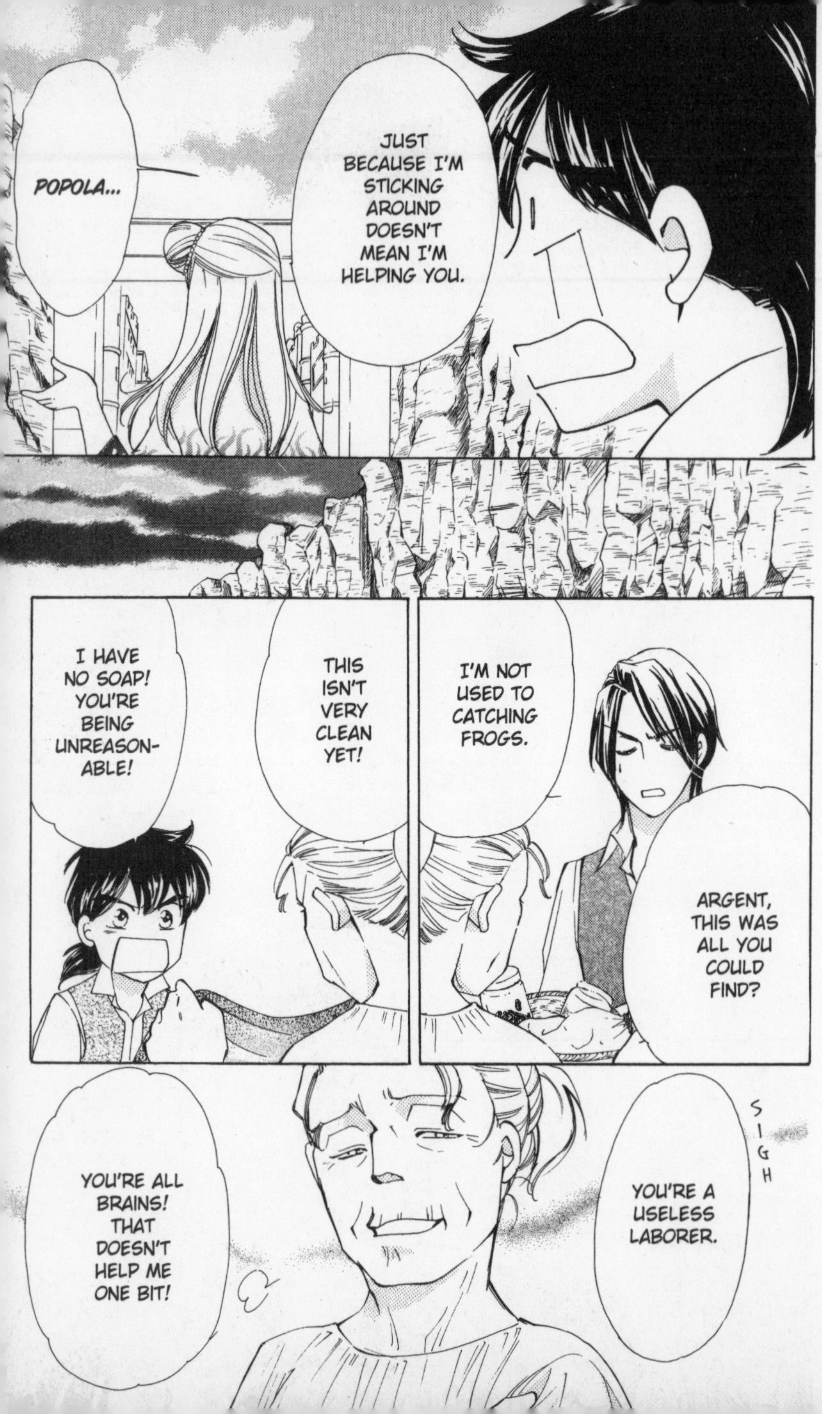
JUST BECAUSE I'M STICKING AROUND DOESN'T MEAN I'M HELPING YOU.
POPOLA...
ARGENT, THIS WAS ALL YOU COULD FIND?
I'M NOT USED TO CATCHING FROGS.
THIS ISN'T VERY CLEAN YET!
I HAVE NO SOAP! YOU'RE BEING UNREASON-ABLE!
SIGH
YOU'RE A USELESS LABORER.
YOU'RE ALL BRAINS! THAT DOESN'T HELP ME ONE BIT!

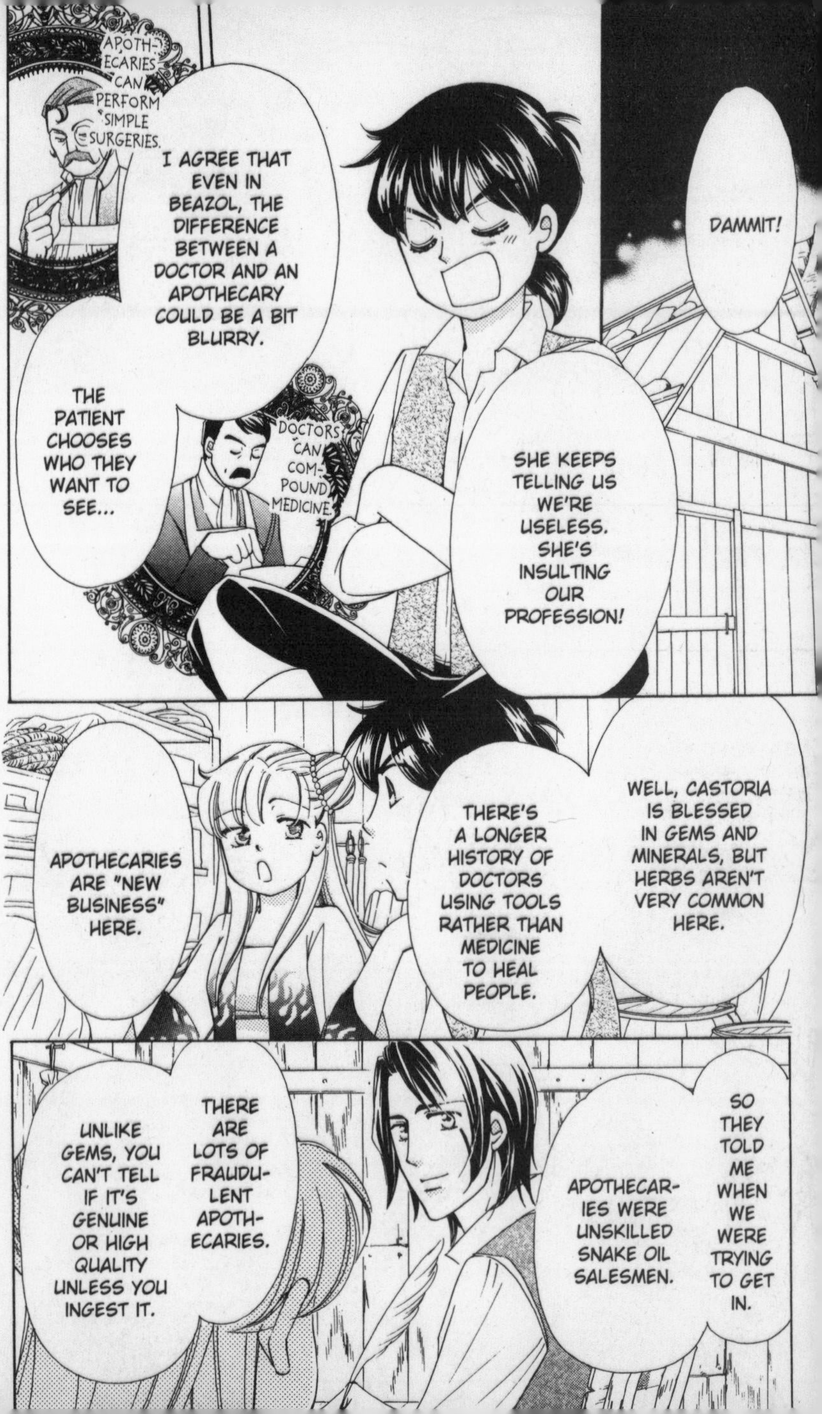
DAMMIT!
SHE KEEPS TELLING US WE'RE USELESS. SHE'S INSULTING OUR PROFESSION!
I AGREE THAT EVEN IN BEAZOL, THE DIFFERENCE BETWEEN A DOCTOR AND AN APOTHECARY COULD BE A BIT BLURRY.
APOTHECARIES CAN PERFORM SIMPLE SURGERIES.
DOCTORS CAN COMPOUND MEDICINE.
THE PATIENT CHOOSES WHO THEY WANT TO SEE...
WELL, CASTORIA IS BLESSED IN GEMS AND MINERALS, BUT HERBS AREN'T VERY COMMON HERE.
THERE'S A LONGER HISTORY OF DOCTORS USING TOOLS RATHER THAN MEDICINE TO HEAL PEOPLE.
APOTHECARIES ARE "NEW BUSINESS" HERE.
SO THEY TOLD ME WHEN WE WERE TRYING TO GET IN.
APOTHECARIES WERE UNSKILLED SNAKE OIL SALESMEN.
THERE ARE LOTS OF FRAUDULENT APOTHECARIES.
UNLIKE GEMS, YOU CAN'T TELL IF IT'S GENUINE OR HIGH QUALITY UNLESS YOU INGEST IT.

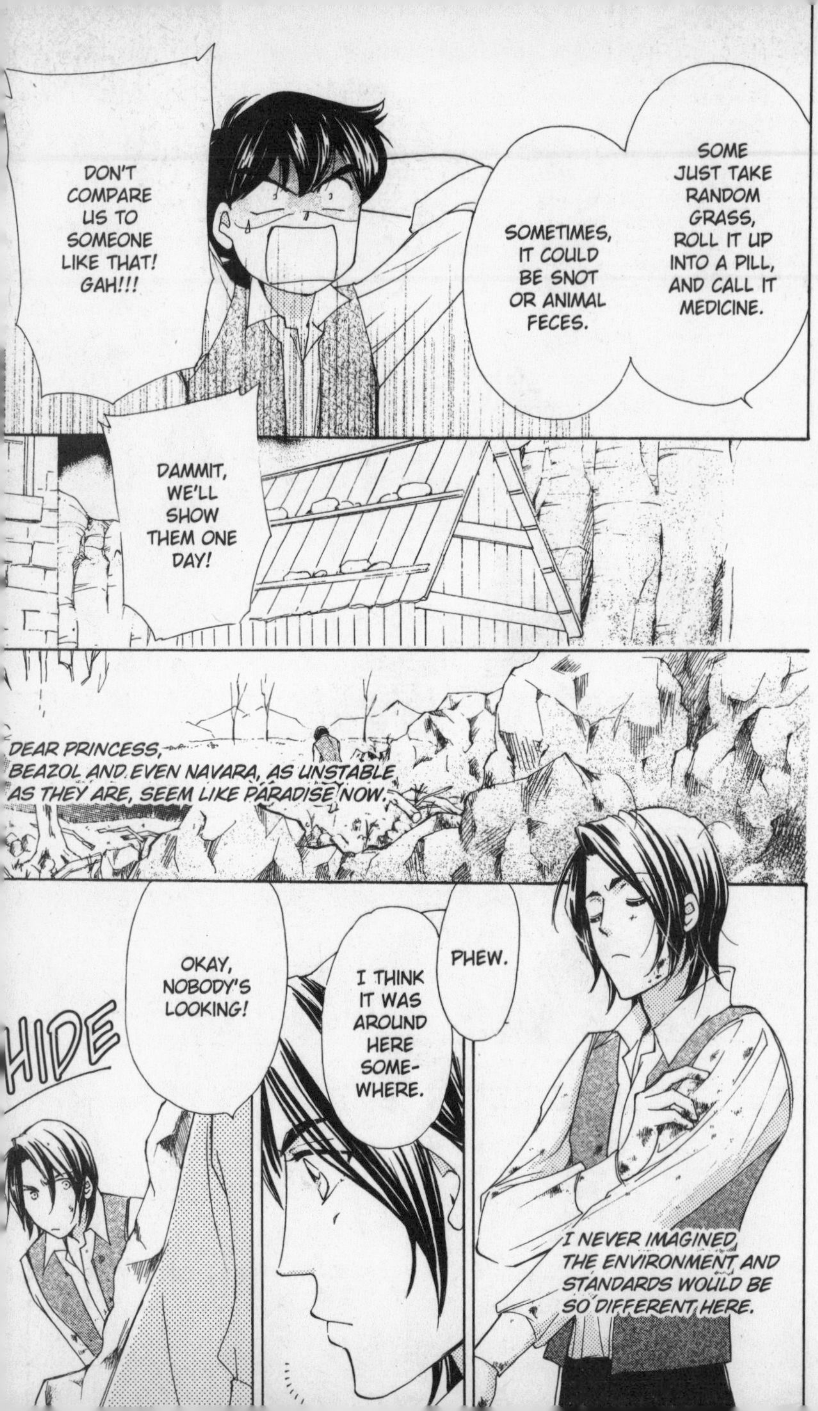
SOME JUST TAKE RANDOM GRASS, ROLL IT UP INTO A PILL, AND CALL IT MEDICINE.
SOMETIMES, IT COULD BE SNOT OR ANIMAL FECES.
DON'T COMPARE US TO SOMEONE LIKE THAT! GAH!!!
DAMMIT, WE'LL SHOW THEM ONE DAY!
DEAR PRINCESS, BEAZOL AND EVEN NAVARA, AS UNSTABLE AS THEY ARE, SEEM LIKE PARADISE NOW.
PHEW.
I NEVER IMAGINED THE ENVIRONMENT AND STANDARDS WOULD BE SO DIFFERENT HERE.
I THINK IT WAS AROUND HERE SOME-WHERE.
OKAY, NOBODY'S LOOKING!
HIDE

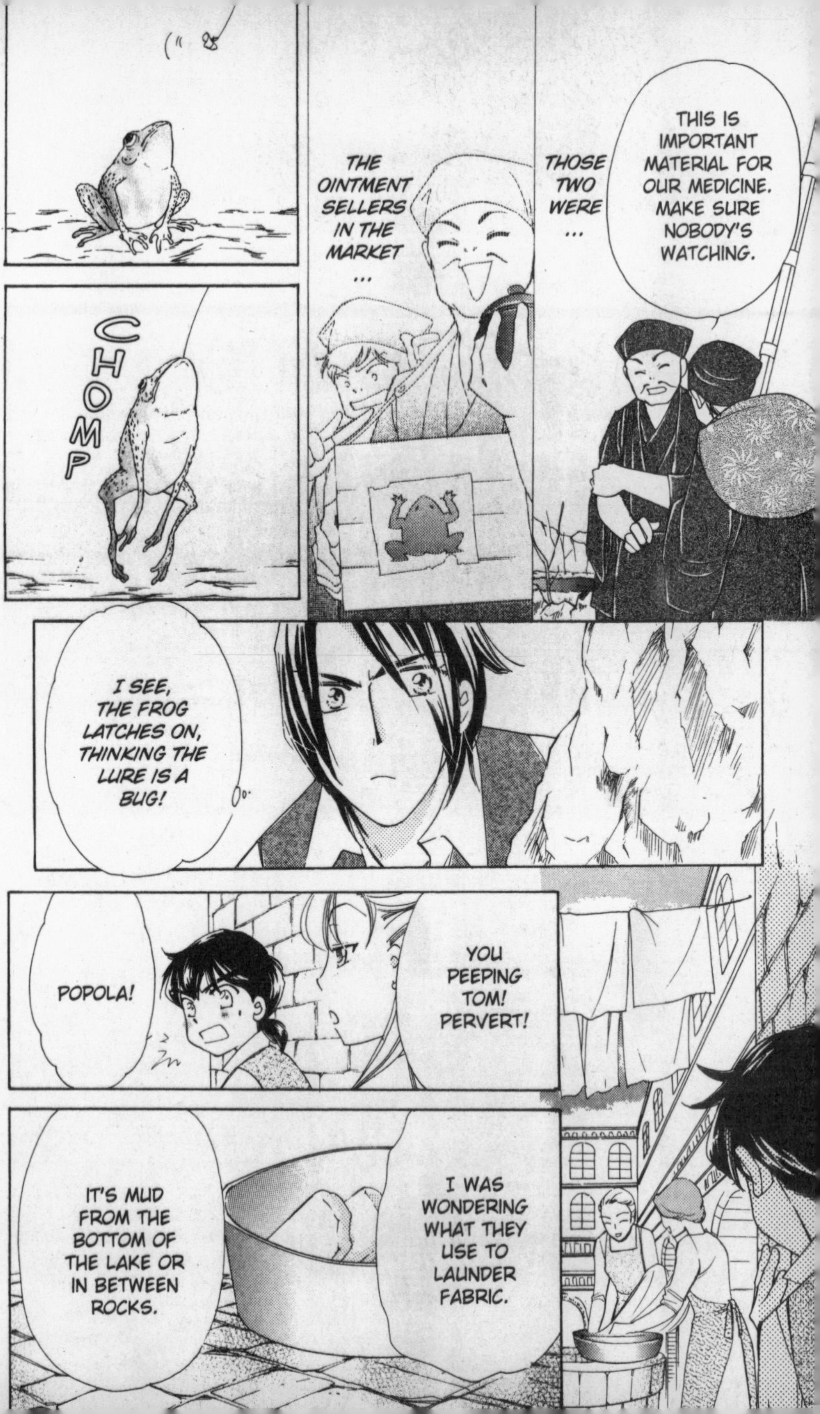
THIS IS IMPORTANT MATERIAL FOR OUR MEDICINE. MAKE SURE NOBODY'S WATCHING.
THOSE TWO WERE ...
THE OINTMENT SELLERS IN THE MARKET ...
CHOMP
I SEE, THE FROG LATCHES ON, THINKING THE LURE IS A BUG!
YOU PEEPING TOM! PERVERT!
POPOLA!
I WAS WONDERING WHAT THEY USE TO LAUNDER FABRIC.
IT'S MUD FROM THE BOTTOM OF THE LAKE OR IN BETWEEN ROCKS.

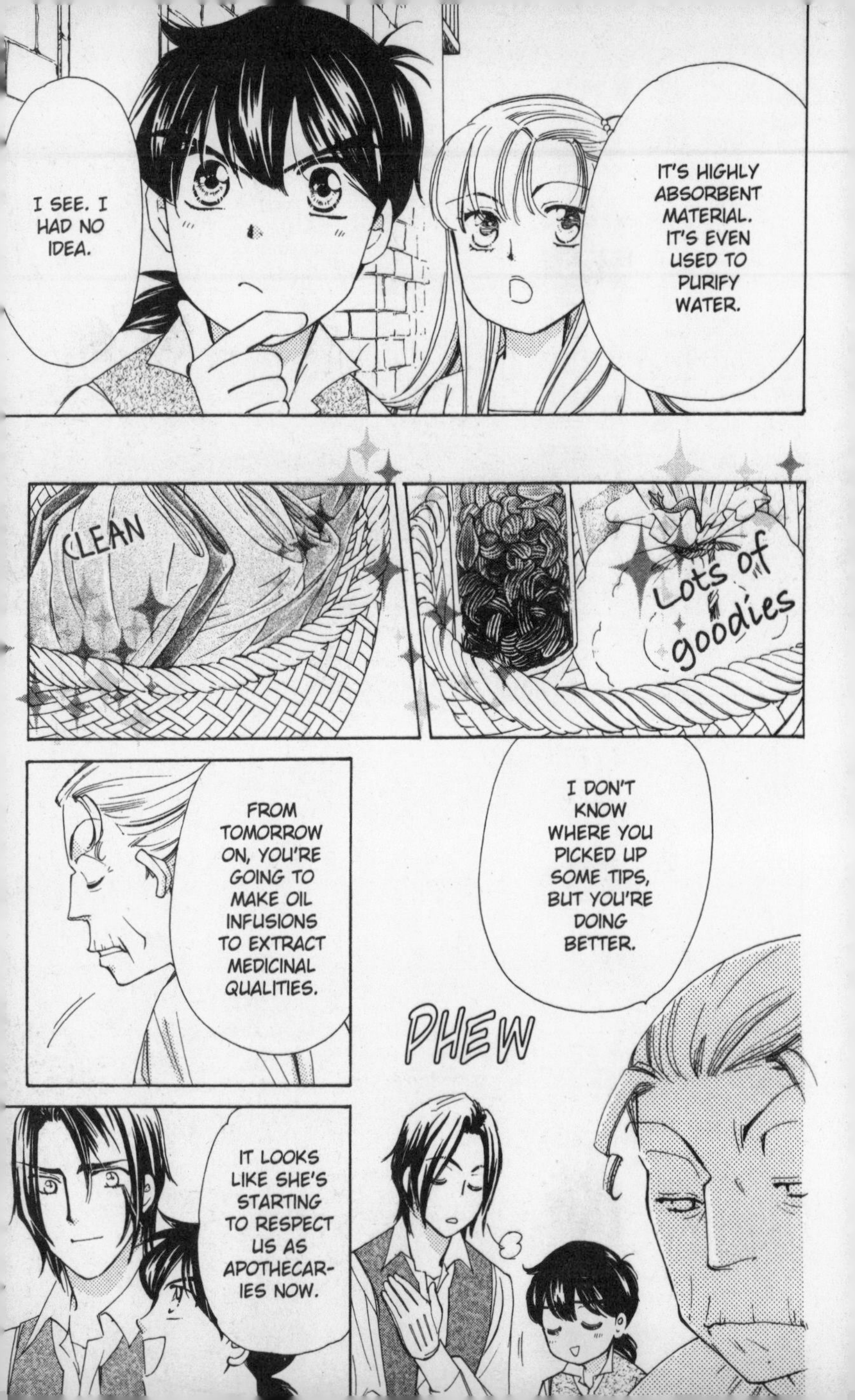
IT'S HIGHLY ABSORBENT MATERIAL. IT'S EVEN USED TO PURIFY WATER.
I SEE. I HAD NO IDEA.
Lots of goodies
CLEAN
I DON'T KNOW WHERE YOU PICKED UP SOME TIPS, BUT YOU'RE DOING BETTER.
PHEW
FROM TOMORROW ON, YOU'RE GOING TO MAKE OIL INFUSIONS TO EXTRACT MEDICINAL QUALITIES.
IT LOOKS LIKE SHE'S STARTING TO RESPECT US AS APOTHECAR-IES NOW.

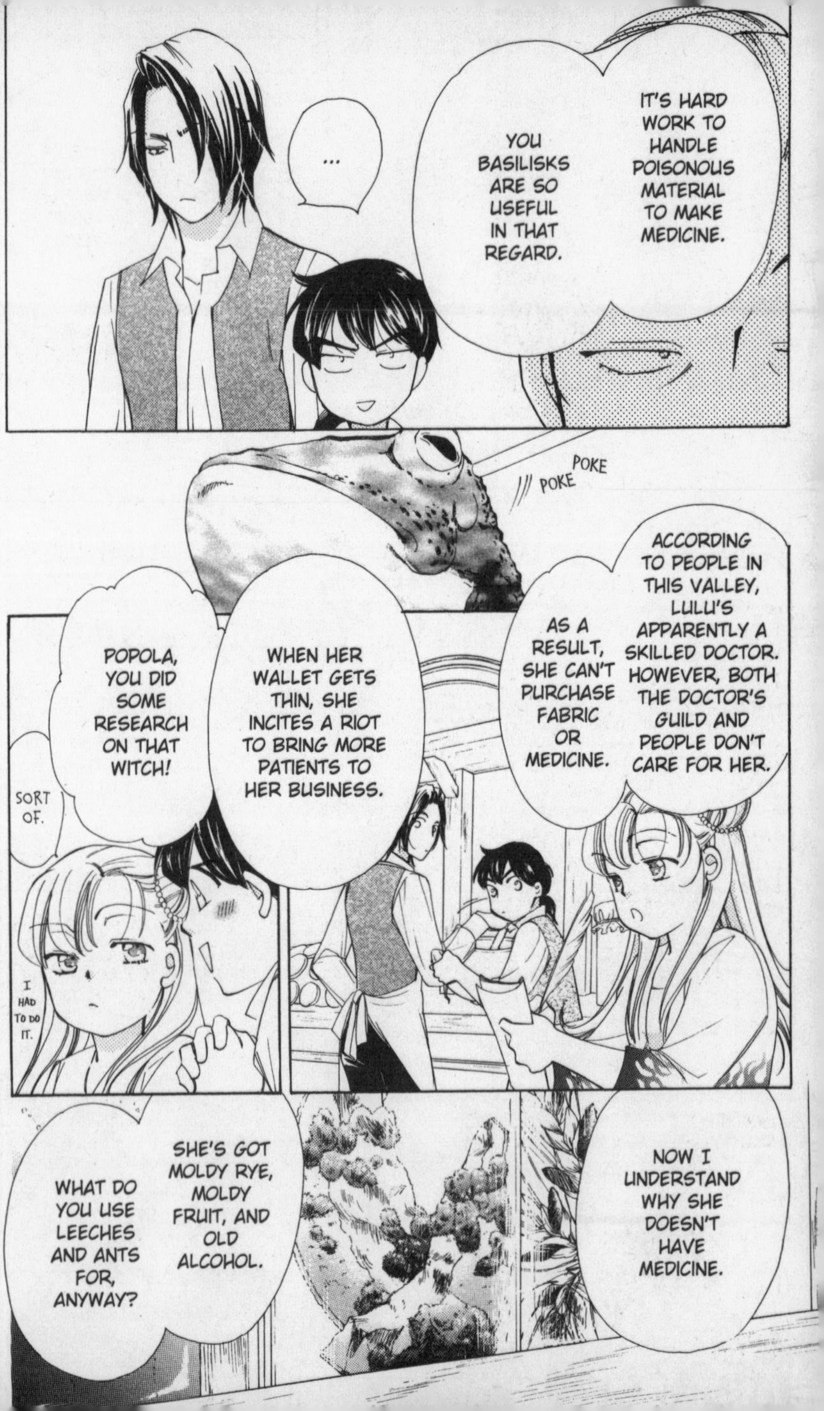
IT'S HARD WORK TO HANDLE POISONOUS MATERIAL TO MAKE MEDICINE.
YOU BASILISKS ARE SO USEFUL IN THAT REGARD.
...
POKE POKE
ACCORDING TO PEOPLE IN THIS VALLEY, LULU'S APPARENTLY A SKILLED DOCTOR. HOWEVER, BOTH THE DOCTOR'S GUILD AND PEOPLE DON'T CARE FOR HER.
AS A RESULT, SHE CAN'T PURCHASE FABRIC OR MEDICINE.
WHEN HER WALLET GETS THIN, SHE INCITES A RIOT TO BRING MORE PATIENTS TO HER BUSINESS.
POPOLA, YOU DID SOME RESEARCH ON THAT WITCH!
SORT OF.
I HAD TO DO IT.
NOW I UNDERSTAND WHY SHE DOESN'T HAVE MEDICINE.
SHE'S GOT MOLDY RYE, MOLDY FRUIT, AND OLD ALCOHOL.
WHAT DO YOU USE LEECHES AND ANTS FOR, ANYWAY?

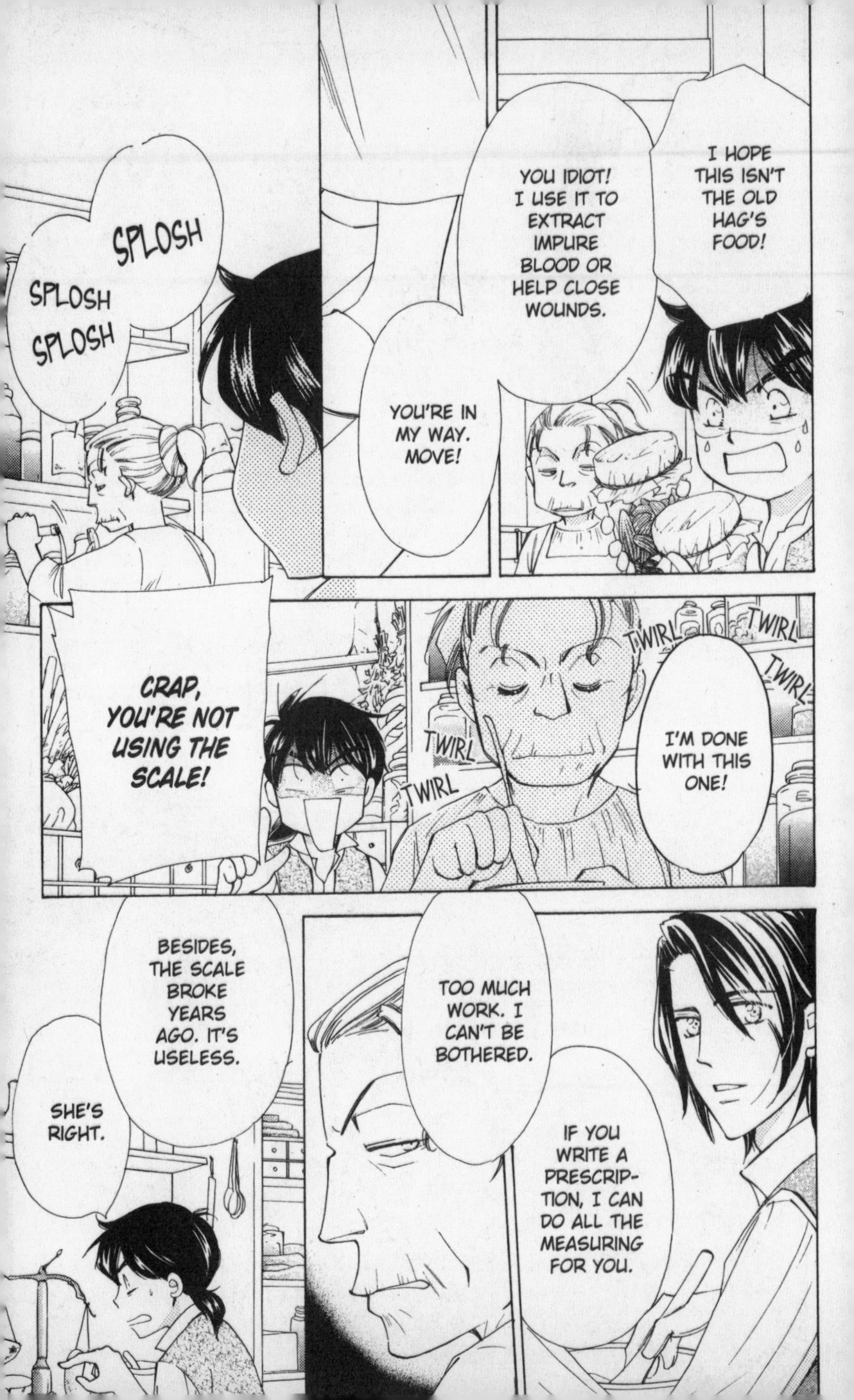
I HOPE THIS ISN'T THE OLD HAG'S FOOD!
YOU IDIOT! I USE IT TO EXTRACT IMPURE BLOOD OR HELP CLOSE WOUNDS.
YOU'RE IN MY WAY. MOVE!
SPLOSH
SPLOSH
SPLOSH
TWIRL TWIRL TWIRL
I'M DONE WITH THIS ONE!
TWIRL TWIRL
CRAP, YOU'RE NOT USING THE SCALE!
TOO MUCH WORK. I CAN'T BE BOTHERED.
IF YOU WRITE A PRESCRIP-TION, I CAN DO ALL THE MEASURING FOR YOU.
BESIDES, THE SCALE BROKE YEARS AGO. IT'S USELESS.
SHE'S RIGHT.

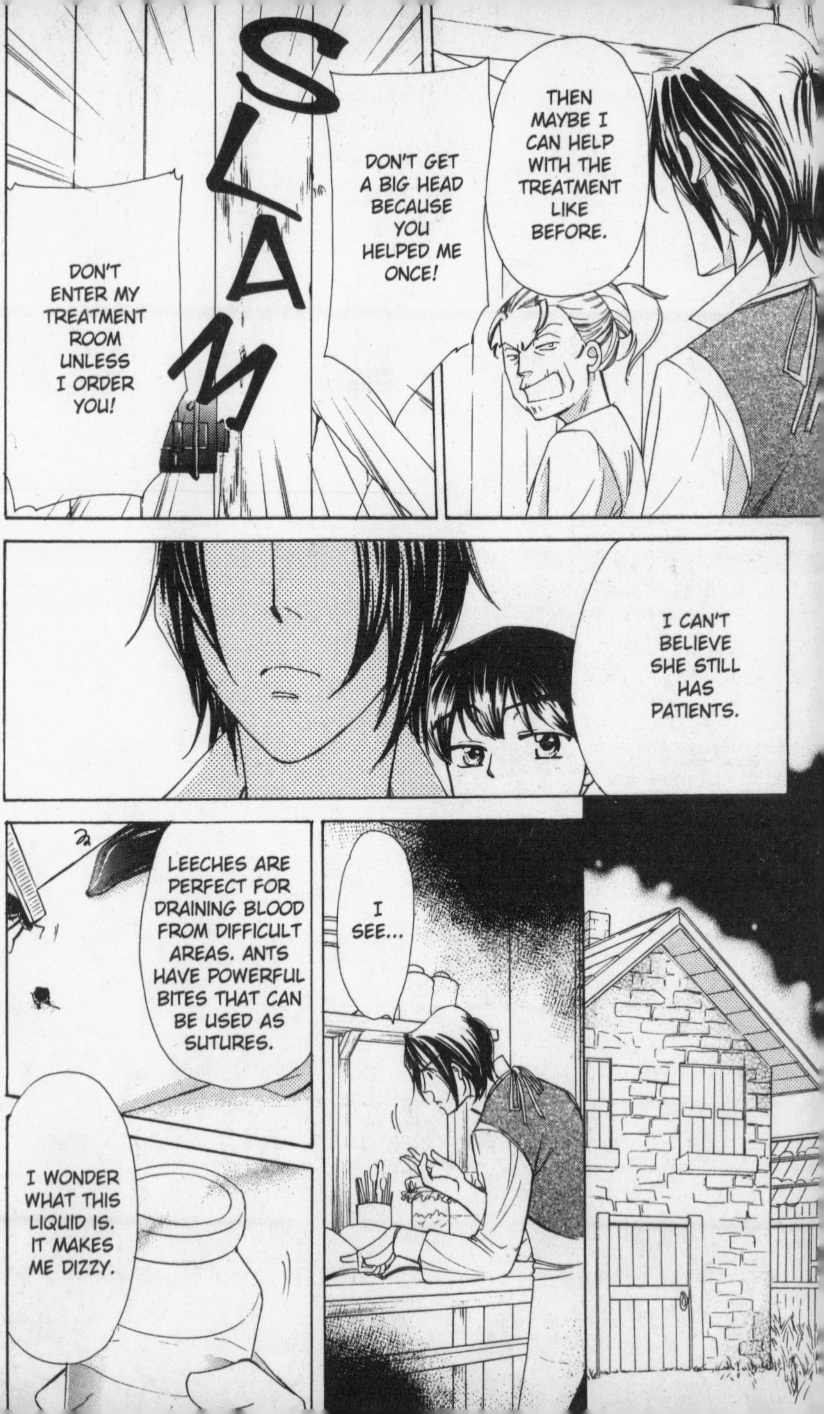
THEN MAYBE I CAN HELP WITH THE TREATMENT LIKE BEFORE.
DON'T GET A BIG HEAD BECAUSE YOU HELPED ME ONCE!
SLAM
DON'T ENTER MY TREATMENT ROOM UNLESS I ORDER YOU!
I CAN'T BELIEVE SHE STILL HAS PATIENTS.
I SEE...
LEECHES ARE PERFECT FOR DRAINING BLOOD FROM DIFFICULT AREAS. ANTS HAVE POWERFUL BITES THAT CAN BE USED AS SUTURES.
I WONDER WHAT THIS LIQUID IS. IT MAKES ME DIZZY.

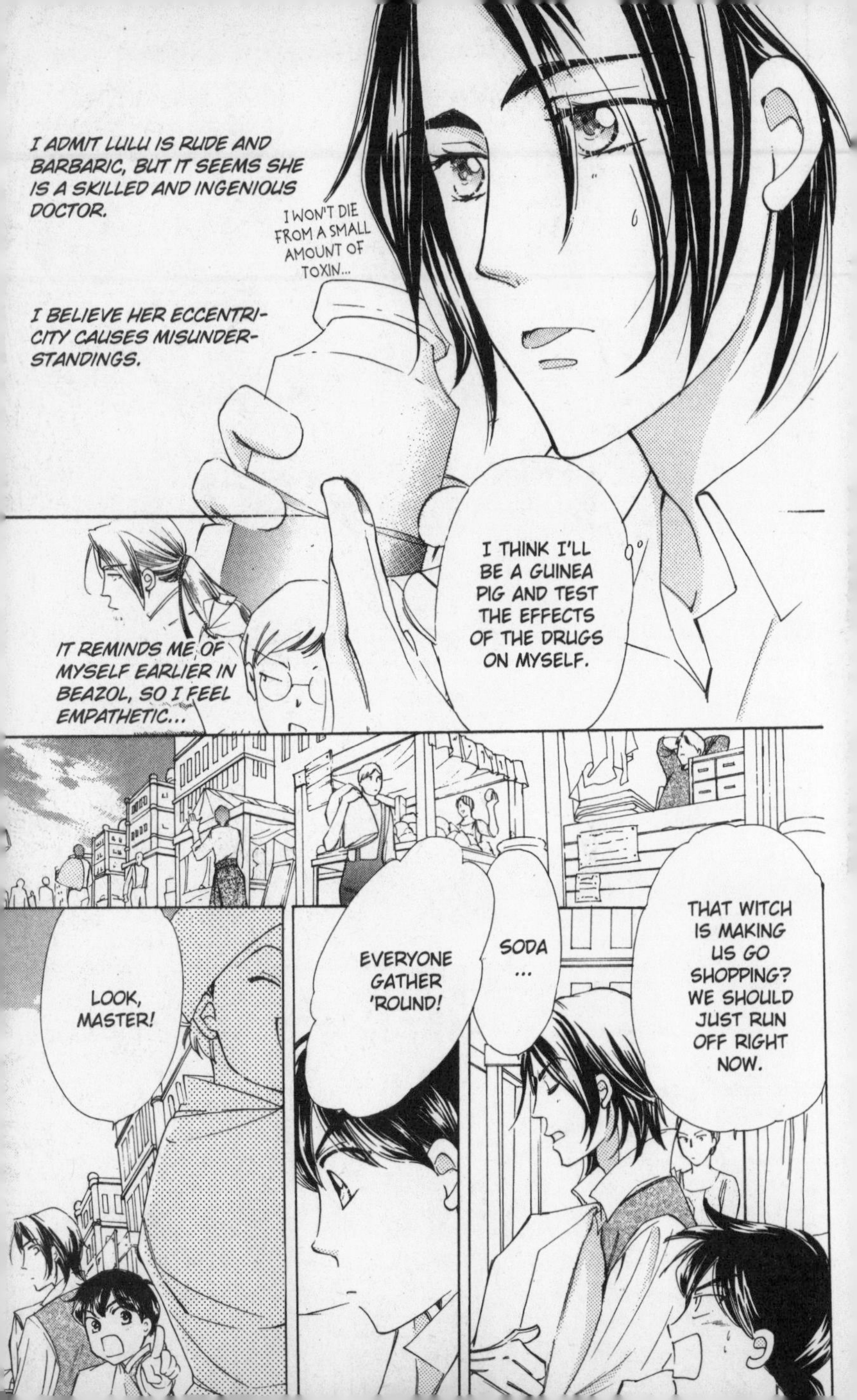

I ADMIT LULU IS RUDE AND BARBARIC, BUT IT SEEMS SHE IS A SKILLED AND INGENIOUS DOCTOR.
I WON'T DIE FROM A SMALL AMOUNT OF TOXIN...
I BELIEVE HER ECCENTRICITY CAUSES MISUNDERSTANDINGS.
I THINK I'LL BE A GUINEA PIG AND TEST THE EFFECTS OF THE DRUGS ON MYSELF.
IT REMINDS ME OF MYSELF EARLIER IN BEAZOL, SO I FEEL EMPATHETIC...
THAT WITCH IS MAKING US GO SHOPPING? WE SHOULD JUST RUN OFF RIGHT NOW.
SODA...
EVERYONE GATHER 'ROUND!
LOOK, MASTER!

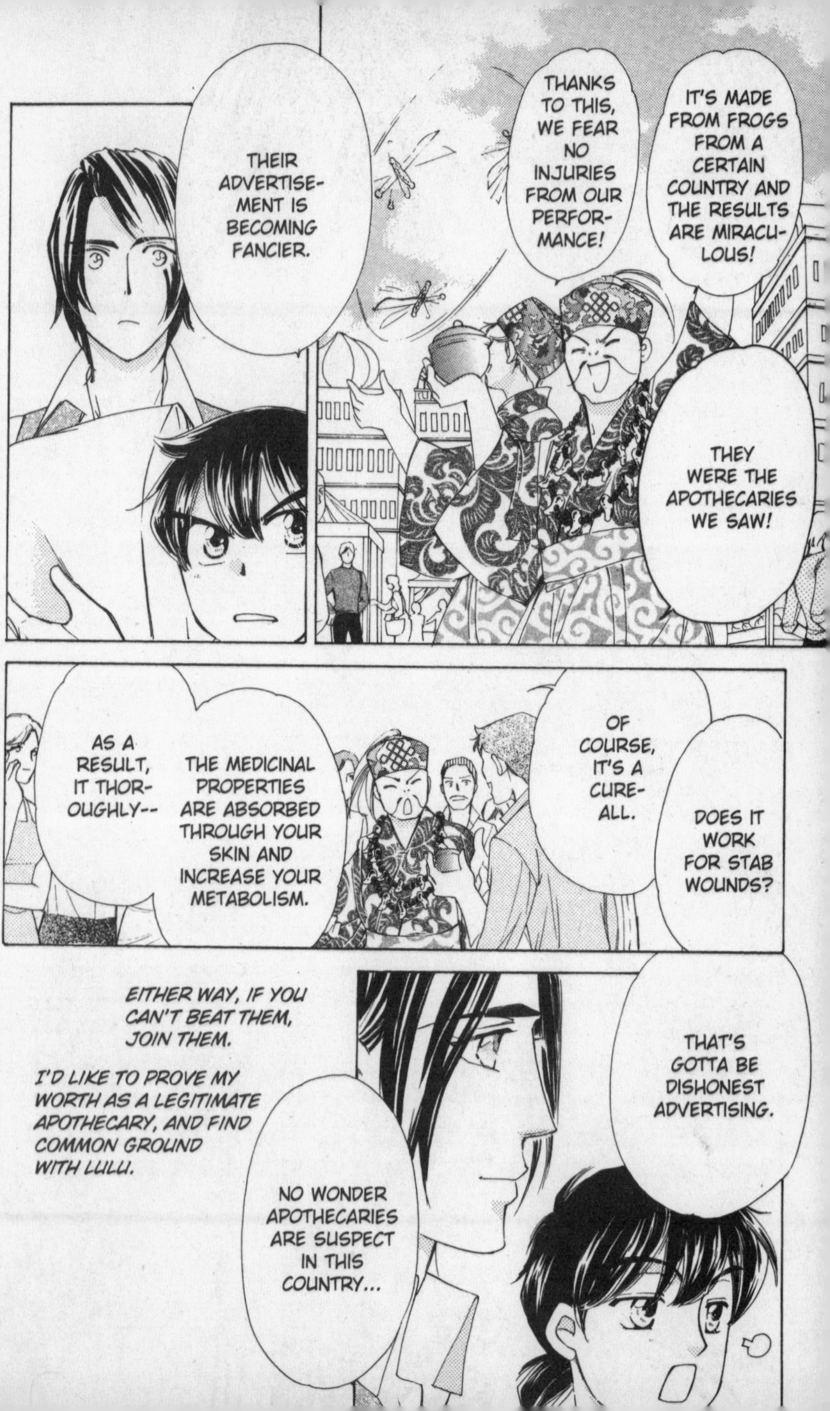
IT'S MADE FROM FROGS FROM A CERTAIN COUNTRY AND THE RESULTS ARE MIRACULOUS!
THANKS TO THIS, WE FEAR NO INJURIES FROM OUR PERFORMANCE!
THEY WERE THE APOTHECARIES WE SAW!
THEIR ADVERTISEMENT IS BECOMING FANCIER.
DOES IT WORK FOR STAB WOUNDS?
OF COURSE, IT'S A CURE-ALL.
THE MEDICINAL PROPERTIES ARE ABSORBED THROUGH YOUR SKIN AND INCREASE YOUR METABOLISM.
AS A RESULT, IT THOROUGHLY--
THAT'S GOTTA BE DISHONEST ADVERTISING.
NO WONDER APOTHECARIES ARE SUSPECT IN THIS COUNTRY...
EITHER WAY, IF YOU CAN'T BEAT THEM, JOIN THEM.
I'D LIKE TO PROVE MY WORTH AS A LEGITIMATE APOTHECARY, AND FIND COMMON GROUND WITH LULU.

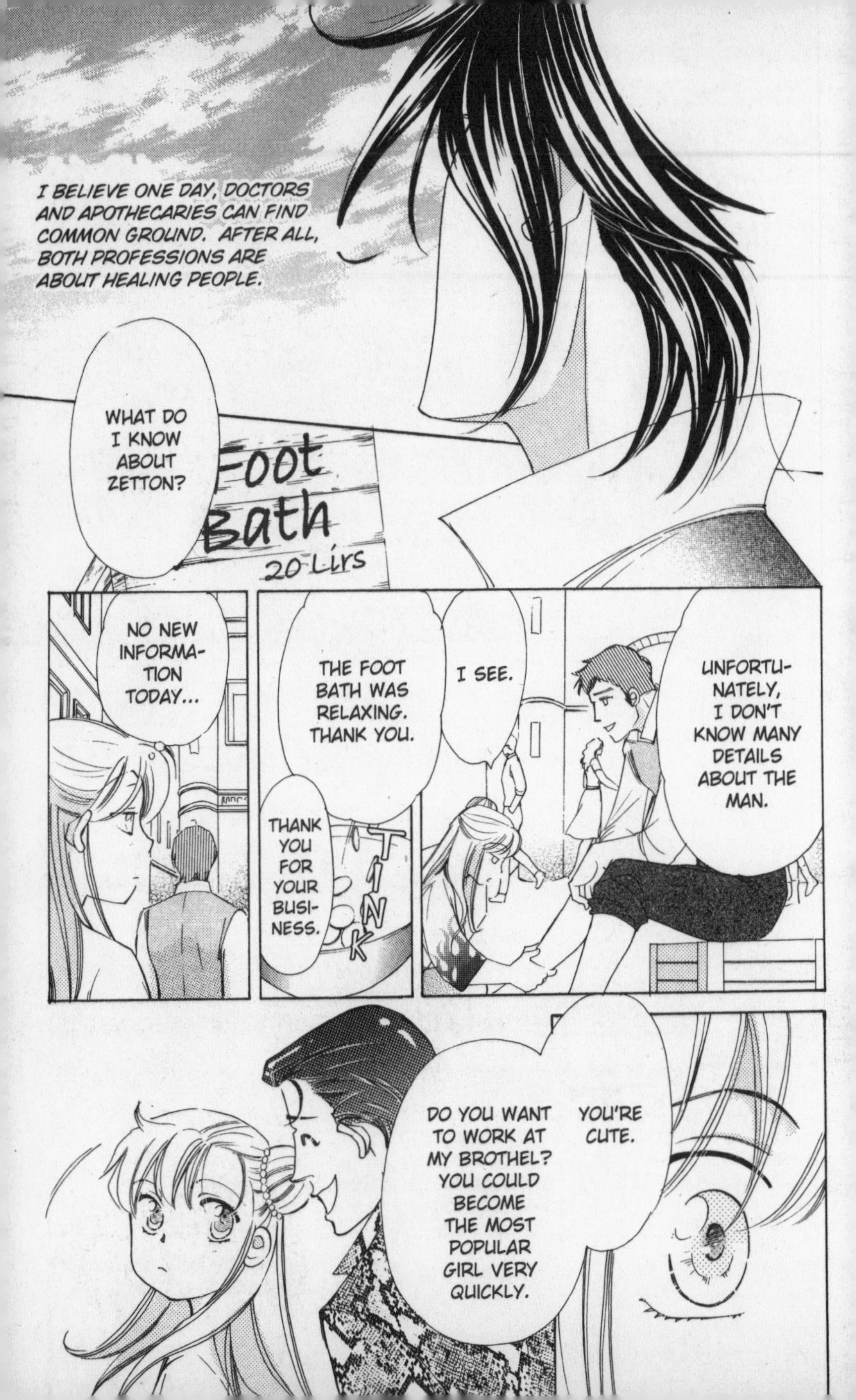
I BELIEVE ONE DAY, DOCTORS AND APOTHECARIES CAN FIND COMMON GROUND. AFTER ALL, BOTH PROFESSIONS ARE ABOUT HEALING PEOPLE.
WHAT DO I KNOW ABOUT ZETTON?
Foot Bath 20 Lirs
UNFORTUNATELY, I DON'T KNOW MANY DETAILS ABOUT THE MAN.
I SEE.
THE FOOT BATH WAS RELAXING. THANK YOU.
THANK YOU FOR YOUR BUSINESS.
TINK
NO NEW INFORMATION TODAY...
YOU'RE CUTE.
DO YOU WANT TO WORK AT MY BROTHEL? YOU COULD BECOME THE MOST POPULAR GIRL VERY QUICKLY.

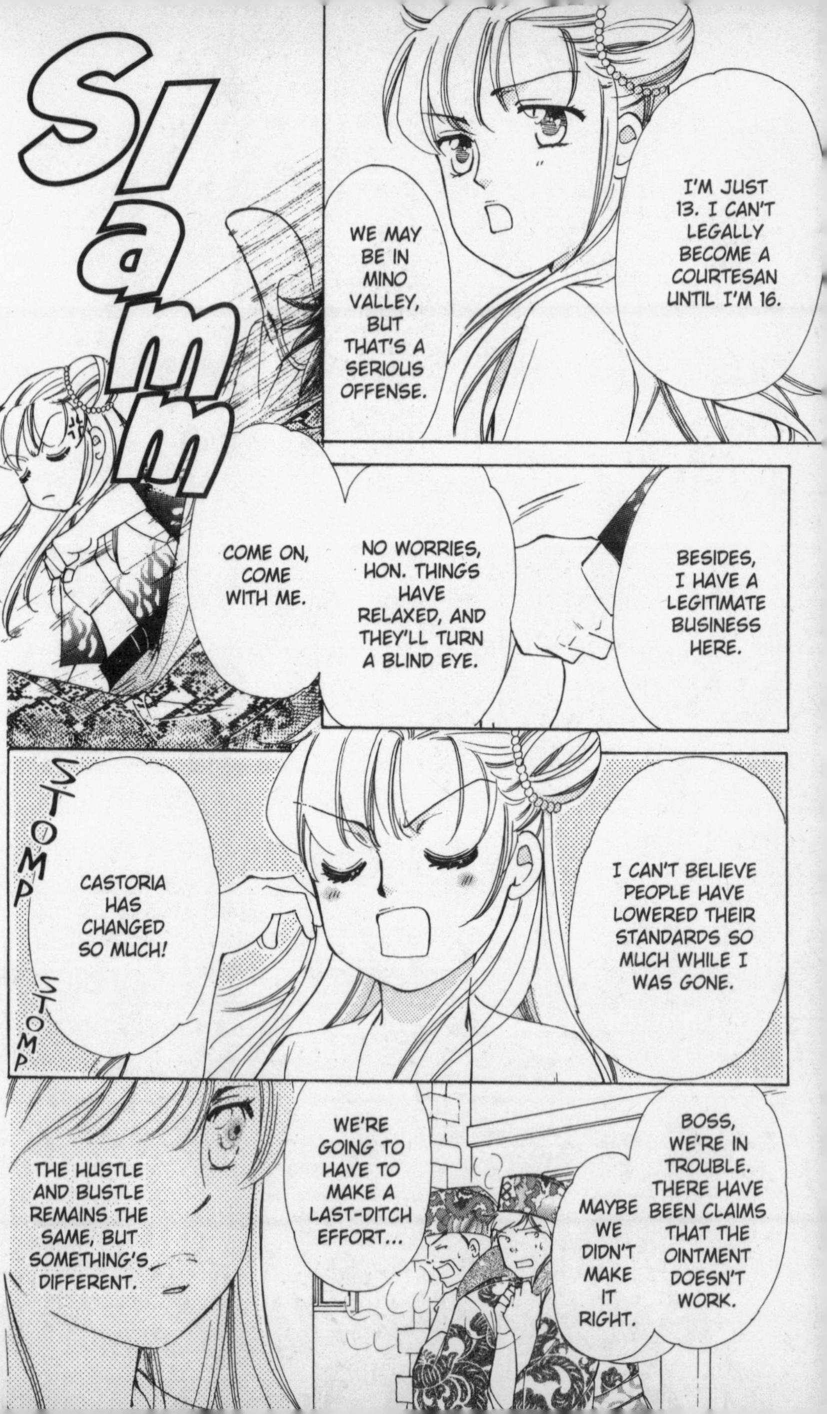
I'M JUST 13. I CAN'T LEGALLY BECOME A COURTESAN UNTIL I'M 16.
WE MAY BE IN MINO VALLEY, BUT THAT'S A SERIOUS OFFENSE.
BESIDES, I HAVE A LEGITIMATE BUSINESS HERE.
NO WORRIES, HON. THINGS HAVE RELAXED, AND THEY'LL TURN A BLIND EYE.
COME ON, COME WITH ME.
Slamm
I CAN'T BELIEVE PEOPLE HAVE LOWERED THEIR STANDARDS SO MUCH WHILE I WAS GONE.
CASTORIA HAS CHANGED SO MUCH!
STOMP
STOMP
BOSS, WE'RE IN TROUBLE. THERE HAVE BEEN CLAIMS THAT THE OINTMENT DOESN'T WORK.
MAYBE WE DIDN'T MAKE IT RIGHT.
WE'RE GOING TO HAVE TO MAKE A LAST-DITCH EFFORT...
THE HUSTLE AND BUSTLE REMAINS THE SAME, BUT SOMETHING'S DIFFERENT.

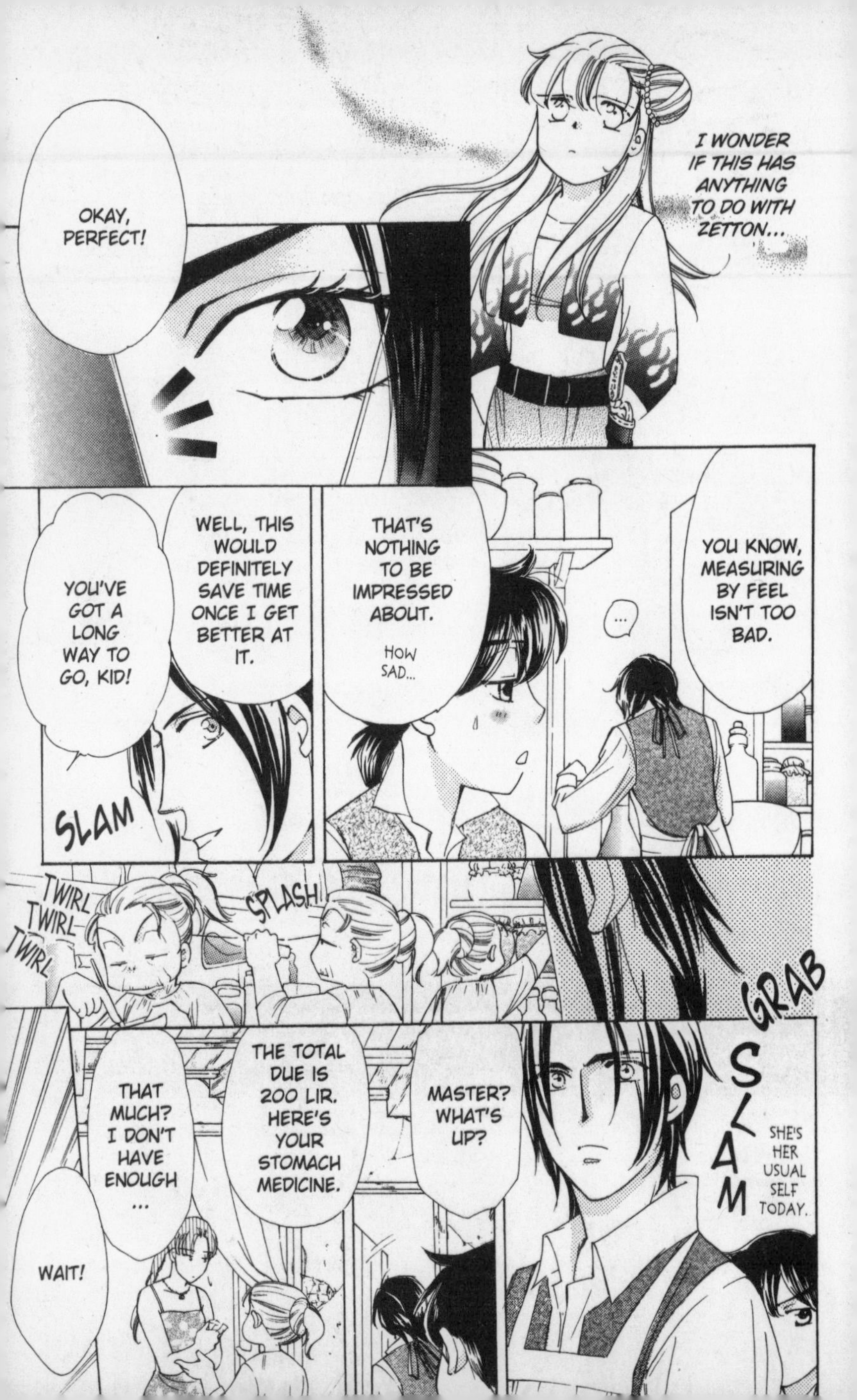
I WONDER IF THIS HAS ANYTHING TO DO WITH ZETTON...
OKAY, PERFECT!
YOU KNOW, MEASURING BY FEEL ISN'T TOO BAD.
...
THAT'S NOTHING TO BE IMPRESSED ABOUT.
HOW SAD...
WELL, THIS WOULD DEFINITELY SAVE TIME ONCE I GET BETTER AT IT.
YOU'VE GOT A LONG WAY TO GO, KID!
SLAM
GRAB
SPLASH
TWIRL TWIRL TWIRL
SLAM
SHE'S HER USUAL SELF TODAY.
MASTER? WHAT'S UP?
THE TOTAL DUE IS 200 LIR. HERE'S YOUR STOMACH MEDICINE.
THAT MUCH? I DON'T HAVE ENOUGH ...
WAIT!

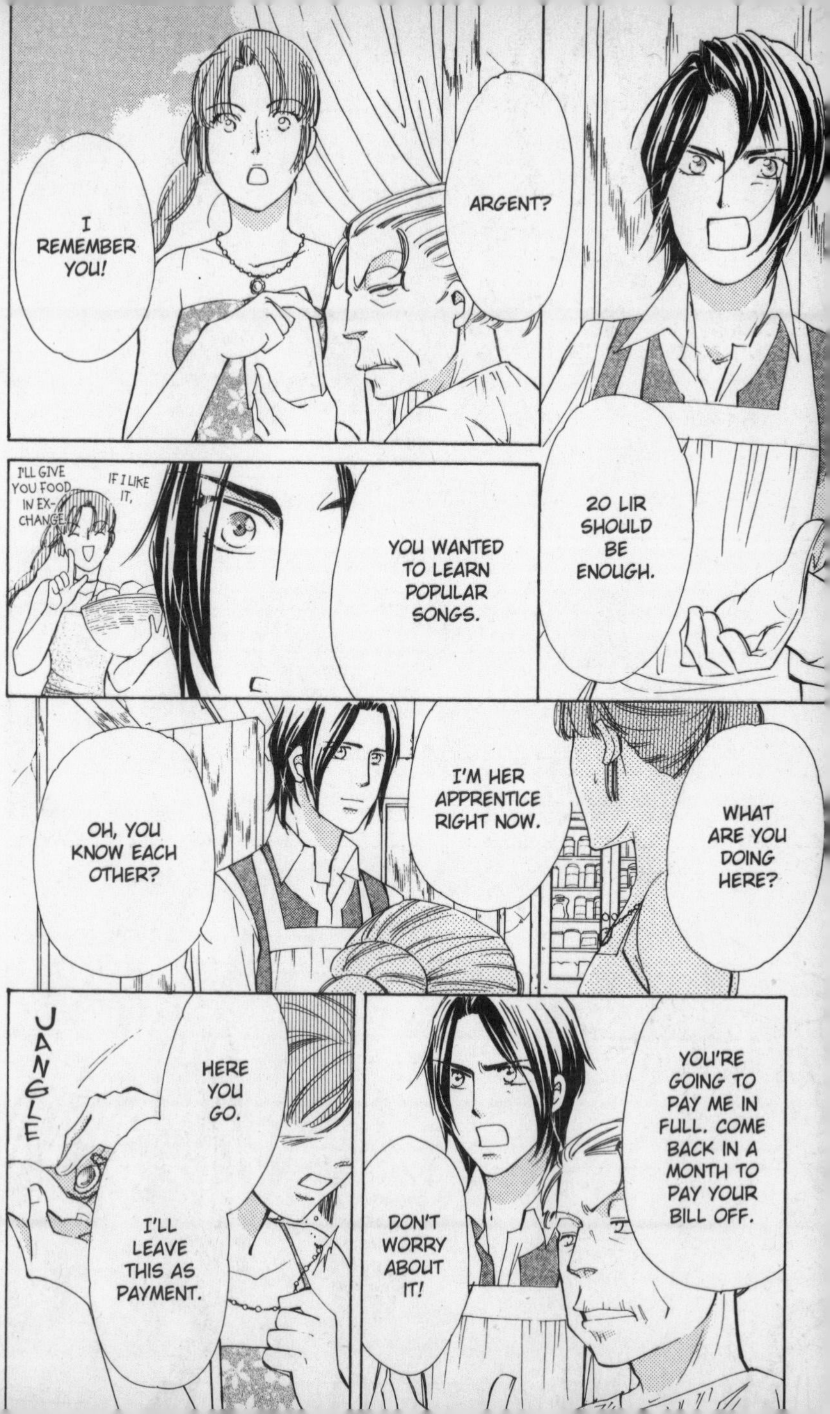
20 LIR SHOULD BE ENOUGH.
ARGENT?
I REMEMBER YOU!
YOU WANTED TO LEARN POPULAR SONGS.
IF I LIKE IT,
I'LL GIVE YOU FOOD IN EX-CHANGE.
WHAT ARE YOU DOING HERE?
I'M HER APPRENTICE RIGHT NOW.
OH, YOU KNOW EACH OTHER?
YOU'RE GOING TO PAY ME IN FULL. COME BACK IN A MONTH TO PAY YOUR BILL OFF.
DON'T WORRY ABOUT IT!
JANGLE
HERE YOU GO.
I'LL LEAVE THIS AS PAYMENT.

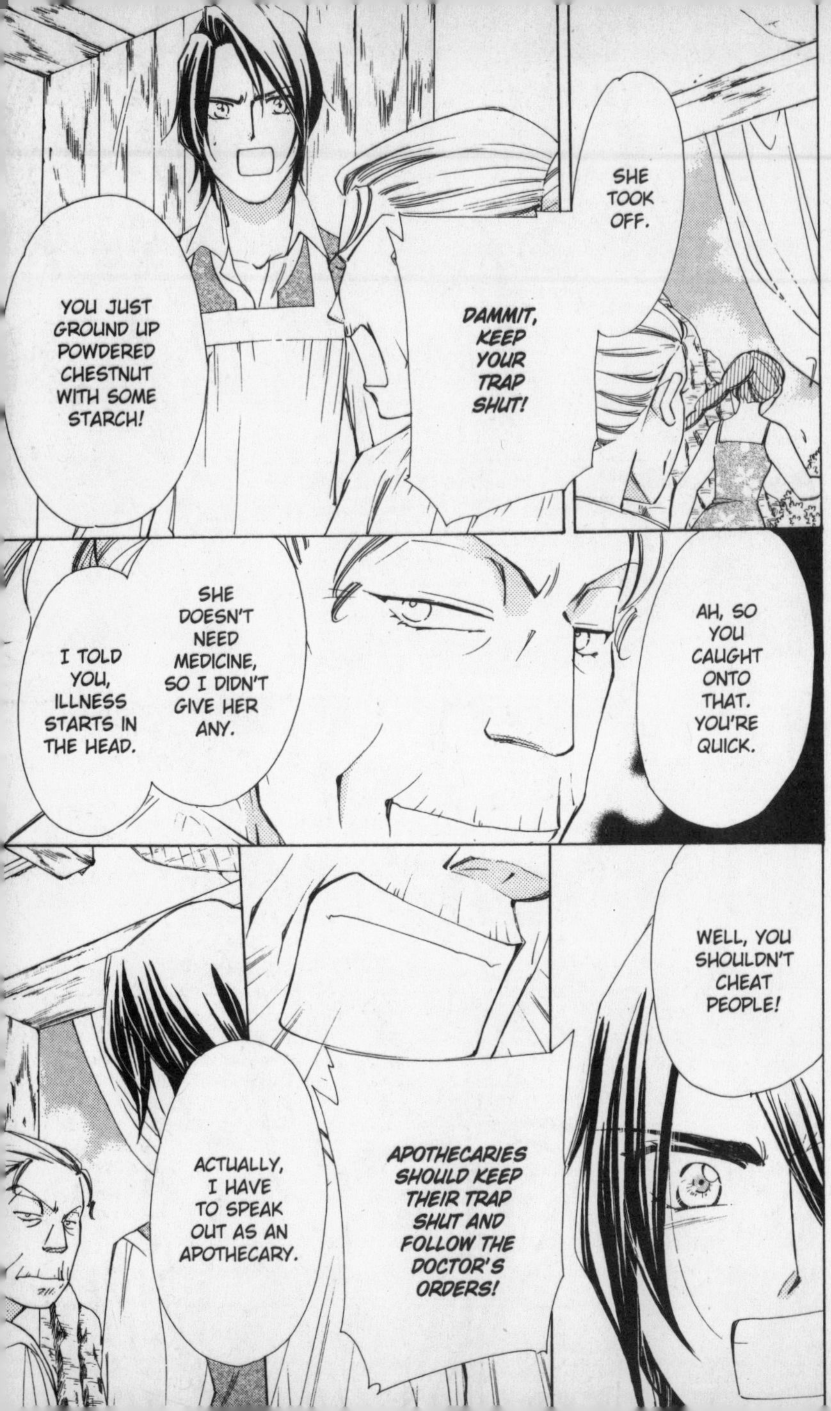
SHE TOOK OFF.
DAMMIT, KEEP YOUR TRAP SHUT!
YOU JUST GROUND UP POWDERED CHESTNUT WITH SOME STARCH!
AH, SO YOU CAUGHT ONTO THAT. YOU'RE QUICK.
SHE DOESN'T NEED MEDICINE, SO I DIDN'T GIVE HER ANY.
I TOLD YOU, ILLNESS STARTS IN THE HEAD.
WELL, YOU SHOULDN'T CHEAT PEOPLE!
APOTHECARIES SHOULD KEEP THEIR TRAP SHUT AND FOLLOW THE DOCTOR'S ORDERS!
ACTUALLY, I HAVE TO SPEAK OUT AS AN APOTHECARY.

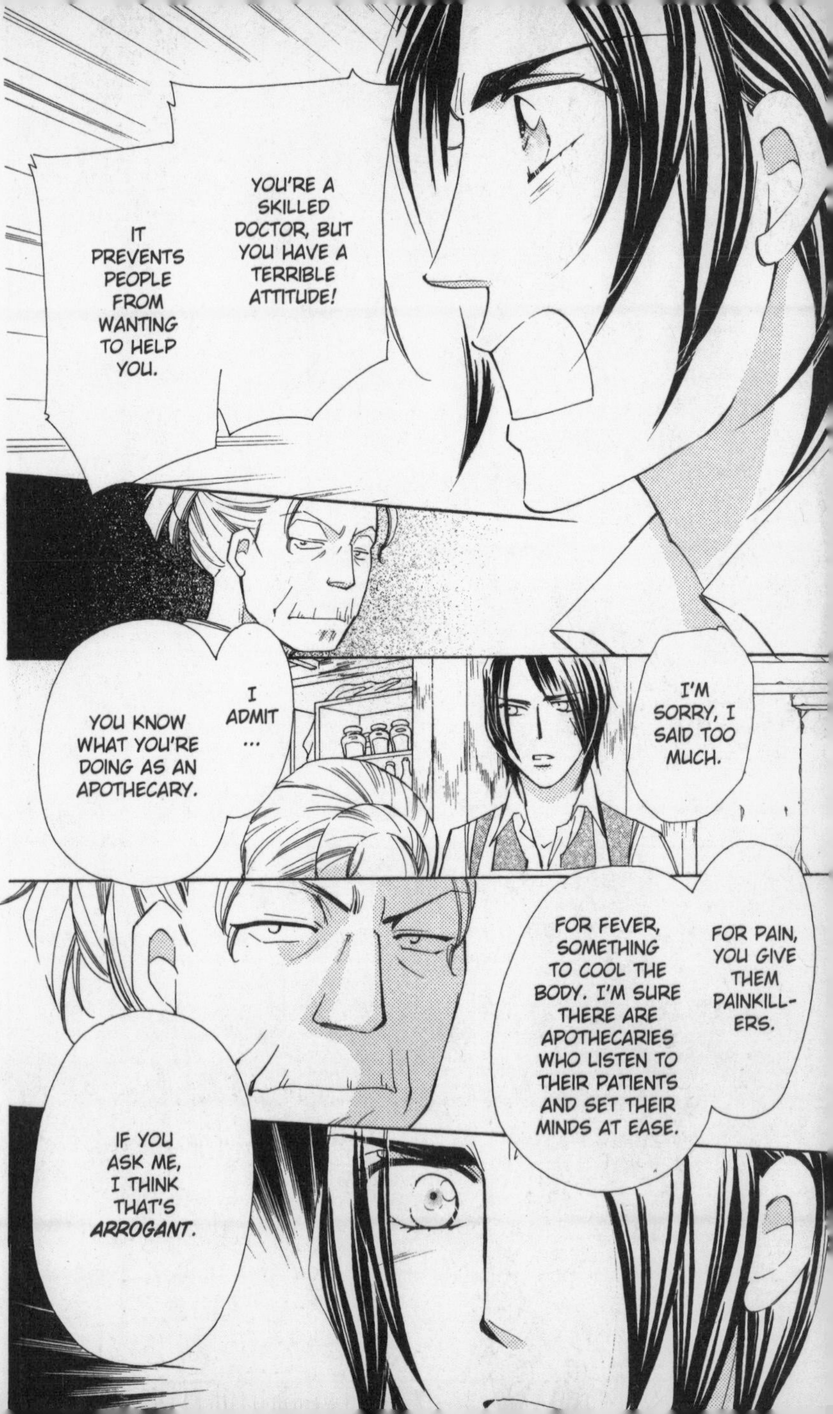
YOU'RE A SKILLED DOCTOR, BUT YOU HAVE A TERRIBLE ATTITUDE!
IT PREVENTS PEOPLE FROM WANTING TO HELP YOU.
I'M SORRY, I SAID TOO MUCH.
I ADMIT ...
YOU KNOW WHAT YOU'RE DOING AS AN APOTHECARY.
FOR PAIN, YOU GIVE THEM PAINKILL-ERS.
FOR FEVER, SOMETHING TO COOL THE BODY. I'M SURE THERE ARE APOTHECARIES WHO LISTEN TO THEIR PATIENTS AND SET THEIR MINDS AT EASE.
IF YOU ASK ME, I THINK THAT'S *ARROGANT*.

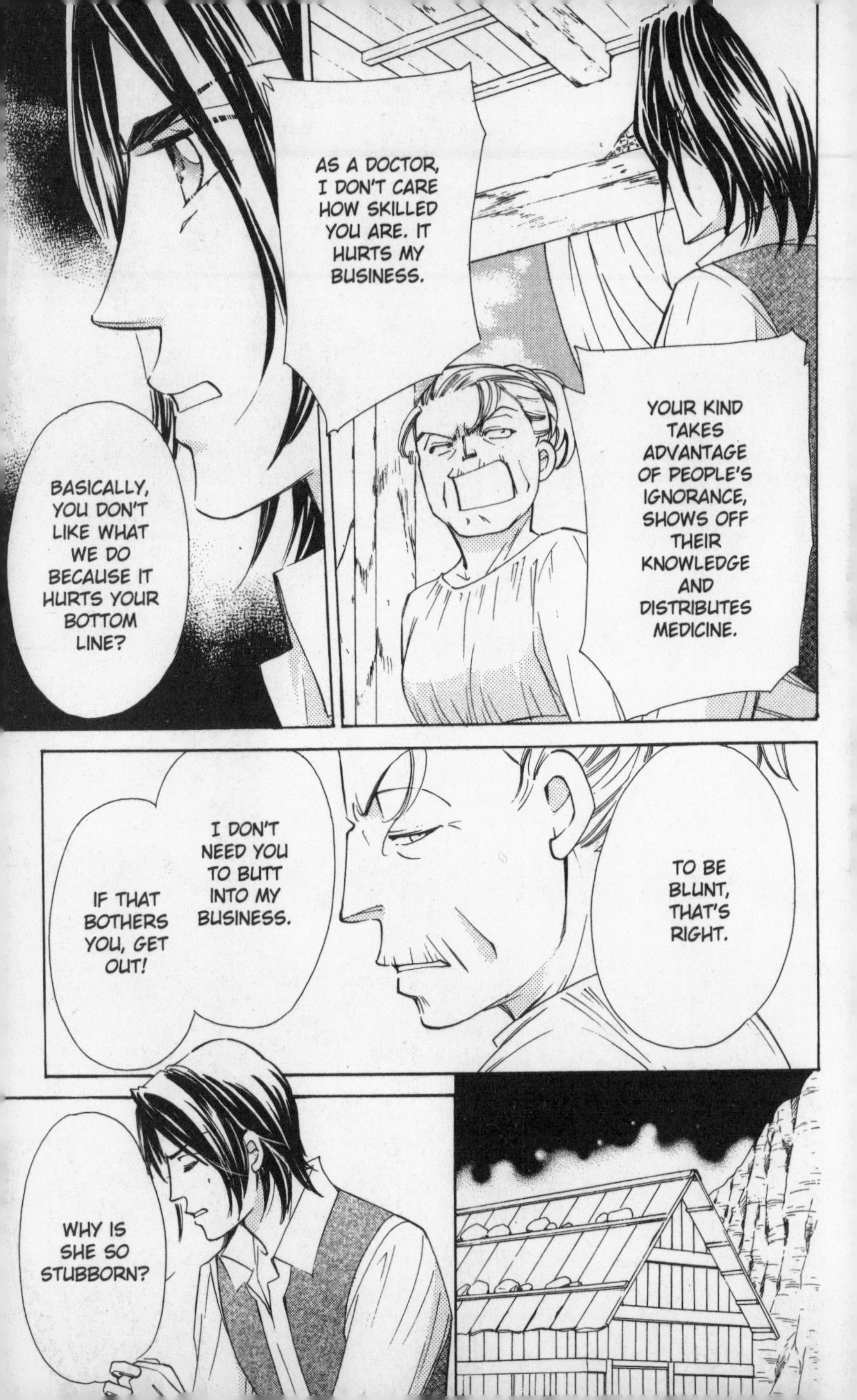
YOUR KIND TAKES ADVANTAGE OF PEOPLE'S IGNORANCE, SHOWS OFF THEIR KNOWLEDGE AND DISTRIBUTES MEDICINE.
AS A DOCTOR, I DON'T CARE HOW SKILLED YOU ARE. IT HURTS MY BUSINESS.
BASICALLY, YOU DON'T LIKE WHAT WE DO BECAUSE IT HURTS YOUR BOTTOM LINE?
TO BE BLUNT, THAT'S RIGHT.
I DON'T NEED YOU TO BUTT INTO MY BUSINESS.
IF THAT BOTHERS YOU, GET OUT!
WHY IS SHE SO STUBBORN?

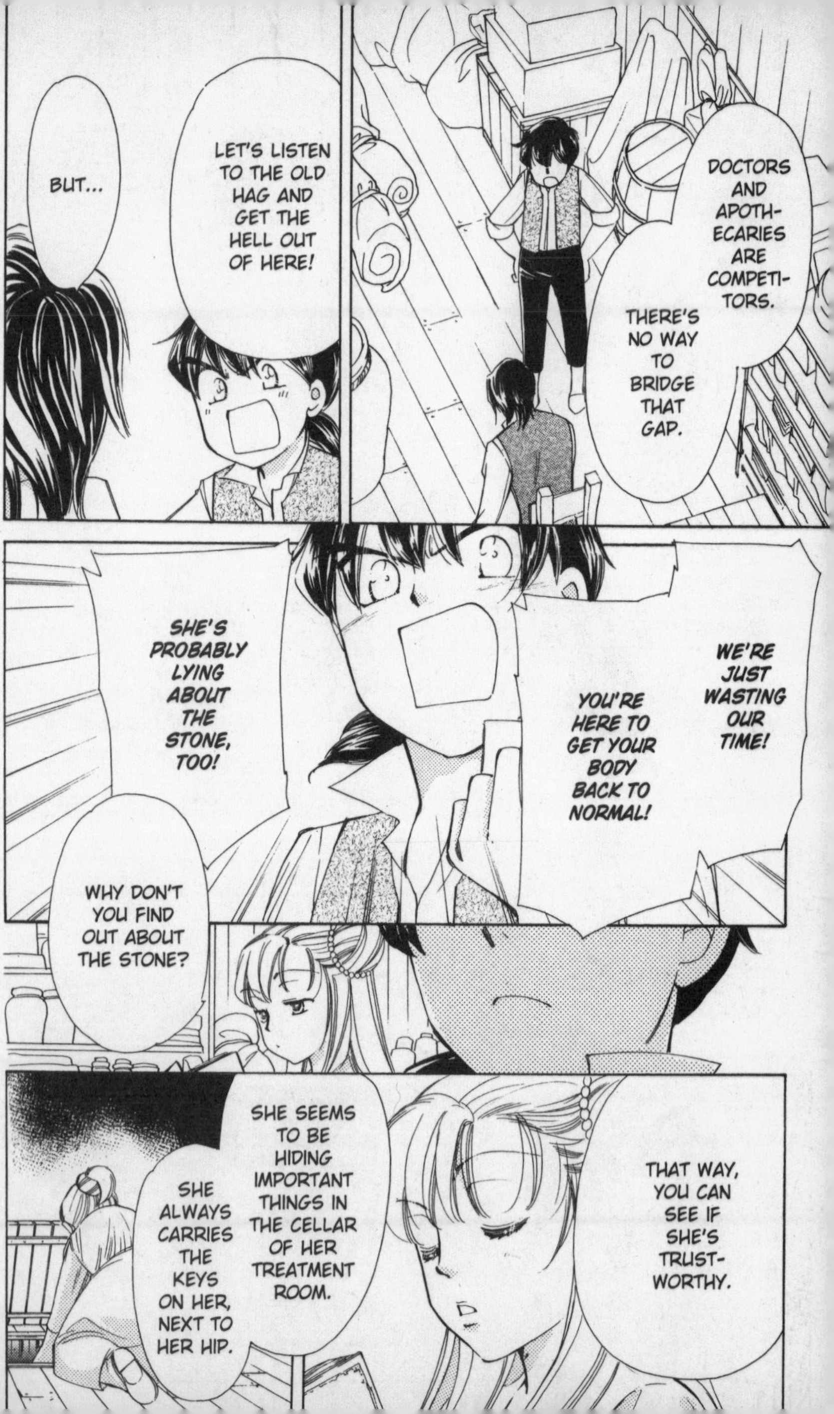
DOCTORS AND APOTHECARIES ARE COMPETITORS.
THERE'S NO WAY TO BRIDGE THAT GAP.
LET'S LISTEN TO THE OLD HAG AND GET THE HELL OUT OF HERE!
BUT...
WE'RE JUST WASTING OUR TIME!
YOU'RE HERE TO GET YOUR BODY BACK TO NORMAL!
SHE'S PROBABLY LYING ABOUT THE STONE, TOO!
WHY DON'T YOU FIND OUT ABOUT THE STONE?
THAT WAY, YOU CAN SEE IF SHE'S TRUST-WORTHY.
SHE SEEMS TO BE HIDING IMPORTANT THINGS IN THE CELLAR OF HER TREATMENT ROOM.
SHE ALWAYS CARRIES THE KEYS ON HER, NEXT TO HER HIP.

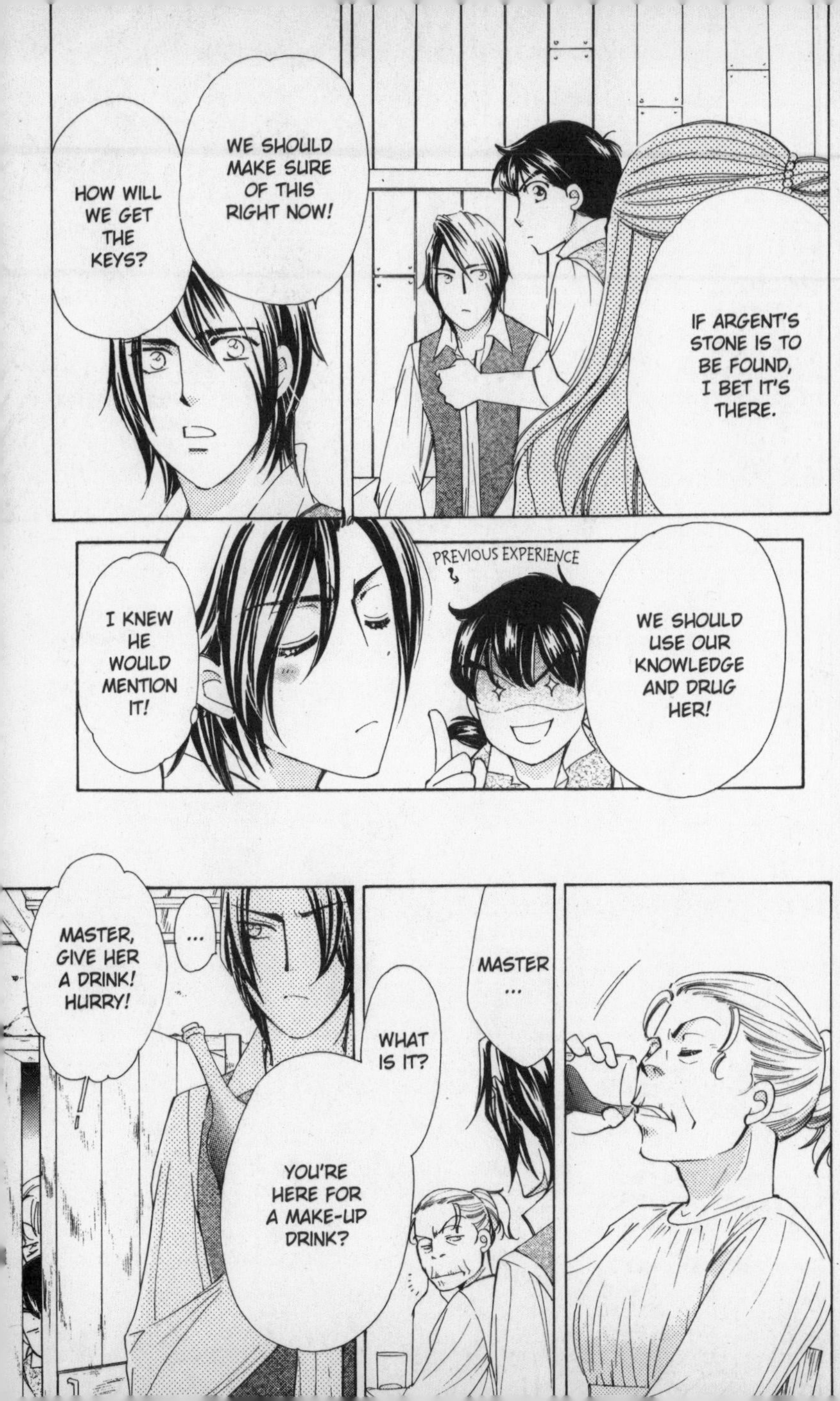
IF ARGENT'S STONE IS TO BE FOUND, I BET IT'S THERE.
WE SHOULD MAKE SURE OF THIS RIGHT NOW!
HOW WILL WE GET THE KEYS?
WE SHOULD USE OUR KNOWLEDGE AND DRUG HER!
PREVIOUS EXPERIENCE
I KNEW HE WOULD MENTION IT!
MASTER ...
WHAT IS IT?
YOU'RE HERE FOR A MAKE-UP DRINK?
...
MASTER, GIVE HER A DRINK! HURRY!

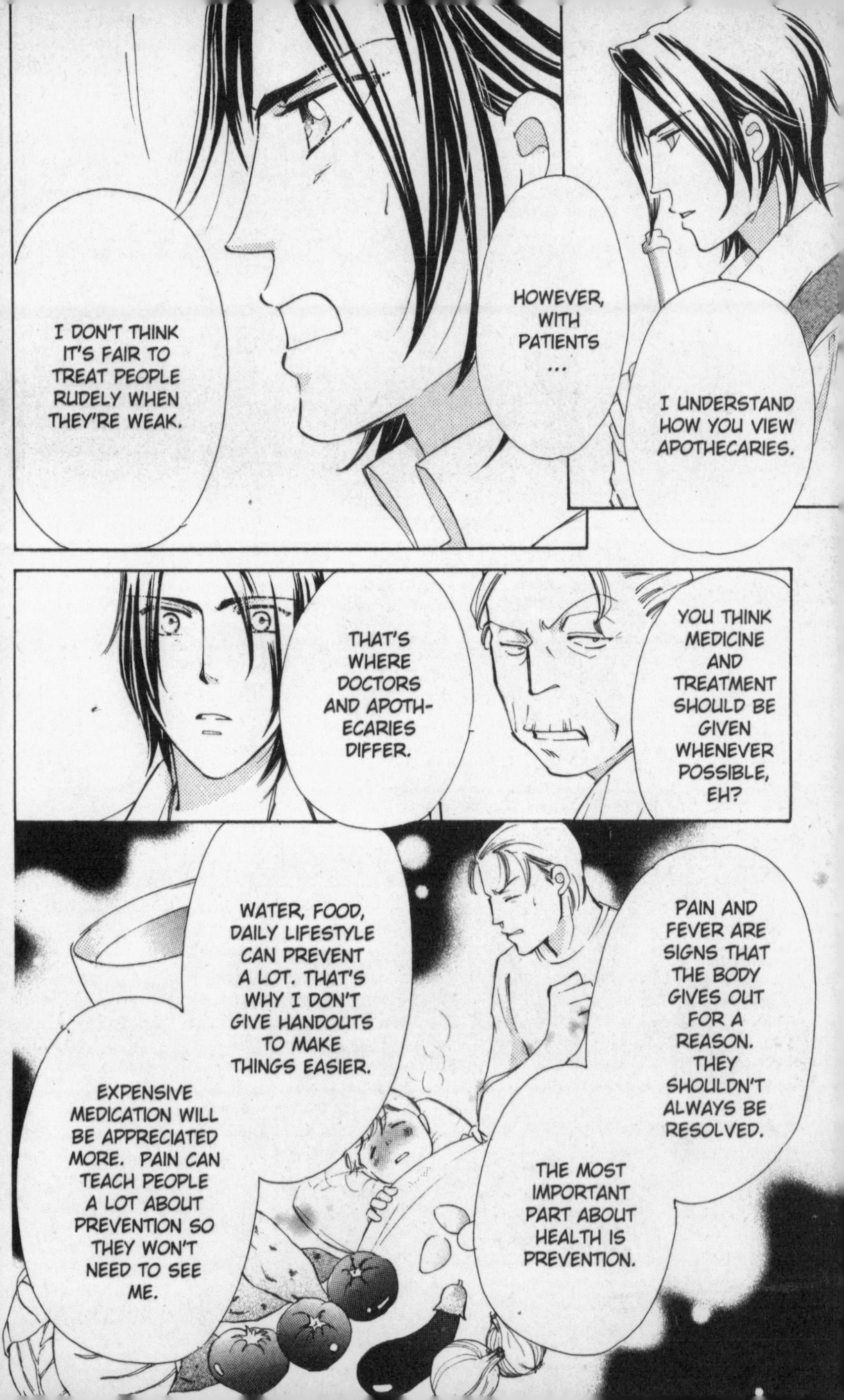
I UNDERSTAND HOW YOU VIEW APOTHECARIES.
HOWEVER, WITH PATIENTS...
I DON'T THINK IT'S FAIR TO TREAT PEOPLE RUDELY WHEN THEY'RE WEAK.
YOU THINK MEDICINE AND TREATMENT SHOULD BE GIVEN WHENEVER POSSIBLE, EH?
THAT'S WHERE DOCTORS AND APOTH-ECARIES DIFFER.
PAIN AND FEVER ARE SIGNS THAT THE BODY GIVES OUT FOR A REASON. THEY SHOULDN'T ALWAYS BE RESOLVED.
THE MOST IMPORTANT PART ABOUT HEALTH IS PREVENTION.
WATER, FOOD, DAILY LIFESTYLE CAN PREVENT A LOT. THAT'S WHY I DON'T GIVE HANDOUTS TO MAKE THINGS EASIER.
EXPENSIVE MEDICATION WILL BE APPRECIATED MORE. PAIN CAN TEACH PEOPLE A LOT ABOUT PREVENTION SO THEY WON'T NEED TO SEE ME.

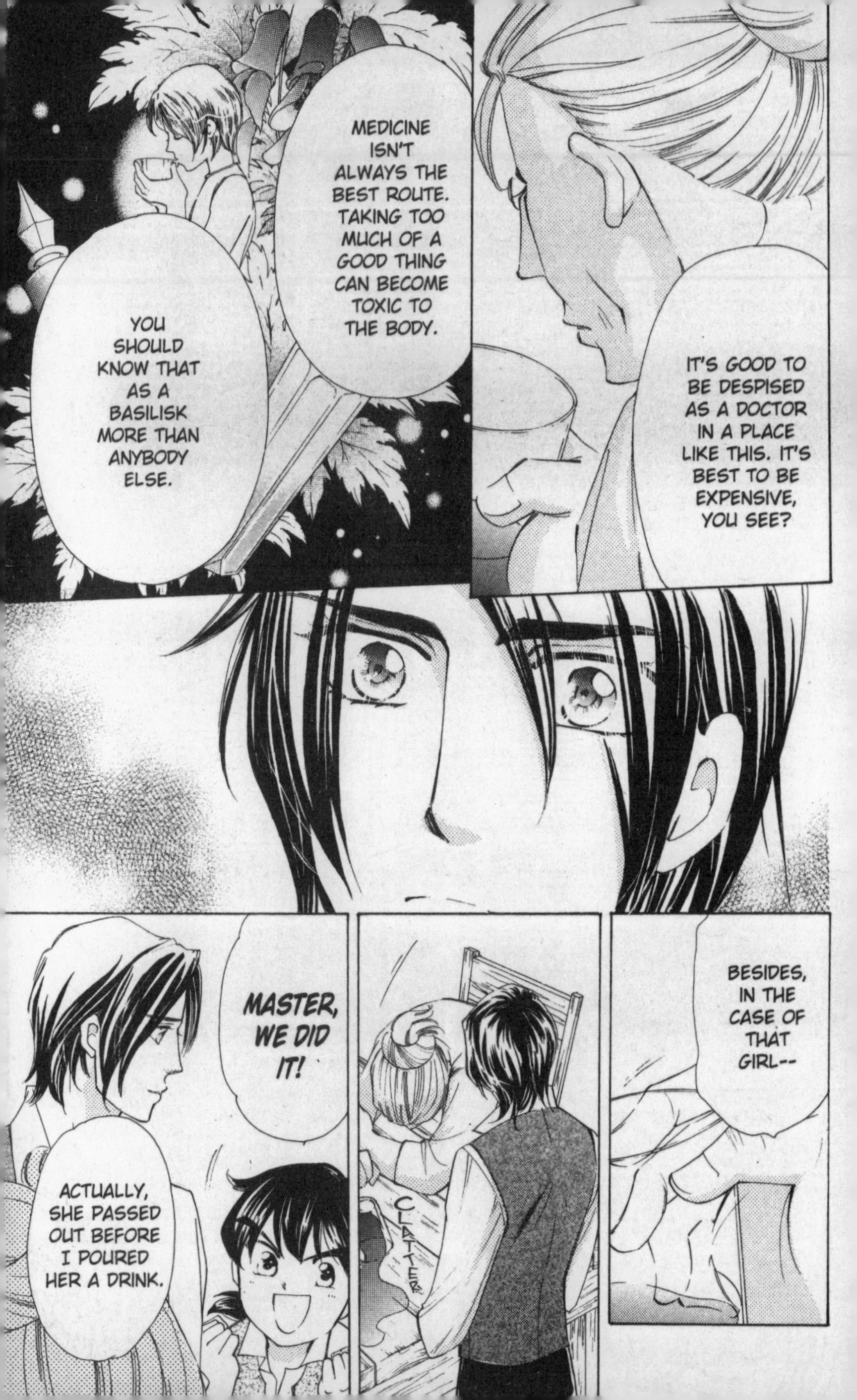
IT'S GOOD TO BE DESPISED AS A DOCTOR IN A PLACE LIKE THIS. IT'S BEST TO BE EXPENSIVE, YOU SEE?
MEDICINE ISN'T ALWAYS THE BEST ROUTE. TAKING TOO MUCH OF A GOOD THING CAN BECOME TOXIC TO THE BODY.
YOU SHOULD KNOW THAT AS A BASILISK MORE THAN ANYBODY ELSE.
BESIDES, IN THE CASE OF THAT GIRL--
CLATTER
MASTER, WE DID IT!
ACTUALLY, SHE PASSED OUT BEFORE I POURED HER A DRINK.

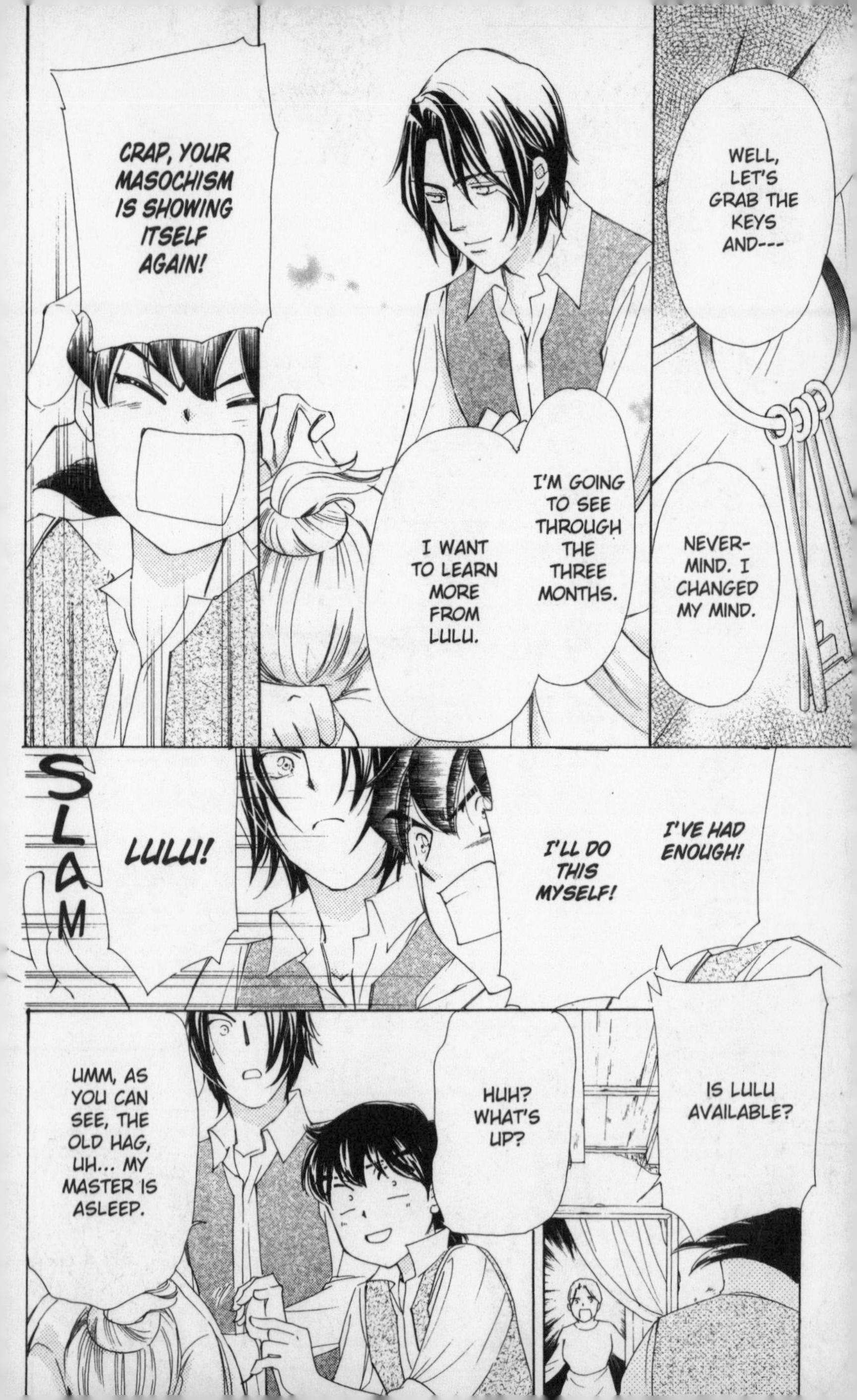
WELL, LET'S GRAB THE KEYS AND---
NEVER-MIND. I CHANGED MY MIND.
I'M GOING TO SEE THROUGH THE THREE MONTHS.
I WANT TO LEARN MORE FROM LULU.
CRAP, YOUR MASOCHISM IS SHOWING ITSELF AGAIN!
I'VE HAD ENOUGH!
I'LL DO THIS MYSELF!
LULU!
SLAM
IS LULU AVAILABLE?
HUH? WHAT'S UP?
UMM, AS YOU CAN SEE, THE OLD HAG, UH... MY MASTER IS ASLEEP.

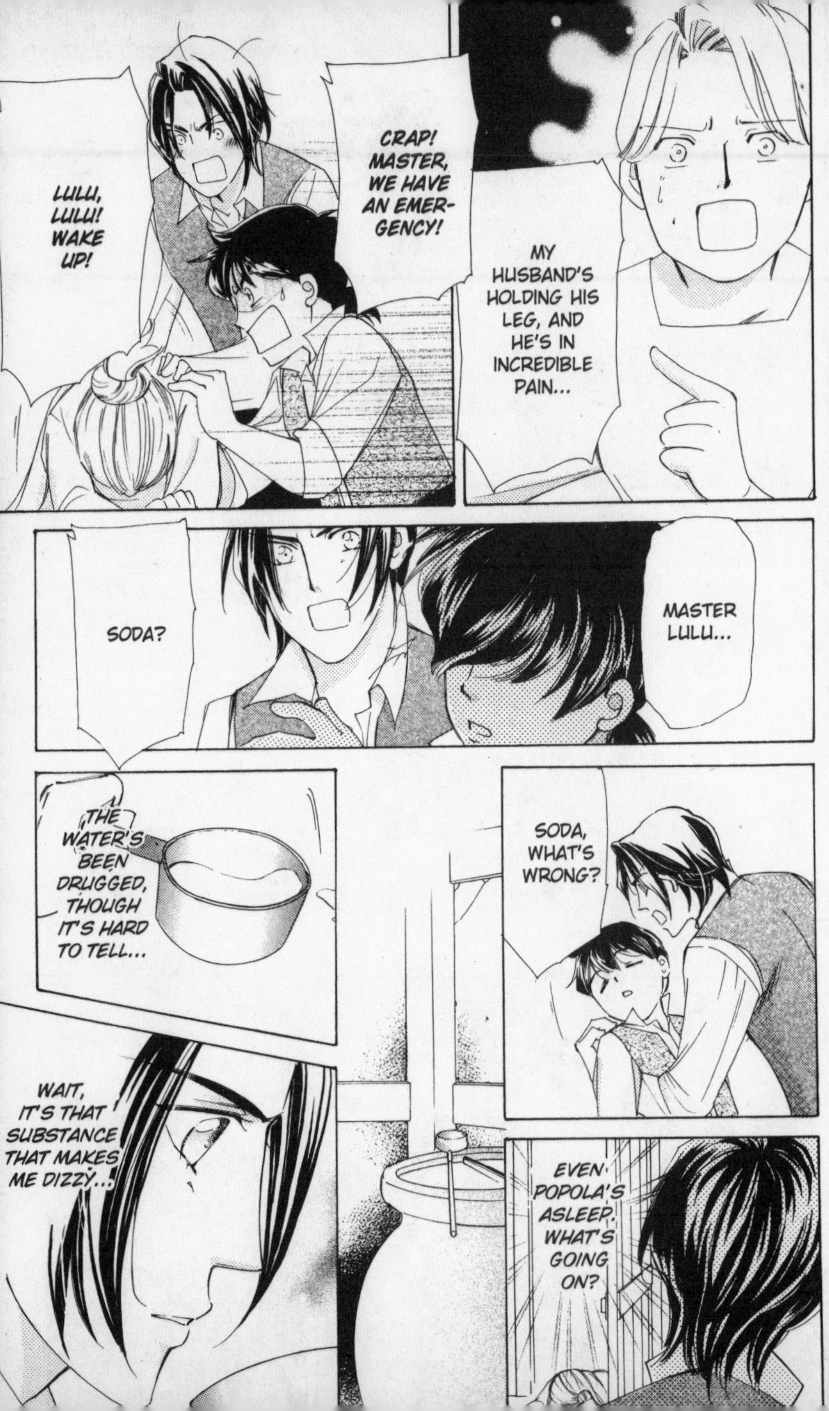
MY HUSBAND'S HOLDING HIS LEG, AND HE'S IN INCREDIBLE PAIN...
CRAP! MASTER, WE HAVE AN EMERGENCY!
LULU, LULU! WAKE UP!
MASTER LULU...
SODA?
SODA, WHAT'S WRONG?
EVEN POPOLA'S ASLEEP. WHAT'S GOING ON?
THE WATER'S BEEN DRUGGED, THOUGH IT'S HARD TO TELL...
WAIT, IT'S THAT SUBSTANCE THAT MAKES ME DIZZY...

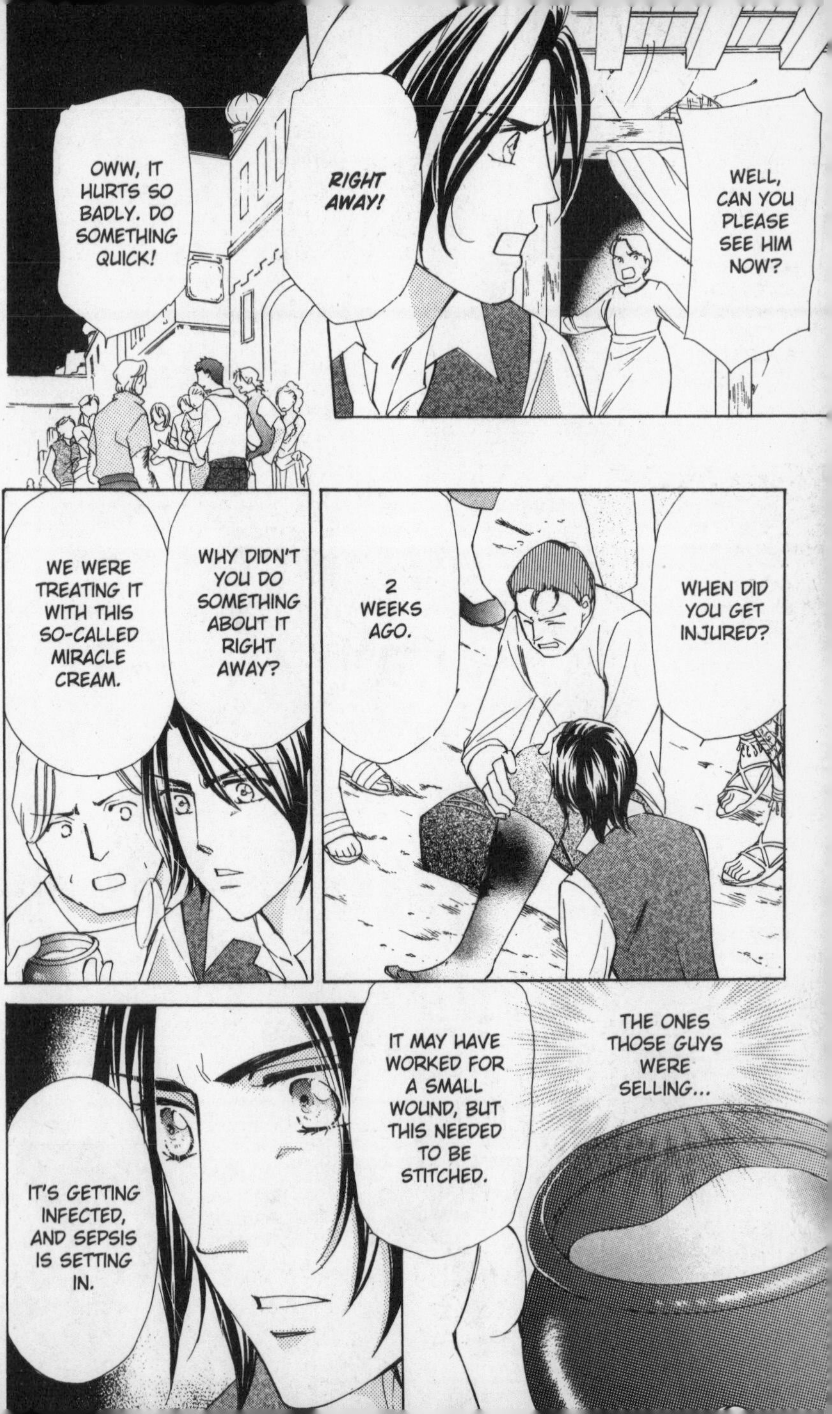
WELL, CAN YOU PLEASE SEE HIM NOW?
RIGHT AWAY!
OWW, IT HURTS SO BADLY. DO SOMETHING QUICK!
WHEN DID YOU GET INJURED?
2 WEEKS AGO.
WHY DIDN'T YOU DO SOMETHING ABOUT IT RIGHT AWAY?
WE WERE TREATING IT WITH THIS SO-CALLED MIRACLE CREAM.
THE ONES THOSE GUYS WERE SELLING...
IT MAY HAVE WORKED FOR A SMALL WOUND, BUT THIS NEEDED TO BE STITCHED.
IT'S GETTING INFECTED, AND SEPSIS IS SETTING IN.

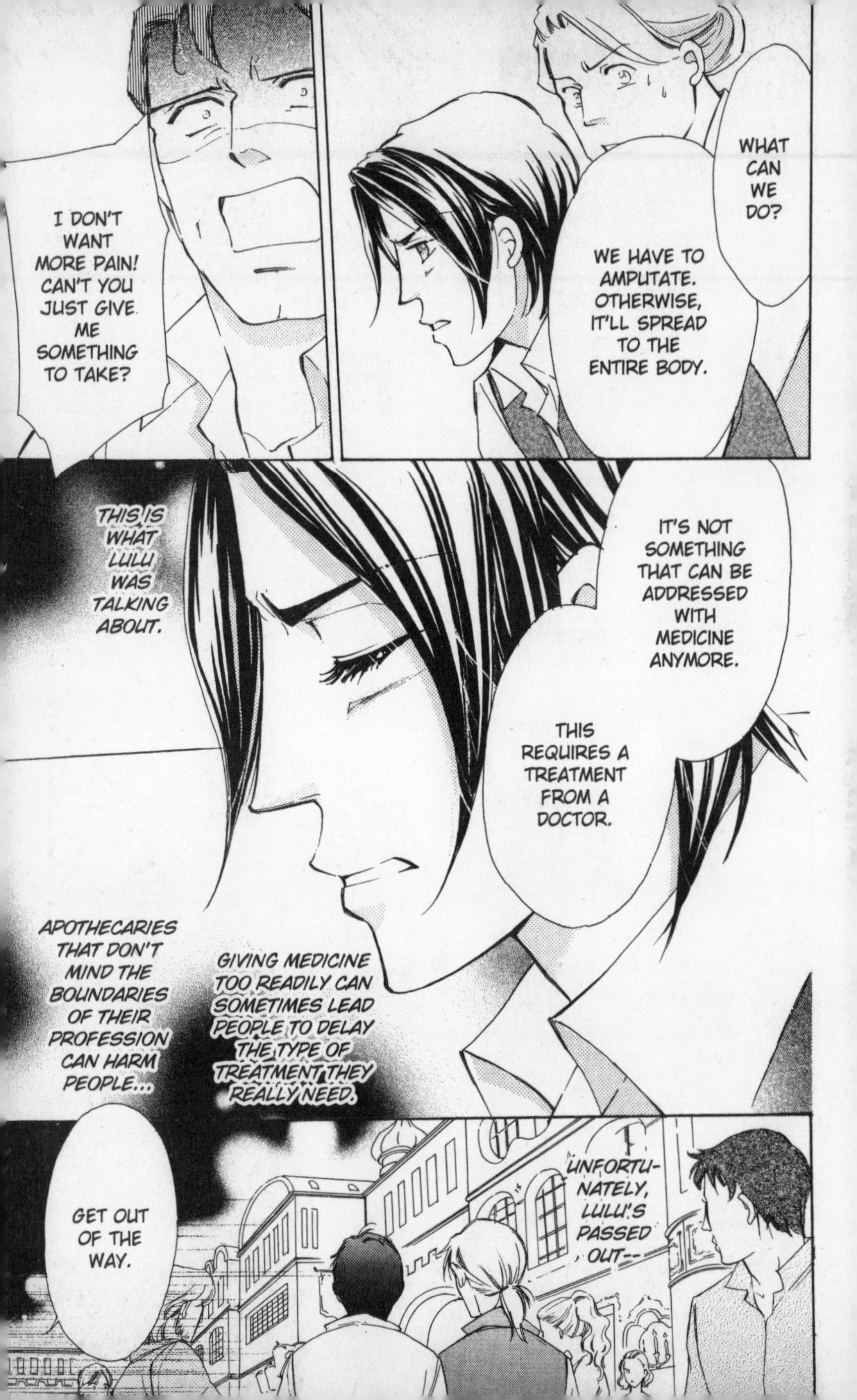
WHAT CAN WE DO?
WE HAVE TO AMPUTATE. OTHERWISE, IT'LL SPREAD TO THE ENTIRE BODY.
I DON'T WANT MORE PAIN! CAN'T YOU JUST GIVE ME SOMETHING TO TAKE?
IT'S NOT SOMETHING THAT CAN BE ADDRESSED WITH MEDICINE ANYMORE.
THIS REQUIRES A TREATMENT FROM A DOCTOR.
THIS IS WHAT LULU WAS TALKING ABOUT.
GIVING MEDICINE TOO READILY CAN SOMETIMES LEAD PEOPLE TO DELAY THE TYPE OF TREATMENT THEY REALLY NEED.
APOTHECARIES THAT DON'T MIND THE BOUNDARIES OF THEIR PROFESSION CAN HARM PEOPLE...
UNFORTU-NATELY, LULU'S PASSED OUT--
GET OUT OF THE WAY.

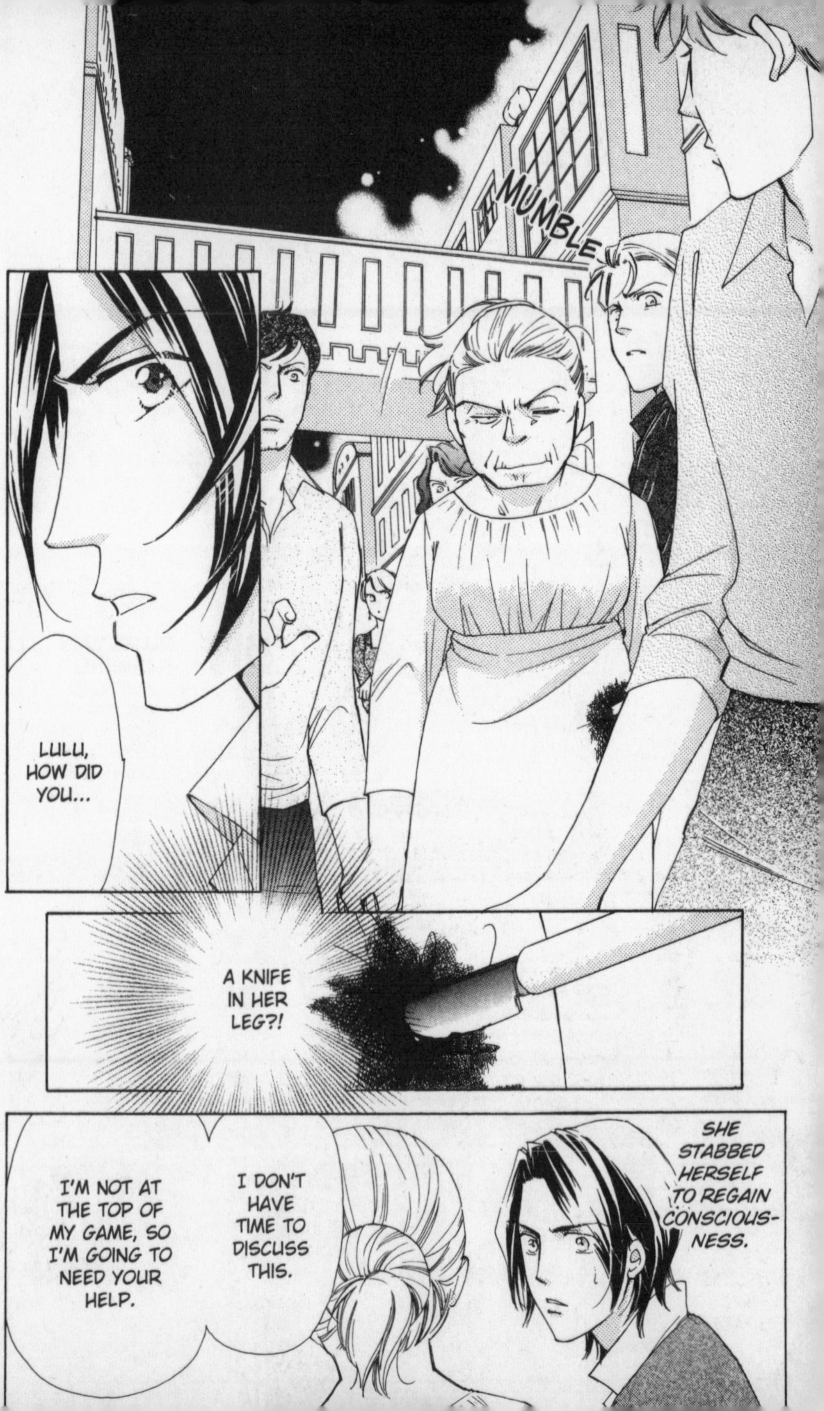

MUMBLE
LULU, HOW DID YOU...
A KNIFE IN HER LEG?!
SHE STABBED HERSELF TO REGAIN CONSCIOUS-NESS.
I DON'T HAVE TIME TO DISCUSS THIS.
I'M NOT AT THE TOP OF MY GAME, SO I'M GOING TO NEED YOUR HELP.

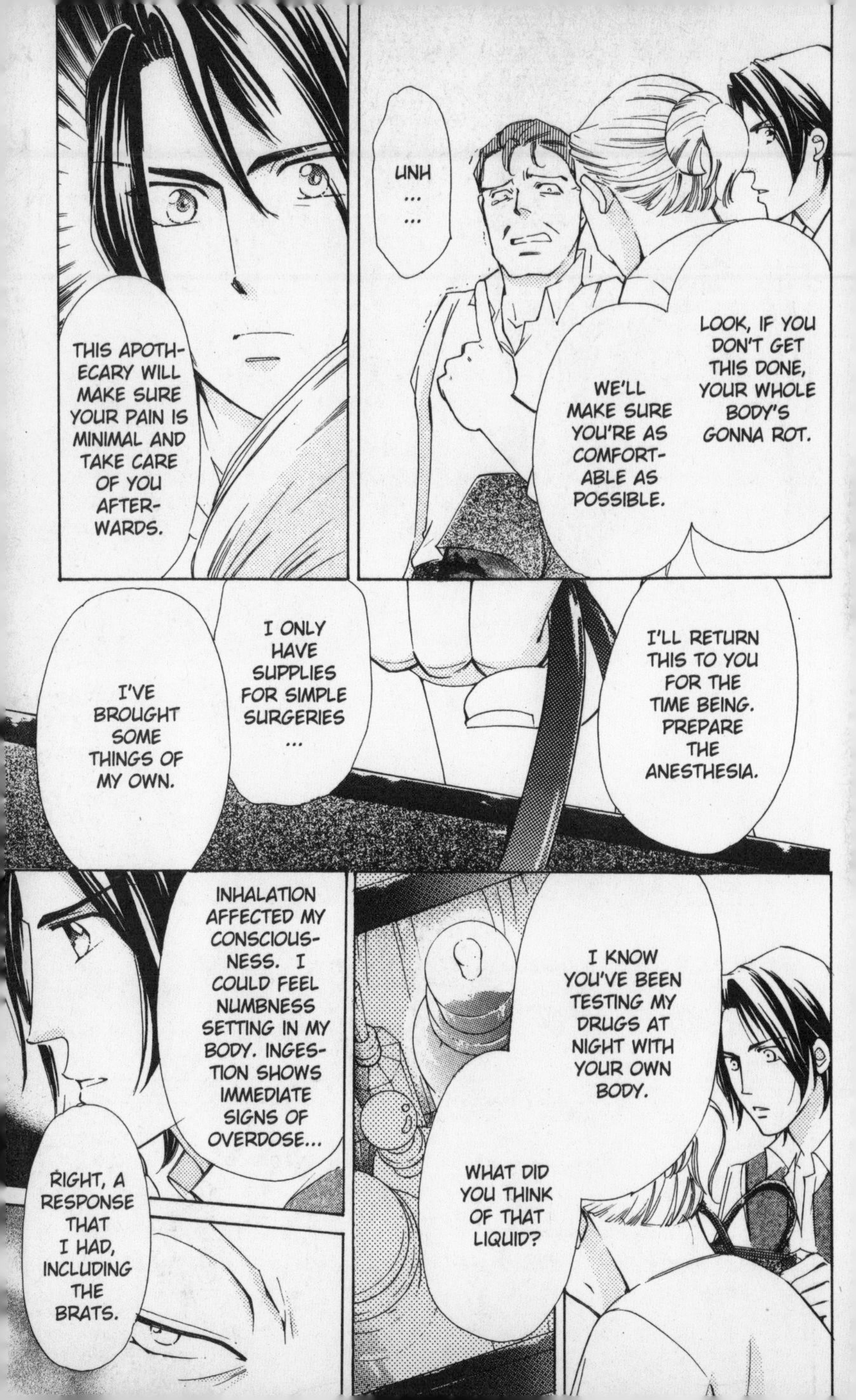
LOOK, IF YOU DON'T GET THIS DONE, YOUR WHOLE BODY'S GONNA ROT.
WE'LL MAKE SURE YOU'RE AS COMFORTABLE AS POSSIBLE.
UNH ... ...
THIS APOTHECARY WILL MAKE SURE YOUR PAIN IS MINIMAL AND TAKE CARE OF YOU AFTERWARDS.
I'LL RETURN THIS TO YOU FOR THE TIME BEING. PREPARE THE ANESTHESIA.
I ONLY HAVE SUPPLIES FOR SIMPLE SURGERIES ...
I'VE BROUGHT SOME THINGS OF MY OWN.
I KNOW YOU'VE BEEN TESTING MY DRUGS AT NIGHT WITH YOUR OWN BODY.
WHAT DID YOU THINK OF THAT LIQUID?
INHALATION AFFECTED MY CONSCIOUSNESS. I COULD FEEL NUMBNESS SETTING IN MY BODY. INGESTION SHOWS IMMEDIATE SIGNS OF OVERDOSE...
RIGHT, A RESPONSE THAT I HAD, INCLUDING THE BRATS.

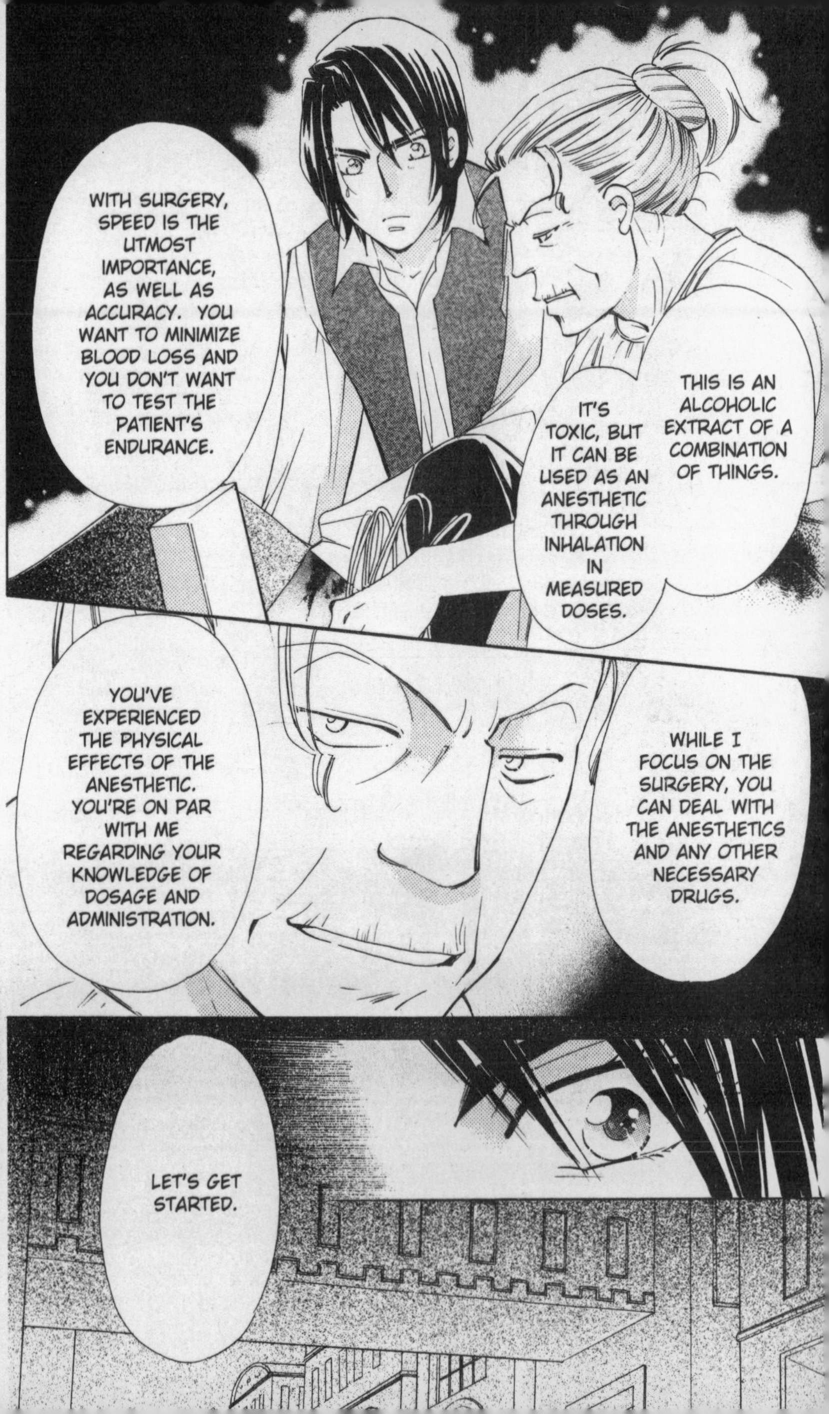
THIS IS AN ALCOHOLIC EXTRACT OF A COMBINATION OF THINGS.
IT'S TOXIC, BUT IT CAN BE USED AS AN ANESTHETIC THROUGH INHALATION IN MEASURED DOSES.
WITH SURGERY, SPEED IS THE UTMOST IMPORTANCE, AS WELL AS ACCURACY. YOU WANT TO MINIMIZE BLOOD LOSS AND YOU DON'T WANT TO TEST THE PATIENT'S ENDURANCE.
WHILE I FOCUS ON THE SURGERY, YOU CAN DEAL WITH THE ANESTHETICS AND ANY OTHER NECESSARY DRUGS.
YOU'VE EXPERIENCED THE PHYSICAL EFFECTS OF THE ANESTHETIC. YOU'RE ON PAR WITH ME REGARDING YOUR KNOWLEDGE OF DOSAGE AND ADMINISTRATION.
LET'S GET STARTED.

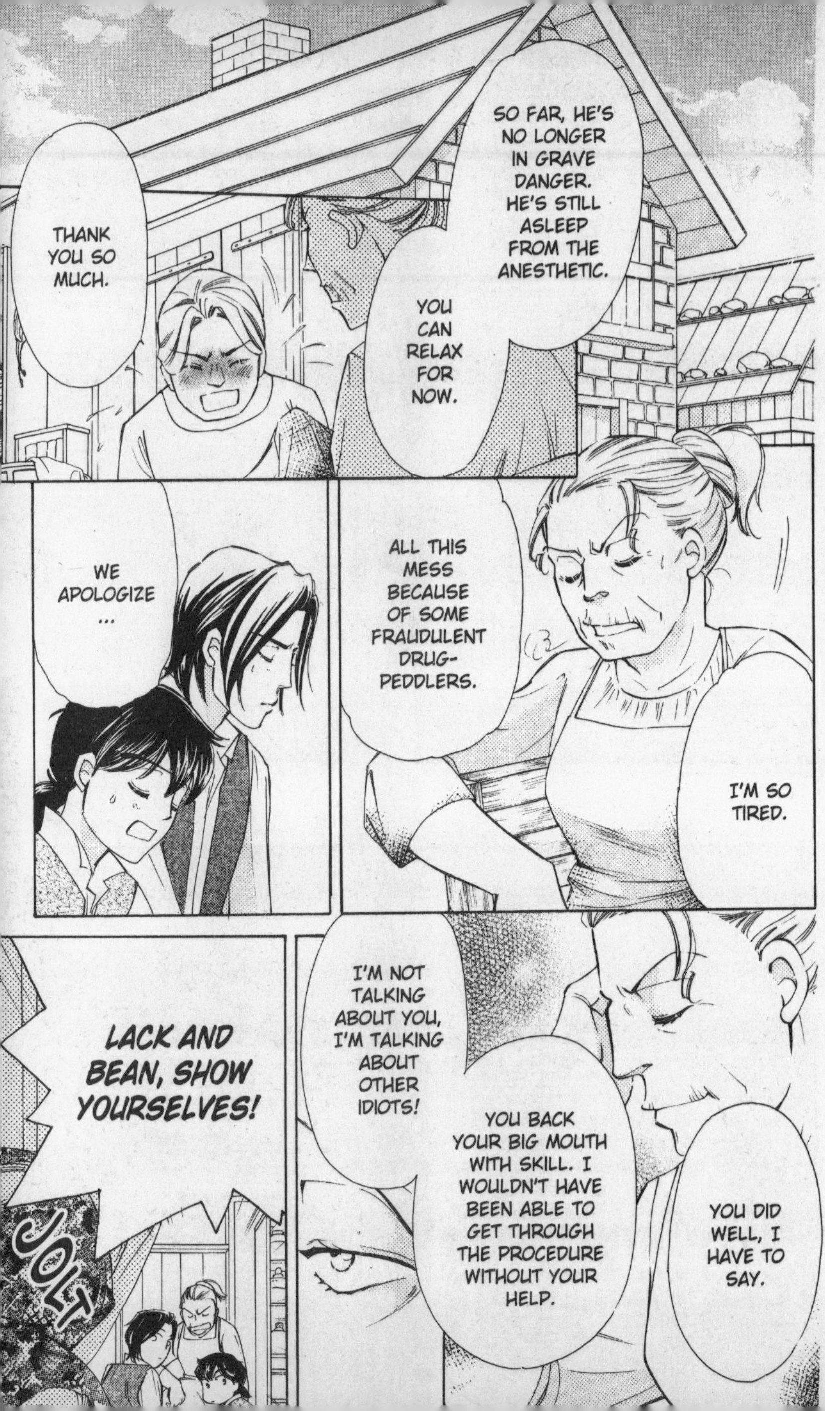
SO FAR, HE'S NO LONGER IN GRAVE DANGER. HE'S STILL ASLEEP FROM THE ANESTHETIC.
YOU CAN RELAX FOR NOW.
THANK YOU SO MUCH.
ALL THIS MESS BECAUSE OF SOME FRAUDULENT DRUG-PEDDLERS.
I'M SO TIRED.
WE APOLOGIZE ...
I'M NOT TALKING ABOUT YOU, I'M TALKING ABOUT OTHER IDIOTS!
YOU DID WELL, I HAVE TO SAY.
YOU BACK YOUR BIG MOUTH WITH SKILL. I WOULDN'T HAVE BEEN ABLE TO GET THROUGH THE PROCEDURE WITHOUT YOUR HELP.
LACK AND BEAN, SHOW YOURSELVES!
JOLT

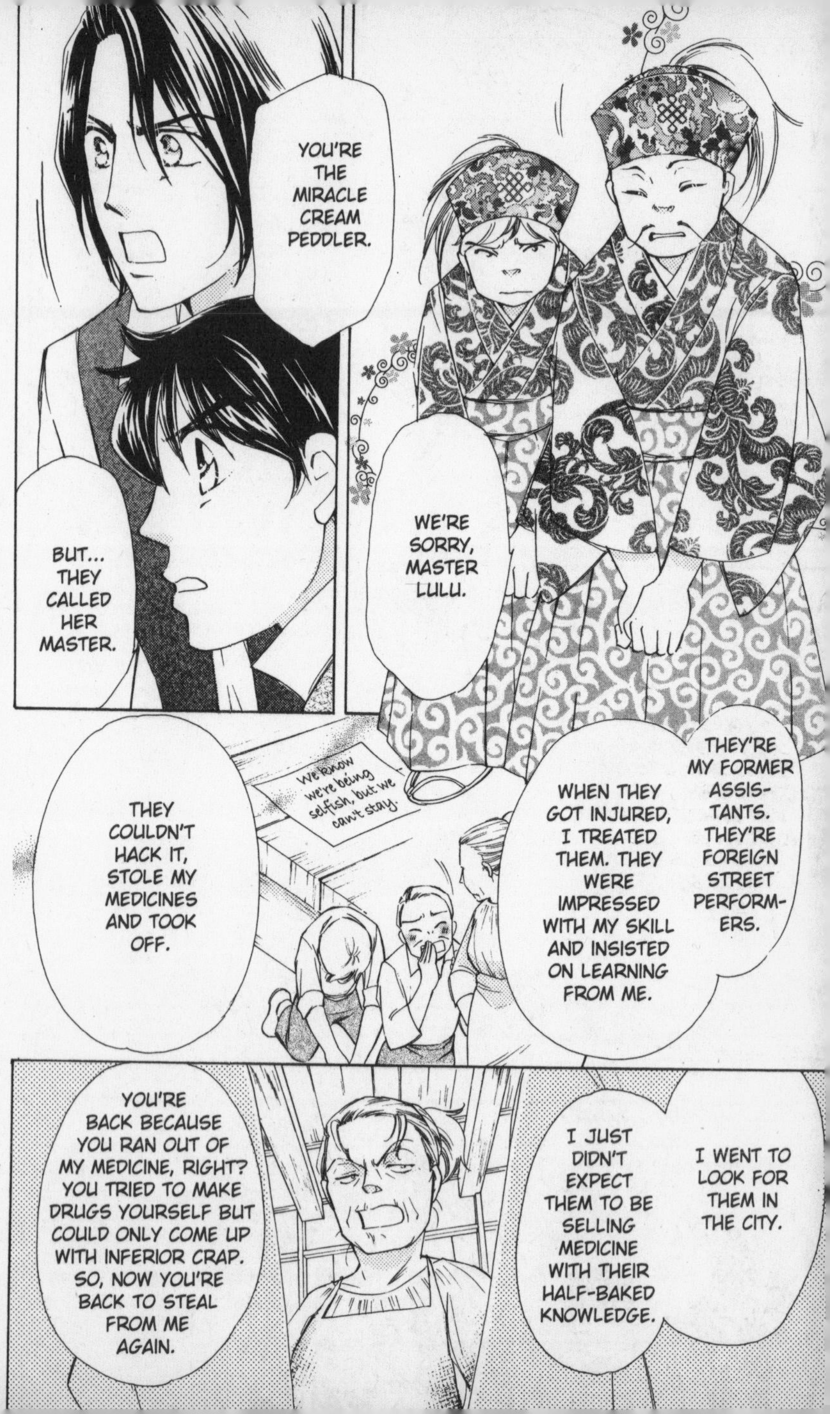
WE'RE SORRY, MASTER LULU.
YOU'RE THE MIRACLE CREAM PEDDLER.
BUT... THEY CALLED HER MASTER.
THEY'RE MY FORMER ASSIS-TANTS. THEY'RE FOREIGN STREET PERFORM-ERS.
WHEN THEY GOT INJURED, I TREATED THEM. THEY WERE IMPRESSED WITH MY SKILL AND INSISTED ON LEARNING FROM ME.
We know we're being selfish, but we can't stay.
THEY COULDN'T HACK IT, STOLE MY MEDICINES AND TOOK OFF.
I WENT TO LOOK FOR THEM IN THE CITY.
I JUST DIDN'T EXPECT THEM TO BE SELLING MEDICINE WITH THEIR HALF-BAKED KNOWLEDGE.
YOU'RE BACK BECAUSE YOU RAN OUT OF MY MEDICINE, RIGHT? YOU TRIED TO MAKE DRUGS YOURSELF BUT COULD ONLY COME UP WITH INFERIOR CRAP. SO, NOW YOU'RE BACK TO STEAL FROM ME AGAIN.

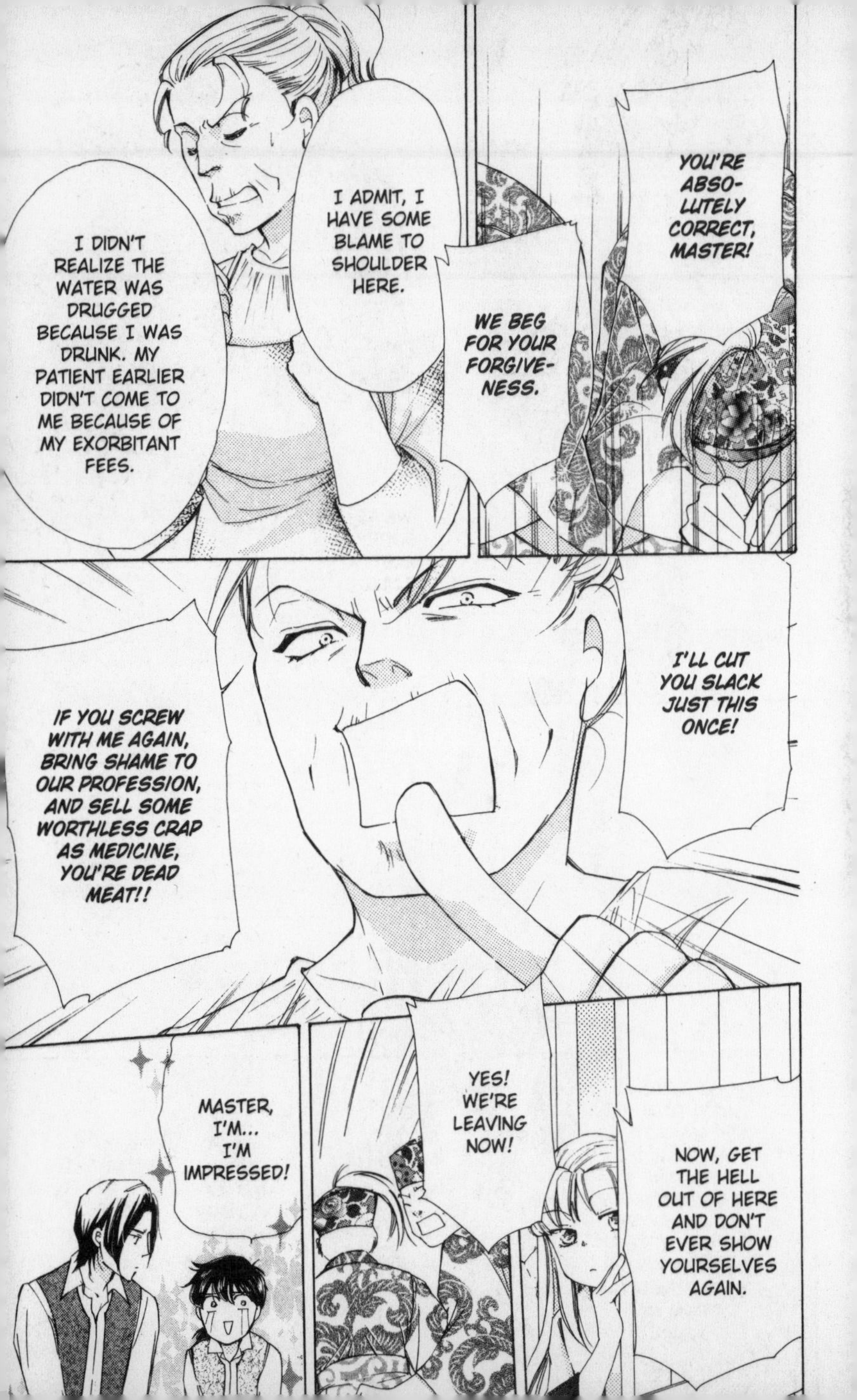
YOU'RE ABSO-LUTELY CORRECT, MASTER!
WE BEG FOR YOUR FORGIVE-NESS.
I ADMIT, I HAVE SOME BLAME TO SHOULDER HERE.
I DIDN'T REALIZE THE WATER WAS DRUGGED BECAUSE I WAS DRUNK. MY PATIENT EARLIER DIDN'T COME TO ME BECAUSE OF MY EXORBITANT FEES.
I'LL CUT YOU SLACK JUST THIS ONCE!
IF YOU SCREW WITH ME AGAIN, BRING SHAME TO OUR PROFESSION, AND SELL SOME WORTHLESS CRAP AS MEDICINE, YOU'RE DEAD MEAT!!
NOW, GET THE HELL OUT OF HERE AND DON'T EVER SHOW YOURSELVES AGAIN.
YES! WE'RE LEAVING NOW!
MASTER, I'M... I'M IMPRESSED!

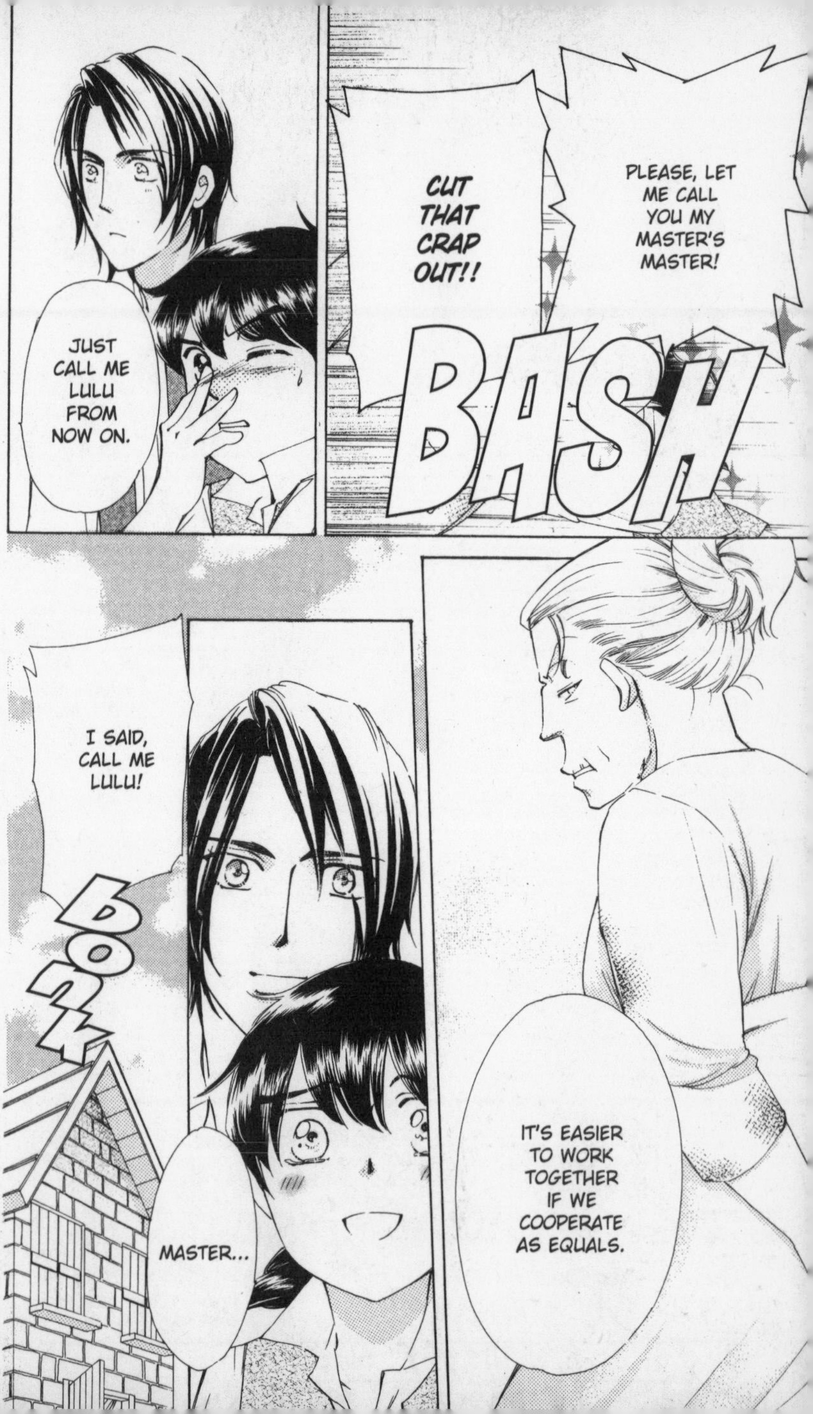
PLEASE, LET ME CALL YOU MY MASTER'S MASTER!
CUT THAT CRAP OUT!!
BASH
JUST CALL ME LULU FROM NOW ON.
IT'S EASIER TO WORK TOGETHER IF WE COOPERATE AS EQUALS.
MASTER...
I SAID, CALL ME LULU!
BONK

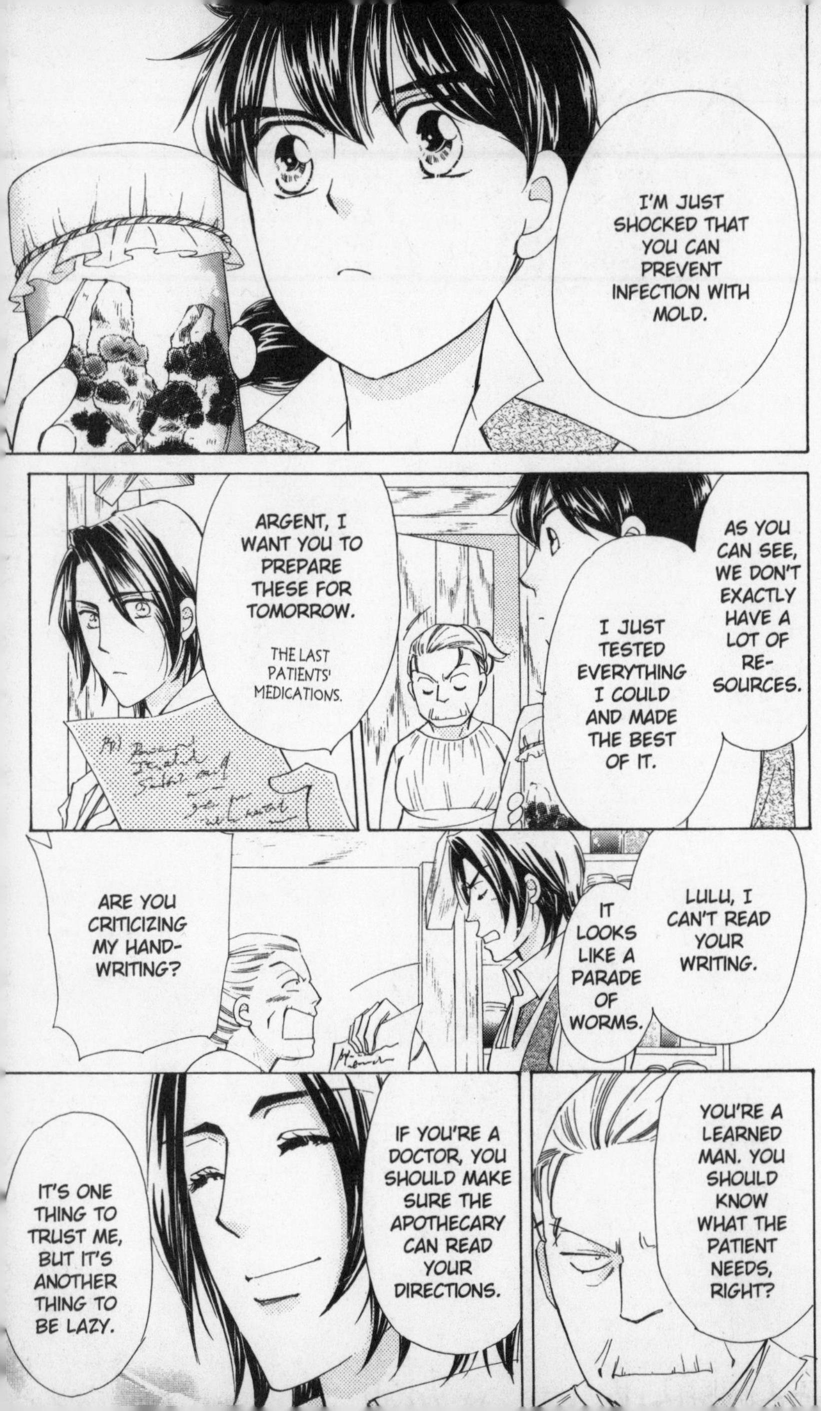
I'M JUST SHOCKED THAT YOU CAN PREVENT INFECTION WITH MOLD.
AS YOU CAN SEE, WE DON'T EXACTLY HAVE A LOT OF RE-SOURCES.
I JUST TESTED EVERYTHING I COULD AND MADE THE BEST OF IT.
ARGENT, I WANT YOU TO PREPARE THESE FOR TOMORROW.
THE LAST PATIENTS' MEDICATIONS.
LULU, I CAN'T READ YOUR WRITING.
IT LOOKS LIKE A PARADE OF WORMS.
ARE YOU CRITICIZING MY HAND-WRITING?
YOU'RE A LEARNED MAN. YOU SHOULD KNOW WHAT THE PATIENT NEEDS, RIGHT?
IF YOU'RE A DOCTOR, YOU SHOULD MAKE SURE THE APOTHECARY CAN READ YOUR DIRECTIONS.
IT'S ONE THING TO TRUST ME, BUT IT'S ANOTHER THING TO BE LAZY.

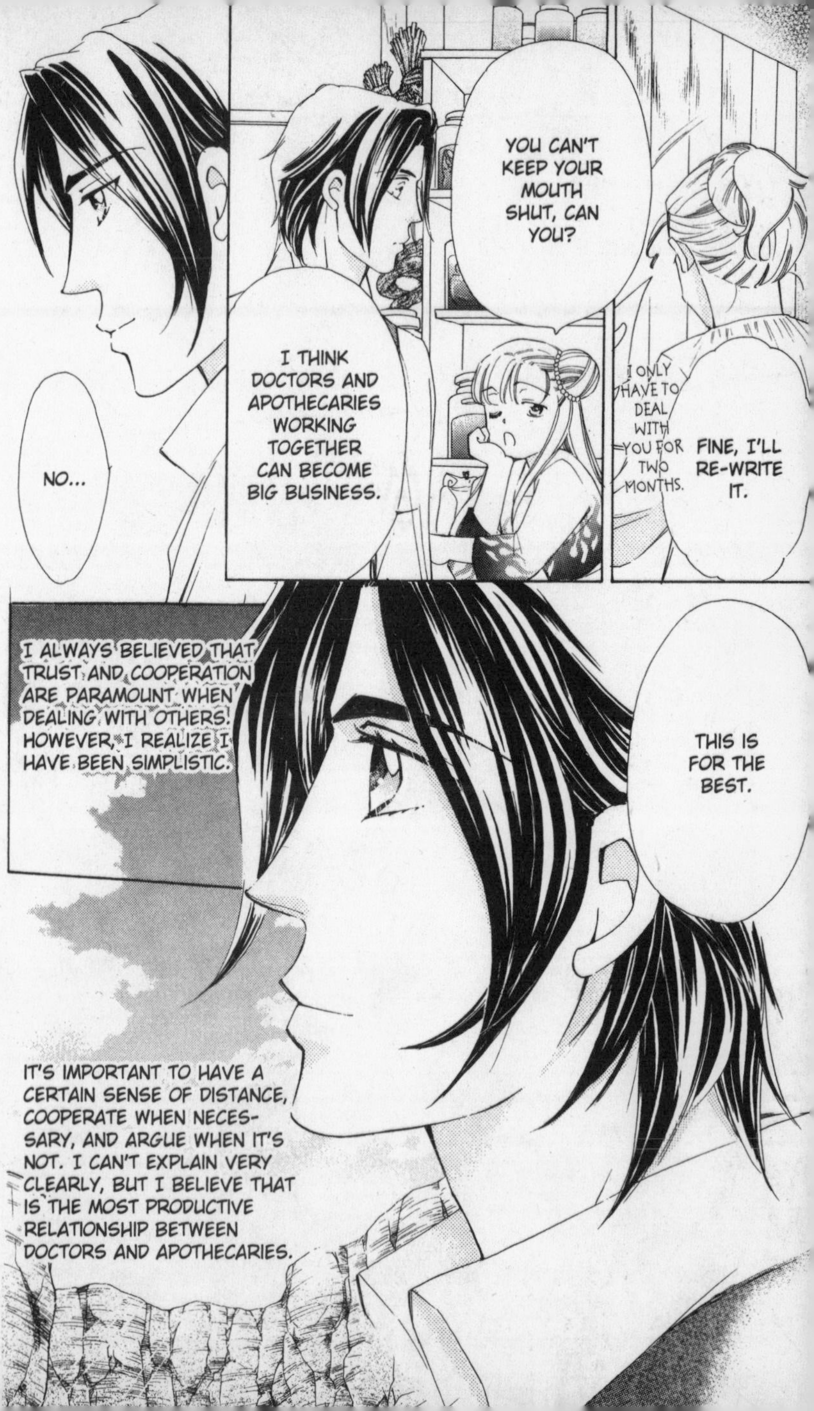
FINE, I'LL RE-WRITE IT.
I ONLY HAVE TO DEAL WITH YOU FOR TWO MONTHS.
YOU CAN'T KEEP YOUR MOUTH SHUT, CAN YOU?
I THINK DOCTORS AND APOTHECARIES WORKING TOGETHER CAN BECOME BIG BUSINESS.
NO...
THIS IS FOR THE BEST.
I ALWAYS BELIEVED THAT TRUST AND COOPERATION ARE PARAMOUNT WHEN DEALING WITH OTHERS. HOWEVER, I REALIZE I HAVE BEEN SIMPLISTIC.
IT'S IMPORTANT TO HAVE A CERTAIN SENSE OF DISTANCE, COOPERATE WHEN NECES-SARY, AND ARGUE WHEN IT'S NOT. I CAN'T EXPLAIN VERY CLEARLY, BUT I BELIEVE THAT IS THE MOST PRODUCTIVE RELATIONSHIP BETWEEN DOCTORS AND APOTHECARIES.

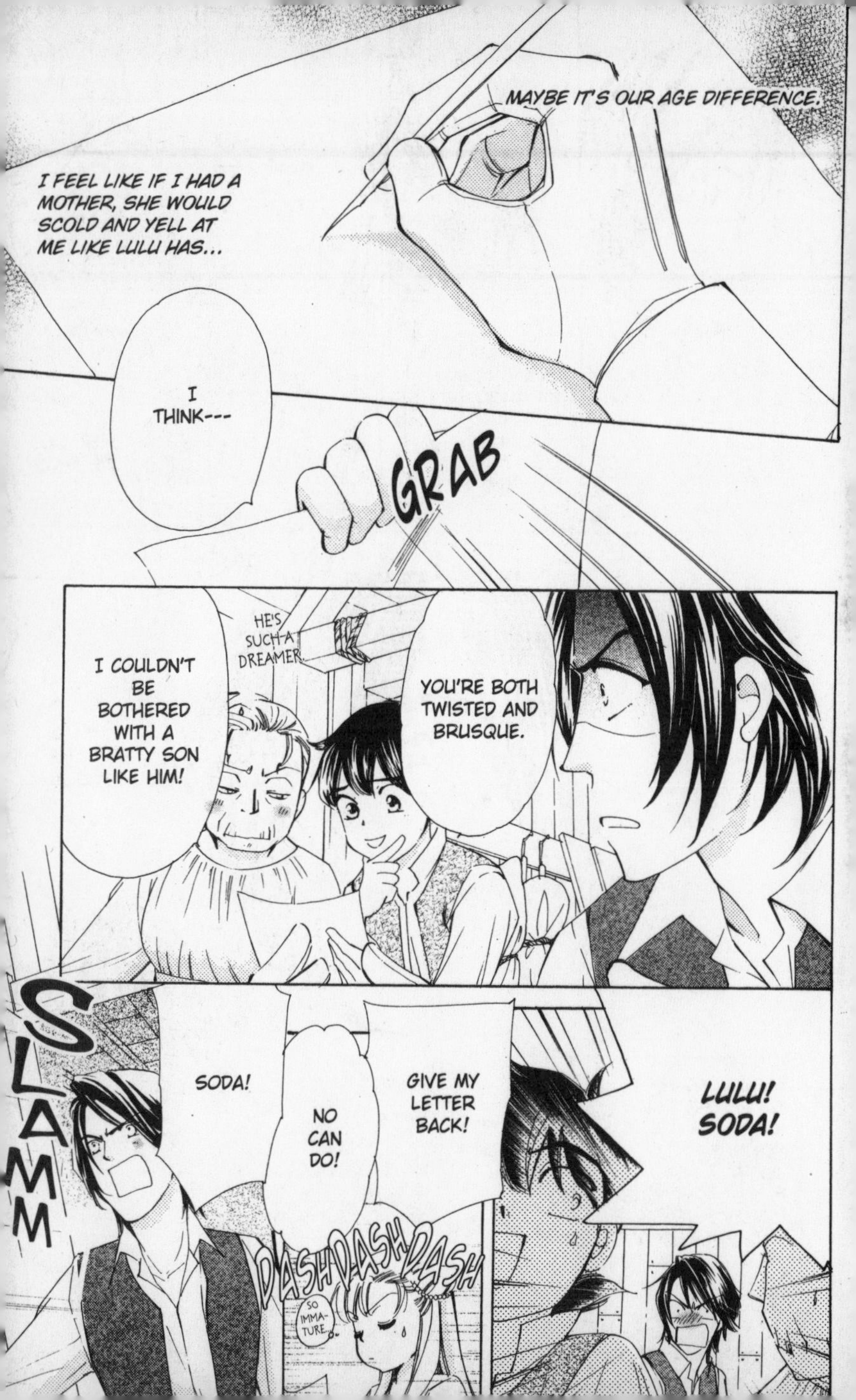
MAYBE IT'S OUR AGE DIFFERENCE.
I FEEL LIKE IF I HAD A MOTHER, SHE WOULD SCOLD AND YELL AT ME LIKE LULU HAS...
I THINK---
GRAB
YOU'RE BOTH TWISTED AND BRUSQUE.
HE'S SUCH A DREAMER.
I COULDN'T BE BOTHERED WITH A BRATTY SON LIKE HIM!
LULU! SODA!
GIVE MY LETTER BACK!
NO CAN DO!
SODA!
SLAMM
DASH DASH DASH
SO IMMATURE...

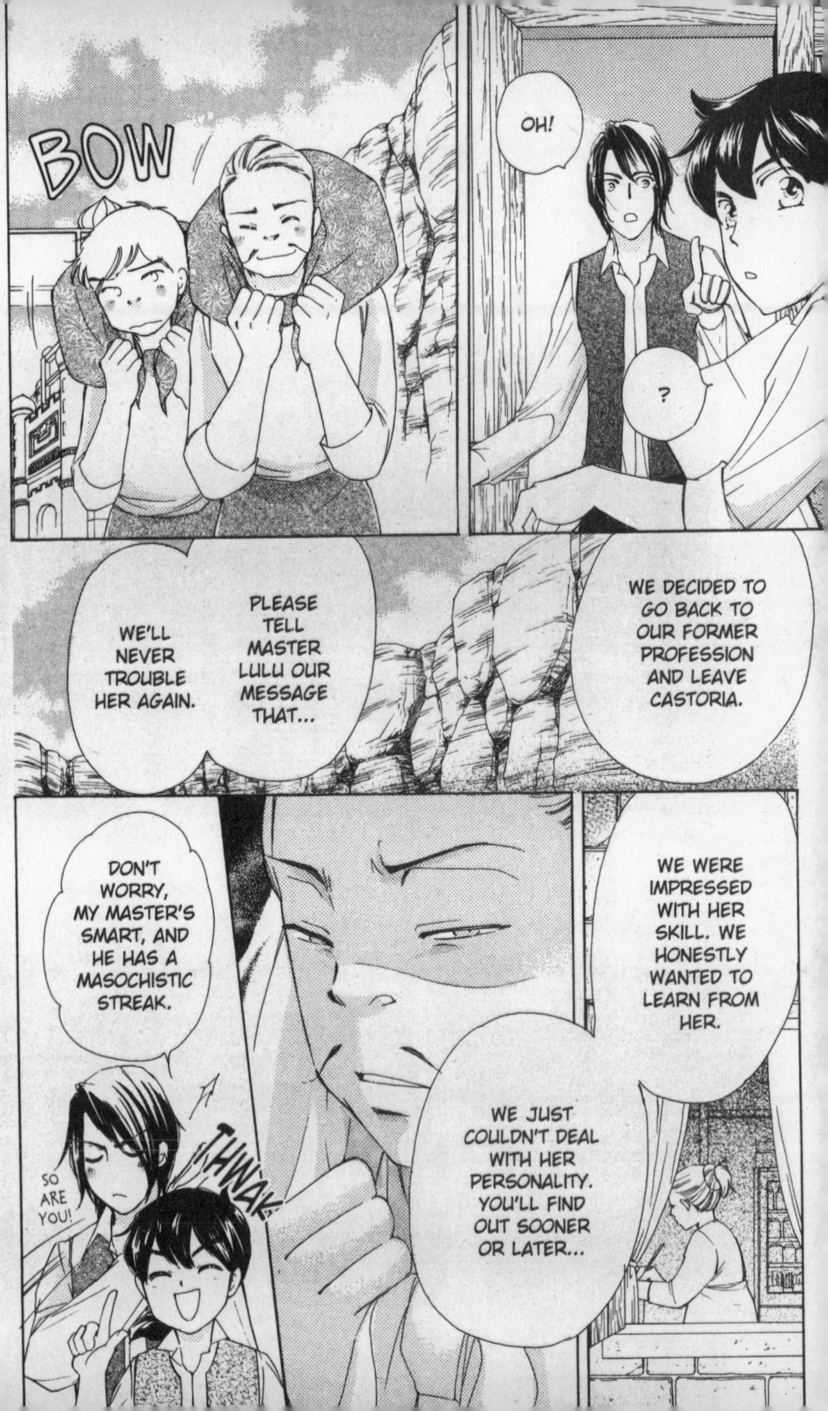
OH!
?
BOW
WE DECIDED TO GO BACK TO OUR FORMER PROFESSION AND LEAVE CASTORIA.
PLEASE TELL MASTER LULU OUR MESSAGE THAT...
WE'LL NEVER TROUBLE HER AGAIN.
WE WERE IMPRESSED WITH HER SKILL. WE HONESTLY WANTED TO LEARN FROM HER.
WE JUST COULDN'T DEAL WITH HER PERSONALITY. YOU'LL FIND OUT SOONER OR LATER...
DON'T WORRY, MY MASTER'S SMART, AND HE HAS A MASOCHISTIC STREAK.
THWAK
SO ARE YOU!

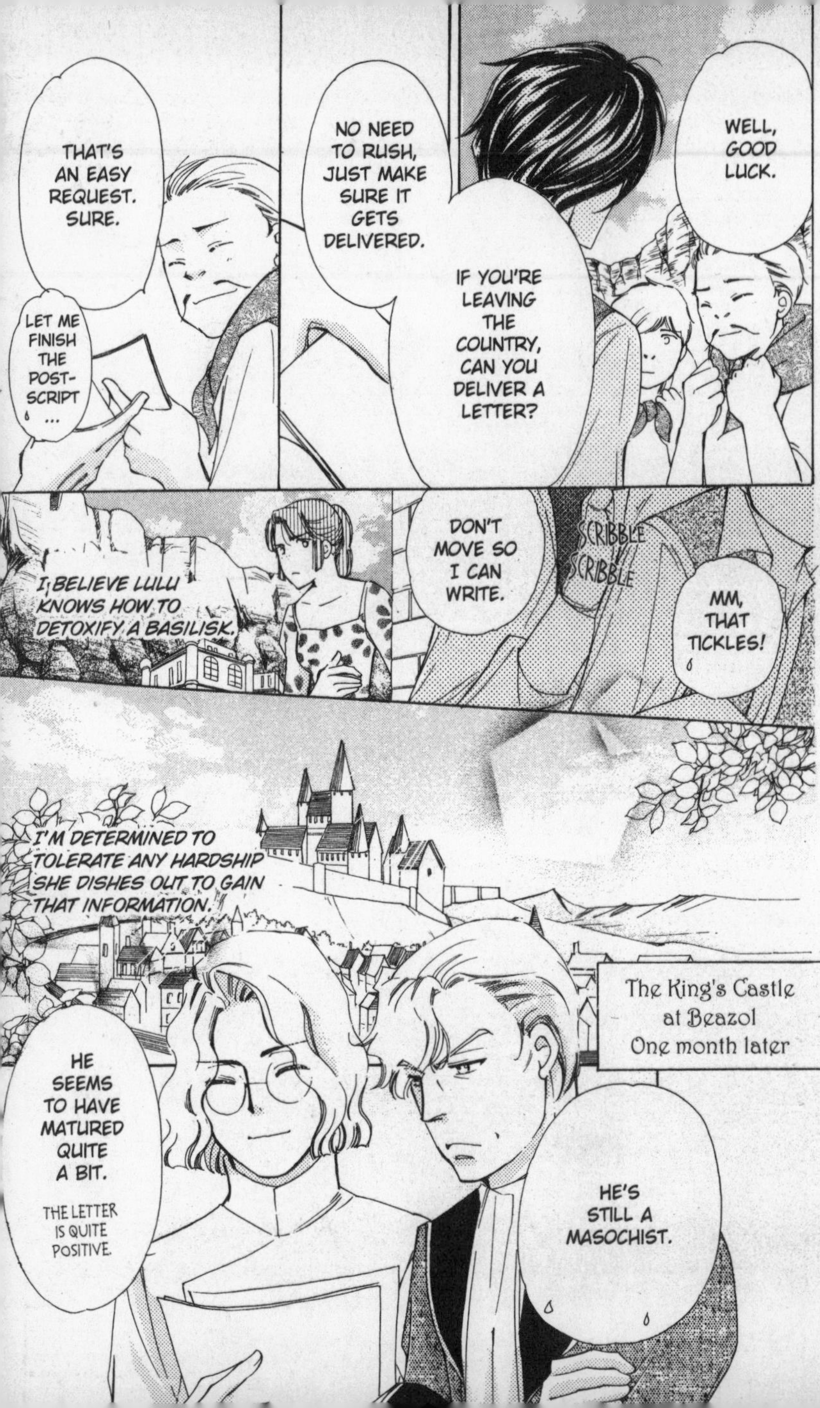
WELL, GOOD LUCK.
IF YOU'RE LEAVING THE COUNTRY, CAN YOU DELIVER A LETTER?
NO NEED TO RUSH, JUST MAKE SURE IT GETS DELIVERED.
THAT'S AN EASY REQUEST. SURE.
LET ME FINISH THE POST-SCRIPT...
MM, THAT TICKLES!
SCRIBBLE SCRIBBLE
DON'T MOVE SO I CAN WRITE.
I BELIEVE LULU KNOWS HOW TO DETOXIFY A BASILISK.
I'M DETERMINED TO TOLERATE ANY HARDSHIP SHE DISHES OUT TO GAIN THAT INFORMATION.
The King's Castle at Beazol One month later
HE SEEMS TO HAVE MATURED QUITE A BIT.
THE LETTER IS QUITE POSITIVE.
HE'S STILL A MASOCHIST.

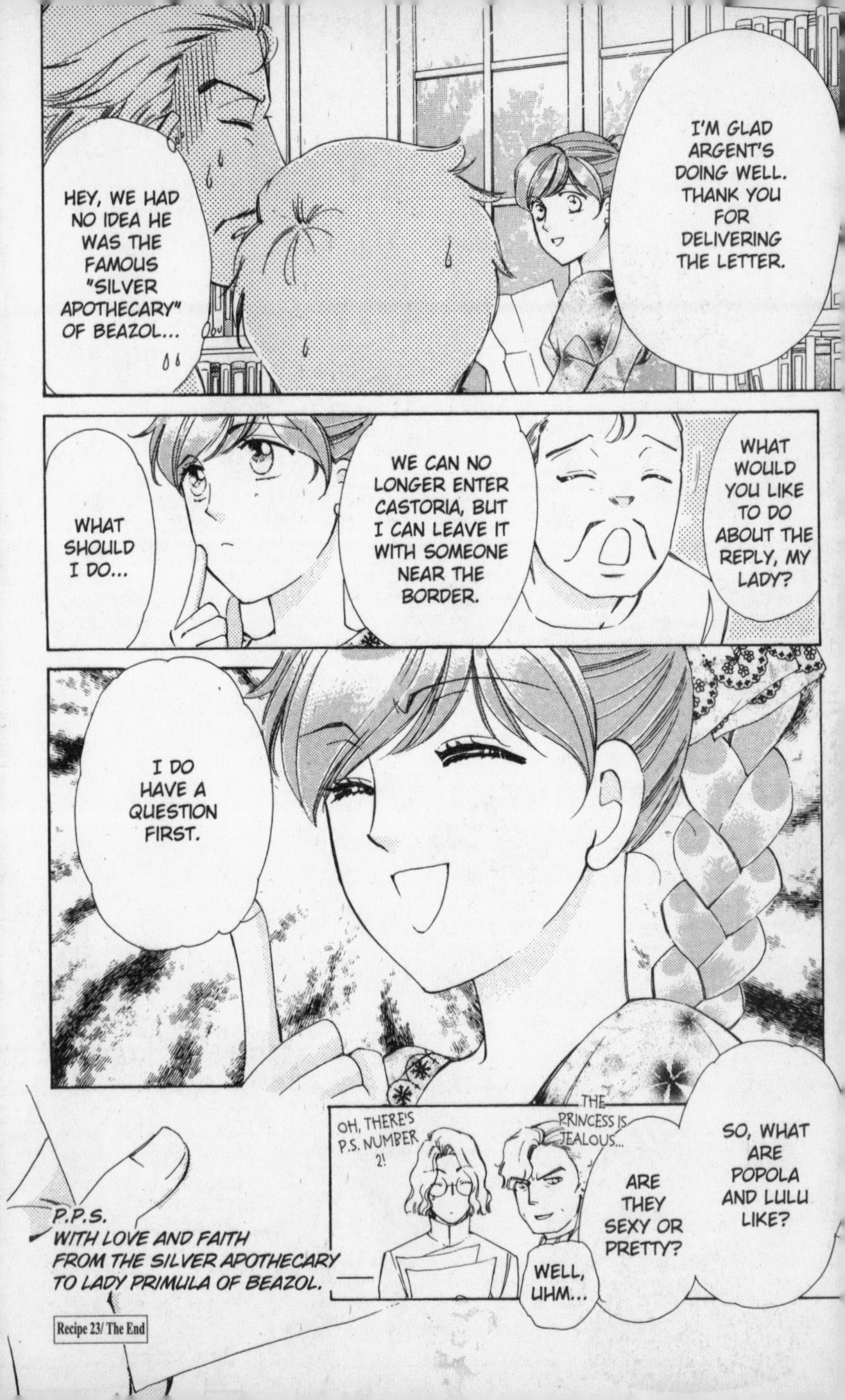
I'M GLAD ARGENT'S DOING WELL. THANK YOU FOR DELIVERING THE LETTER.
HEY, WE HAD NO IDEA HE WAS THE FAMOUS "SILVER APOTHECARY" OF BEAZOL...
WHAT WOULD YOU LIKE TO DO ABOUT THE REPLY, MY LADY?
WE CAN NO LONGER ENTER CASTORIA, BUT I CAN LEAVE IT WITH SOMEONE NEAR THE BORDER.
WHAT SHOULD I DO...
I DO HAVE A QUESTION FIRST.
SO, WHAT ARE POPOLA AND LULU LIKE?
ARE THEY SEXY OR PRETTY?
THE PRINCESS IS JEALOUS...
OH, THERE'S P.S. NUMBER 2!
WELL, UHM...
P.P.S.
WITH LOVE AND FAITH FROM THE SILVER APOTHECARY TO LADY PRIMULA OF BEAZOL.

Recipe 23/ The End

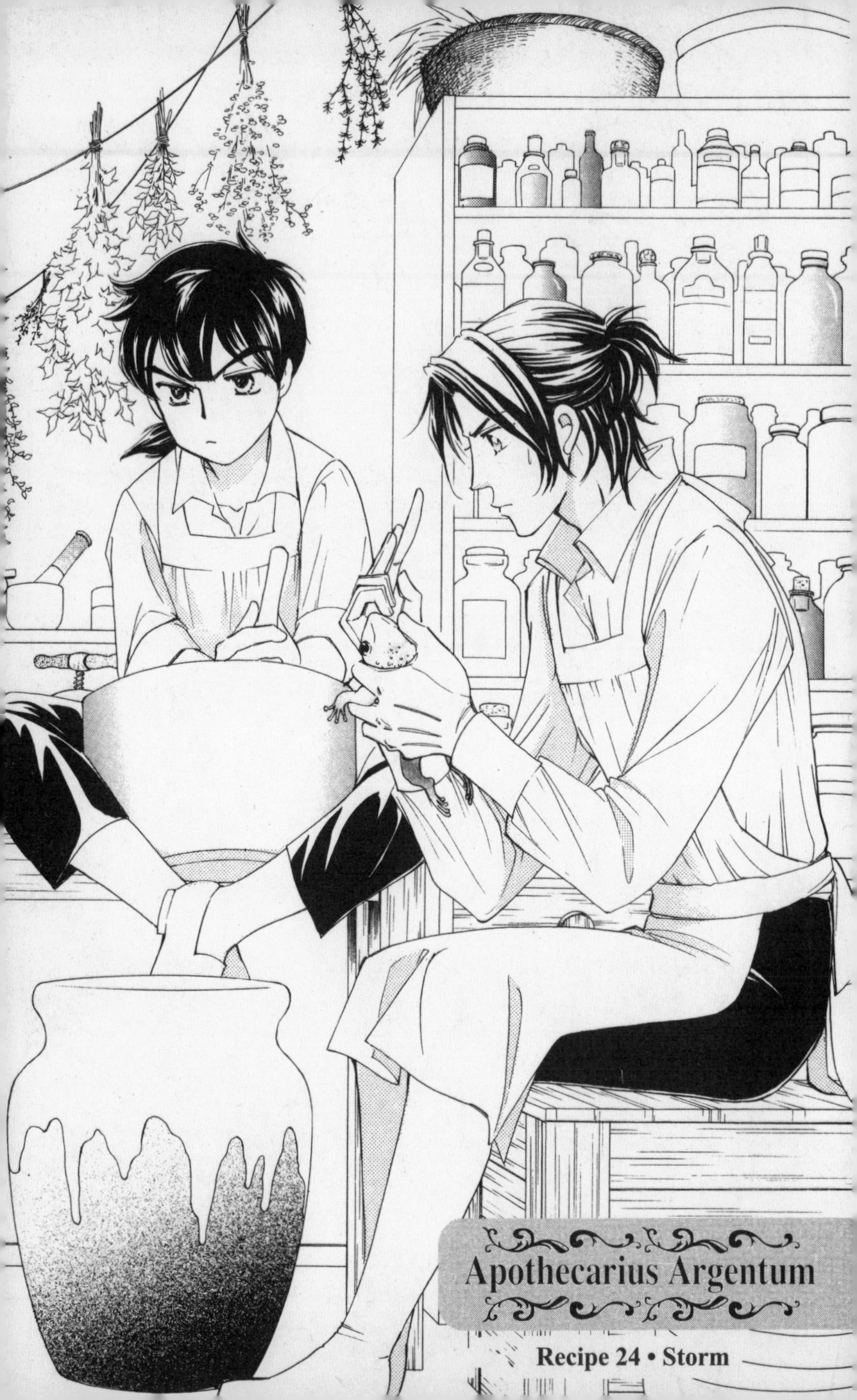
Apothecarius Argentum
Recipe 24 • Storm

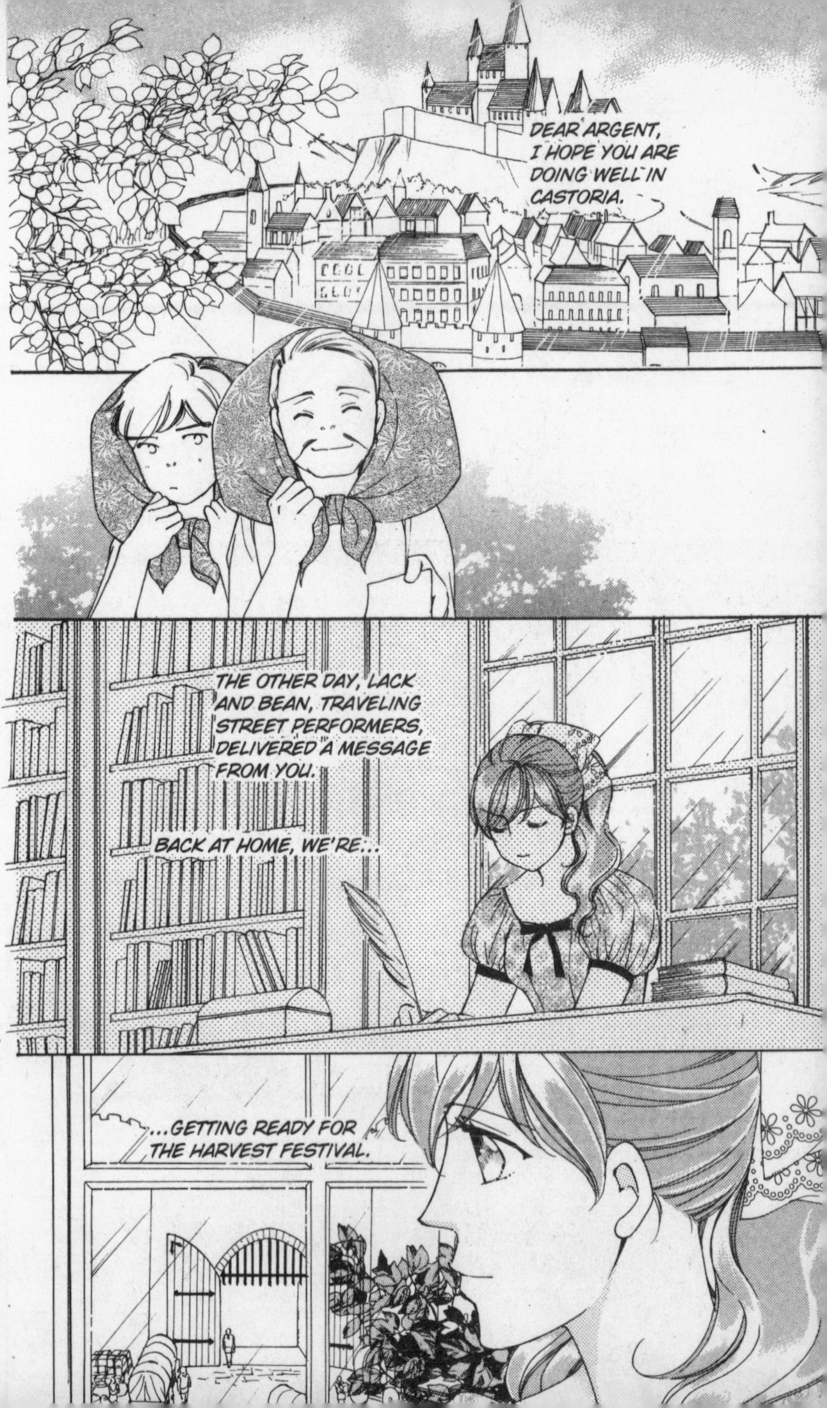
DEAR ARGENT, I HOPE YOU ARE DOING WELL IN CASTORIA.
THE OTHER DAY, LACK AND BEAN, TRAVELING STREET PERFORMERS, DELIVERED A MESSAGE FROM YOU.
BACK AT HOME, WE'RE...
...GETTING READY FOR THE HARVEST FESTIVAL.

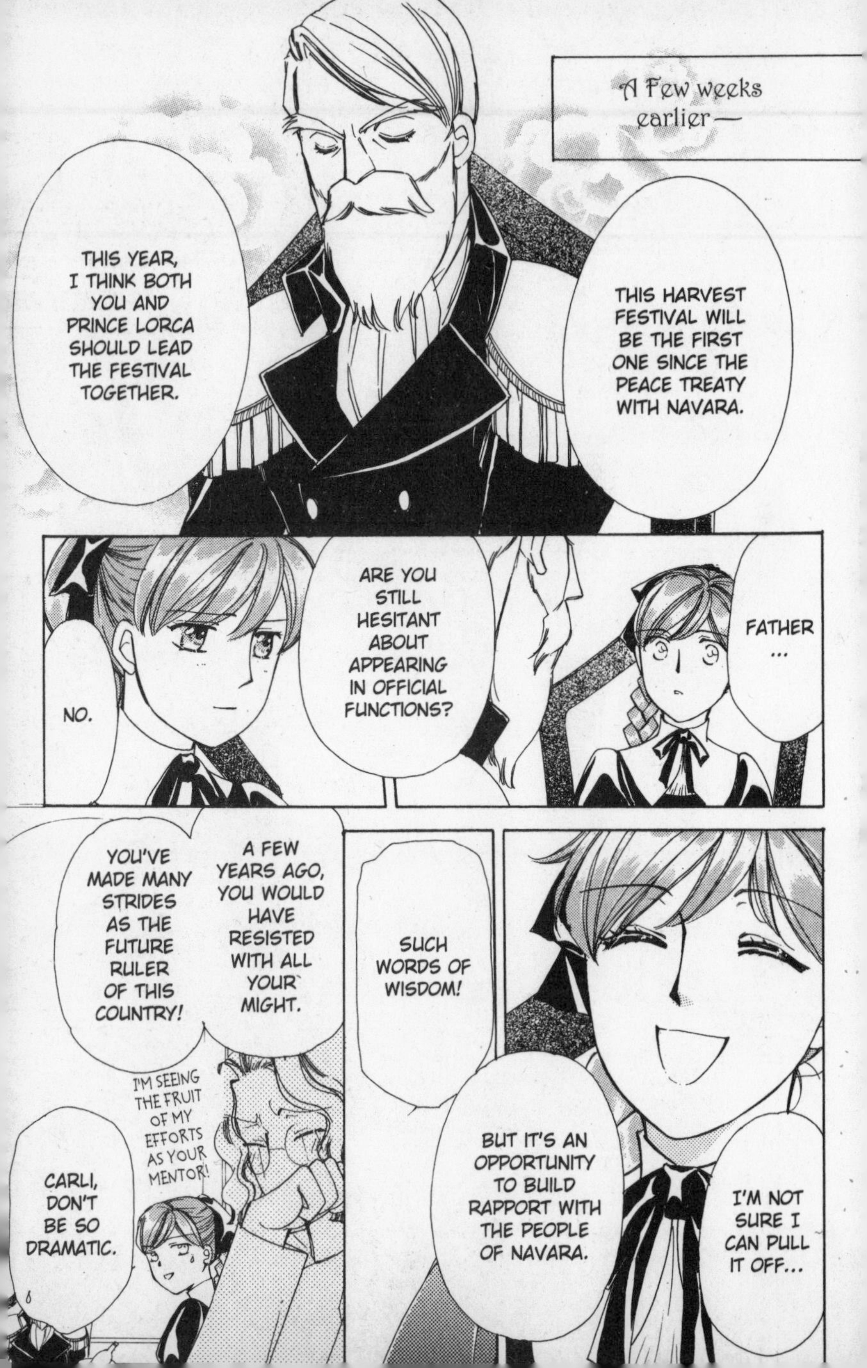
A Few weeks earlier—
THIS HARVEST FESTIVAL WILL BE THE FIRST ONE SINCE THE PEACE TREATY WITH NAVARA.
THIS YEAR, I THINK BOTH YOU AND PRINCE LORCA SHOULD LEAD THE FESTIVAL TOGETHER.
FATHER ...
ARE YOU STILL HESITANT ABOUT APPEARING IN OFFICIAL FUNCTIONS?
NO.
I'M NOT SURE I CAN PULL IT OFF...
BUT IT'S AN OPPORTUNITY TO BUILD RAPPORT WITH THE PEOPLE OF NAVARA.
SUCH WORDS OF WISDOM!
A FEW YEARS AGO, YOU WOULD HAVE RESISTED WITH ALL YOUR MIGHT.
YOU'VE MADE MANY STRIDES AS THE FUTURE RULER OF THIS COUNTRY!
I'M SEEING THE FRUIT OF MY EFFORTS AS YOUR MENTOR!
CARLI, DON'T BE SO DRAMATIC.

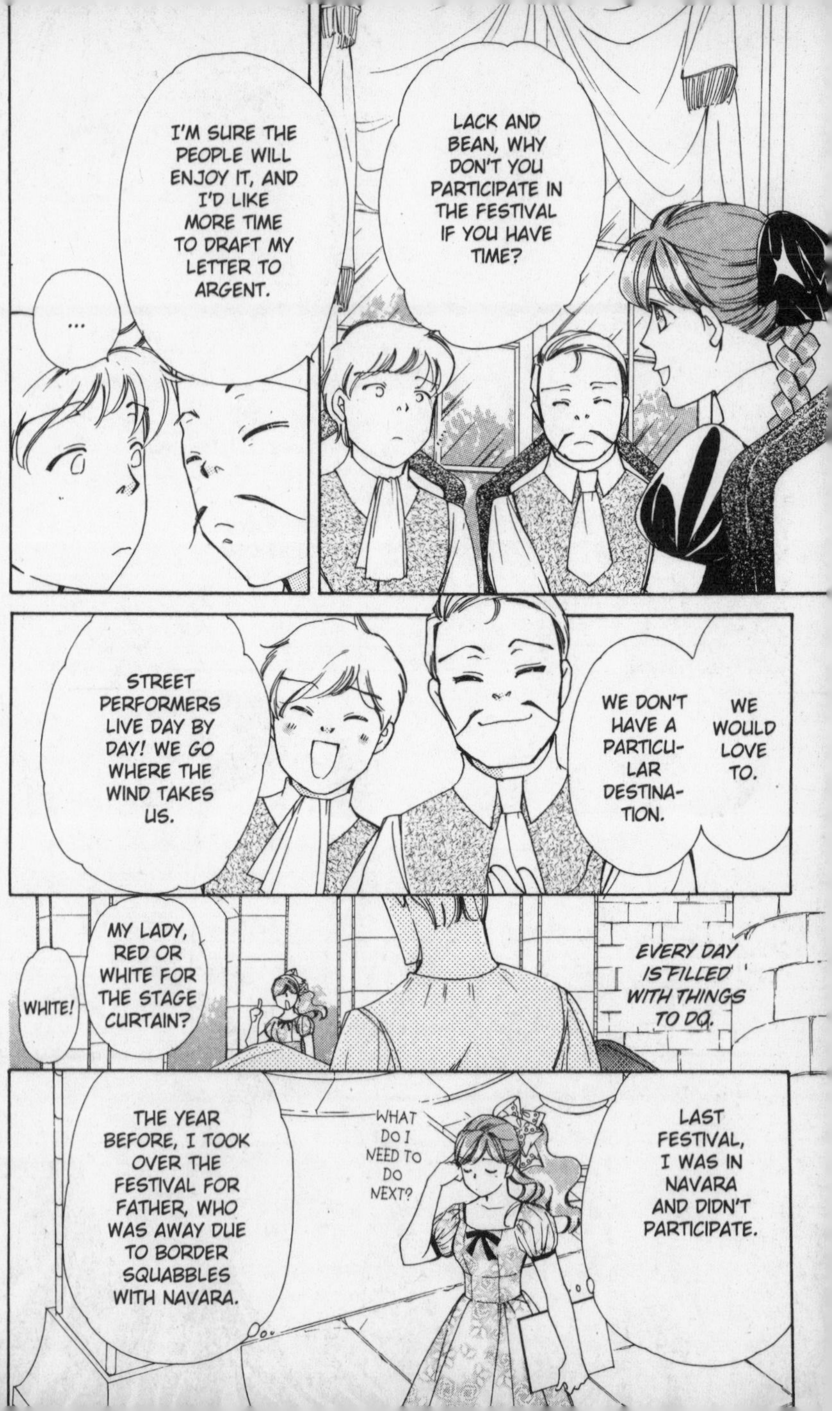
LACK AND BEAN, WHY DON'T YOU PARTICIPATE IN THE FESTIVAL IF YOU HAVE TIME?
I'M SURE THE PEOPLE WILL ENJOY IT, AND I'D LIKE MORE TIME TO DRAFT MY LETTER TO ARGENT.
...
WE WOULD LOVE TO.
WE DON'T HAVE A PARTICULAR DESTINATION.
STREET PERFORMERS LIVE DAY BY DAY! WE GO WHERE THE WIND TAKES US.
EVERY DAY IS FILLED WITH THINGS TO DO.
MY LADY, RED OR WHITE FOR THE STAGE CURTAIN?
WHITE!
LAST FESTIVAL, I WAS IN NAVARA AND DIDN'T PARTICIPATE.
WHAT DO I NEED TO DO NEXT?
THE YEAR BEFORE, I TOOK OVER THE FESTIVAL FOR FATHER, WHO WAS AWAY DUE TO BORDER SQUABBLES WITH NAVARA.

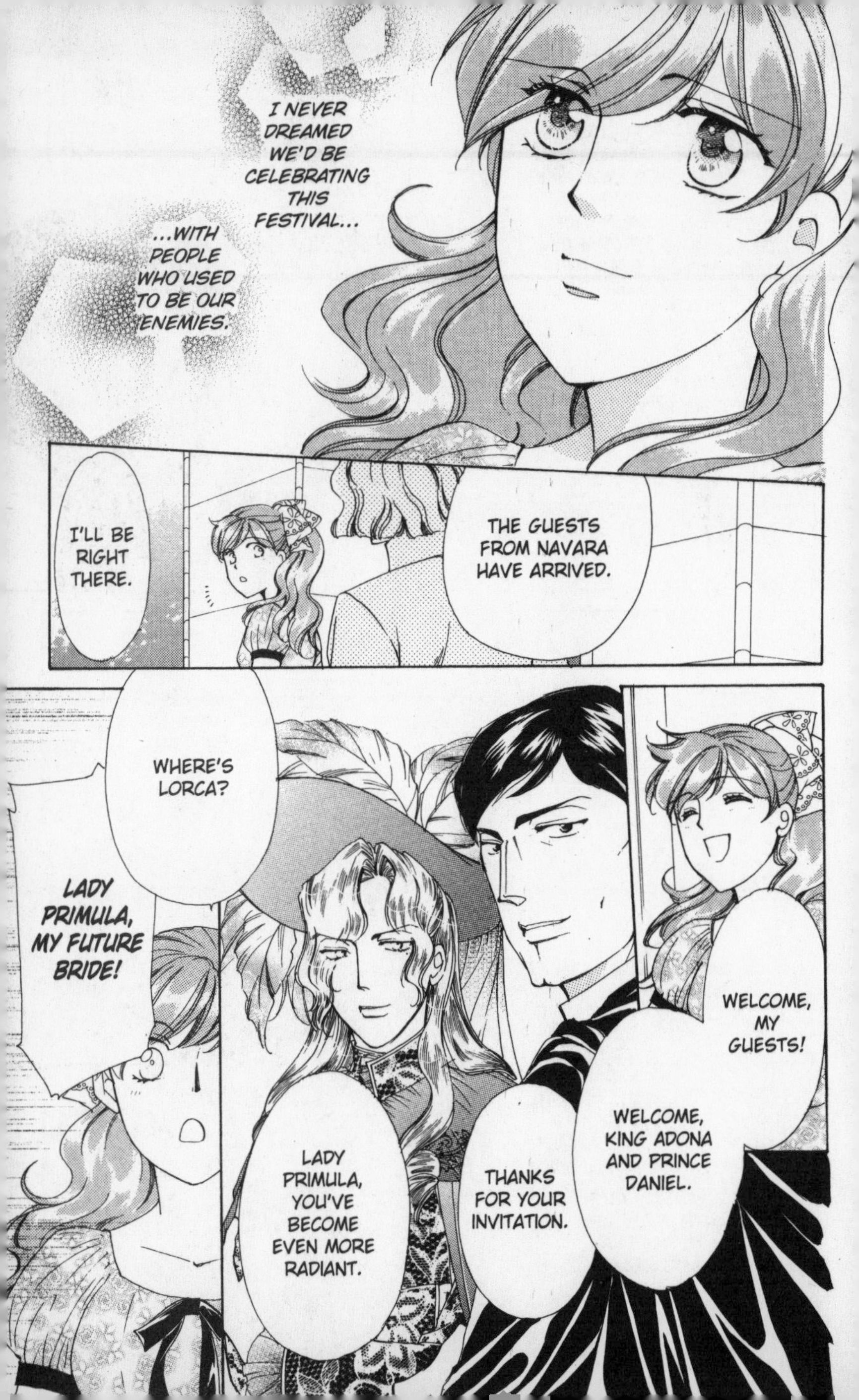
I NEVER DREAMED WE'D BE CELEBRATING THIS FESTIVAL...
...WITH PEOPLE WHO USED TO BE OUR ENEMIES.
THE GUESTS FROM NAVARA HAVE ARRIVED.
I'LL BE RIGHT THERE.
WELCOME, MY GUESTS!
WELCOME, KING ADONA AND PRINCE DANIEL.
THANKS FOR YOUR INVITATION.
LADY PRIMULA, YOU'VE BECOME EVEN MORE RADIANT.
WHERE'S LORCA?
LADY PRIMULA, MY FUTURE BRIDE!

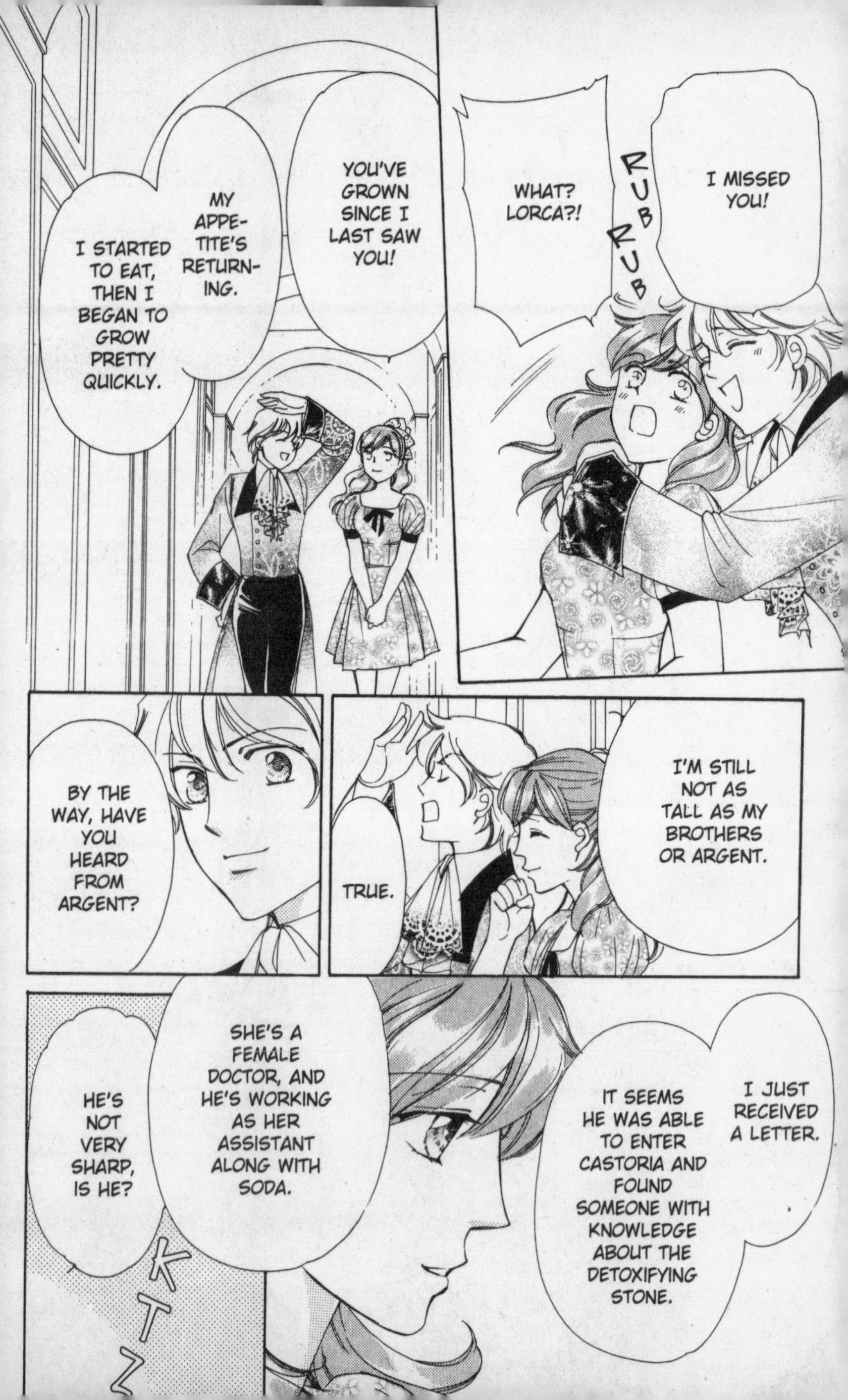
I MISSED YOU!
RUB RUB
WHAT? LORCA?!
YOU'VE GROWN SINCE I LAST SAW YOU!
MY APPE-TITE'S RETURN-ING.
I STARTED TO EAT, THEN I BEGAN TO GROW PRETTY QUICKLY.
I'M STILL NOT AS TALL AS MY BROTHERS OR ARGENT.
TRUE.
BY THE WAY, HAVE YOU HEARD FROM ARGENT?
I JUST RECEIVED A LETTER.
IT SEEMS HE WAS ABLE TO ENTER CASTORIA AND FOUND SOMEONE WITH KNOWLEDGE ABOUT THE DETOXIFYING STONE.
SHE'S A FEMALE DOCTOR, AND HE'S WORKING AS HER ASSISTANT ALONG WITH SODA.
HE'S NOT VERY SHARP, IS HE?
KTZ

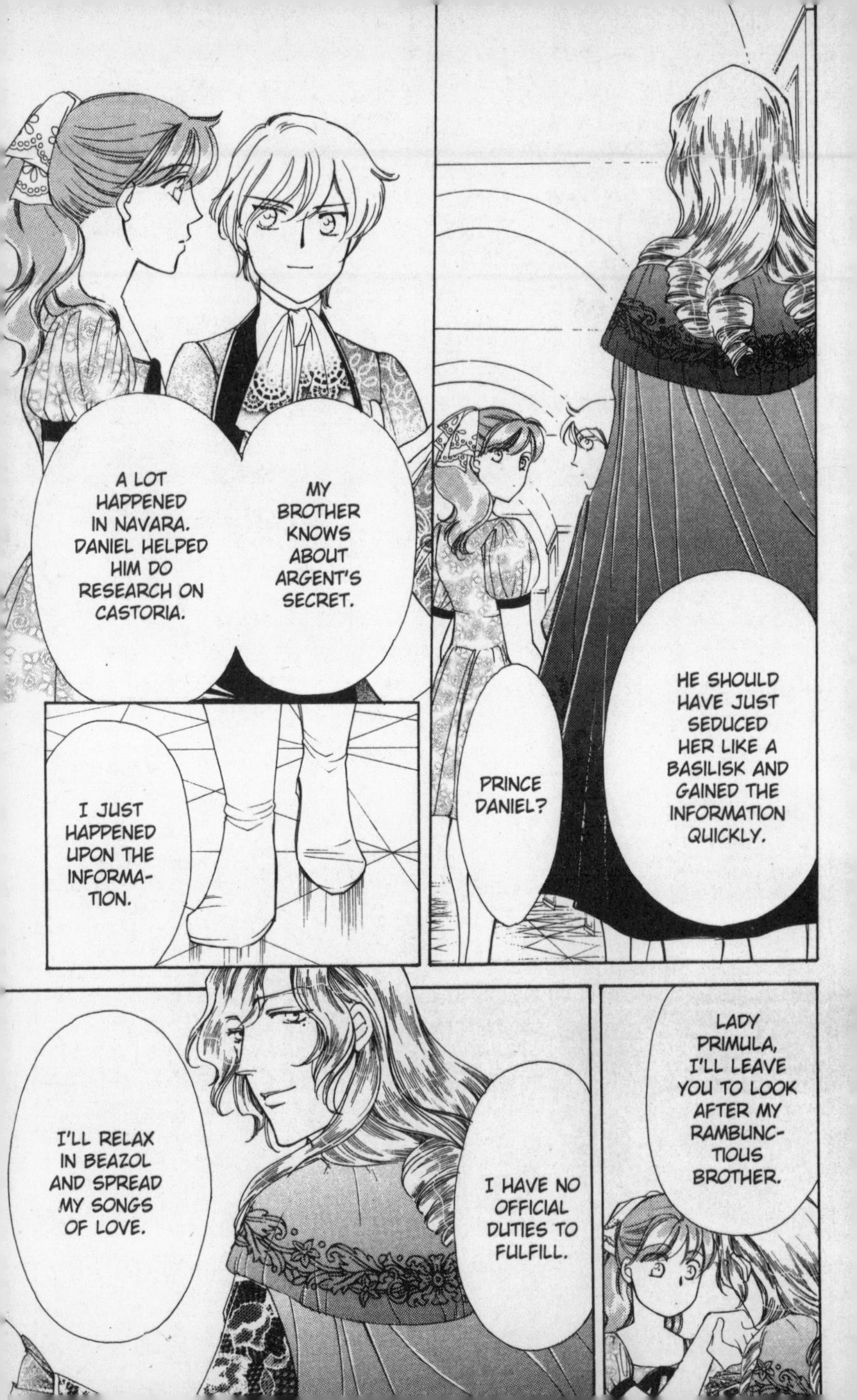
HE SHOULD HAVE JUST SEDUCED HER LIKE A BASILISK AND GAINED THE INFORMATION QUICKLY.
PRINCE DANIEL?
MY BROTHER KNOWS ABOUT ARGENT'S SECRET.
A LOT HAPPENED IN NAVARA. DANIEL HELPED HIM DO RESEARCH ON CASTORIA.
I JUST HAPPENED UPON THE INFORMA-TION.
LADY PRIMULA, I'LL LEAVE YOU TO LOOK AFTER MY RAMBUNC-TIOUS BROTHER.
I HAVE NO OFFICIAL DUTIES TO FULFILL.
I'LL RELAX IN BEAZOL AND SPREAD MY SONGS OF LOVE.

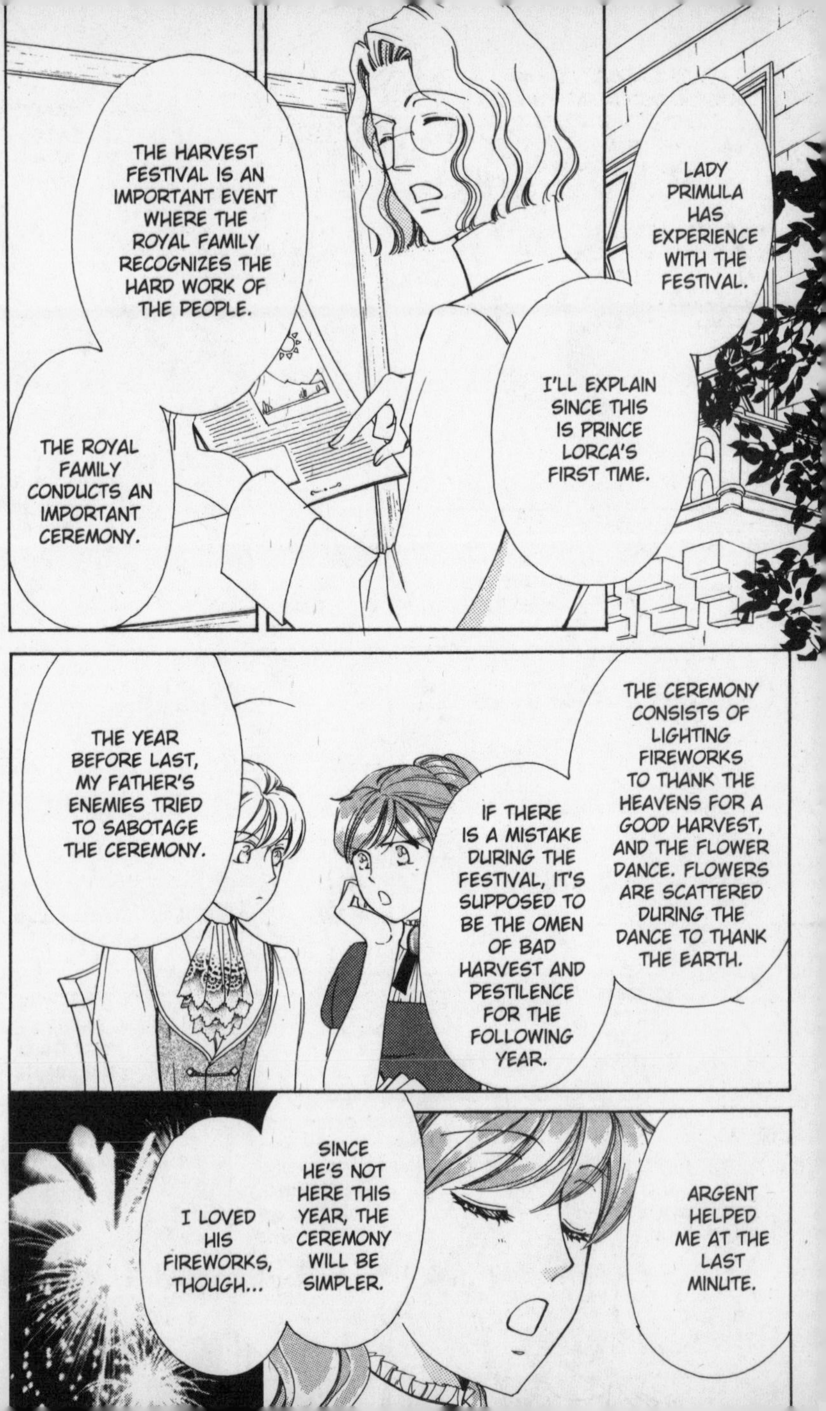
LADY PRIMULA HAS EXPERIENCE WITH THE FESTIVAL.
I'LL EXPLAIN SINCE THIS IS PRINCE LORCA'S FIRST TIME.
THE HARVEST FESTIVAL IS AN IMPORTANT EVENT WHERE THE ROYAL FAMILY RECOGNIZES THE HARD WORK OF THE PEOPLE.
THE ROYAL FAMILY CONDUCTS AN IMPORTANT CEREMONY.
THE CEREMONY CONSISTS OF LIGHTING FIREWORKS TO THANK THE HEAVENS FOR A GOOD HARVEST, AND THE FLOWER DANCE. FLOWERS ARE SCATTERED DURING THE DANCE TO THANK THE EARTH.
IF THERE IS A MISTAKE DURING THE FESTIVAL, IT'S SUPPOSED TO BE THE OMEN OF BAD HARVEST AND PESTILENCE FOR THE FOLLOWING YEAR.
THE YEAR BEFORE LAST, MY FATHER'S ENEMIES TRIED TO SABOTAGE THE CEREMONY.
ARGENT HELPED ME AT THE LAST MINUTE.
SINCE HE'S NOT HERE THIS YEAR, THE CEREMONY WILL BE SIMPLER.
I LOVED HIS FIREWORKS, THOUGH...

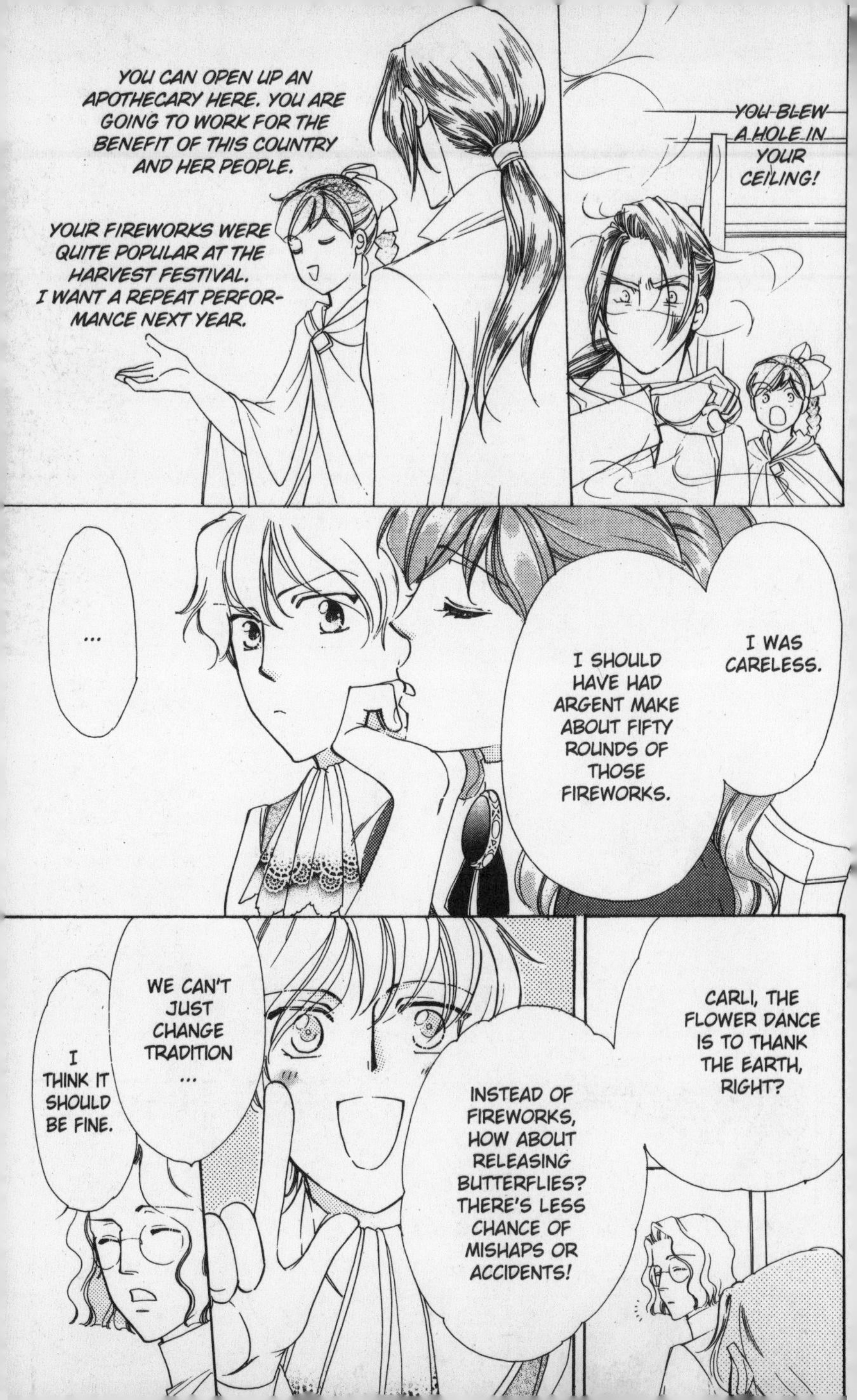
YOU BLEW A HOLE IN YOUR CEILING!
YOU CAN OPEN UP AN APOTHECARY HERE. YOU ARE GOING TO WORK FOR THE BENEFIT OF THIS COUNTRY AND HER PEOPLE.
YOUR FIREWORKS WERE QUITE POPULAR AT THE HARVEST FESTIVAL. I WANT A REPEAT PERFORMANCE NEXT YEAR.
I WAS CARELESS.
I SHOULD HAVE HAD ARGENT MAKE ABOUT FIFTY ROUNDS OF THOSE FIREWORKS.
...
CARLI, THE FLOWER DANCE IS TO THANK THE EARTH, RIGHT?
INSTEAD OF FIREWORKS, HOW ABOUT RELEASING BUTTERFLIES? THERE'S LESS CHANCE OF MISHAPS OR ACCIDENTS!
WE CAN'T JUST CHANGE TRADITION ...
I THINK IT SHOULD BE FINE.

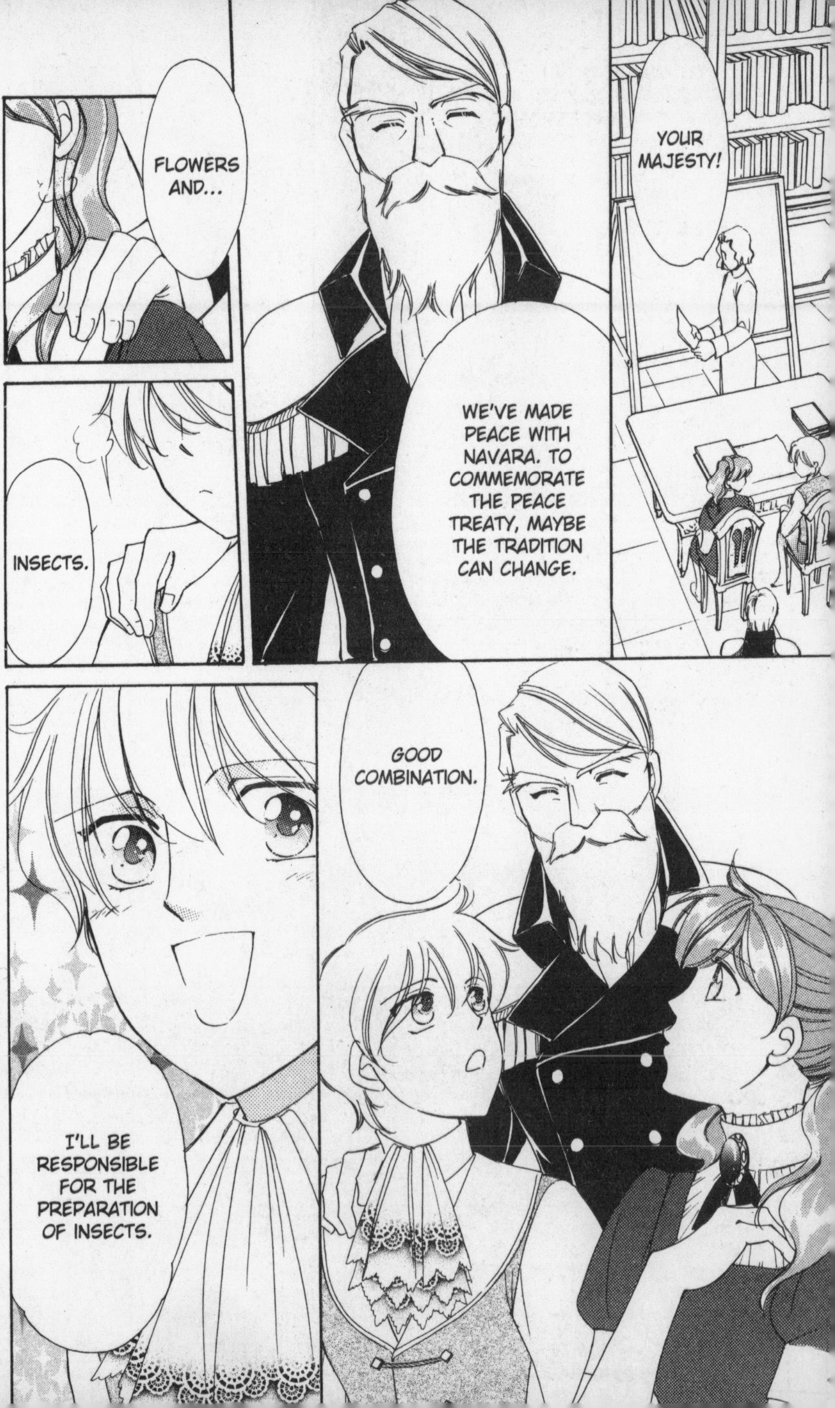
YOUR MAJESTY!
WE'VE MADE PEACE WITH NAVARA. TO COMMEMORATE THE PEACE TREATY, MAYBE THE TRADITION CAN CHANGE.
FLOWERS AND...
INSECTS.
GOOD COMBINATION.
I'LL BE RESPONSIBLE FOR THE PREPARATION OF INSECTS.

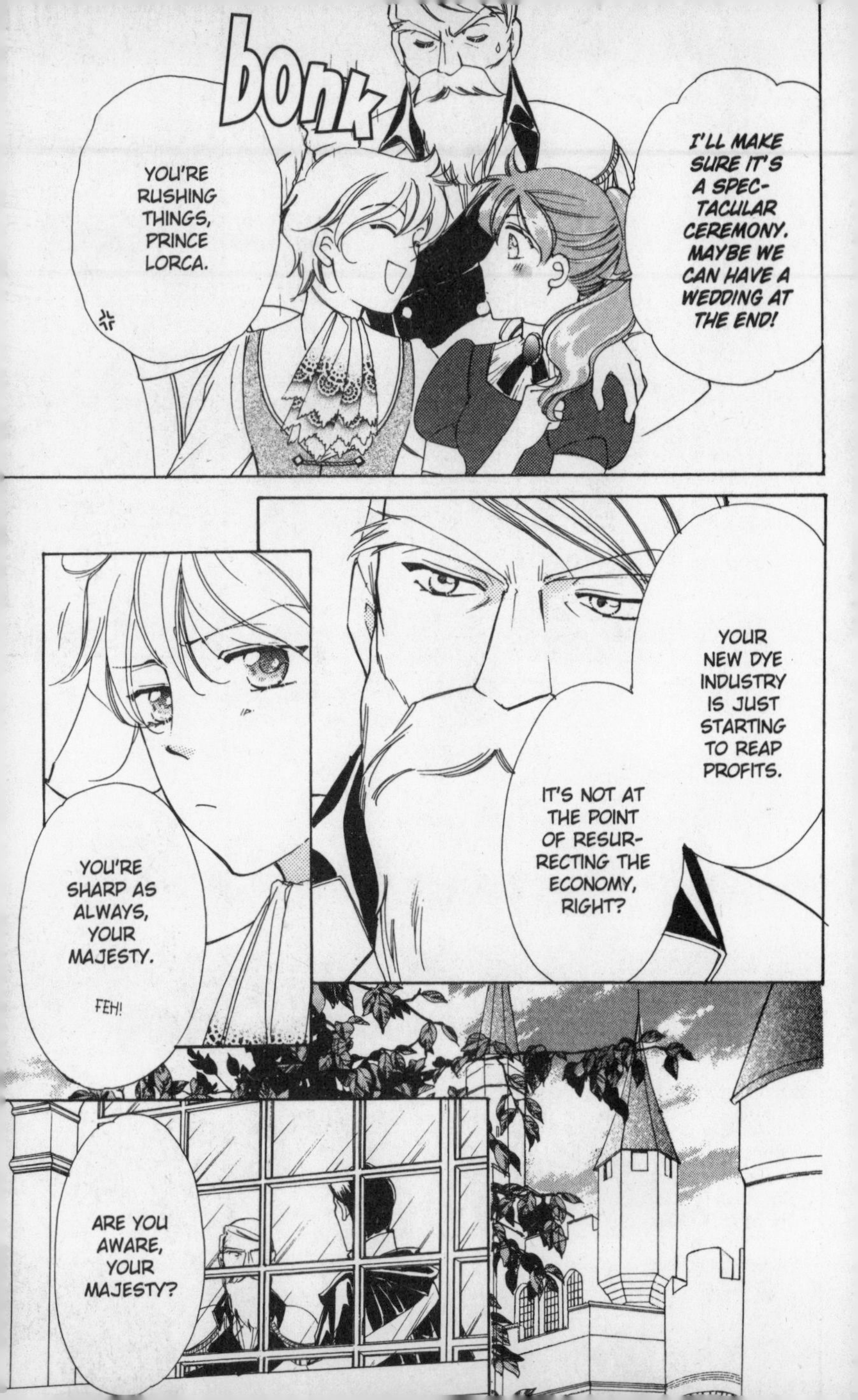
I'LL MAKE SURE IT'S A SPECTACULAR CEREMONY. MAYBE WE CAN HAVE A WEDDING AT THE END!
bonk
YOU'RE RUSHING THINGS, PRINCE LORCA.
YOUR NEW DYE INDUSTRY IS JUST STARTING TO REAP PROFITS.
IT'S NOT AT THE POINT OF RESURRECTING THE ECONOMY, RIGHT?
YOU'RE SHARP AS ALWAYS, YOUR MAJESTY.
FEH!
ARE YOU AWARE, YOUR MAJESTY?

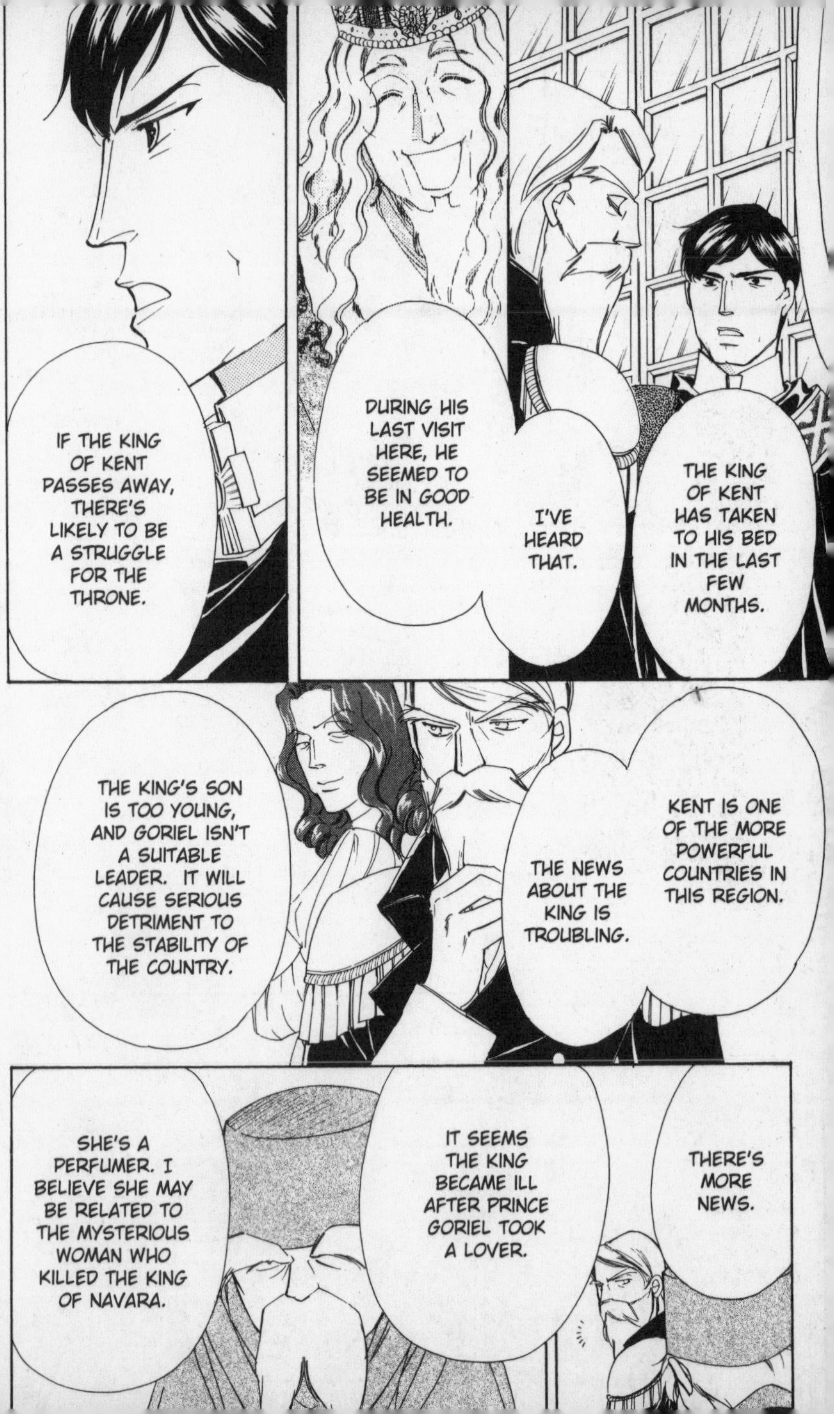
THE KING OF KENT HAS TAKEN TO HIS BED IN THE LAST FEW MONTHS.
I'VE HEARD THAT.
DURING HIS LAST VISIT HERE, HE SEEMED TO BE IN GOOD HEALTH.
IF THE KING OF KENT PASSES AWAY, THERE'S LIKELY TO BE A STRUGGLE FOR THE THRONE.
KENT IS ONE OF THE MORE POWERFUL COUNTRIES IN THIS REGION.
THE NEWS ABOUT THE KING IS TROUBLING.
THE KING'S SON IS TOO YOUNG, AND GORIEL ISN'T A SUITABLE LEADER. IT WILL CAUSE SERIOUS DETRIMENT TO THE STABILITY OF THE COUNTRY.
THERE'S MORE NEWS.
IT SEEMS THE KING BECAME ILL AFTER PRINCE GORIEL TOOK A LOVER.
SHE'S A PERFUMER. I BELIEVE SHE MAY BE RELATED TO THE MYSTERIOUS WOMAN WHO KILLED THE KING OF NAVARA.

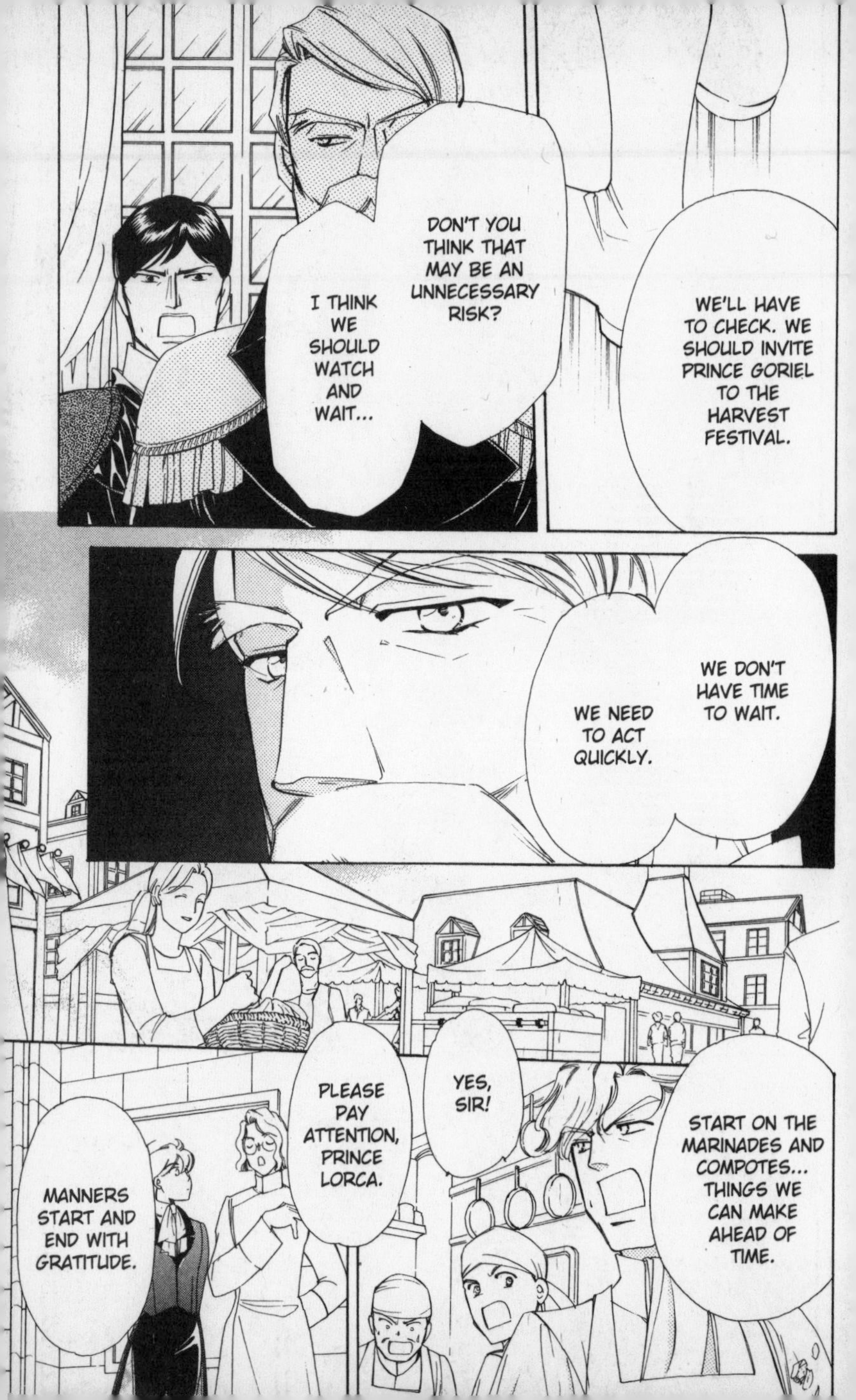
WE'LL HAVE TO CHECK. WE SHOULD INVITE PRINCE GORIEL TO THE HARVEST FESTIVAL.
DON'T YOU THINK THAT MAY BE AN UNNECESSARY RISK?
I THINK WE SHOULD WATCH AND WAIT...
WE DON'T HAVE TIME TO WAIT.
WE NEED TO ACT QUICKLY.
START ON THE MARINADES AND COMPOTES... THINGS WE CAN MAKE AHEAD OF TIME.
YES, SIR!
PLEASE PAY ATTENTION, PRINCE LORCA.
MANNERS START AND END WITH GRATITUDE.

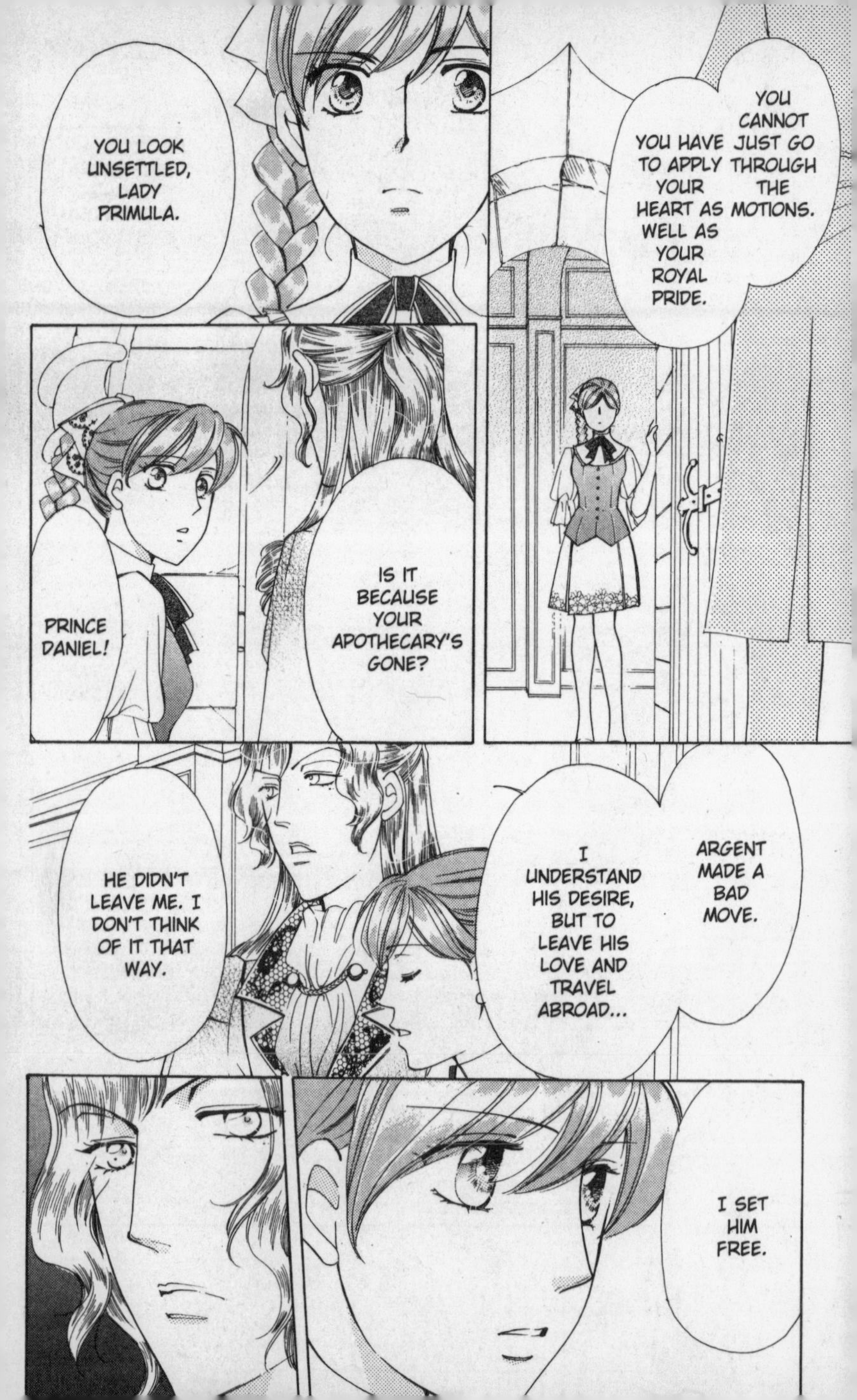
YOU CANNOT JUST GO THROUGH THE MOTIONS.
YOU HAVE TO APPLY YOUR HEART AS WELL AS YOUR ROYAL PRIDE.
YOU LOOK UNSETTLED, LADY PRIMULA.
IS IT BECAUSE YOUR APOTHECARY'S GONE?
PRINCE DANIEL!
ARGENT MADE A BAD MOVE.
I UNDERSTAND HIS DESIRE, BUT TO LEAVE HIS LOVE AND TRAVEL ABROAD...
HE DIDN'T LEAVE ME. I DON'T THINK OF IT THAT WAY.
I SET HIM FREE.

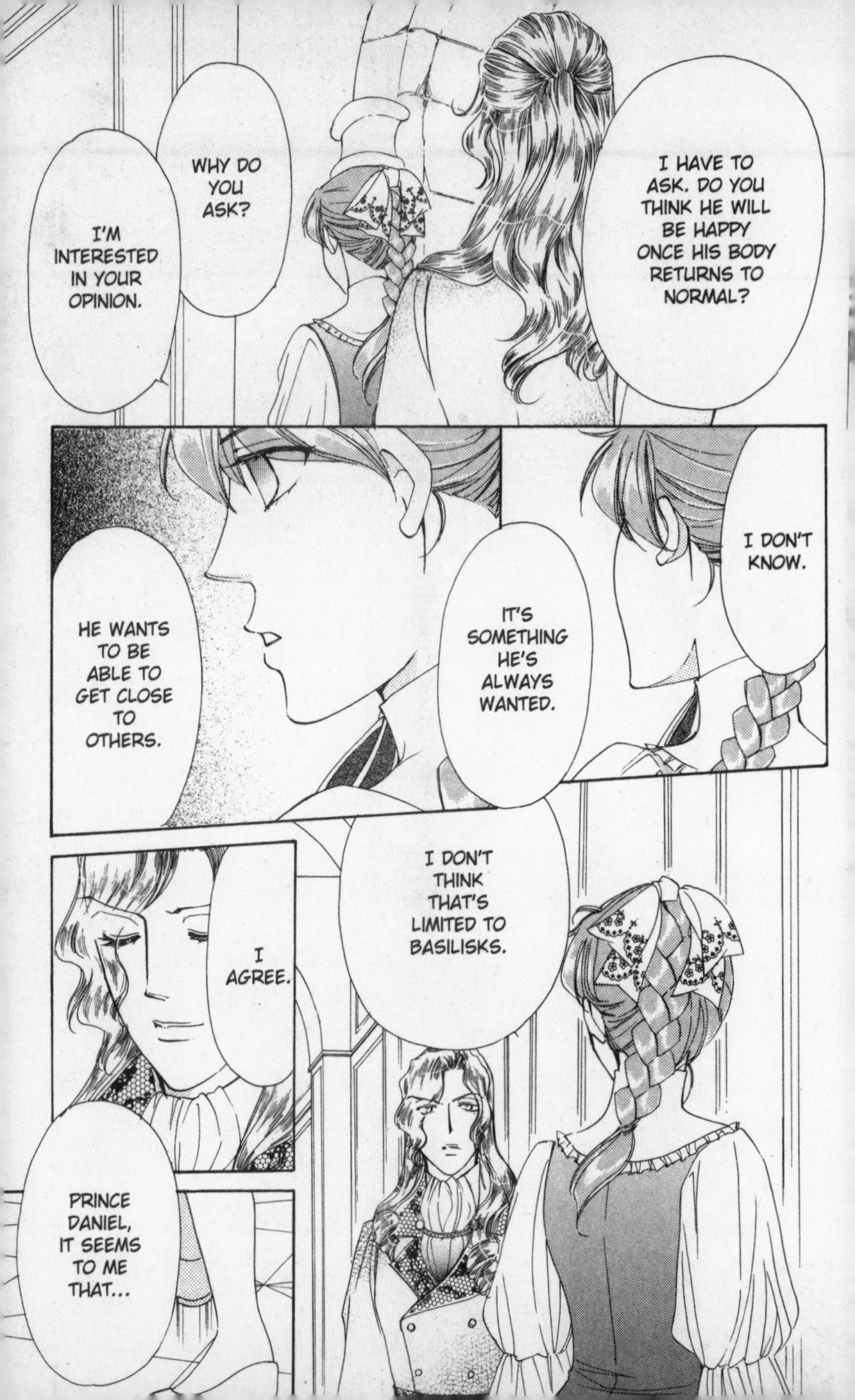
I HAVE TO ASK. DO YOU THINK HE WILL BE HAPPY ONCE HIS BODY RETURNS TO NORMAL?
WHY DO YOU ASK?
I'M INTERESTED IN YOUR OPINION.
I DON'T KNOW.
IT'S SOMETHING HE'S ALWAYS WANTED.
HE WANTS TO BE ABLE TO GET CLOSE TO OTHERS.
I DON'T THINK THAT'S LIMITED TO BASILISKS.
I AGREE.
PRINCE DANIEL, IT SEEMS TO ME THAT...

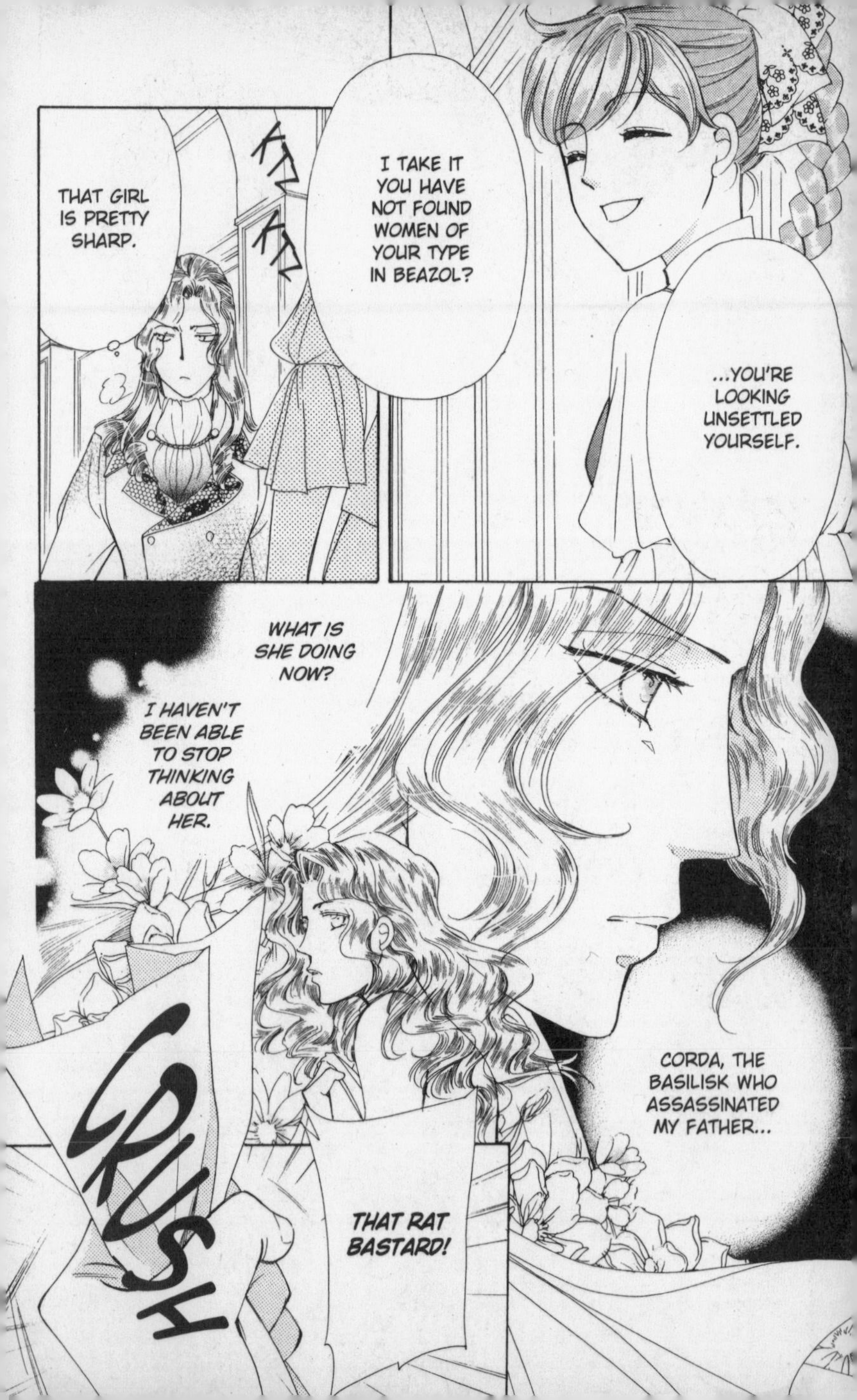
I TAKE IT YOU HAVE NOT FOUND WOMEN OF YOUR TYPE IN BEAZOL?
...YOU'RE LOOKING UNSETTLED YOURSELF.
KTZ KTZ
THAT GIRL IS PRETTY SHARP.
WHAT IS SHE DOING NOW?
I HAVEN'T BEEN ABLE TO STOP THINKING ABOUT HER.
CORDA, THE BASILISK WHO ASSASSINATED MY FATHER...
THAT RAT BASTARD!
CRUSH

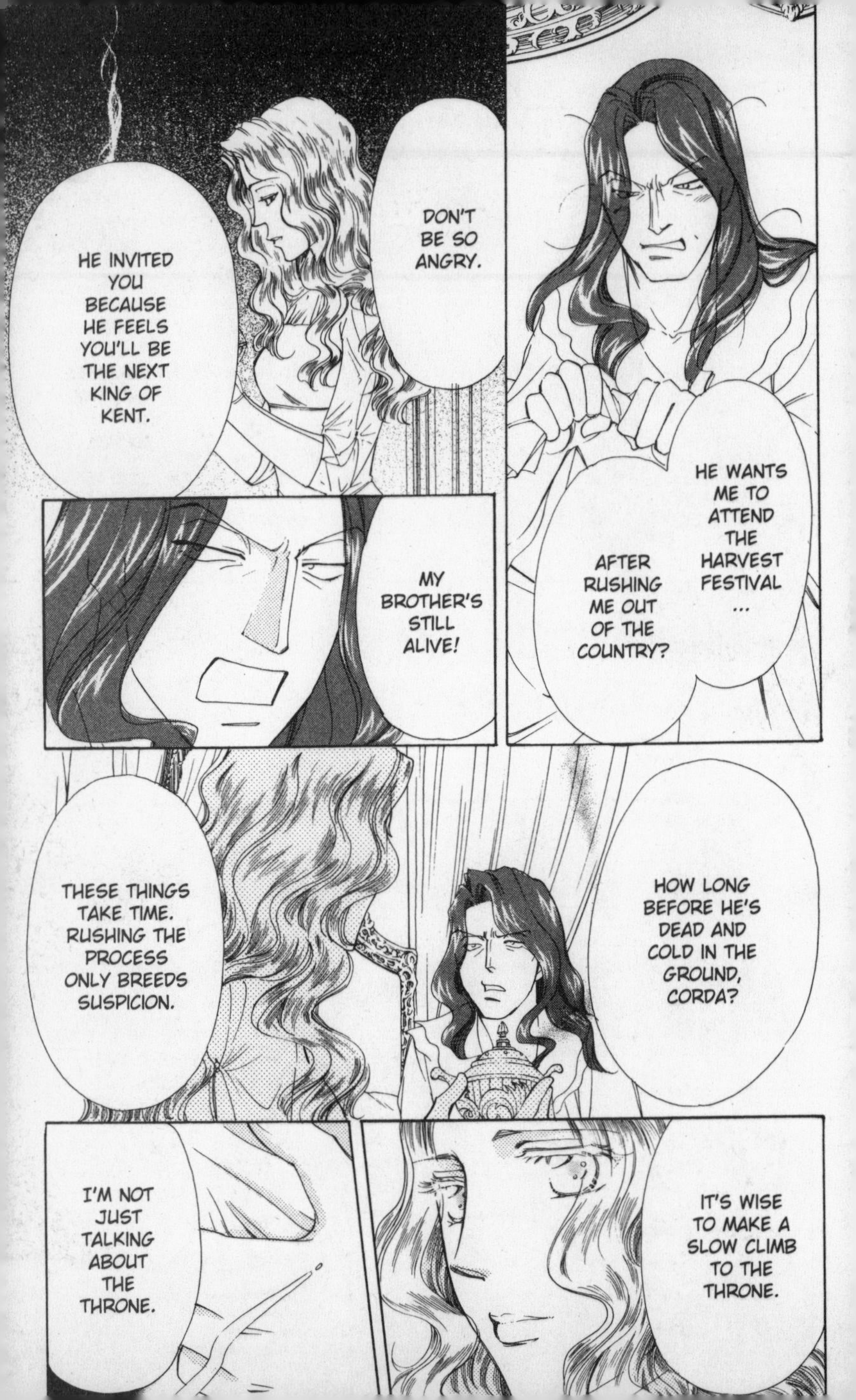
HE WANTS ME TO ATTEND THE HARVEST FESTIVAL ...
AFTER RUSHING ME OUT OF THE COUNTRY?
DON'T BE SO ANGRY.
HE INVITED YOU BECAUSE HE FEELS YOU'LL BE THE NEXT KING OF KENT.
MY BROTHER'S STILL ALIVE!
HOW LONG BEFORE HE'S DEAD AND COLD IN THE GROUND, CORDA?
THESE THINGS TAKE TIME. RUSHING THE PROCESS ONLY BREEDS SUSPICION.
IT'S WISE TO MAKE A SLOW CLIMB TO THE THRONE.
I'M NOT JUST TALKING ABOUT THE THRONE.

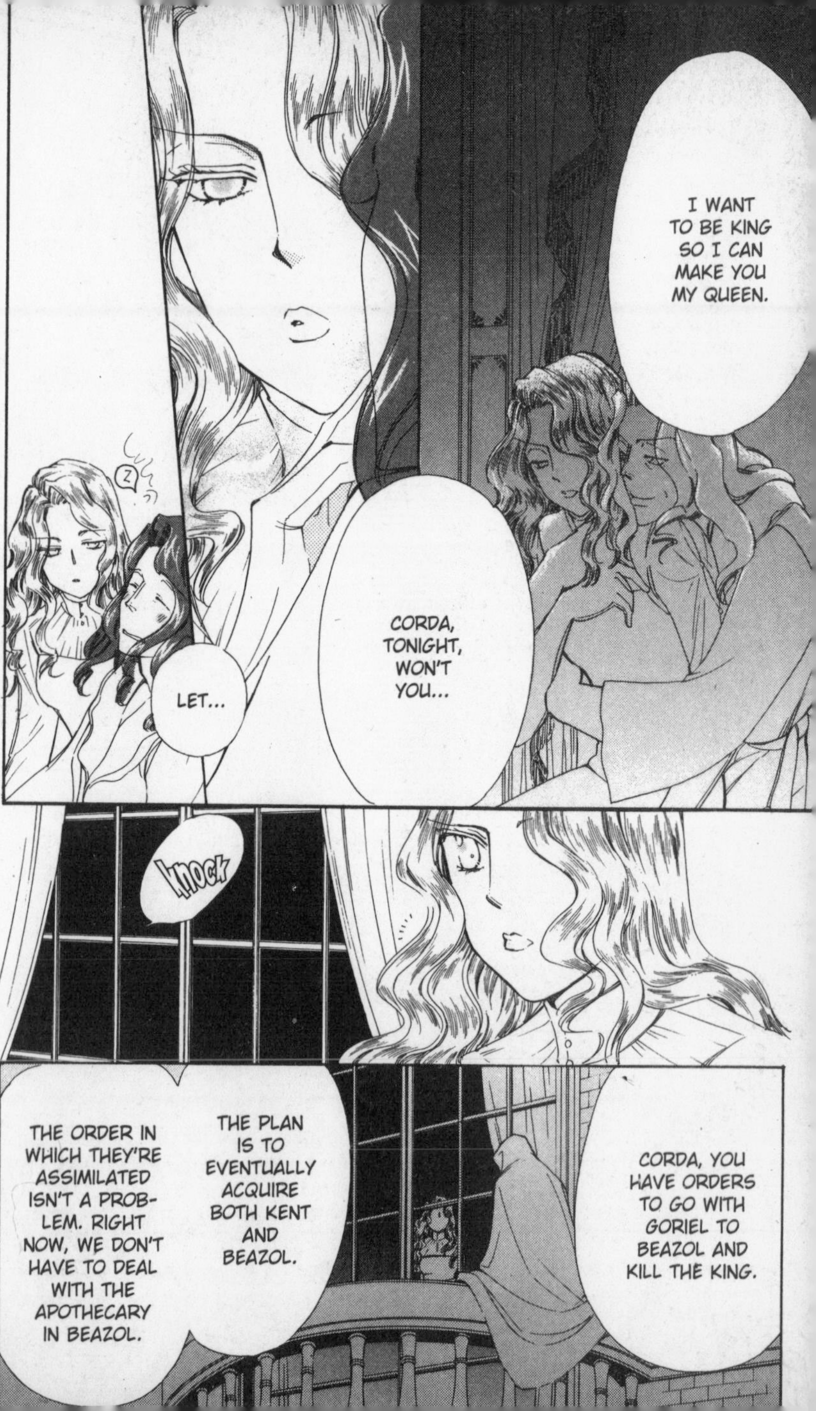
I WANT TO BE KING SO I CAN MAKE YOU MY QUEEN.
CORDA, TONIGHT, WON'T YOU...
LET...
knock
CORDA, YOU HAVE ORDERS TO GO WITH GORIEL TO BEAZOL AND KILL THE KING.
THE PLAN IS TO EVENTUALLY ACQUIRE BOTH KENT AND BEAZOL.
THE ORDER IN WHICH THEY'RE ASSIMILATED ISN'T A PROB-LEM. RIGHT NOW, WE DON'T HAVE TO DEAL WITH THE APOTHECARY IN BEAZOL.

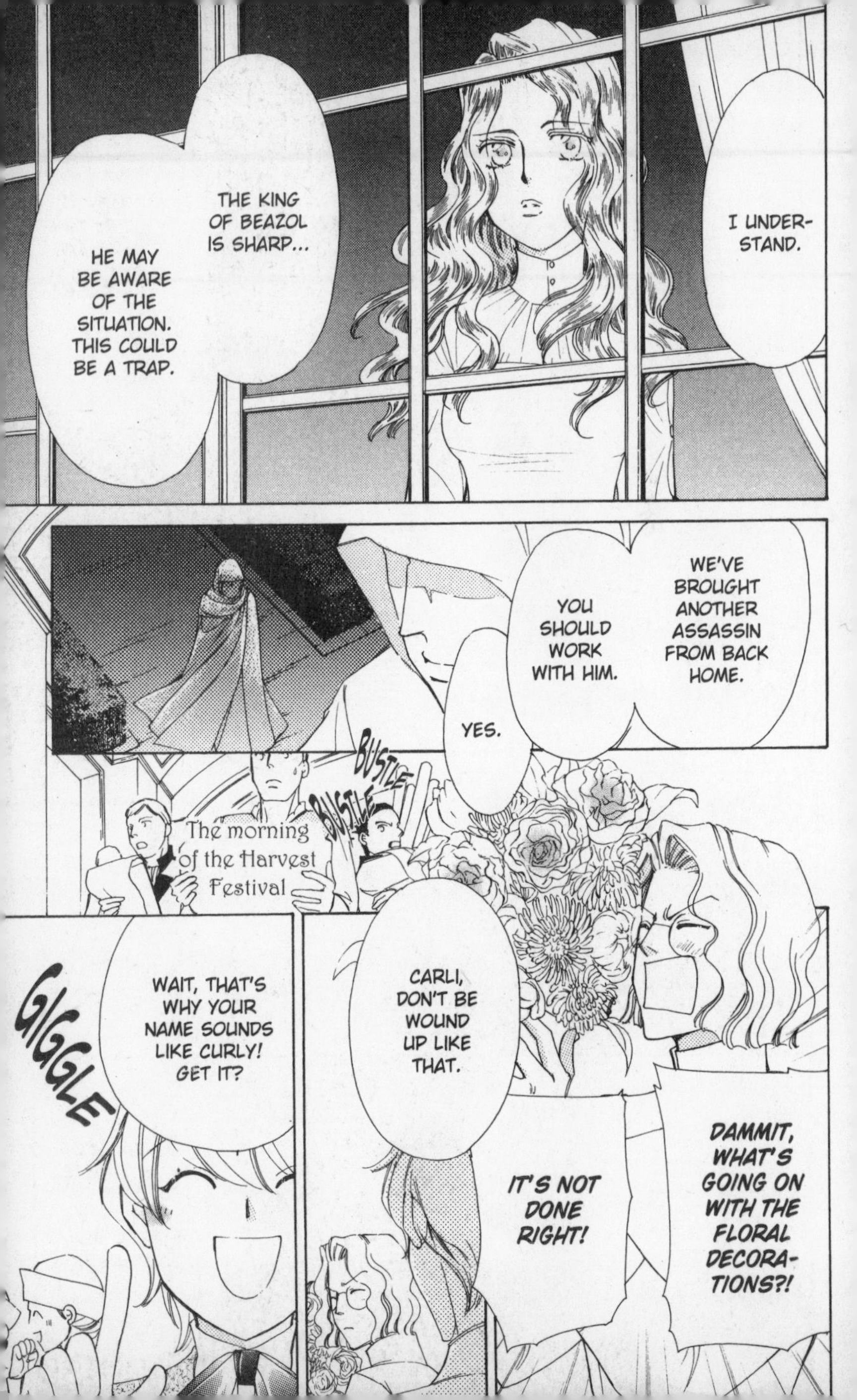
I UNDER-STAND.
THE KING OF BEAZOL IS SHARP...
HE MAY BE AWARE OF THE SITUATION. THIS COULD BE A TRAP.
WE'VE BROUGHT ANOTHER ASSASSIN FROM BACK HOME.
YOU SHOULD WORK WITH HIM.
YES.
BUSTLE
BUSTLE
The morning of the Harvest Festival
DAMMIT, WHAT'S GOING ON WITH THE FLORAL DECORA-TIONS?!
IT'S NOT DONE RIGHT!
CARLI, DON'T BE WOUND UP LIKE THAT.
WAIT, THAT'S WHY YOUR NAME SOUNDS LIKE CURLY! GET IT?
GIGGLE

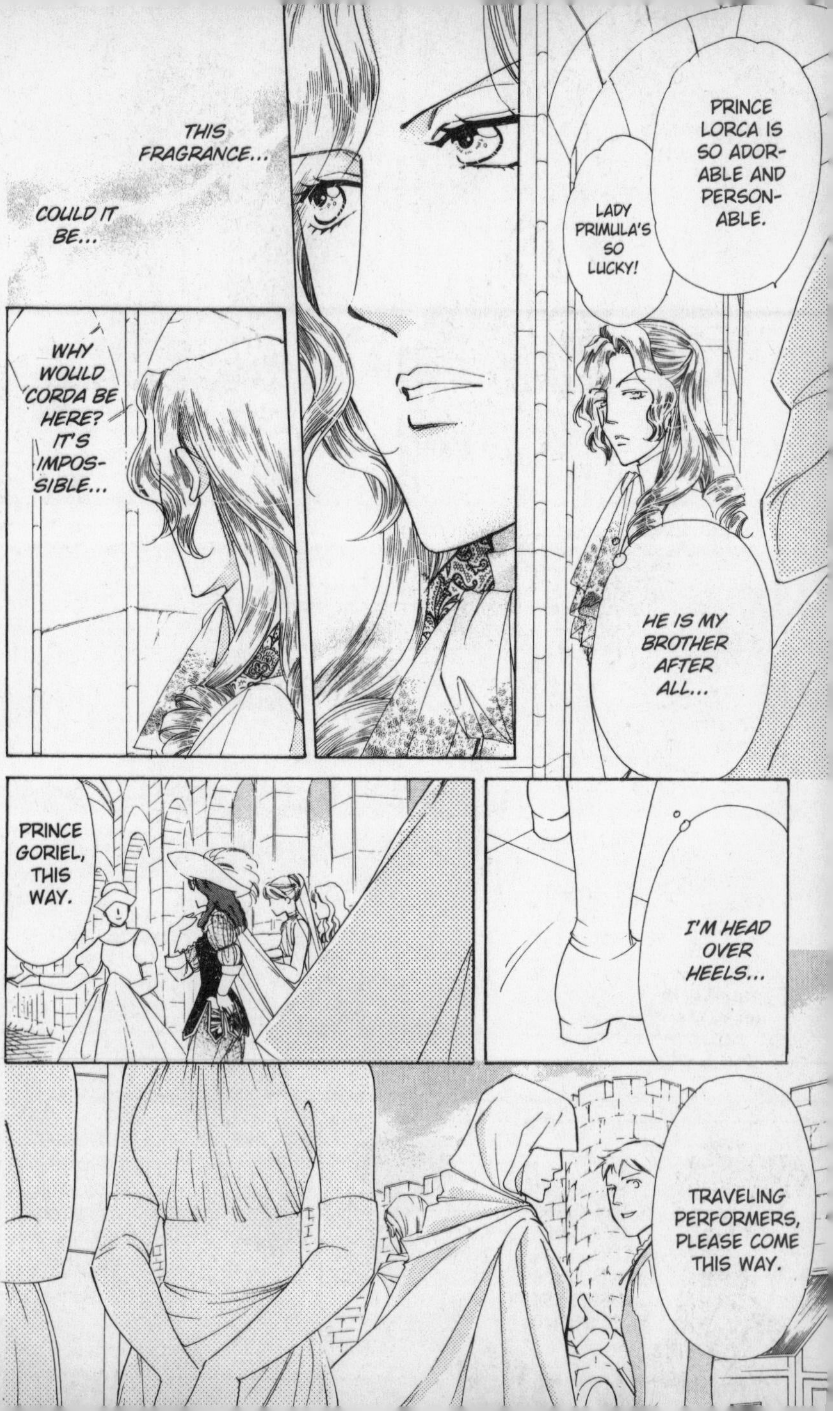
PRINCE LORCA IS SO ADORABLE AND PERSONABLE.
LADY PRIMULA'S SO LUCKY!
HE IS MY BROTHER AFTER ALL...
THIS FRAGRANCE...
COULD IT BE...
WHY WOULD CORDA BE HERE? IT'S IMPOSSIBLE...
I'M HEAD OVER HEELS...
PRINCE GORIEL, THIS WAY.
TRAVELING PERFORMERS, PLEASE COME THIS WAY.

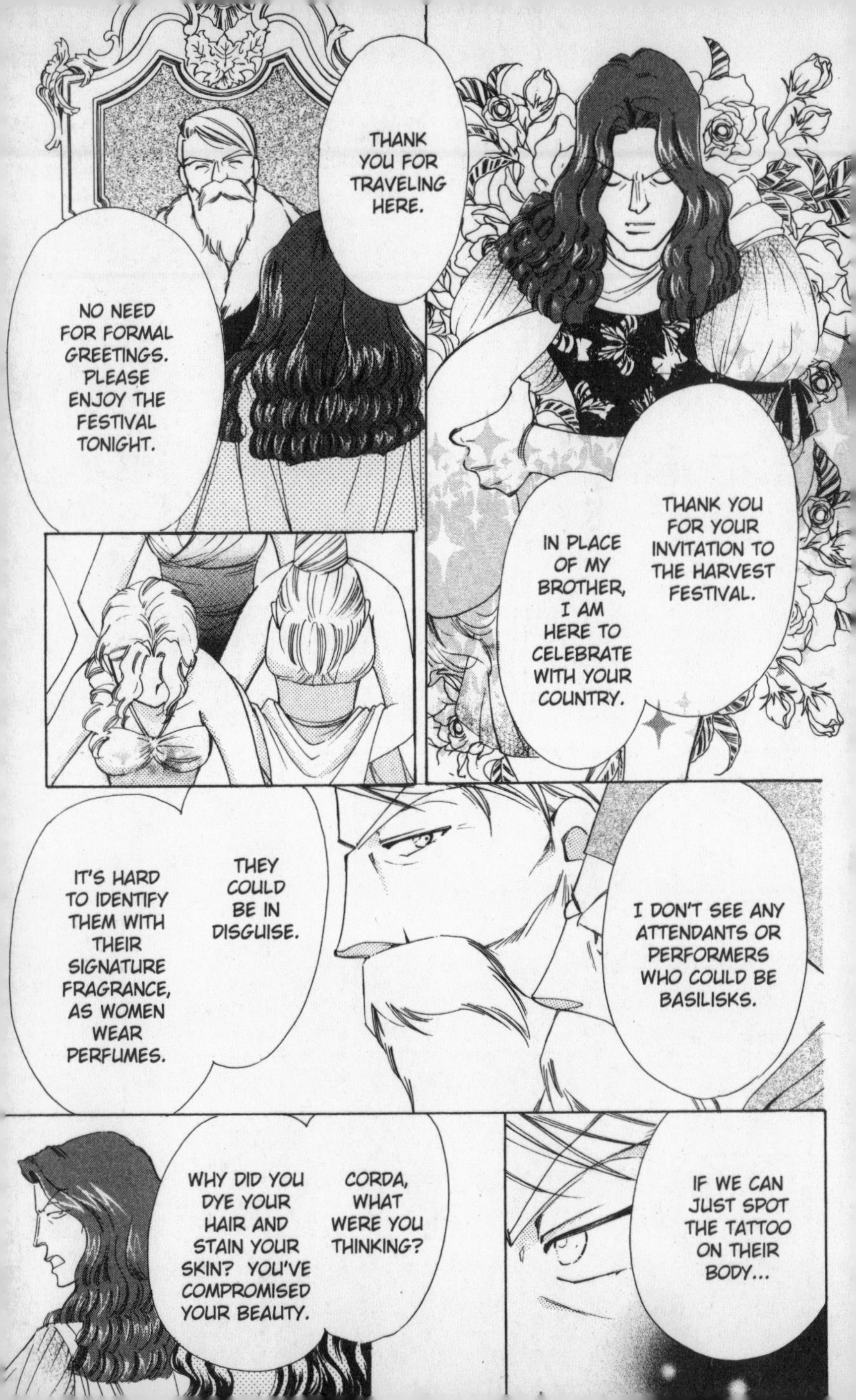
THANK YOU FOR YOUR INVITATION TO THE HARVEST FESTIVAL.
IN PLACE OF MY BROTHER, I AM HERE TO CELEBRATE WITH YOUR COUNTRY.
THANK YOU FOR TRAVELING HERE.
NO NEED FOR FORMAL GREETINGS. PLEASE ENJOY THE FESTIVAL TONIGHT.
I DON'T SEE ANY ATTENDANTS OR PERFORMERS WHO COULD BE BASILISKS.
THEY COULD BE IN DISGUISE.
IT'S HARD TO IDENTIFY THEM WITH THEIR SIGNATURE FRAGRANCE, AS WOMEN WEAR PERFUMES.
IF WE CAN JUST SPOT THE TATTOO ON THEIR BODY...
CORDA, WHAT WERE YOU THINKING?
WHY DID YOU DYE YOUR HAIR AND STAIN YOUR SKIN? YOU'VE COMPROMISED YOUR BEAUTY.

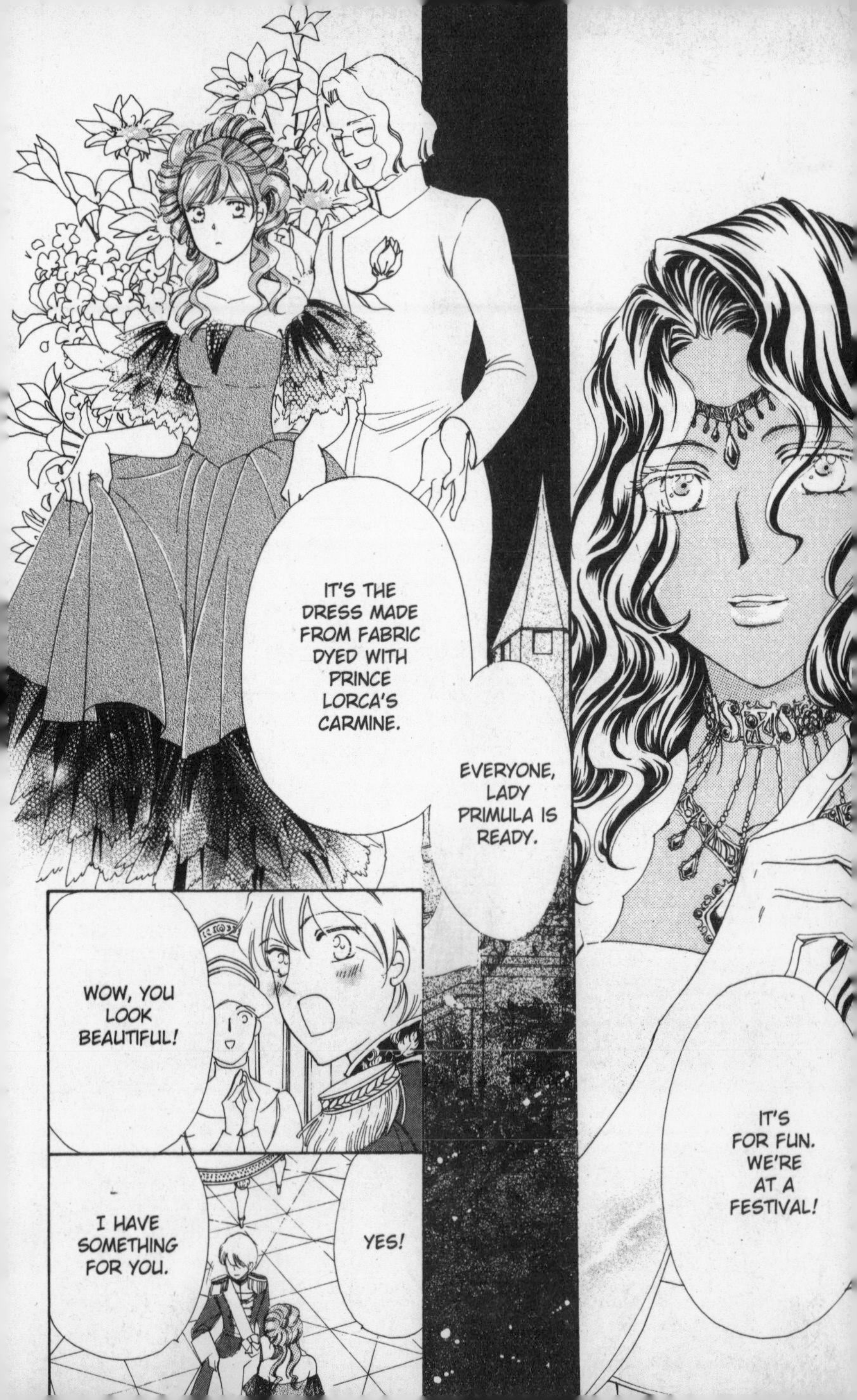
IT'S FOR FUN. WE'RE AT A FESTIVAL!
EVERYONE, LADY PRIMULA IS READY.
IT'S THE DRESS MADE FROM FABRIC DYED WITH PRINCE LORCA'S CARMINE.
WOW, YOU LOOK BEAUTIFUL!
YES!
I HAVE SOMETHING FOR YOU.

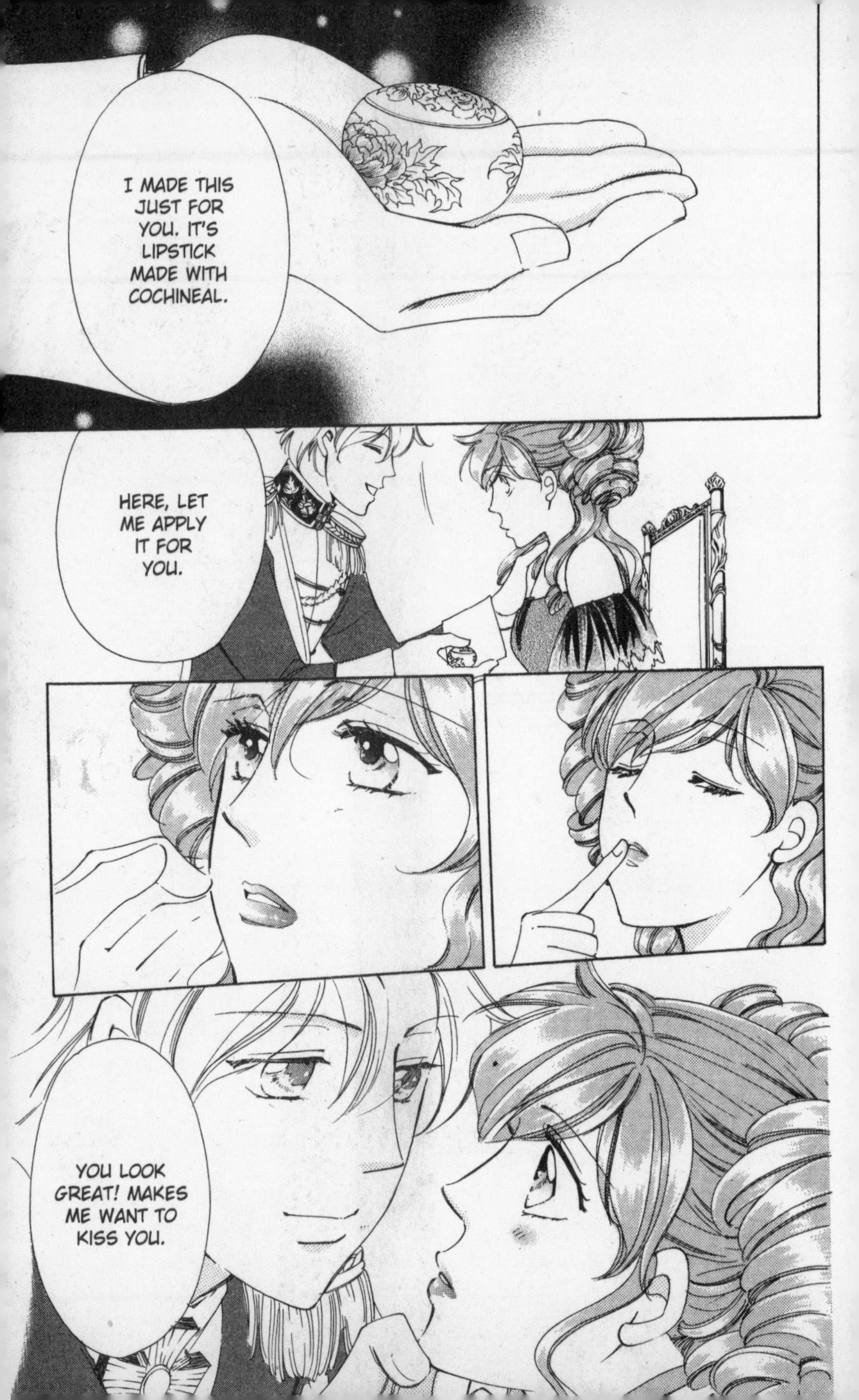
I MADE THIS JUST FOR YOU. IT'S LIPSTICK MADE WITH COCHINEAL.
HERE, LET ME APPLY IT FOR YOU.
YOU LOOK GREAT! MAKES ME WANT TO KISS YOU.

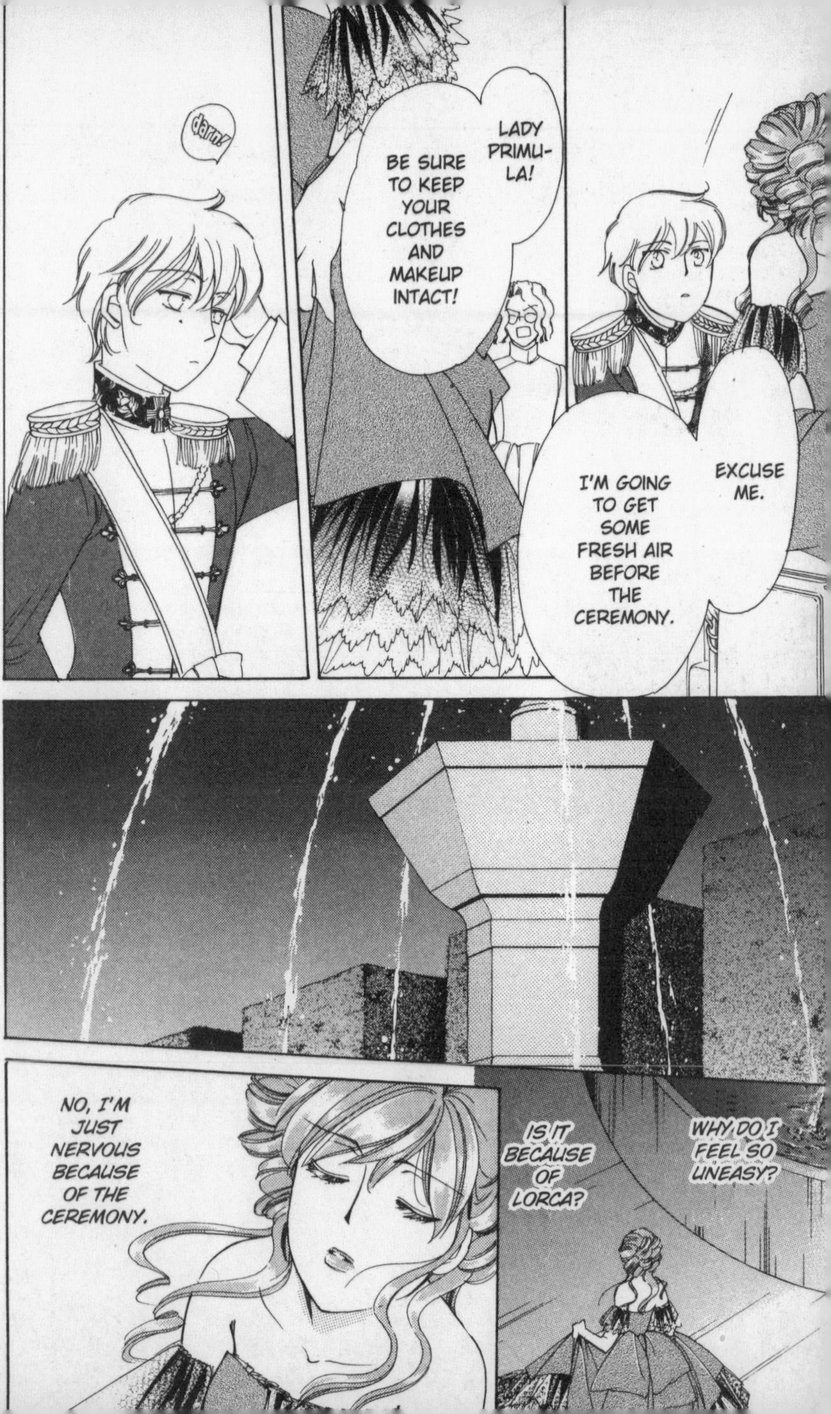
EXCUSE ME.
I'M GOING TO GET SOME FRESH AIR BEFORE THE CEREMONY.
LADY PRIMULA!
BE SURE TO KEEP YOUR CLOTHES AND MAKEUP INTACT!
darn!
WHY DO I FEEL SO UNEASY?
IS IT BECAUSE OF LORCA?
NO, I'M JUST NERVOUS BECAUSE OF THE CEREMONY.

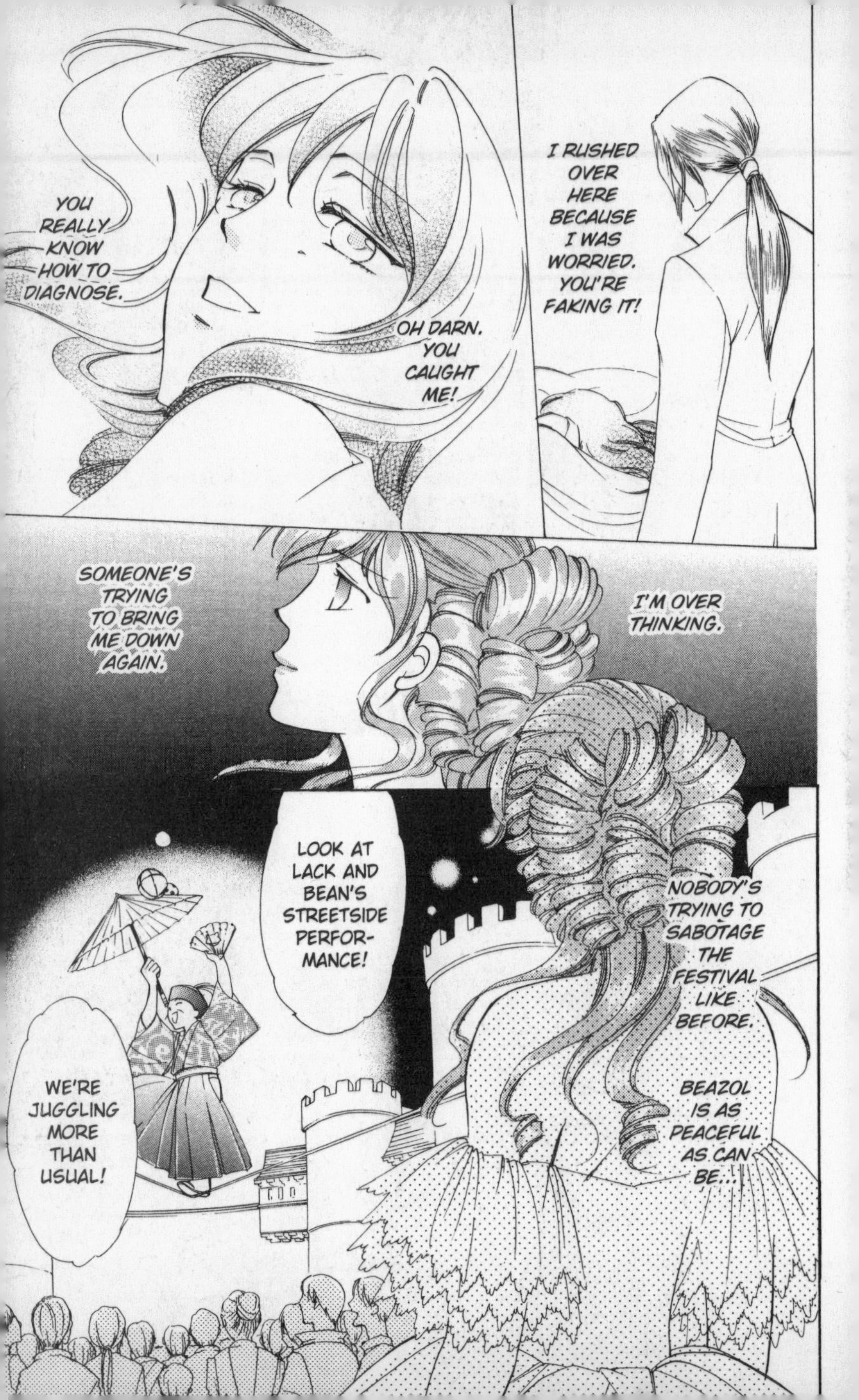
I RUSHED OVER HERE BECAUSE I WAS WORRIED. YOU'RE FAKING IT!
OH DARN. YOU CAUGHT ME!
YOU REALLY KNOW HOW TO DIAGNOSE.
SOMEONE'S TRYING TO BRING ME DOWN AGAIN.
I'M OVER THINKING.
NOBODY'S TRYING TO SABOTAGE THE FESTIVAL LIKE BEFORE.
BEAZOL IS AS PEACEFUL AS CAN BE...
LOOK AT LACK AND BEAN'S STREETSIDE PERFOR-MANCE!
WE'RE JUGGLING MORE THAN USUAL!

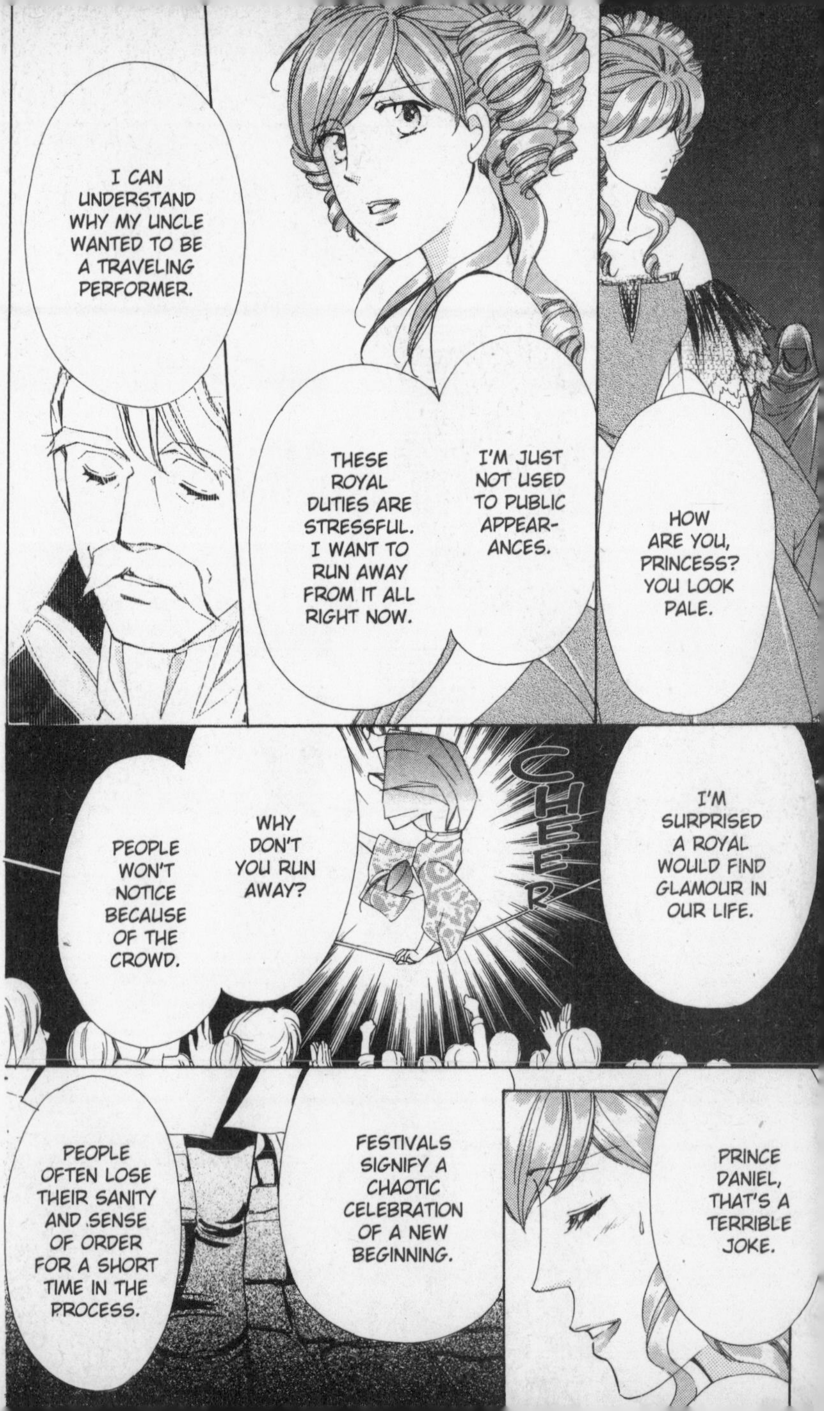
HOW ARE YOU, PRINCESS? YOU LOOK PALE.
I'M JUST NOT USED TO PUBLIC APPEARANCES.
THESE ROYAL DUTIES ARE STRESSFUL. I WANT TO RUN AWAY FROM IT ALL RIGHT NOW.
I CAN UNDERSTAND WHY MY UNCLE WANTED TO BE A TRAVELING PERFORMER.
I'M SURPRISED A ROYAL WOULD FIND GLAMOUR IN OUR LIFE.
CHEER
WHY DON'T YOU RUN AWAY?
PEOPLE WON'T NOTICE BECAUSE OF THE CROWD.
PRINCE DANIEL, THAT'S A TERRIBLE JOKE.
FESTIVALS SIGNIFY A CHAOTIC CELEBRATION OF A NEW BEGINNING.
PEOPLE OFTEN LOSE THEIR SANITY AND SENSE OF ORDER FOR A SHORT TIME IN THE PROCESS.

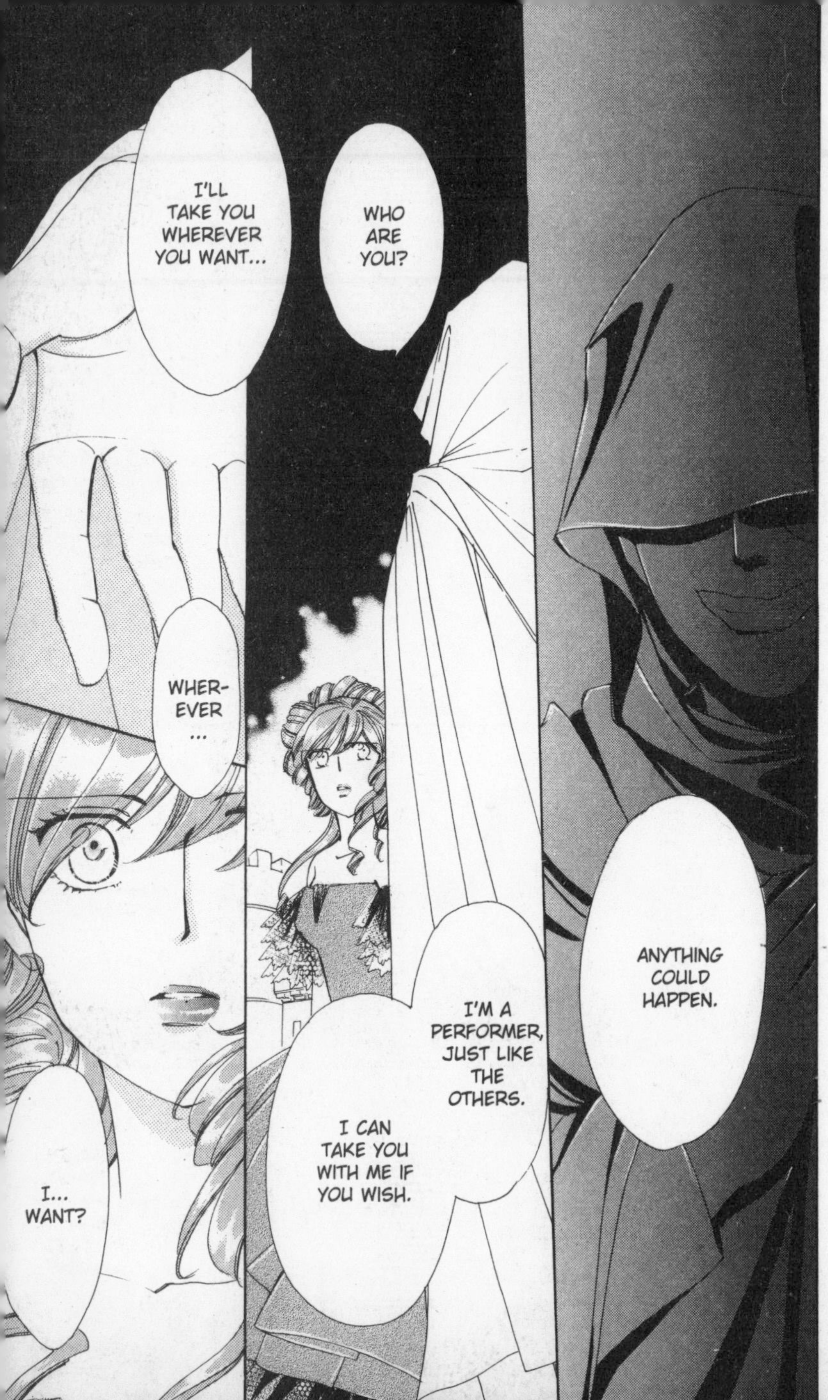
ANYTHING COULD HAPPEN.
WHO ARE YOU?
I'M A PERFORMER, JUST LIKE THE OTHERS.
I CAN TAKE YOU WITH ME IF YOU WISH.
I'LL TAKE YOU WHEREVER YOU WANT...
WHER-EVER ...
I... WANT?

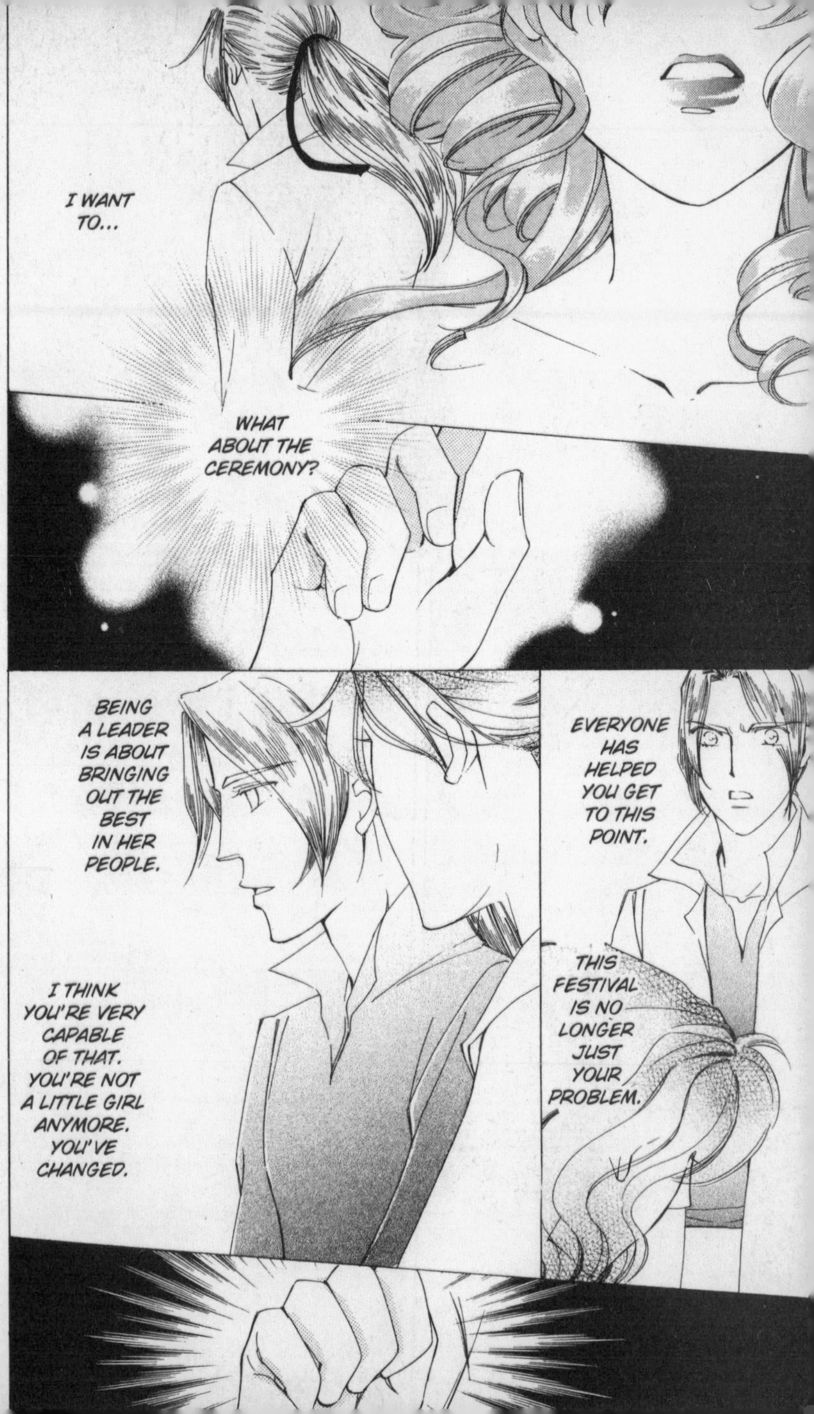
I WANT TO...
WHAT ABOUT THE CEREMONY?
EVERYONE HAS HELPED YOU GET TO THIS POINT.
THIS FESTIVAL IS NO LONGER JUST YOUR PROBLEM.
BEING A LEADER IS ABOUT BRINGING OUT THE BEST IN HER PEOPLE.
I THINK YOU'RE VERY CAPABLE OF THAT. YOU'RE NOT A LITTLE GIRL ANYMORE. YOU'VE CHANGED.

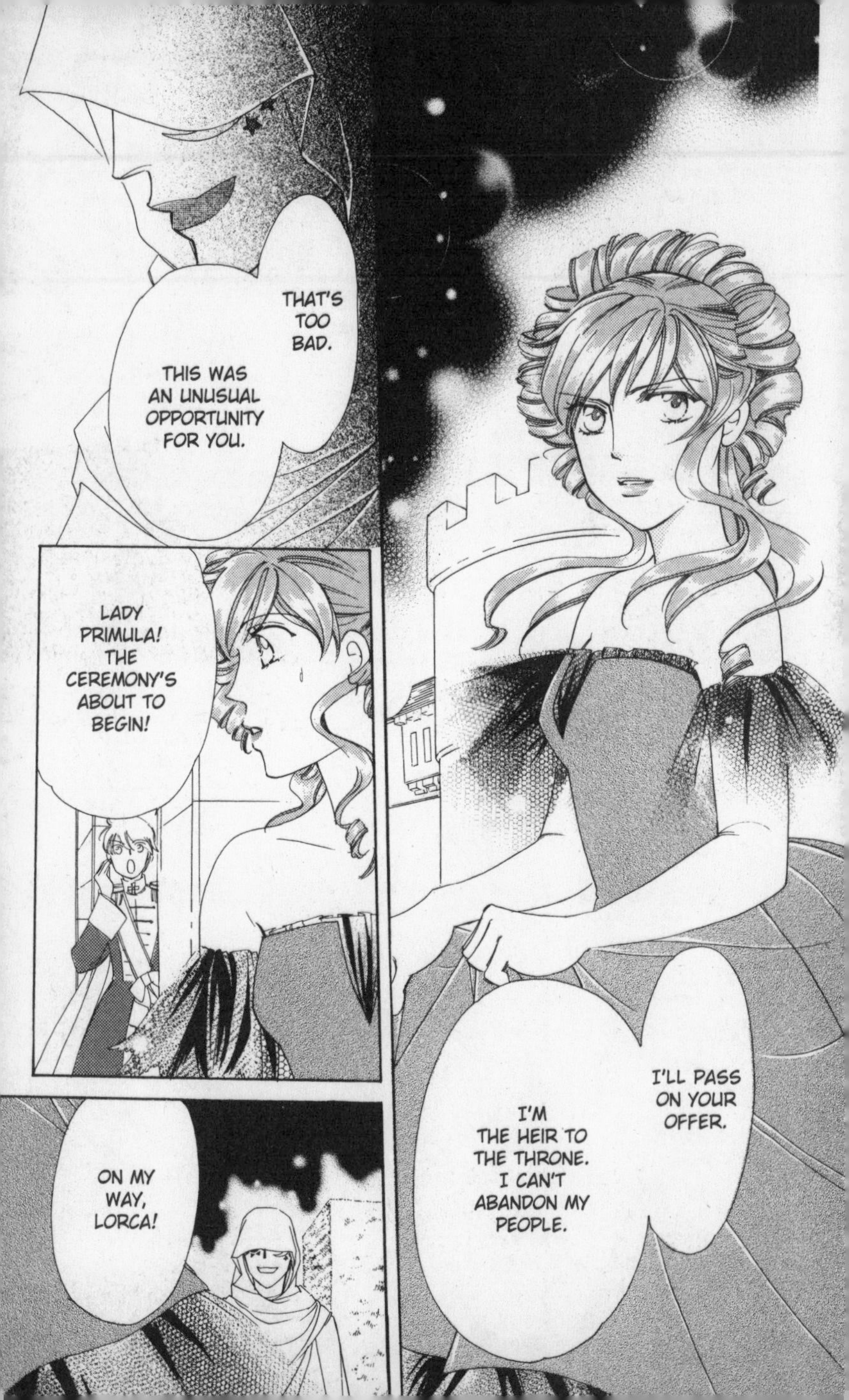
I'LL PASS ON YOUR OFFER.
I'M THE HEIR TO THE THRONE. I CAN'T ABANDON MY PEOPLE.
THAT'S TOO BAD.
THIS WAS AN UNUSUAL OPPORTUNITY FOR YOU.
LADY PRIMULA! THE CEREMONY'S ABOUT TO BEGIN!
ON MY WAY, LORCA!

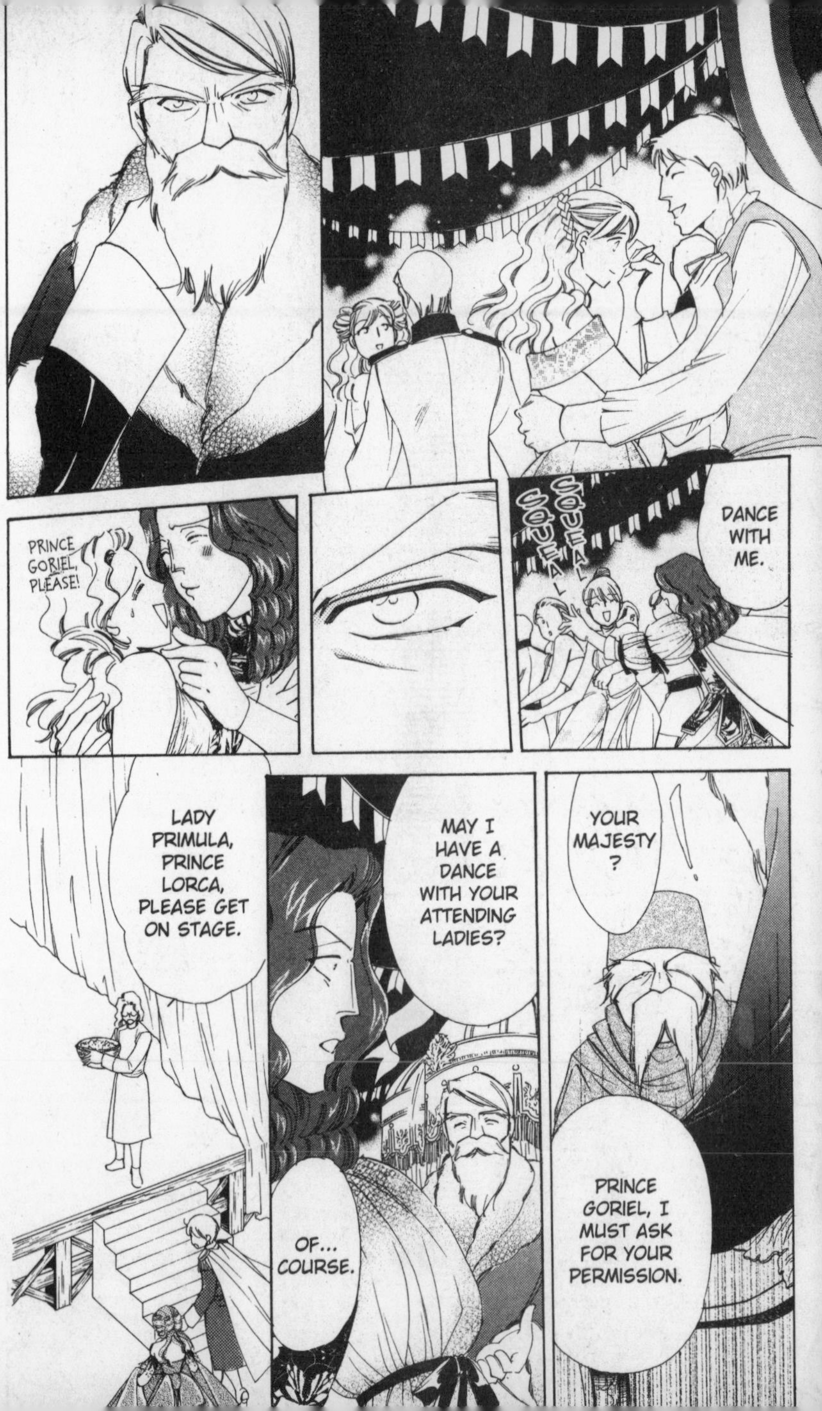
DANCE WITH ME.
SQUEAL
SQUEAL
PRINCE GORIEL, PLEASE!
YOUR MAJESTY ?
PRINCE GORIEL, I MUST ASK FOR YOUR PERMISSION.
MAY I HAVE A DANCE WITH YOUR ATTENDING LADIES?
OF... COURSE.
LADY PRIMULA, PRINCE LORCA, PLEASE GET ON STAGE.

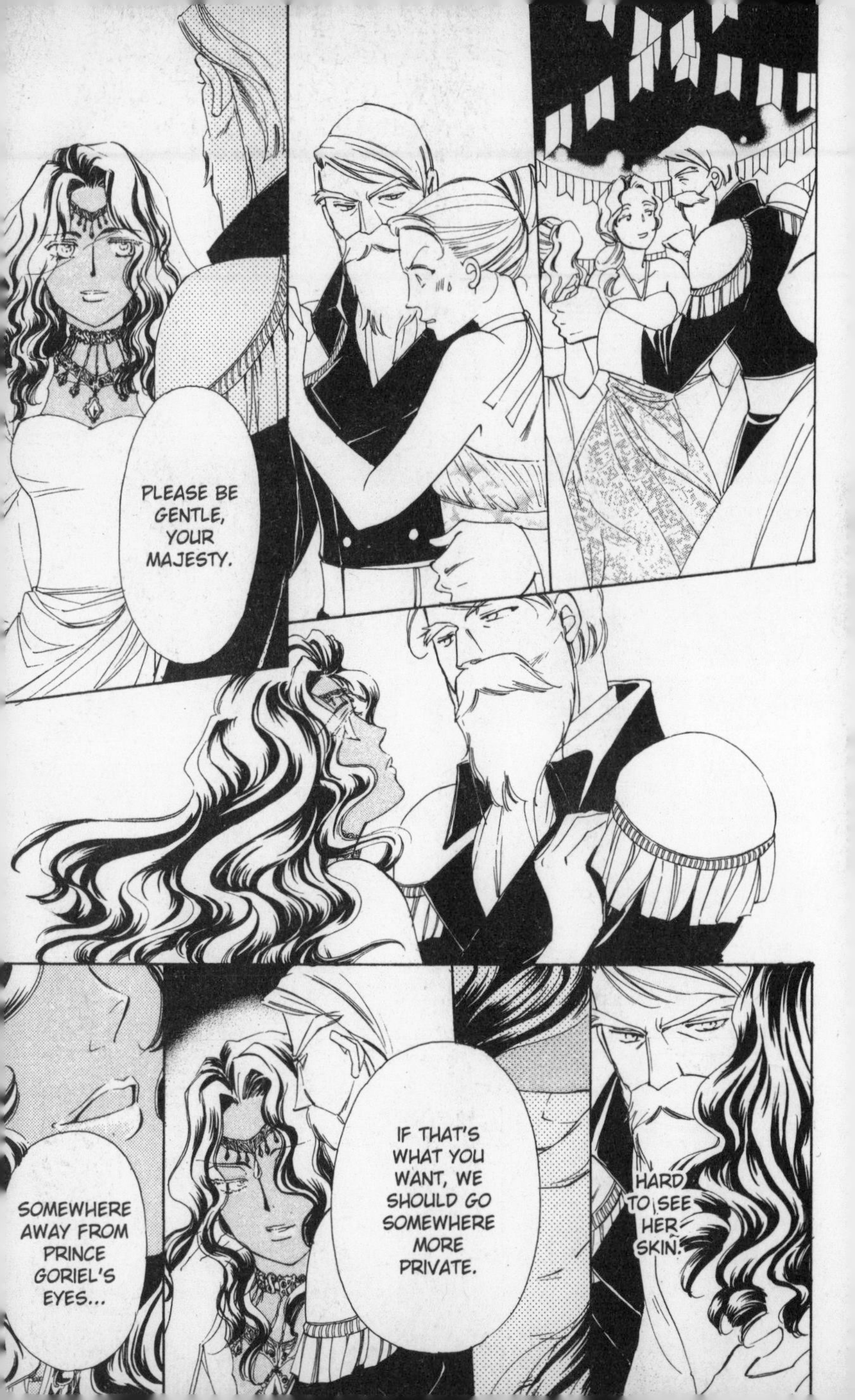
PLEASE BE GENTLE, YOUR MAJESTY.
HARD TO SEE HER SKIN.
IF THAT'S WHAT YOU WANT, WE SHOULD GO SOMEWHERE MORE PRIVATE.
SOMEWHERE AWAY FROM PRINCE GORIEL'S EYES...

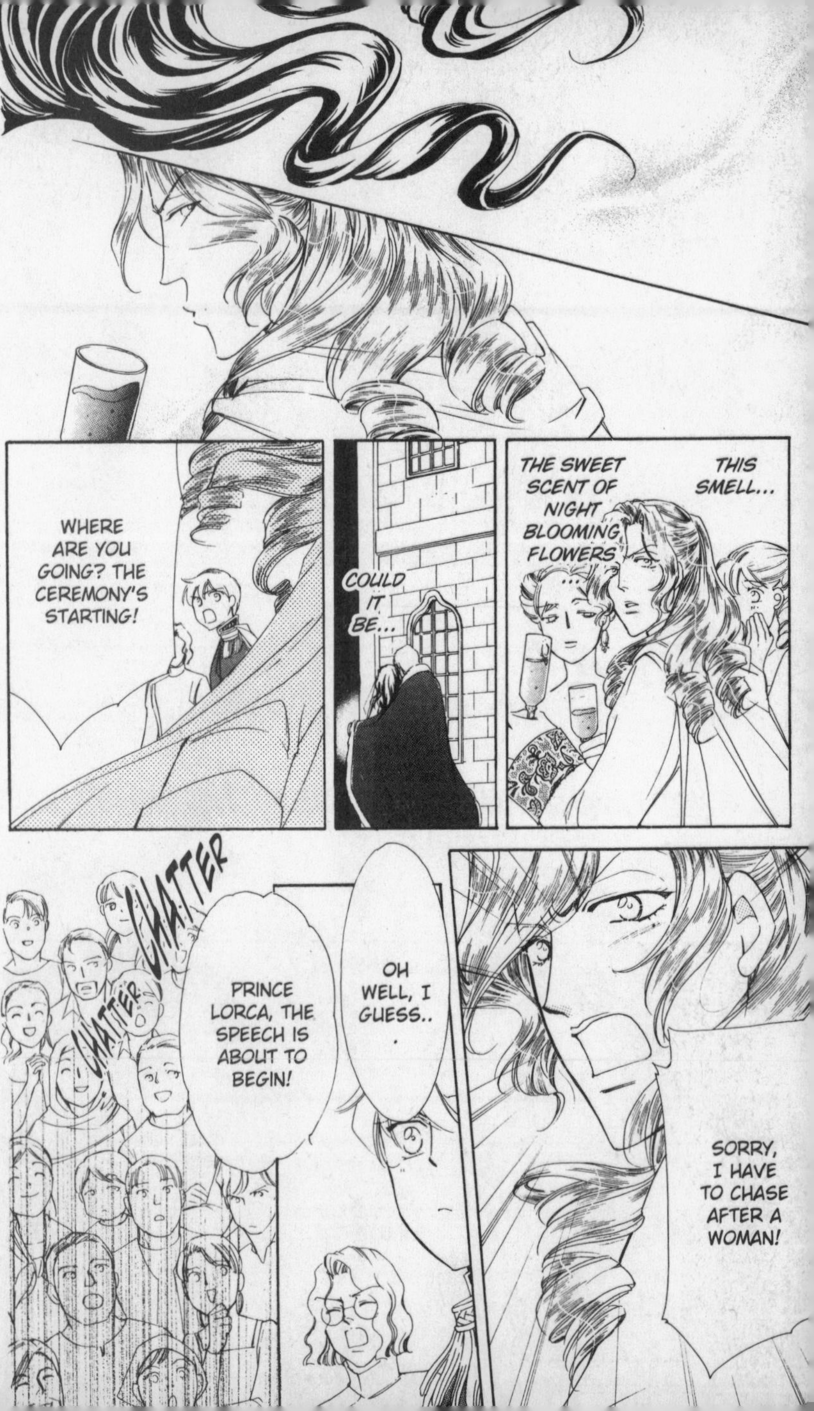
THIS SMELL...
THE SWEET SCENT OF NIGHT BLOOMING FLOWERS
...
COULD IT BE...
WHERE ARE YOU GOING? THE CEREMONY'S STARTING!
SORRY, I HAVE TO CHASE AFTER A WOMAN!
OH WELL, I GUESS...
PRINCE LORCA, THE SPEECH IS ABOUT TO BEGIN!
CHATTER
CHATTER

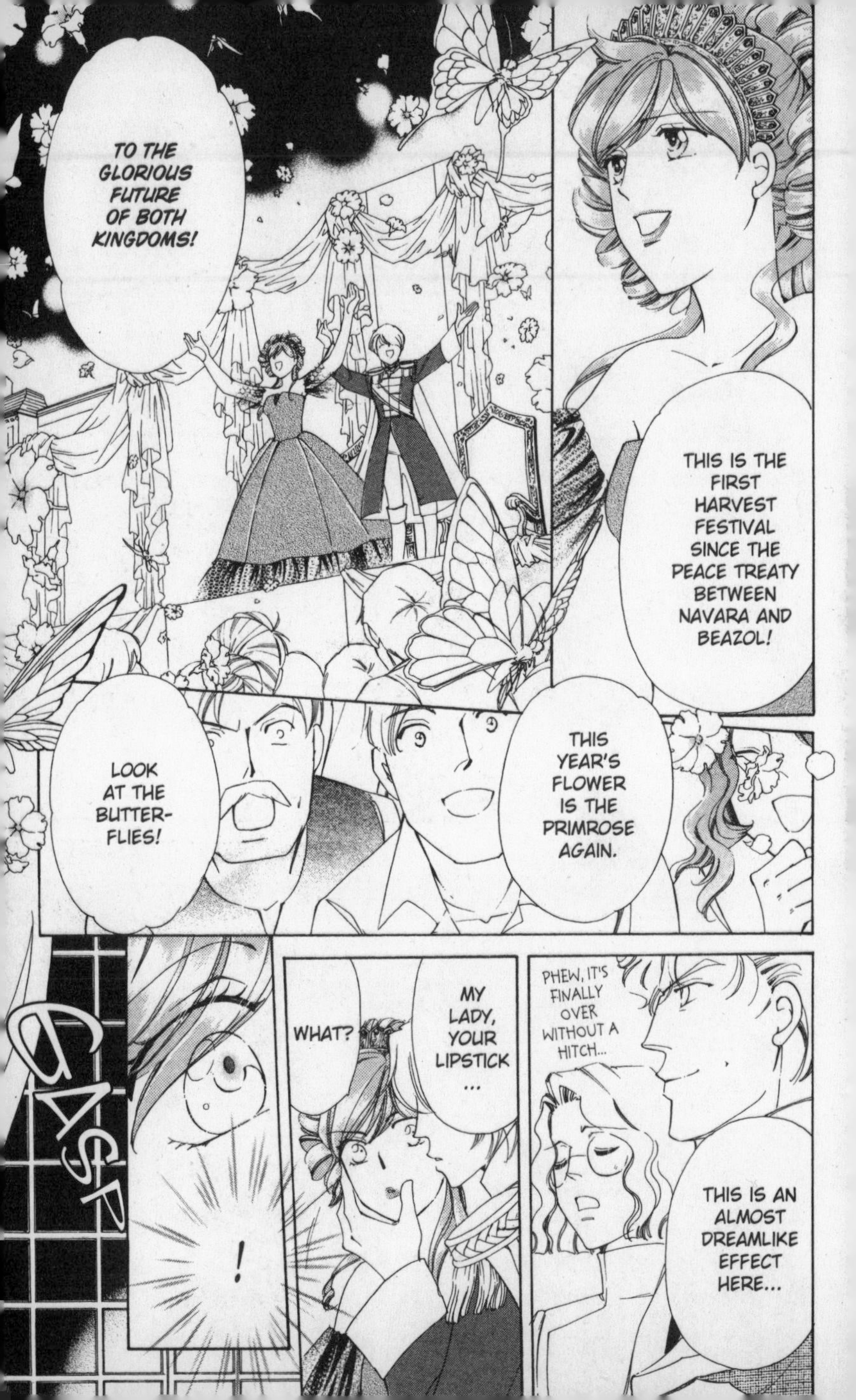
THIS IS THE FIRST HARVEST FESTIVAL SINCE THE PEACE TREATY BETWEEN NAVARA AND BEAZOL!
TO THE GLORIOUS FUTURE OF BOTH KINGDOMS!
THIS YEAR'S FLOWER IS THE PRIMROSE AGAIN.
LOOK AT THE BUTTER-FLIES!
PHEW, IT'S FINALLY OVER WITHOUT A HITCH...
THIS IS AN ALMOST DREAMLIKE EFFECT HERE...
MY LADY, YOUR LIPSTICK ...
WHAT?
GASP
!

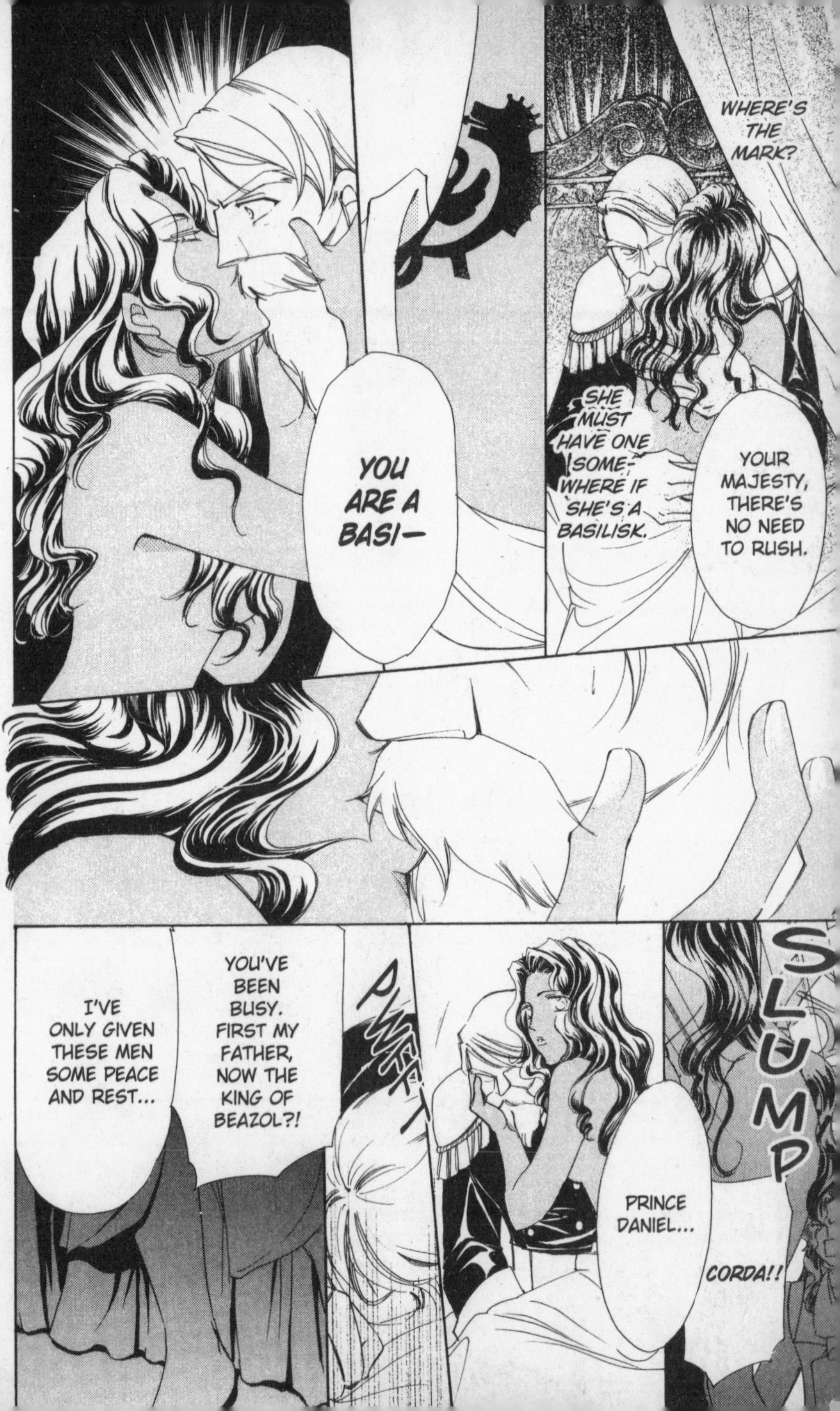
WHERE'S THE MARK?
YOUR MAJESTY, THERE'S NO NEED TO RUSH.
SHE MUST HAVE ONE SOME-WHERE IF SHE'S A BASILISK.
YOU ARE A BASI—
SLUMP
CORDA!!
PRINCE DANIEL...
PWFFT
YOU'VE BEEN BUSY. FIRST MY FATHER, NOW THE KING OF BEAZOL?!
I'VE ONLY GIVEN THESE MEN SOME PEACE AND REST...

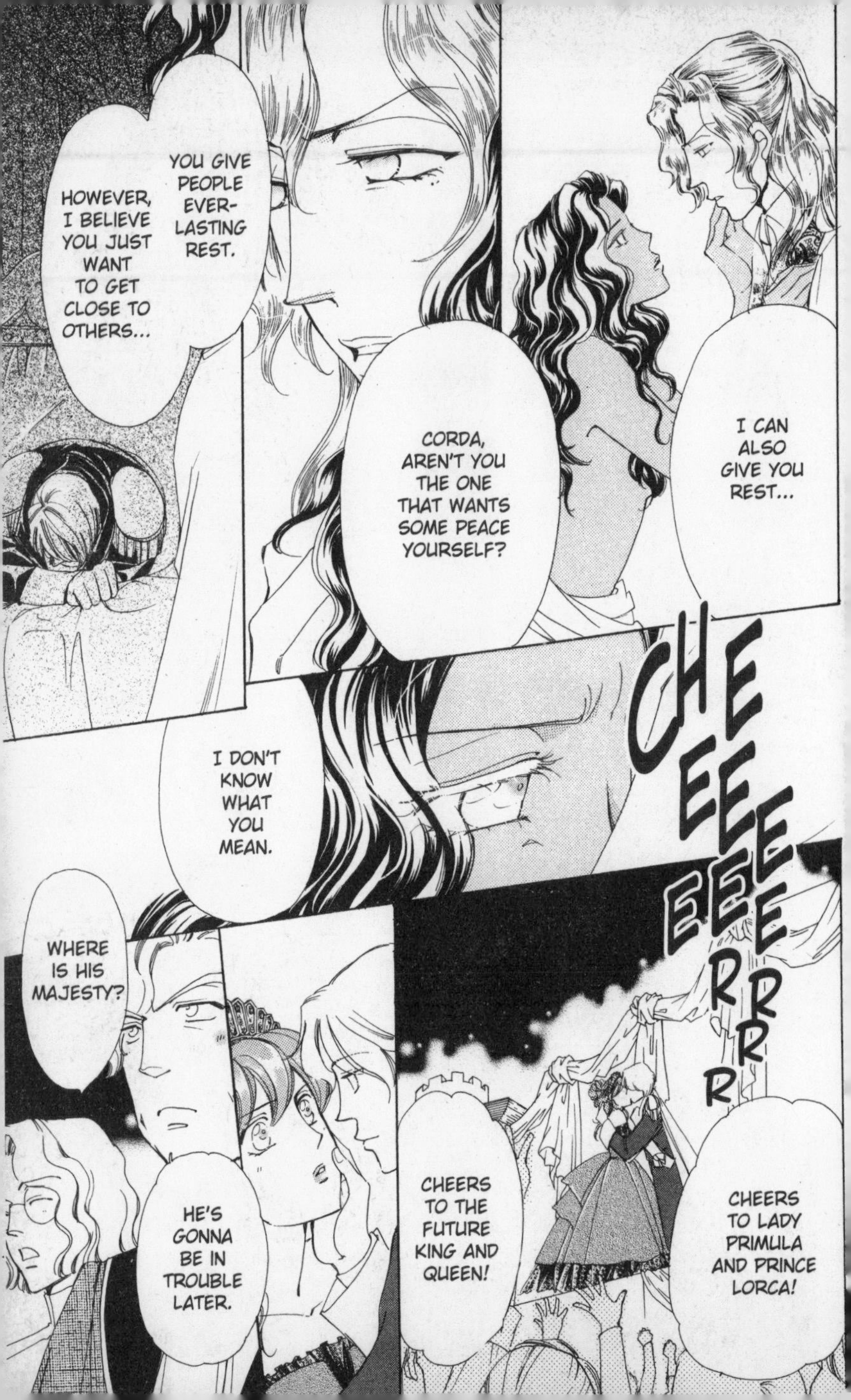

I CAN ALSO GIVE YOU REST...
YOU GIVE PEOPLE EVER-LASTING REST.
HOWEVER, I BELIEVE YOU JUST WANT TO GET CLOSE TO OTHERS...
CORDA, AREN'T YOU THE ONE THAT WANTS SOME PEACE YOURSELF?
I DON'T KNOW WHAT YOU MEAN.
CHEEEEEEEERRRRR
CHEERS TO LADY PRIMULA AND PRINCE LORCA!
CHEERS TO THE FUTURE KING AND QUEEN!
WHERE IS HIS MAJESTY?
HE'S GONNA BE IN TROUBLE LATER.

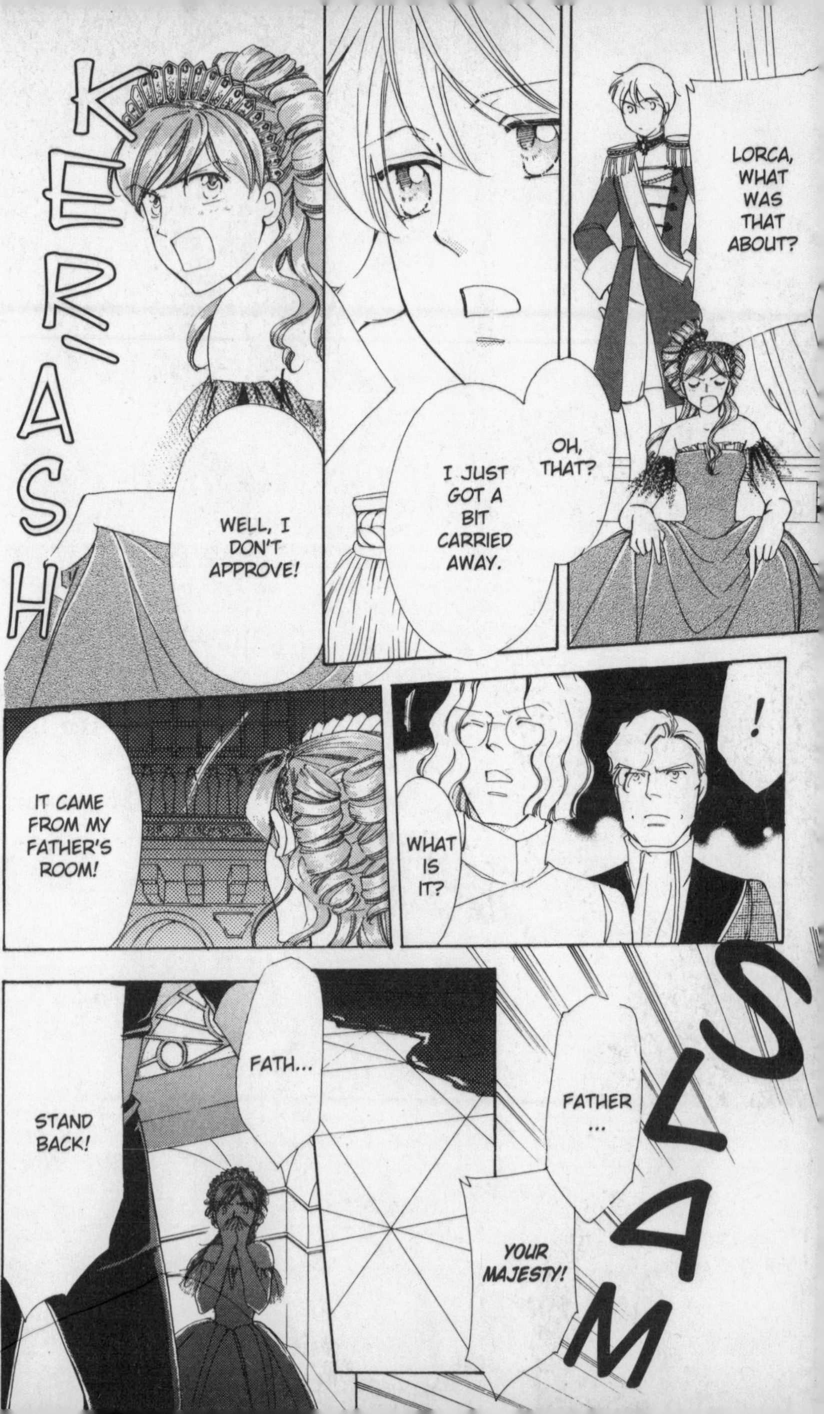
LORCA, WHAT WAS THAT ABOUT?
OH, THAT?
I JUST GOT A BIT CARRIED AWAY.
WELL, I DON'T APPROVE!
KERASH
!
WHAT IS IT?
IT CAME FROM MY FATHER'S ROOM!
SLAM
YOUR MAJESTY!
FATHER...
FATH...
STAND BACK!

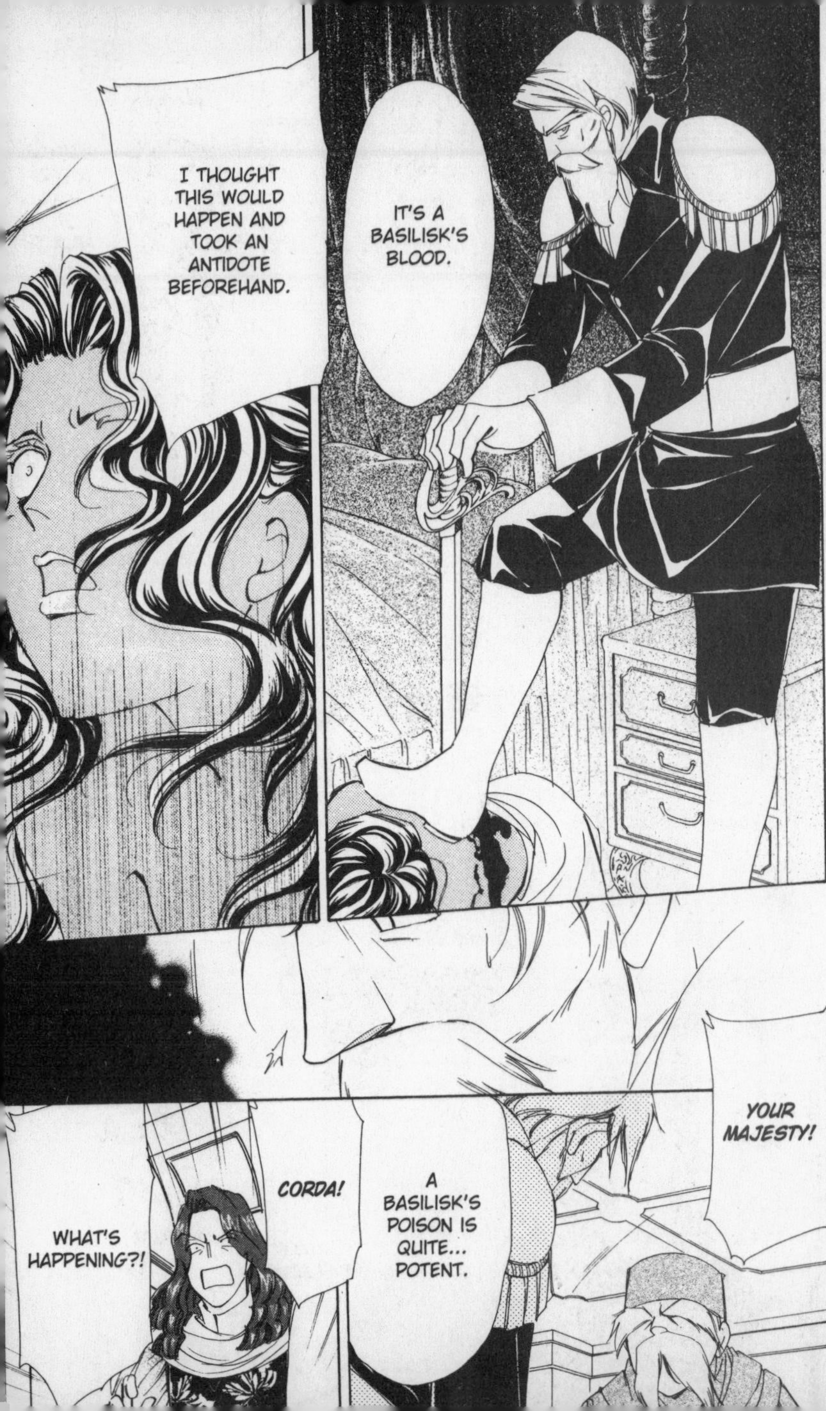
IT'S A BASILISK'S BLOOD.
I THOUGHT THIS WOULD HAPPEN AND TOOK AN ANTIDOTE BEFOREHAND.
YOUR MAJESTY!
A BASILISK'S POISON IS QUITE... POTENT.
CORDA!
WHAT'S HAPPENING?!

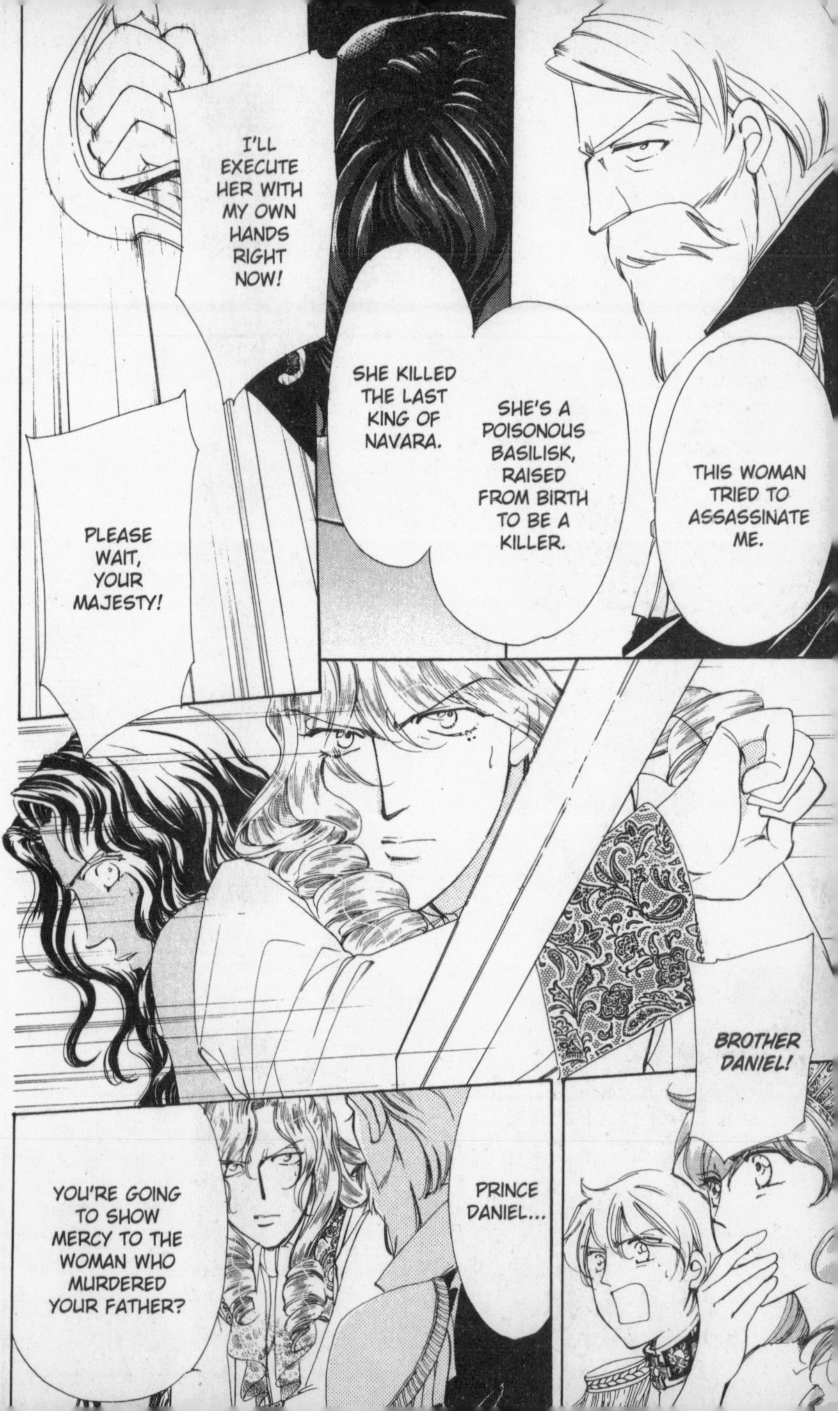
THIS WOMAN TRIED TO ASSASSINATE ME.
SHE'S A POISONOUS BASILISK, RAISED FROM BIRTH TO BE A KILLER.
SHE KILLED THE LAST KING OF NAVARA.
I'LL EXECUTE HER WITH MY OWN HANDS RIGHT NOW!
PLEASE WAIT, YOUR MAJESTY!
BROTHER DANIEL!
PRINCE DANIEL...
YOU'RE GOING TO SHOW MERCY TO THE WOMAN WHO MURDERED YOUR FATHER?

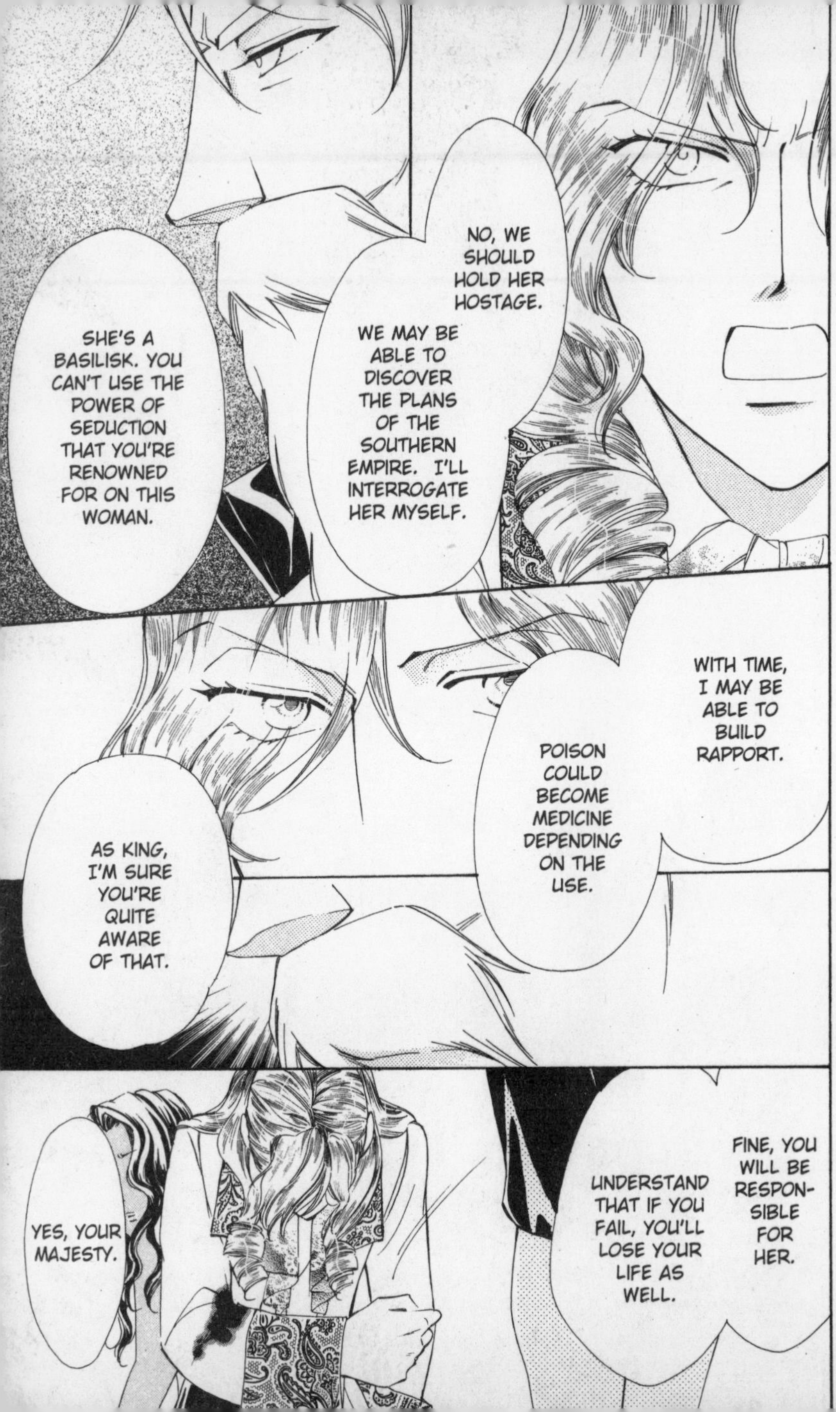
NO, WE SHOULD HOLD HER HOSTAGE.
WE MAY BE ABLE TO DISCOVER THE PLANS OF THE SOUTHERN EMPIRE. I'LL INTERROGATE HER MYSELF.
SHE'S A BASILISK. YOU CAN'T USE THE POWER OF SEDUCTION THAT YOU'RE RENOWNED FOR ON THIS WOMAN.
WITH TIME, I MAY BE ABLE TO BUILD RAPPORT.
POISON COULD BECOME MEDICINE DEPENDING ON THE USE.
AS KING, I'M SURE YOU'RE QUITE AWARE OF THAT.
FINE, YOU WILL BE RESPON-SIBLE FOR HER.
UNDERSTAND THAT IF YOU FAIL, YOU'LL LOSE YOUR LIFE AS WELL.
YES, YOUR MAJESTY.

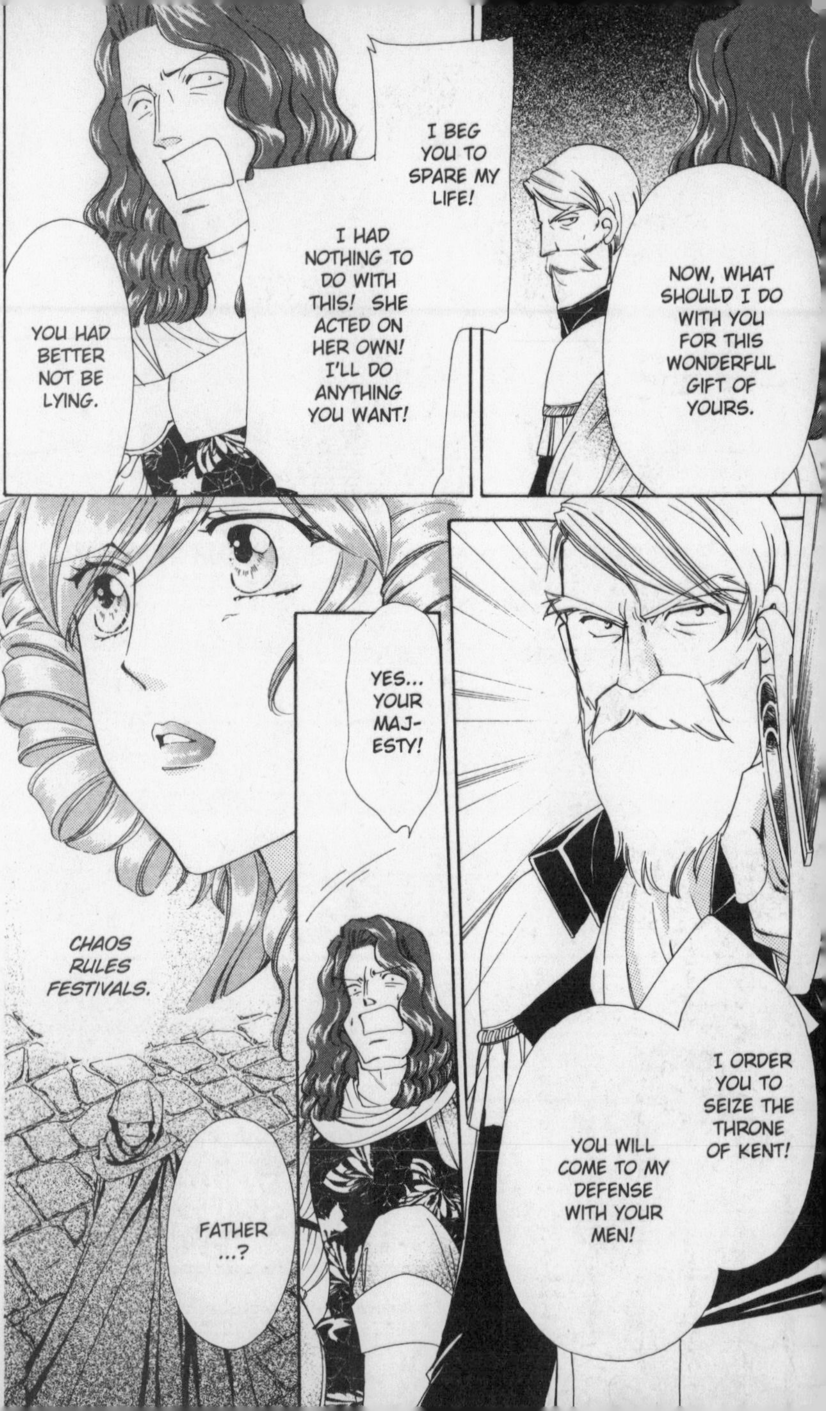
NOW, WHAT SHOULD I DO WITH YOU FOR THIS WONDERFUL GIFT OF YOURS.
I BEG YOU TO SPARE MY LIFE!
I HAD NOTHING TO DO WITH THIS! SHE ACTED ON HER OWN! I'LL DO ANYTHING YOU WANT!
YOU HAD BETTER NOT BE LYING.
I ORDER YOU TO SEIZE THE THRONE OF KENT!
YOU WILL COME TO MY DEFENSE WITH YOUR MEN!
YES... YOUR MAJ-ESTY!
CHAOS RULES FESTIVALS.
FATHER ...?

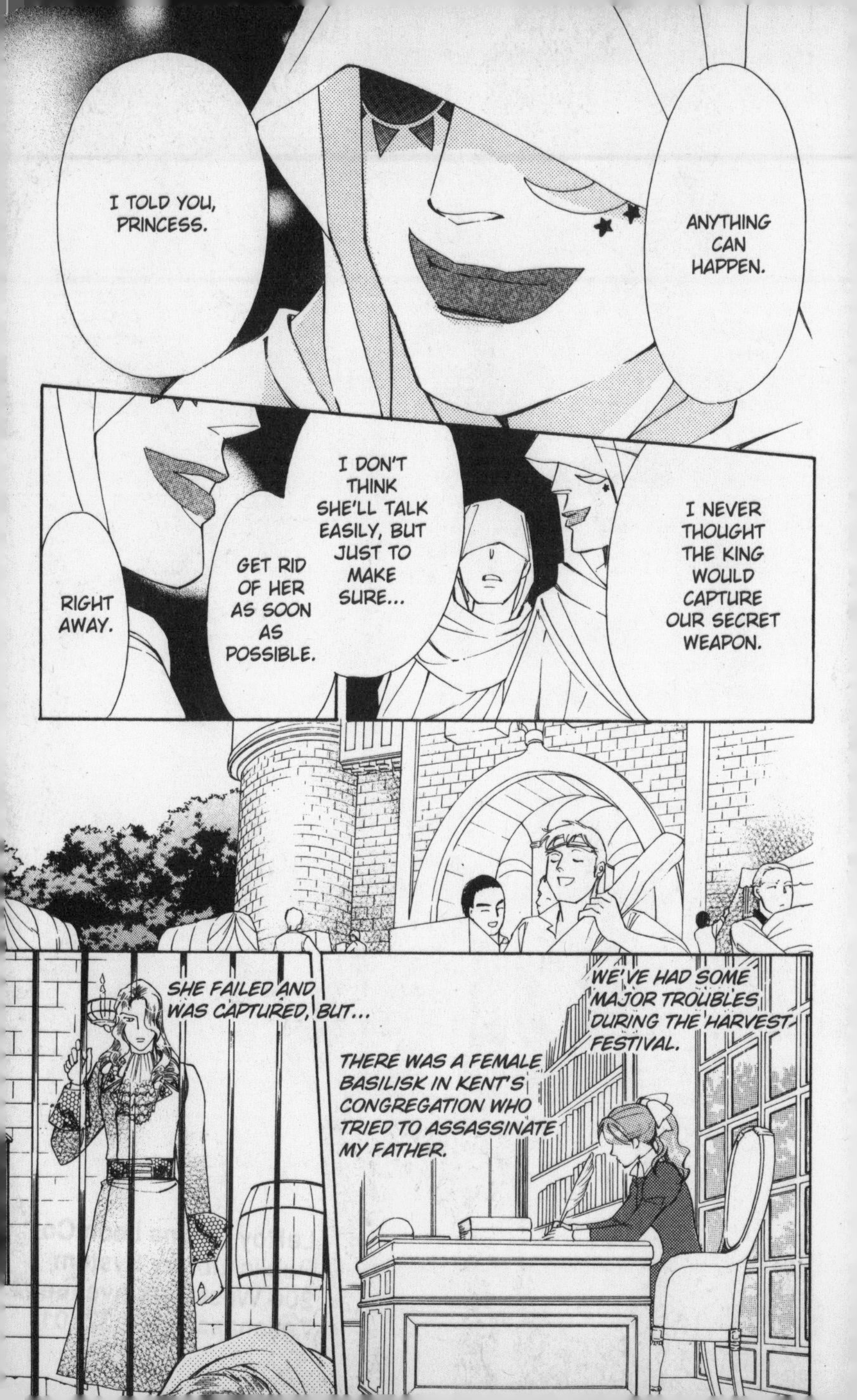
ANYTHING CAN HAPPEN.
I TOLD YOU, PRINCESS.
I NEVER THOUGHT THE KING WOULD CAPTURE OUR SECRET WEAPON.
I DON'T THINK SHE'LL TALK EASILY, BUT JUST TO MAKE SURE...
GET RID OF HER AS SOON AS POSSIBLE.
RIGHT AWAY.
WE'VE HAD SOME MAJOR TROUBLES DURING THE HARVEST FESTIVAL.
THERE WAS A FEMALE BASILISK IN KENT'S CONGREGATION WHO TRIED TO ASSASSINATE MY FATHER.
SHE FAILED AND WAS CAPTURED, BUT...

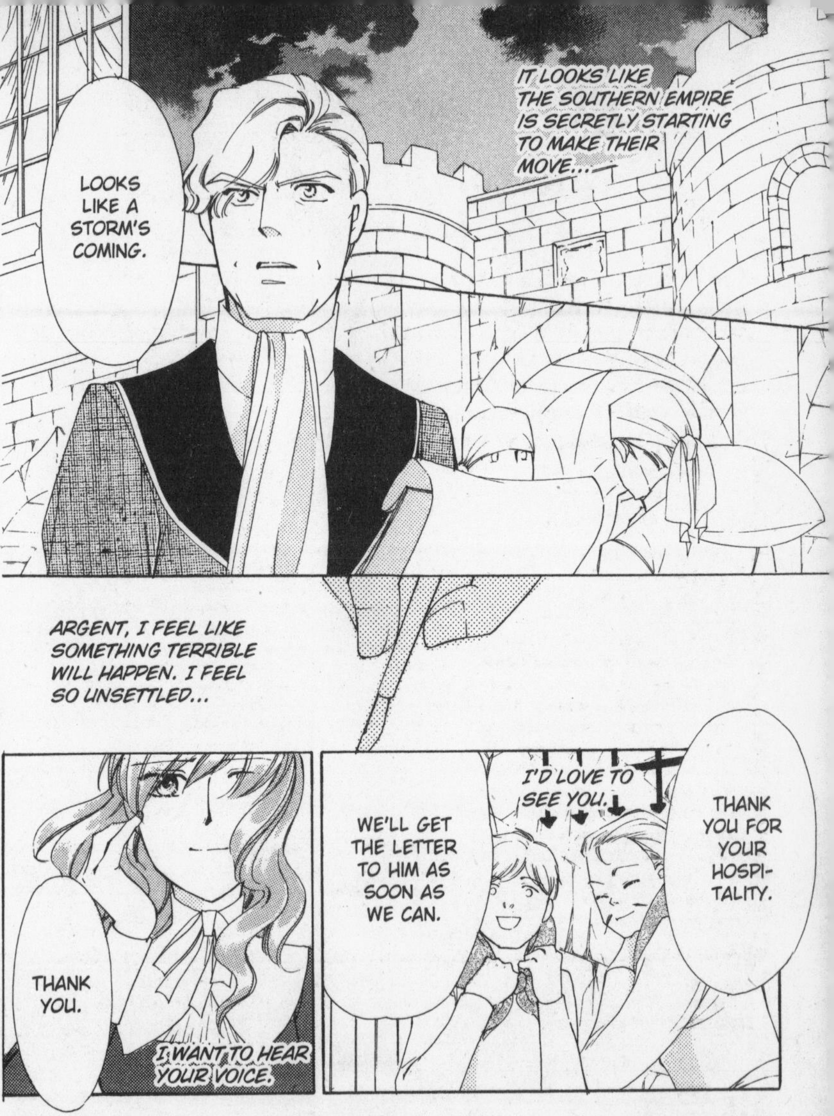
IT LOOKS LIKE THE SOUTHERN EMPIRE IS SECRETLY STARTING TO MAKE THEIR MOVE...
LOOKS LIKE A STORM'S COMING.
ARGENT, I FEEL LIKE SOMETHING TERRIBLE WILL HAPPEN. I FEEL SO UNSETTLED...
THANK YOU FOR YOUR HOSPI-TALITY.
I'D LOVE TO SEE YOU.
WE'LL GET THE LETTER TO HIM AS SOON AS WE CAN.
THANK YOU.
I WANT TO HEAR YOUR VOICE.

NEED YOU MORE THAN
EVER RIGHT NOW...

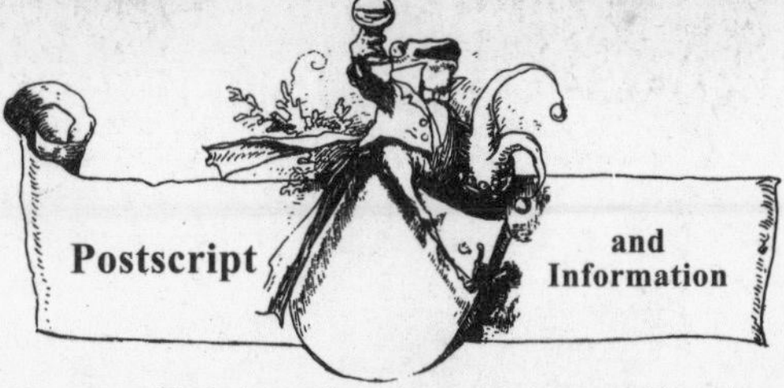
Postscript
and
Information

I hope you enjoyed volume 6. Soda's first love, the antagonism between doctors and apothecaries... I always wanted to create a story around this subject, but due to issues like civil unrest and trouble with neighbors, it's taken a while to appear. Meanwhile, Soda, Popola and Lulu's characters have evolved. People have written about Argent and Soda's masochistic combination. I've laughed about it, but it's about time they graduate from that label. I'm furiously working on that. Next volume, can they escape the masochism, and will Argent be reunited with Lady Primula? I hope you look forward to their adventures.

Yamashita

Toad Venom Extract
Bufonis Venenum
(Chapter 22, 23)

Toad venom is the dehydrated secretion of the auricular and skin glands of Bufo bufo gargarizans Cantor or Bufo melanotictus Bchneider, Bufonidae. It contains steroids such as Resibufogenin and Bufotalin. It is a cardiotonic and eases inflammations. It can also be used as a local anesthetic. The cardiotonic qualities are similar to digitalis, but unlike the digitalis, it does not build up in the body. During the Edo era, street vendors often sold boiled and dried toad and centipede extracts to be used for skin scrapes and irritations. The main ingredient was fat from horses.

Leech (Chapter 23)

Leeches have been used medicinally since the time of the Ancient Egyptians, all the way to Europe in the 20th century. Their bloodsucking qualities were used medicinally for conditions such as stroke, glaucoma, and bruising. They were also used to assist in encouraging circulation post amputation and the prevention of gangrene. Bloodletting fell out of favor and leeches were phased out in modern medicine. However, leeches are making a comeback in today's medicine due to many beneficial chemicals that leeching produces, such as anticoagulants and anti-arthritic compounds.

Ethyl Ether (Chapter 23)

First synthesized in 1540 by Valerius Cordus, it was introduced as a general anesthetic in 1840 by Morton. The administration requires very little equipment. It can be administered through inhalation through a mask. As a result, it was used as an anesthetic for children as well. It is no longer used as an anesthetic due to its flammability and negative side effects.

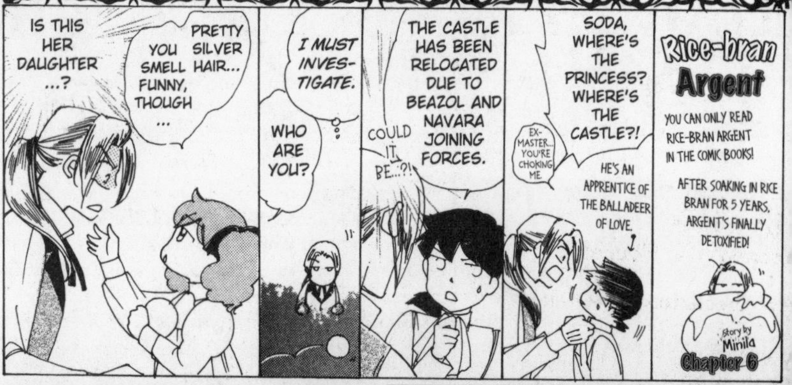
Rice-bran Argent
YOU CAN ONLY READ RICE-BRAN ARGENT IN THE COMIC BOOKS!
AFTER SOAKING IN RICE BRAN FOR 5 YEARS, ARGENT'S FINALLY DETOXIFIED!
Story by Minila
Chapter 6
SODA, WHERE'S THE PRINCESS? WHERE'S THE CASTLE?!
EX-MASTER... YOU'RE CHOKING ME.
HE'S AN APPRENTICE OF THE BALLADEER OF LOVE.
THE CASTLE HAS BEEN RELOCATED DUE TO BEAZOL AND NAVARA JOINING FORCES.
COULD IT BE...?!
I MUST INVES-TIGATE.
WHO ARE YOU?
PRETTY SILVER HAIR... YOU SMELL FUNNY, THOUGH ...
IS THIS HER DAUGHTER ...?

I've got a bad feeling... tune in next time!

Apothecarius Argentum 6/ The End

Apothecarius Argentum c/o CMX
888 Prospect Street, Suite 240,
La Jolla CA 92037

CATCH UP NOW WITH ANY VOLUMES YOU'VE MISSED!

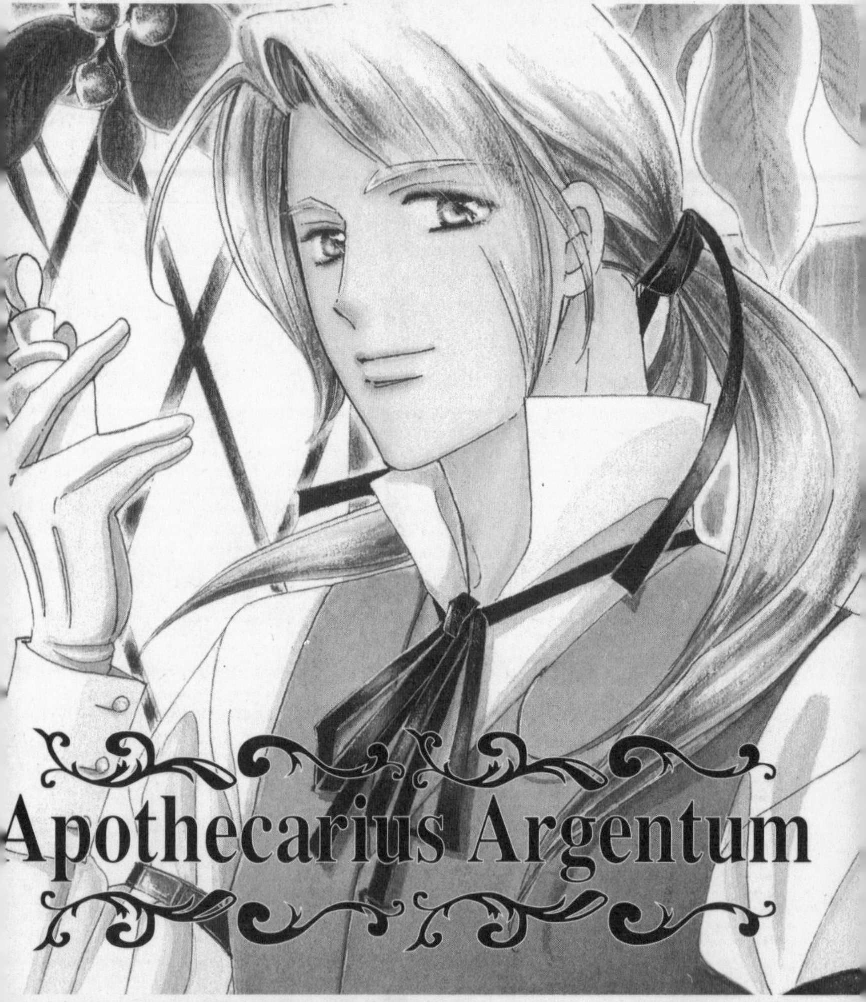
Apothecarius Argentum

y Tomomi Yamashita. With Argent away and tensions mounting back in Beazol, hat's going to happen next? If you've missed any of the previous volumes and are curious oout how things got to this point, now would be a good time find out. Learn about Argent's outhful training as a Basilisk and how he first came to the King of Beazol's attention. xperience his early relationship with Princess Primula, discover why he left the kingdom, nd find out why he came back. Then be sure to join us next year for APOTHECARIUS RGENTUM Volume 7.

YAKUSHI ARGIAN Vol. 6 © 2007 Tomomi Yamashita. All
rights reserved. First published in Japan in 2007 by Akita
Publishing Co., Ltd.

APOTHECARIUS ARGENTUM Volume 6, published by
WildStorm Productions, an imprint of DC Comics, 888
Prospect St. #240, La Jolla, CA 92037. English Translation
© 2008. All Rights Reserved. English translation rights in
U.S.A. And Canada arranged with Akita Publishing Co.,
Ltd., through Tuttle-Mori Agency, Inc., Tokyo. CMX is a
trademark of DC Comics. The stories, characters, and
incidents mentioned in this magazine are entirely fictional.
Printed on recyclable paper. WildStorm does not read or
accept unsolicited submissions of ideas, stories or artwork.
Printed in Canada.

DC Comics, A Warner Bros. Entertainment Company.

Ikoi Hiroe – Translation and Adaptation
Kathryn Renta – Lettering
Larry Berry – Design
Jim Chadwick – Editor

ISBN: 978-1-4012-1766-2

All the pages in this book were created—and are printed here—in Japanese RIGHT-to-LEFT format. No artwork has been reversed or altered, so you can read the stories the way the creators meant for them to be read.

RIGHT TO LEFT?!

Traditional Japanese manga starts at the upper right-hand corner, and moves right-to-left as it goes down the page. Follow this guide for an easy understanding.

For more information and sneak previews, visit cmxmanga.com. Call 1-888-COMIC BOOK for the nearest comics shop or head to your local book store.

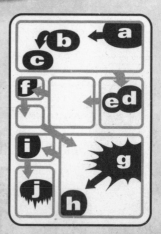